Edition <kes>

With modern computer technology everywhere, the importance of data integrity and the security of IT systems has increased immensely. Given the complexity and rapid progress of information technology, IT professionals need in-depth knowledge in this field.

The series Edition <kes> provides the required know-how, promoting risk awareness and helping in the development and implementation of security solutions of IT systems and their environment.

<kes> – Journal of Information Security (see www.kes.info), bimonthly published by DATAKONTEXT GmbH, covers all subjects from audits and security policies to encryption and access control. It also provides information about new security hard- and software as well as the relevant legislation for multimedia and data security.

Furthermore, authors of the journal and the book series Edition <kes> help users in basic and expert seminars to implement information security in a practice-oriented manner (see www.itsecuritycircles.de).

More information about this series at
http://www.springer.com/series/12374

Eberhard von Faber · Wolfgang Behnsen

Secure ICT Service Provisioning for Cloud, Mobile and Beyond

ESARIS: The Answer to the Demands of Industrialized IT Production Balancing Between Buyers and Providers

2nd updated and extended Edition

Springer Vieweg

Eberhard von Faber
T-Systems
Bonn, Germany

Wolfgang Behnsen
Erlangen, Germany

Edition <kes>
ISBN 978-3-658-16481-2   ISBN 978-3-658-16482-9 (eBook)
DOI 10.1007/978-3-658-16482-9

Library of Congress Control Number: 2017936049

Springer Vieweg
© Springer Fachmedien Wiesbaden GmbH 2012, 2017

Printed on acid-free paper

This Springer Vieweg imprint is published by Springer Nature
The registered company is Springer Fachmedien Wiesbaden GmbH
The registered company address is: Abraham-Lincoln-Strasse 46, 65189 Wiesbaden, Germany

Foreword

Companies can gain a decisive market advantage through information and communication technology (ICT). Clouds providing central computing services, mobile access, networking, and machine-to-machine communication are the basis for processing high volumes of business-relevant data, and are at the core of new business concepts and greater performance in existing ones. ICT is used in almost all businesses to automate business processes and increase speed and quality. This "digitalization" has two major consequences. Firstly, enterprises, authorities and even consumers are much more dependent on ICT. The value of the data being processed is going up and up, while adversaries, including hostile hackers, organized crime and industrial spies, are unfortunately highly motivated and active as well. Secondly, ICT is now a ubiquitous part of everyday life. This increases the attack surfaces that adversaries can, and do, exploit.

ICT infrastructures and applications are attacked effectively and both enterprises and consumers suffer considerable losses. Though managers and officials know that they have to invest in protecting their ICT, many stakeholders still consider appropriate security to be inconvenient and expensive. At the end of the day, it is about "which party must do what."

Technology, business models and trends in the economy lead to an immense centralization of computing power mastered by large-scale IT production. Cost pressure and other customer demands in turn reinforce the need to deliver ICT services in an industrialized manner. User organizations are increasingly using ICT services from ICT service providers instead of producing these services in-house themselves. They demand reliability and seek trustworthy, dependable suppliers offering secure ICT services: A sufficient level of security is an essential and intrinsic element for the successful digitalization of industries, administration, and our society as a whole. The word "intrinsic" is important here. Users demand reliable ICT services and want to concentrate on making the most of them in their business, requiring the security to be integrated "almost invisibly" and "with ease." Nonetheless, it is up to the user to demand and reimburse the appropriate protection of ICT. In fact, every party in the supply chain must make their contribution to security, since the chain is only as strong as its weakest link. However, this cannot be taken as a given but must be arranged systematically.

This 2nd, updated and extended edition of the book presents methods and measures for dealing with information security in today's IT industry that were developed and proven in our corporation, with our customers, and with suppliers and partners. This book is intended to help the reader to implement security measures throughout a complex ICT delivery infrastructure in organizations, processes and technology, from design to service management, while taking into consideration effectiveness as regards customer requirements, and efficiency relating to costs. The book should also help user organizations to understand the security aspects of ICT provision and to select the correct provider and the correct services in terms of information security. In this way, the workable architecture presented here aims to find a balance between buyers and providers: requirements and deliverables must correspond. *Secure ICT Service Provisioning for Cloud, Mobile and Beyond* is of utmost concern to both parties.

Reinhard Clemens

Member of the Board of Management at Deutsche Telekom

CEO of T-Systems

Preface

The task of making ICT services secure is important and mission critical for any ICT service provider paid to deliver secure ICT services for cloud, mobile and beyond. Such providers are challenged to turn requirements into real material security in a way that is verifiable for customers. This puts leading ICT service providers in a very specific and (does it come as a surprise?) very complicated and truly complex situation. The reasons are easy to see. The provider is facing an almost unmanageable multitude of different sets of requirements that are all to be met by its single ICT service delivery infrastructure. Moreover, the provider must produce the ICT services efficiently, which in turn requires as much standardizing and harmonizing as possible.

In the past, security was managed in "customer silos." However, security requirements have increased dramatically in number, coverage and depth in recent years. At the same time, the customers of the ICT service provider demand a significant cost reduction while retaining or even enhancing performance and flexibility, and at the same time being provided with more security transparency and assurance.

This situation was the starting point some years ago when a number of security managers from T-Systems sat down together with the authors of this book to discuss precisely the issues described above. We decided to take a big step forward. We invented the idea of "industrializing security" or adapting ICT security to an industrialized ICT provision method. That was the birth of ESARIS, the subject of this book. That approach, and its realization, have proven to be very successful. We decided to publish large parts of the work in order to contribute to *Secure ICT Service Provisioning for Cloud, Mobile and Beyond*. At the same time, we wanted to encourage customers and a wider audience to discuss the concepts and to adopt useful ideas. In this way, the industry should be able to progress in balancing the requirements of user organizations and the measures that are provided by ICT service providers.

With the 1st edition of this book, major concepts of ESARIS were published at the beginning of 2013. Since then, our corporation has gained more experience in applying the new methods and measures in practice, and has also developed new ones. Four years later, this 2nd, updated and extended edition presents an even more complete set of concepts, methods and measures. It provides deeper insight, improved rationales and more background information. T-Systems' Board of Management decided to implement ESARIS in our corporation and initiated a longer-lasting program for introducing it in all subsidiaries around the world. This book reports on real-world experience from this Transformation program. Moreover, it considers feedback from our customers as well as experience gained from using

ESARIS while managing numerous big and complex deals throughout their IT outsourcing phases, including Sales, Manage the Deal, Transition and Transformation, and Operations. Recently, T-Systems initiated the foundation of the Zero Outage Industry Standard association in which technology leaders are aiming to provide the highest quality and security against outages of IT infrastructure. The work in this association and other examples show that ESARIS closed a substantial gap in the literature about information security. ESARIS "takes operational requirements into account and focuses on user requirements, thus facing the reality in the market economy." It addresses efficiency, standardization and quality in the realm of security; and it helps to manage security in large-scale IT production characterized by a high degree of division of labor and specialization. I consider this book an essential contribution to the successful industrialization of ICT: Users require ICT services that are secure, at an affordable cost.

Heike Bayerl

Vice President of international Security, Compliance & Quality Management

T-Systems, IT Division

About this book

Managing a large-scale IT production is a challenge. Providing information and communication services ("ICT services") in a *secure* manner while meeting the *security* requirements of the user organizations adds further difficulty. The technical solutions including firewall & Co. are, however, not the issue! Large IT organizations must be able to define, communicate and correctly apply thousands of single measures in a large-scale, industrial environment with thousands of employees located in many countries. This is a real problem and this book will provide solutions to this. Moreover, large IT organizations usually have many customers which are supplied with a complex of different ICT services. Hence, the interaction with those customers is a critical success factor for both sides.

This book describes concepts, methods and measures which enable ICT service providers to provide secure ICT services in the beginning second half of the information age, characterized by large-scale IT production with rigorous specialization and division of labor along the complete supply chain. This book is for suppliers playing their role in this environment. Even more important, user organizations are given deep insight in secure IT production which allows them to make the best out of cloud, mobile and beyond.

The subject of this book is rather new! The "architectural approach" in this book is one of the first comprehensive ventures providing mainly IT producers with a "security toolset" to tackle the challenges of upcoming business and production models. The authors abstain from repeating known security practices. The content of this book is rather new, but already tested and proven. The concepts, models and underlying security measures have been developed and deployed by a large ICT company so that this book can also report on practical experiences.

The following slide controls may provide further information.

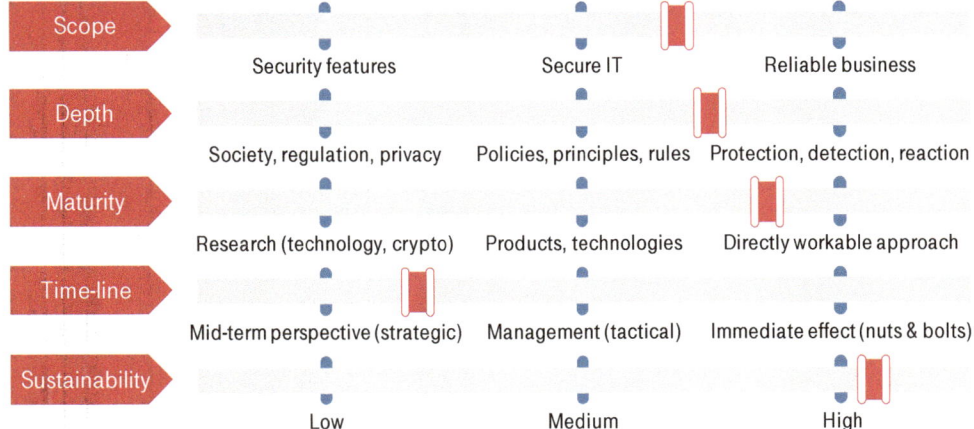

Table of Contents

Part 1: Foundation 1

1   Subject (from pain to pleasure) 3
1.1 Challenges 3
1.2 Areas of activity beyond „Protection, Detection, Reaction" 6
     1.2.1 Transparency 9
     1.2.2 Interfaces and interaction 14
     1.2.3 Standardization 18
1.3 Solutions 21

2   Environment 25
2.1 Frameworks for ESARIS 26
2.2 Perspectives: corporate versus product security 30

3   Main building blocks and general set-up 33
3.1 ESARIS Dimensions 33
3.2 ESARIS Work Areas 35
3.3 ESARIS Collaboration Model 37
3.4 Hierarchy of Security Standards 42
     3.4.1 Overview 42
     3.4.2 Level 1: Corporate Security Policy 44
     3.4.3 Level 2: Corporate Security Rules 44
     3.4.4 Level 3: ICT Security Principles 45
     3.4.5 Level 4: ICT Security Standards 46
     3.4.6 Level 5: ICT Security Baselines 46
3.5 ESARIS Concept of Double Direction Standards 47

4   ESARIS Security Taxonomy 51
4.1 Design criteria for the ESARIS Security Taxonomy 51
4.2 Structure of the ESARIS Security Taxonomy 55
4.3 Areas and the ICT Security Standards at a glance 61
     4.3.1 Networks 62
     4.3.2 Data center 63
     4.3.3 Customer and users.. 66
     4.3.4 Evidence and Customer Relation 67
     4.3.5 Service Management 69
     4.3.6 Risk Management and Certification.................................. 71
4.4 Summary of standards and taxonomy.. 72
4.5 Provider Scope of Control 74

5   Secured by definition – integration with core business (ITSM) 81
5.1   ITSM processes and why security must be integrated into them 81
5.2   Division of labor between IT and IT security 88
5.3   How the integration looks like and actually works 91

Part 2: Core activities...97

6   Standardization – ensuring quality and efficiency...99
6.1   Understanding standardization, its necessity and benefits..........................99
6.2   ESARIS Industrialization Concept 103
        6.2.1   Dealing with requirements 103
        6.2.2   Composition of services 105
6.3   ESARIS Security Specification Concept 106
6.4   Obstacles towards standardization and solutions...113

7   Attainment – achieving compliance with ESARIS standards....................121
7.1   Foundation 121
7.2   Requirements engineering and elaboration and application of ESARIS
        standards 123
7.3   ESARIS Attainment Levels and verification of compliance 128
7.4   Service offering portfolio integration 134

8   Fulfillment – meeting customer demands 139
8.1   Foundation 139
8.2   IT outsourcing...142
8.3   Assurance for customers 148
        8.3.1   Contractual evidence 148
        8.3.2   Operational evidence...153
        8.3.3   Contractual and other changes 155

9   Flexibility – managing the supplier network 159
9.1   Roles and types of suppliers 159
9.2   Third party integration model...162

Part 3: Implementation 171

10   Maintenance – requirements, documents, improvements...........................173
10.1   Document IDs and more 173
10.2   Virtual organization, roles and processes 179
10.3   Library, versions and consistency...182
10.4   Protecting intellectual property 186

11   Transformation – implementing ESARIS sustainably...........................189
11.1   Mission: induce a massive change 189
11.2   Approach: ESARIS Maturity Level and master plan 192
11.3   Enablement: training and communication 200
11.4   Voyage of ICT services 205

12 Implementation – IT production and its protection in practice 209
12.1 Evidence and Customer Relation 209
    12.1.1 Match – (Im)Prove – Correct 210
    12.1.2 Accomplishing security 214
12.2 Service Management 220
    12.2.1 Plan – Build – Change 222
    12.2.2 Accomplishing security 229
    12.2.3 Stocktake – Assemble – Preserve 236
    12.2.4 Accomplishing security 241
12.3 ICT Service Access 246
    12.3.1 Transportation 247
    12.3.2 Customer side and endpoints 249
    12.3.3 Connectivity 253
    12.3.4 Securing transportation 256
    12.3.5 Securing workplaces 258
    12.3.6 Securing connectivity 265
12.4 IT Service Production 267
    12.4.1 The lower IT stack 268
    12.4.2 IT management and data center premises 274
    12.4.3 Applications 279
    12.4.4 Securing the lower IT stack 282
    12.4.5 Securing IT management and data center premises 286
    12.4.6 Securing applications 290
12.5 Risk Management and Certification 297

13 Routine – day-to-day security management using ESARIS 303
13.1 Fourteen tasks for managing security using ESARIS 303
13.2 Three ways of verifying compliance with security standards 309
13.3 A number of tips to deal with trouble and confusion 313
13.4 Buyers and providers: joint security management 316

14 Conclusion 325

Annexes 331
A Authors and acknowledgement 331
B Glossary (terms and definitions) 336
B.1 Fundamental terms 336
B.2 Terms relating to security organization 338
B.3 Terms relating to difficulties and restoration 342
B.4 Major concepts and models at a glance 343
C Literature 359
D Abbreviations 363
E Index 364

Overview: Fig. 1 below provides a quick point of reference.

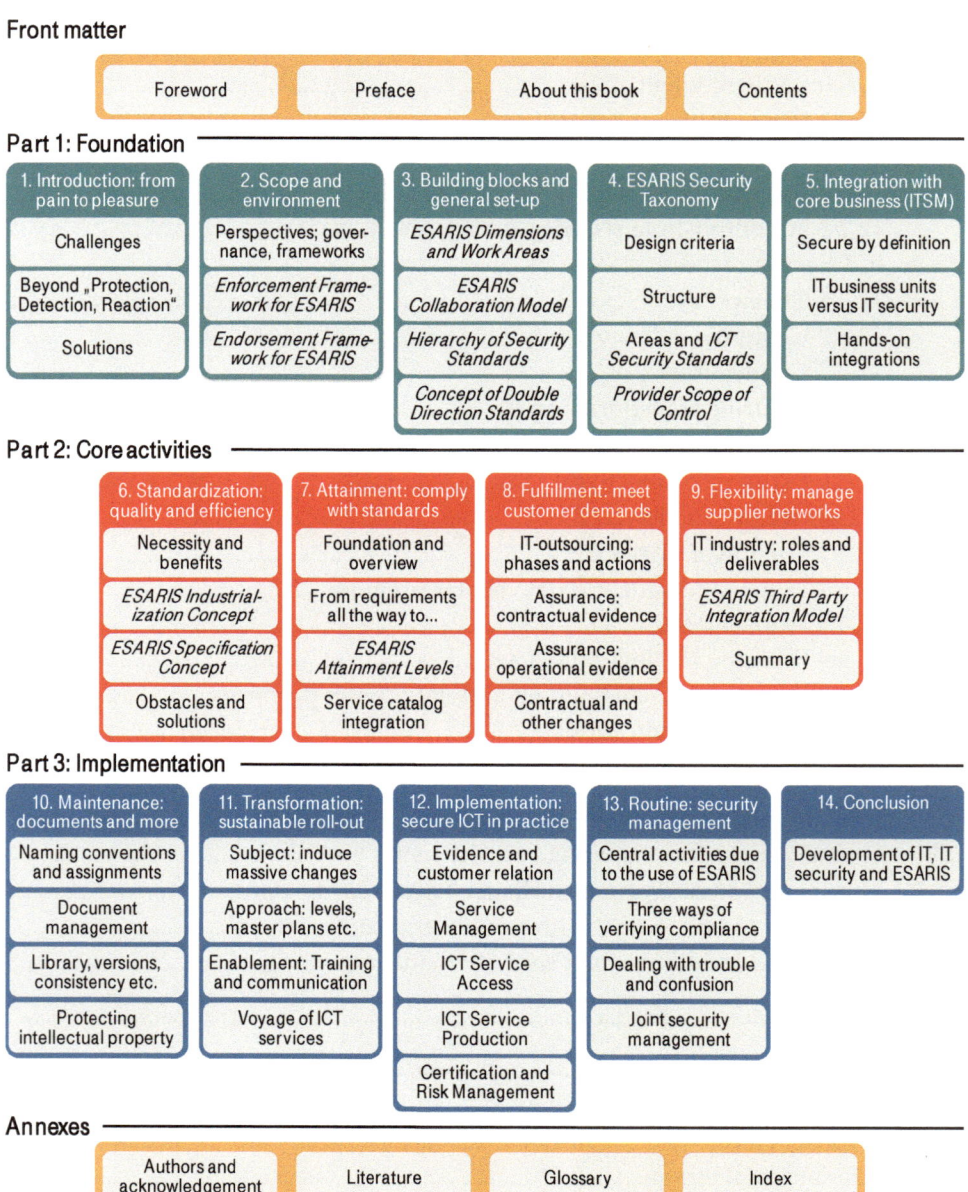

Fig. 1: Structure of this book

Part 1: Foundation

Protecting ICT services in a large-scale, distributed IT production is a challenge that requires an effective classification and organization schema. In order to ensure that security really works in such an environment, the IT security management and the provider's core processes are being integrated. Today, quality, security and efficiency count. That's why the standardization and harmonization is crucial. Modularity is required so that all businesses und the supply chain can be supported. Agreements on security and transparency need to be managed as a sound basis for relationships with customers and suppliers. These central topics are shown in Fig. 2.

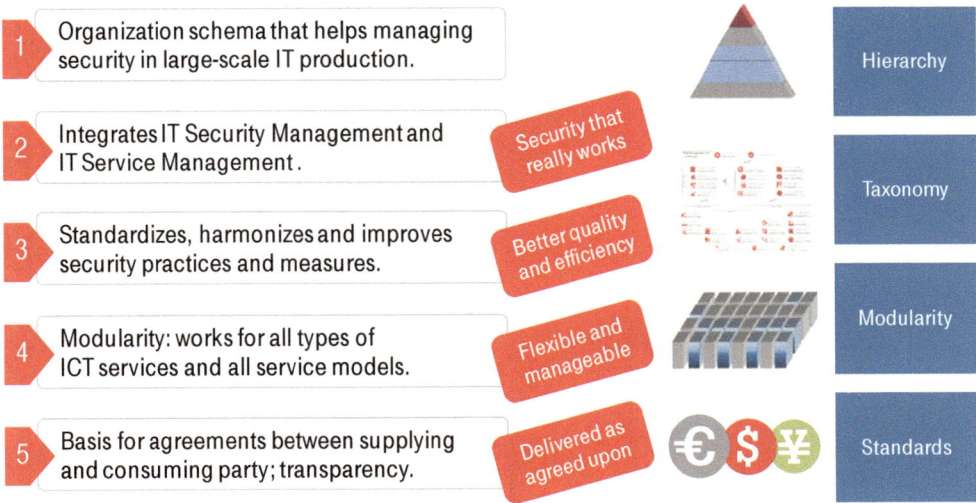

Fig. 2: Goals and benefits of ESARIS

1   Subject (from pain to pleasure)

Introduction and summary: Every textbook about IT security shall provide new information and deliver workable guidance to solve problems, master challenges, or manage security in a more effective or efficient way. This book promises to deliver. The best recipe for making things better is to understand the problem or challenge first. Consequently, Sect. 1.1 will rapidly come to the point and present a list of twelve challenges in form of questions. ICT[1] service providers are expected not being able to reply with "yes, we can, this is our practice". Sect. 1.2 summarizes the approach described in this book and describes some of the means suitable to tackle the twelve challenges. Background information is also given. Finally, Sect. 1.3 outlines solutions for all twelve challenges. The details are subject of the remainder of this book.

1.1   Challenges

Introduction and summary: This section looks at security from the perspective of ICT service providers which must deliver secure ICT services to their customers. Challenges are highlighted.

Operating and actively managing about 50 computers (server systems) can be demanding for a small team though the people being involved may know each other and be able to directly communicate. The operation of 5,000 servers, however, is quite different. Being responsible for 50,000 servers is a real challenge and a large IT company may have even more servers if the business is distributed amongst many countries around the world. Whereas in the first case of 50 server systems not even a real data center is required, the installation of 50,000 servers requires the space of about 9,000 square meters only for IT (for the sake of comparison: a soccer pitch has about 7,100 square meters). Note that air-conditioning, power supply etc. additionally consume several times the amount of space used for the IT. And who knows how many virtual machines (servers) are actually running on each (physical) server system?

The numbers might be impressive or not, but the implications are great. In a large or even huge IT department, the IT personnel can e.g. no longer know each other and directly communicate. Their working model is characterized by a high degree

---

[1] "ICT" stands for "information and communication technology" covering "IT" (information technology) and "TC" (telecommunication technology). "ICT" is used whenever this book refers to services for users or to the parties providing such services (mainly the ICT Service Provider). Though both types of technology might be referred to, the abbreviation "IT" is still used in terms like "IT security", "IT production", "IT department" etc. since ICT is not seen to be frequently used in such contexts.

of division of labor. Everybody is highly specialized and executes well-defined tasks while working along predefined processes. Specialization and division of labor requires defining roles and responsibilities as well as interfaces for their interaction. Such an organization is required for managing such a large-scale IT. It is also required to realize the economies of scale and competitive advantages as the result thereof. The ICT is growing fast on this planet and becomes bigger since ICT is used in more and more areas and businesses. The ICT becomes more and more centralized since an industrialized operation of ICT is cheaper and mostly better through the economies of scale. The second half of the information age is characterized by a novel mode: the IT production takes the place of traditional IT and TC.

What does this mean for security? The ICT becomes more complex. Is it a problem that this bigger ICT boosts the effort for security? No, this should scale well. Is it difficult to implement novel security measures which are required to secure the advanced ICT platforms used nowadays? Though the security measures might be different to those used in traditional systems, many manufacturers are specialized to deliver the required solutions. This should also not be the problem. There are many standards, products, and best practices that provide the necessary technical and procedural security measures.

Larger IT departments and specialized ICT Service Providers must be able to define, communicate and correctly apply hundreds and thousands of single security measures in a large-scale, industrial environment with thousands of employees located in many countries, each being highly specialized. This is a real problem and this book will provide solutions to this.

There is another aspect. In the second half of the information age, the IT production gets centralized. This means that specialized IT companies (called "ICT Service Providers" from now on) provide a large portion of the ICT services that are purchased by user organizations or end-users. This trend towards using ICT services from third parties (ICT Service Providers) is called "IT outsourcing". Third-party services are used since they are cheaper and mostly better. Only an industrialized, large-scale IT production can realize these economies of scale. Such an ICT Service Provider will offer and produce its ICT services for many customers (user organizations). Each customer can have different requirements, also with respect to security. The user organizations' business differ which lead to different security requirements. Note that there are many different ICT services ranging from workplace services and network services all the way to numerous ICT services including the delivery of application, platform or infrastructure services. This adds further complexity to the ICT Service Provider's business and makes managing the security in this IT production more difficult. Though people not being involved in such a business may tend to underestimate this complexity, this is really critical.

What is needed? Table 1 shows twelve challenges for ICT Service Providers. This book promises to provide answers and solutions to those questions and challenges.

It is recommended to read the latter carefully. Most IT departments and IT companies will not be able to answer many of the questions with "yes".

Table 1: Challenges which ICT Service Providers have to respond to

Challenges
1. Reliability/transparency. Can the ICT Service Provider make statements off the cuff that are not only short and precise, but also meaningful and reliable (e.g., for an RfI or RfP)? Is this the case for all possible aspects that influence the security of the ICT services offered? Does this apply for all ICT services and platforms offered?
2. Industrialization. Has the ICT Service Provider standardized all its IT security measures to such an extent that it can industrialize its production? Are the IT security measures modularized to such an extent that they can flexibly meet customer requirements?
3. Work areas. Is the ICT Service Provider well-prepared to support and coordinate the following three, organizationally different work areas in terms of security? The work areas are: customer-independent development projects, customer-related projects for winning, processing and implementing orders, and ongoing IT operation that is not organized based on projects.
4. Interaction with customers. Does the ICT Service Provider have the necessary staff and organization to provide its customers with the required degree of transparency? Does the ICT Service Provider simultaneously provide personnel and procedural interfaces to allow information to be exchanged between the user company and itself during every phase of the business relationship?
5. Contract design. Are the ICT Service Provider's security standards suitable as a basis for contracts with user companies? Are measures taken to ensure that the contractual regulations and implementation of the security standards do not diverge?
6. Standardization. Are tried and tested technical concepts and solutions systematically documented and standardized? Is the expertise of security specialists who are only available to a limited extent thus opened up to the entire company and made possible to use? Is the architecture sufficiently flexible to allow new methods and measures to be added and existing ones to be updated?
7. ITIL integration/enabling. Can IT staff and other staff understand the security architecture and apply the security guidelines and not only IT security experts? Does the architecture ensure that the security measures are integrated into the core production processes (ITIL) so that their implementation can be ensured?

Challenges
<u>8. Efficiency</u>. Does the ICT Service Provider have an architecture to support the standardization? Does this constitute a means of making complexity manageable? Does it offer concepts to achieve economies of scale through reuse? Are costs reduced and quality increased as a result?
<u>9. Hierarchy</u>. Does the architecture contain a hierarchy in which the IT security measures are progressively refined so that statements can be made with differing degrees of detail? Does this make it possible to demonstrate that the IT security measures support the achievement of the company goals and form an integrated, mutually supportive and secure whole?
<u>10. Division of labor</u>. Does the ICT Service Provider have an architecture that supports various models of the division of labor and allows the standardized IT security measures to be assigned to the departments and teams responsible? Does the architecture also accomplish this for the division of labor in the external supply chain with suppliers and partners?
<u>11. Knowledge management</u>. Does the ICT Service Provider's architecture support the effective management of the entire knowledge compiled in the security standards? Is it ensured that all information can be located quickly despite the complexity and the large amount of the information?
<u>12. ISMS integration</u>.[2] Does the ICT Service Provider's architecture support the usual security management activities – in particular, monitoring adherence to standards, drawing up and managing evidence of compliance and implementing measures to eliminate deviations?

1.2   Areas of activity beyond „Protection, Detection, Reaction"

Introduction and summary: Obviously, user organizations expect the ICT services purchased from ICT Service Providers to be secure. But there is more. ICT Service Providers need to meet a wide variety of market requirements. In the more complex IT outsourcing situations, the security management of the ICT Service Provider (producer) and that of the user organization (customer) are interwoven. For these reasons, an entirely different approach is required for securing an IT production than for a traditional IT operation on a low scale and with a low degree of complexity. The new approach outlined in this section takes operational requirements into account and focuses on user requirements, thus facing the reality in the market economy.

---

2   ISMS: Information Security Management System

Editorial note: This section is based on one of the author's earlier publications.[3]

Today's ICT platforms are usually large. The task of an ICT Service Provider's security management department is to ensure the security of ICT services. Although the special features of the platform lead to the need for special security measures, they are described in detail in literature.[4] The actual challenge for an ICT Service Provider's security management department entails adequately implementing these security measures and orchestrating the numerous individual activities connected with them. This is shown in Fig. 3.

Fig. 3: Existing catalogs of measures and the real challenge

User organizations draw on the ICT services of specialized ICT Service Providers. This process, referred to as "IT outsourcing", transfers the responsibility for service provision to the ICT Service Provider. The ICT Service Provider provides the service and is responsible for its quality; in other words, also for ensuring security in the sense of eliminating inacceptable risks.

Although IT outsourcing means that the ICT Service Provider is responsible for (the security of) the ICT services, the associated risk remains with the user organi-

---

[3] Eberhard von Faber: Organisation und Absicherung einer industriellen IT-Produktion, Drei Handlungsfelder jenseits von „Protection, Detection, Reaction"; in: Datenschutz und Datensicherheit - DuD, October 2016, Vol. 40, Issue 10, pp 647–653, ISSN 1614-0702, Springer Fachmedien Wiesbaden 2016 [48]

[4] E.g. Information Security Forum (ISF): The Standard of Good Practice for Information Security 2016 [25]; Cloud Security Alliance (CSA): Security Guidance; Version 3.0, Nov. 2011 [31]; ISO/IEC 27017 – Information technology — Security techniques — Code of practice for information security controls based on ISO/IEC 27002 for cloud services; 2015 [8]

zation. To be more precise, inadequate safeguarding of ICT services poses a business risk for both sides. In the case of the user organization, the risk entails negative impacts on the business processes that are provided with the aid of the ICT services. For the ICT Service Provider, risks arise as a result of failure to meet the expectations and requirements of its customers, that is, the user organizations. It is difficult to say which side tips the balance, and that is not the essential question anyway. Highly industrialized markets are steered in a different way.

So how do ICT Service Providers need to establish themselves as producers in order to their customers' requirements? In this regard, three topic areas arise that represent to a certain extent the products delivered by the ICT Service Provider. The situation is illustrated in Fig. 4.

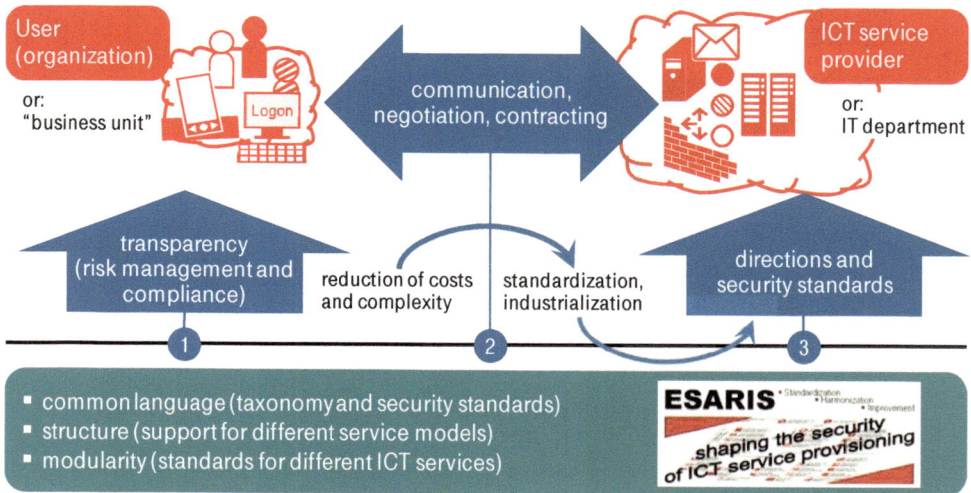

Fig. 4: Situation with regard to requirements and solutions

The three topic areas are:

- Transparency: How is "security" achieved, what does it require and what security measures have been implemented? Such information forms the basis for synchronizing the requirements (of the user organizations) with the security properties implemented in the ICT services (offered by the ICT Service Provider). Transparency is an indispensable basis for business, as it builds up confidence and allows the user organization to conduct operational risk management.

- Interfaces and interaction: User organizations and ICT Service Providers need interfaces and procedures in order to discuss the topic of "security", balance expectations and possibilities, and establish corresponding contractual agreements. This does not entail a one-off comparison that seals the purchase. An ICT service cannot be described like a simple product. Technology and requirements are subject to constant change, meaning that requirements need to be exchanged and synchronized constantly, also during the operating phase.

- Standardization: User organizations expect using external ICT services to have advantages over producing the services themselves. This means that the ICT Service Provider needs to achieve economies of scale – something that is essentially only made possible by the industrialization of IT production and its extensive standardization. Standardization is important on the side of the ICT Service Provider with a view to ensuring high quality at an acceptable cost.

The *Enterprise Security Architecture for Reliable ICT Services (ESARIS)* described in this book focuses on meeting these three market requirements.

We will look into all three elements in more detail in the following sections. A description will be provided of the measures that the ICT Service Provider needs to take and how they benefit the user organizations (its customers).

Note: There are simple cloud or infrastructure services such as memory space, highly standardized platform services and simple applications that can be purchased and configured directly through a web shop. Even when such services are produced industrially, some of the measures described below may not actually be required. Why? This book focuses on IT outsourcing that is characterized by the complexity of the IT applications and their close connection with the user organizations' core business. The ICT Service Provider serves a large number of user organizations and provides them with a fairly extensive range of ICT services. For large user organizations, the ICT services/applications will always be complex as well as industry-specific and company-specific (individual). After all, they need to support a large number of corporate processes while generating significant competitive advantages.

1.2.1 Transparency

The ICT Service Provider ensures the protection of the ICT services. It is also his task to provide the information that the user organizations require in order to assess the IT risks. The ICT Service Provider needs to ensure that the available information is appropriately prepared and maintained. Finally, the user organizations need to know if their security requirements are met. Larger organizations have different requirements because their business is different and they are making business in different environments. Hence, they have to adhere to different legislation, industry standards etc. They are exposed to specific threat scenarios requiring special security solutions, and maybe also their risk appetite is different. This is shown in the upper left of Fig. 5. User organizations should have their own security management organization. This organization is used to work with one framework whereas another corporation uses another framework (shown in the upper right of Fig. 5). ICT Service Providers must be able to provide transparency in a way that shows the connection to such frameworks.

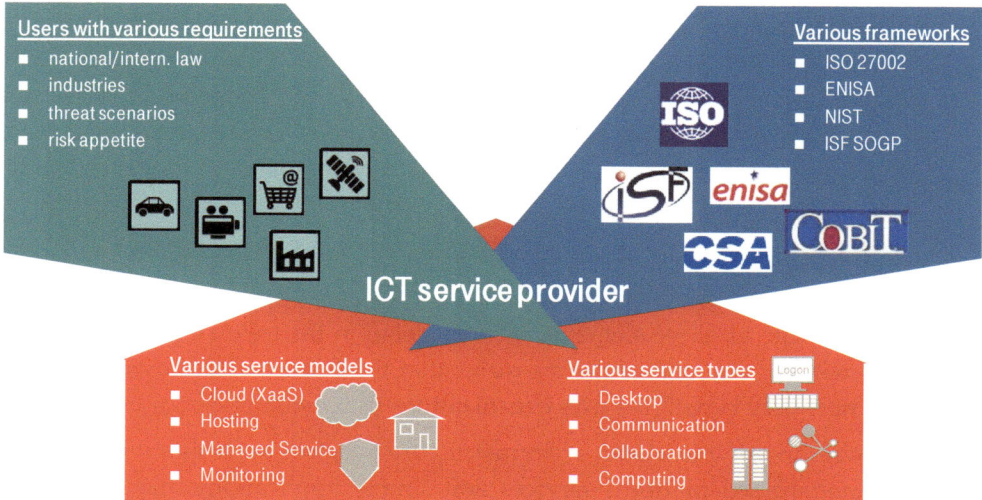

Fig. 5: Transparency; providers must consider four variables/parameters

But there are two more aspects. Transparency means provisioning of information about "how security is achieved". Large ICT Service Providers maintain a service offering portfolio that comprises many different ICT services including e.g. desktop services, network services and computing services. Refer to lower right in Fig. 5. Moreover, these ICT services may be produced and delivered with different service models. What does "service model" mean? Any IT is worthless without an application on top of the IT stack. However, which party provides this and is responsible for it? There are models where the ICT Service Provider only provides infrastructure services without an application. Actually, there are numerous such service models. Tasks relating to the IT service management may also be distributed so that the ICT Service Provider is not responsible for all management activities. Refer to lower left in Fig. 5. Such types and models must also be considered. The ICT Service Provider must be prepared to maintain the information in a way that he is able to respond to the various scenarios.

This will not work in the long term without a corresponding corporate culture. The IT operation and its staff must not concentrate their thoughts and actions entirely on implementation, but must also constantly keep track of the information required by the user organizations (customers). So what exactly is required?

Architecture

Nowadays, the technologies used to provide ICT services are usually highly complex. There are a large number of different ICT services, which differ in terms of functions, means of production, provision models and service parameters. The first step towards achieving transparency is therefore to establish a classification and organization scheme that makes it possible to control this complexity and serves as a shared "platform" for exchanging information. This book describes the *Enterprise Security Architecture for Reliable ICT Services (ESARIS)*, which was developed precisely for this purpose. Without such an architecture it is hardly possible at all to ensure security in a large-scale industrialized IT production with thousands of employees who are organized in a large number of highly specialized teams and departments, and are usually also spread over a large geographical area.

There are other security architectures in the literature like O-ESA[5] and SABSA.[6] In contrast, ESARIS is not a template only nor a framework or a reference for the development of an enterprise security architecture or program. ESARIS is an enterprise security architecture for ICT Service Providers that considers industrialization, division of labor and related trends in today's IT industry. ESARIS is not for experts only but shall be used by everyone (when it comes to security). It does not only tell what to do, but provides detailed guidance how to do it. Table 2 defines the term "security architecture" as being understood and used in this book.

Table 2: Definition of security architecture

Security architecture	Main effect
Security architecture is related to standardization since it aims at solving many similar problems using the same principles. It helps raising the quality and reducing costs.	Lower costs, better quality
Security architecture leads activities for securing ICT services in a holistic manner by describing (1) basic elements (decomposition) and (2) rules for their interaction (integration).	Comprehensive view, approach for realization
Security architecture makes things easier to comprehend and to apply since it reduces to fundamental parts and principles which helps managing complexity. Security architecture always uses illustrations and schematics.	Activation of people, enablement
Security architecture supports the division of labor (decomposition) since every party is contributing to a common overall plan (integration).	Industrialization: match the economic system
Security architecture ensures that all parts and contributions are mutually supportive and provide an integrated secure whole (integration).	Fit for purpose

The elements of the security architecture are classification and organization schemes that divide a complex object into different elements and pinpoint the interconnections between them (similarities, differences, interaction). It must be pos-

---

5   The Open Group: Open Enterprise Security Architecture (O-ESA), A Framework and Template for Policy-Driven Security; Van Haren Publishing, Zaltbommel, 2011, ISBN 978 90 8753 672 5 [38]

6   John Sherwood, Andrew Clark and David Lynas: Enterprise Security Architecture, A Business-Driven Approach; CRC Press, Boca Raton, 2005, ISBN 978 1 57820 318 5 [39]

sible to present each subarchitecture in the form of a diagram or visual representation that fits on one page (with a font size of 14 pt or more). This makes it easily intelligible and allows it to be used as a medium for discussions. The diagrams do not contain all information, but they can be used to explain all important details. Text documents provide all important information; a diagram or visual representation simply gives an idea and represents the "frozen essence". Lists that have simply been provided in the form of a drawing do not count. For an architectural diagram, the sequence is always an important part of the information to be conveyed. This "drawing pictures" is absolutely necessary if several thousand people in a company are to learn something specific, remember it in the long term and discuss it. People take in information predominantly and most easily in visual form. Pictures provide important anchors that aid memory. Defined technical terms, as well as neologisms, the establishment of your own jargon and the use of icons, abbreviations, alternative names, avatars and so on greatly support communication and help people to work in a targeted manner. ICT Service Providers should not underestimate the importance of this type of tool.

Hierarchy and taxonomy which are explained in the following are examples of elements of the ESARIS security architecture.

Hierarchy

As the requirements of the user organizations involve greatly differing degrees of detail and abstraction, the ICT Service Provider's security documentation must also be structured accordingly. This means that the security documentation needs to have a hierarchical structure. More general specifications are refined step by step to form concrete instructions on implementing individual security functions and mechanisms. ESARIS uses two levels for the company ("overarching") and further three levels for the ICT services (the company's "products").

Level 3 contains higher-level security rules that apply for all ICT services, technologies and process areas. It has the purpose of reconciliation with corporate policies as well as industry standards and other standards (e.g., ISO/IEC 27001). The bottom level containing the most details (Level 5) is intended for internal use. It instructs employees as to which security measures they should implement and how, as well as determining what they should do and how they should behave (continuously during development, implementation and operation). User organizations that "outsource" IT want to reduce complexity and delegate tasks. They are therefore not usually interested in these "bits and bytes" and are often not even able to understand this documentation because, with the IT outsourcing, they have reduced the corresponding IT competencies or do not even have any at all.

With a view to allowing information to be exchanged effectively between user organizations and ICT Service Providers, a further level is needed, which has been especially inserted into ESARIS as Level 4. The security documentation at this degree of detail and abstraction should serve the following purpose: it should make it possible to communicate, negotiate and agree on security issues with a large number of major user organizations (customers). The documentation should constitute implementation-independent specifications (no products and versions) that enable the IT production to achieve the required security by implementing various security features. This flexibility benefits both sides, but is also necessary in order for security to be successfully implemented in an environment that is highly dynamic with regard to both economy and technology. Ultimately, the description at this degree of detail and abstraction makes it possible to provide a general overview of all security aspects and to check for completeness and interaction.

Details will be provided later in this book.

Taxonomy

This description level (Level 4 in ESARIS), which is equally important for the user organization and the ICT Service Provider, still comprises up to 500 security measures with sentences in which it may all come down to one word. Not all of these measures are always actually relevant for a customer. When customers purchase backend services, they are not interested in how the ICT Service Provider would safeguard a workstation. In addition, the measures serve as guidelines for the ICT Service Provider's departments and, again, only a few of these measures are really relevant for a particular organizational unit. A further element is therefore needed in the architecture. This is the *ESARIS Security Taxonomy* with 31 areas.

The *ESARIS Security Taxonomy* will be described later in this book in great detail.

Such a consistent modular concept is also important because specifications for all possible ICT services and service models must be included and need to be possible to find. Furthermore, it must be possible to map them to the service portfolio. The same applies when it comes to organizing IT production. As already mentioned, all departments need to be able to identify "their" measures very quickly. In addition, the taxonomy supports the issues of "interfaces and interaction" (see next Sect. 1.2.2) and "standardization" (Sect. 1.2.3).

It is important that the security measures that the ICT Service Provider defines and communicates with the user organizations (its customers) do not solely have a *preventive* character, but also cover *detection* and *reaction*. What does that mean? It may be open to dispute whether the implementation of measures to detect possible security breaches has a preventive character, yet the crucial questions are always as follows: How do I know that the measures have been implemented and are effective? What happens when measures fail or prove to be insufficient? The ICT Service Provider's catalog must therefore include everything that contributes towards security. This is necessary for implementation, and customers need answers to corresponding questions. Here are some examples of detection and response: One measure describes functional and penetration testing. This establishes whether other security measures are effective (*detection* in the sense of evidence). One measure requires "quality gates" with defined checks. This also establishes whether other security measures have actually been implemented. One measure requires the installation of a scanner. This establishes whether certain configuration and hardening guidelines have been observed. Other scanners search for (known) weaknesses by checking product versions and patch levels. Measures are also defined as to how detected weaknesses are to be removed (*reaction*). Another example of measures in the area of *reaction* includes measures regarding incident management.

Summary: The user organizations require information ("transparency") that enables them to assess the IT risks involved in using external ICT services. In ISO/IEC 15408, the Common Criteria [7], the term "assurance" is used here. This entails being sufficiently certain that there are no inacceptable risks and that the ICT services can therefore be considered to be secure for the user organization. The need for information differs greatly, but is generally high in the more complex IT outsourcing situations. The large quantity of information gives rise to the need for a classification scheme in the form of an architecture with elements such as a hierarchy and taxonomy. However, user organizations also need to understand how their ICT Service Provider works. After all, this lays the foundations for concluding valid contracts and being able to influence the ICT Service Provider. The ICT Service Provider's entire documentation should be structured in line with the architecture, in such a way that the required information (or requirements for it) can actually be found.

1.2.2   Interfaces and interaction

ICT Service Providers act in a customer-oriented manner, which does not always seem to be organized in a satisfactory way with regard to the issue of IT security or information security. Security may be just one of many features, but the success and continued existence of companies may depend on it. Customer orientation means being able to obtain and process information from customers – in every phase and at any time.

Extending ITIL

Most large-scale IT organizations are organized in accordance with the IT Infrastructure Library (ITIL).[7] For an ICT Service Provider with numerous customers, however, one important area is missing here, namely the interfaces to the user organization, the customer. Although ITIL includes demand management, service portfolio management and service reporting, the ICT Service Providers ("IT outsourcers") have additionally incorporated sales, deal management, migration phases (transition, transformation) and usually also explicit service delivery management for the operating phase into their process environment. In most cases,

---

[7]   Refer e.g. to: Ahmad K. Shuja: ITIL: Service Management Implementation and Operation; Auerbach Publications, 2010 [35]

though, this has not yet been implemented properly for the issue of IT security. And it is more complicated than it looks at first glance! Standards such as ISO/IEC 27002[8] as well as ISO/IEC 27017[9] do not provide sufficient assistance with regard to how an ICT Service Provider can serve its customers.

Fig. 6 shows a simplified model for IT outsourcing. In the first two phases (sales and deal management), the ICT service/product is only discussed and not delivered. Nonetheless, these phases are very important with respect to security since crucial decisions are taken. Then the ICT Service Provider takes over the IT business (Transition and Transformation) and becomes responsible for features of the ICT services as well as its protection. When possible adaptations are completed, standard operations start using the provider's security standards.

Fig. 6: Interfaces; providers must support interaction

As one can probably imagine, the phases of sales and contract negotiations deserve particular attention. What was said above under "Transparency" needs to be adequately implemented here. This includes support from security experts. Another specific example, "transition and transformation", provides more insight: When the ICT Service Provider takes over the IT business from a user organization or its current service provider, it usually takes on data, applications, often also hardware and sometimes entire data centers with the complete IT stack – possibly including staff and their processes. Even taking on the data is critical, as neither the security measures of the "old" service provider nor those of the "new" one take effect here. This is also the case for the following phases, in which the IT operation is progressively changed over to the standards of the new ICT Service Provider. Individual measures need to be defined for this and laid down in a contract between both parties.

---

8   ISO/IEC 27002 – Information technology – Security techniques – Code of practice for information security management, 2013 [6]

9   ISO/IEC 27017 – Information technology — Security techniques — Code of practice for information security controls based on ISO/IEC 27002 for cloud services; 2015 [8]

The same applies for the operating phase ("run"). This phase not only involves security incidents, with the result that information needs to be exchanged between the ICT Service Provider and the user organization. It is also important that activities on both sides are closely coordinated where necessary. For this purpose, the processes of the respective security management systems (ISMS) need to interact, and the groups of people involved must be prepared for this. These are typical measures in the "reaction" category, although their definition and implementation are of a precautionary nature.

IT is a highly dynamic environment with regard to technologies and provisioning models. However, security requirements also change as a result of changed business requirements or new usage models. And even the threats are subject to constant change. Thus, IT and IT security never stand still. It is necessary to establish whether the interface is prepared to master critical patches with downtime during the operating phase ("run") and subsequently implement or initiate any necessary changes in contracts. The ICT Service Provider's security documentation should also contain statements regarding this, and the elements of its architecture (such as a taxonomy) should provide space for this.

It should be noted that some business models do not allow for or cover any sales, deal management and migration services whatsoever. Simple cloud services are distributed via marketing measures, are defined by standard contracts (general terms and conditions) and comprise neither migration services nor any IT management services. In more complex IT outsourcing situations, in contrast, delivery services and Service Level Agreements (SLA) are negotiated and IT Service Management is actually the object of the outsourcing. Here, dedicated teams or whole departments with hundreds of appropriately specialized employees operate the interfaces in sales, deal management, transition and transformation as well as operations. The aim is to implement this for "IT security" with appropriately qualified employees who have defined roles and responsibilities.

Providing evidence

Interfaces between the user organization and the ICT Service Provider are indispensable, need to be anchored in the relevant processes and must be integrated in terms of both organization and personnel. But what is managed using the interfaces? Some examples have already been provided but, from the viewpoint of the user organization, probably the most important thing to be exchanged is evidence – to be more precise, *assurance*.

ISO/IEC 15408[10] defines "assurance" as grounds for confidence that the security requirements are met. Assurance is "evidence of trustworthiness" and generated by gathering knowledge that no inacceptable risks exist and that the ICT services

---

10   ISO/IEC 15408 – Information technology — Security techniques — Evaluation criteria for
     IT security — Part 1: Introduction and general model; 2009 [9]

can therefore be considered to be "secure". The user organization's security management cannot make do with assumptions, but requires adequate assurance that its security requirements are complied with.

This compliance has two faces. Firstly, the ICT Service Provider needs to comply with a wide range of (its own) security standards and safeguard its ICT services accordingly. Secondly, it must also be ensured that the user organization's security requirements are complied with. The ICT Service Provider needs to verify and ensure both aspects separately. The key instruments for internal compliance (called "attainment") entail developing and managing security standards as well as means for comparing if they are actually implemented. The ICT Service Provider must apply its own security standards and also verify this for itself.

External compliance (evidence of compliance with customer requirements, called "fulfillment") is subdivided into two parts, namely "contractual evidence" and "operational evidence". It would also be possible, and perhaps more appropriate, to speak of "contract-based evidence" and "operational evidence". Considering the example of a car may better explain this. The customer buys a fast car and therefore needs good brakes. At least the maximum speed is specified. The comparison of this value with the customer's requirements constitutes the compliance number one. The customer drives at the promised speed and can brake with ease. This is compliance number two and the operational evidence that the brakes fulfill their purpose.

When it comes to the security of ICT services, basically both is needed, but there are limits. The contract-based evidence is not able to cover everything at every level. The ICT Service Provider should have a great deal more requirements, specifications and checks to safeguard ICT services than a user organization can and wants to regulate in a contract. Why? IT outsourcing is supposed to relieve the user organization! The user organization hasn't gained much if it takes care of (or has to take care of) everything itself again. The ICT Service Provider therefore needs to provide the most important and relevant information. An important role in the operational evidence is played by security reports. These reports summarize information about security management activities (e.g., incidents and patch levels) as well as information about security-relevant events in IT (e.g., the evaluation of log data and alerts) in a previously defined form. Security reports are an important instrument for the user organization: for its own risk management and as evidence for its own customers and auditors.

The assurance that no inacceptable risks exist must be "adequate". The higher the potential risk, the more extensive the evidence should be (higher "assurance level"). Science and industry are still in the finding phase here, which is characterized by deflection in both directions. Some companies, just like many end users, have a tendency towards reckless carelessness. Other companies take a very thorough approach but often fail to cover every area because of limited resources. Instead, the aim should be to achieve a certain coverage with an *adequate* degree of thoroughness.

Summary: Interfaces are required between the user organization and ICT Service Provider in order to be able to reach agreements and develop them further. This is the case for the entire life-cycle and is especially essential in complex IT outsourcing situations. Each of the phases of sales, deal management, migration (transition, transformation) and operation (service delivery management) has its own requirements and requires a separate interface that needs to be defined accordingly and made ready to use. One key task of these interfaces involves exchanging information with regard to the fulfillment of customer requirements. Both sides are active here. This becomes particularly apparent when modifications are required. There are a wide range of reasons for this and both sides may request such modifications. Large, far-reaching modifications in operations are carried out in complex IT outsourcing situations in project mode, often in close interaction between the user organization and the ICT Service Provider. These projects are thus not essentially different from those during the migration (transition, transformation). The interfaces to be installed must also be equipped for such situations.

1.2.3   Standardization

IT security is becoming more and more important. This is a direct consequence of IT being used more and becoming increasingly widespread – also in areas that were not previously supported by IT or which simply did not exist before. As a result, the number of threats is also increasing. Some of them are only becoming possible due to the way in which we use IT and what we do with it.

Another important aspect is the realization that not only IT but also IT security costs money, takes time and requires other resources (such as expertise). As the decisions are relating to business and not personal ones, a cost/benefit analysis needs to be drawn up that is objective and is comprehensible for decision-makers.

IT security managers therefore need to pay more attention to an issue that does not seem to be part of their domain at all: limiting things to that which is found to be necessary. To be more precise, the IT security managers of an ICT Service Provider are increasingly forced to counteract the "escalating" effort involved in safeguarding ICT services, which appears to be arising as a result of the "escalating" usage of the ICT services and their technical complexity. Three measures are recommended for reducing costs of all kinds:

- An architectural classification and organization scheme that makes it possible to direct expenses appropriately to the relevant areas based on risk,

- Integration of IT security management and IT service management (ITIL),

- Consistent standardization.

The *Enterprise Security Architecture for Reliable ICT Services (ESARIS)* described in this book supports all three points.

Fig. 7 shows the development of IT away from custom solutions and towards more standardized ones. The figure also shows consequences for security. In both cases, we see a shift from "exact fit" to "best match". Security managers must face the facts. The environment became different. Nowadays, standardization and modularity are very important.

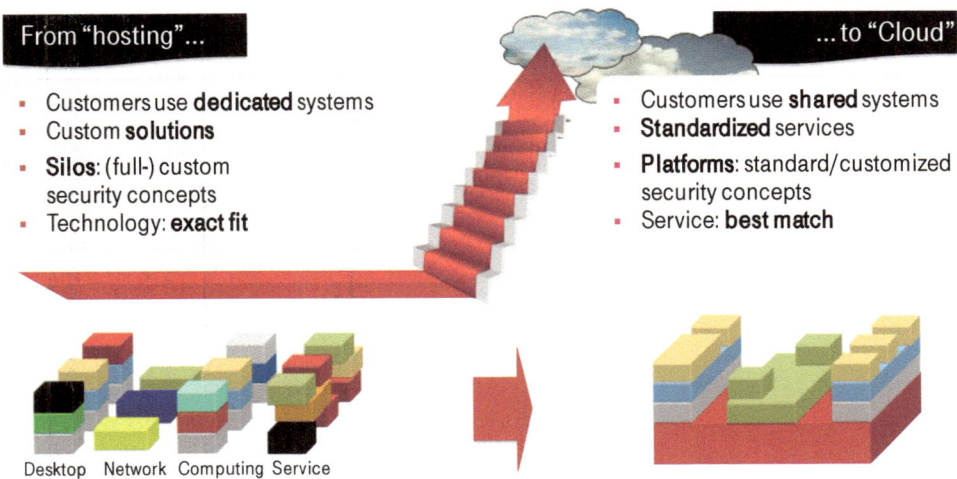

Fig. 7: ESARIS Standardization Philosophy

Integration of IT security management and IT service management (ITIL)

ESARIS integrates IT security management (ISO/IEC 27001) and IT service management (ITIL, ISO/IEC 20000[11]) consistently for the first time. What does this mean? All workflow-related or process-related security measures become part of the ITIL process steps, the tools used and all instructions for the IT personnel. Moreover, they cover all sections of the extended life-cycle (sales, deal management, transition, transformation and operations).

What are the advantages of such integration and where is it necessary? A large-scale industrialized IT production is organized in accordance with ITIL. The integration of security into the actual development and production processes ensures that security really is implemented. It forms the basis for "security by definition". Often, it is not actually possible to separate security and IT. Just think of hardening and other configuration activities, of incidents including system downtime or of patching. Integration also brings security closer to the ICT Service Provider's core competencies and core business. Inevitably, a common language gradually emerges in the company. The consideration of security in all process steps along the (internal) supply chain helps to avoid subsequent corrections, duplicate work and

---

[11]   ISO/IEC 20000 – Information technology – Service management – Part 1: Service management system requirements, Part 2: Guidance on the application of service management systems; 2012 [2]

contradictions. This reduces costs, speeds things up and increases quality. What's more, as a result of the fact that security now becomes "everyone's job", the workload is spread, thus relieving the security organization. At the same time, investments in security become more straightforward, as they become part of organization's core tasks and management begins to value security accordingly. The comprehensive approach makes better use of the time and capabilities of the security experts, as their working results are distributed more effectively. The use of unique IT service management processes for all ICT services and technology areas results in standardization. The integration of unique security measures leads to cost and quality benefits. The *ESARIS Security Taxonomy* mentioned above contains areas and measures that relate to the relevant processes and practices.

Predefinition and reuse

Standardization is generally a feature of industrial production methods and ultimately also spreads to the working results and their components. Cloud services are a good example of this. An ICT Service Provider must now also endeavor to standardize its technical security measures, as they are part of the ICT services. Standardization is indispensable in order for companies to be able to reduce production costs and increase quality through a high degree of reuse.[12]

What does this specifically mean for IT security? Obviously, user organizations also benefit from cost reductions and increased quality. However, there is more to the advantages than that. It is ultimately the standardization of security that makes it possible to achieve the transparency that user organizations need in order to effectively deal with risks. Without standardized classification and organization schemes (for example, hierarchy, taxonomy) companies are soon fighting a losing battle. However, the interfaces between the user organization and the ICT Service Provider are also a result of standardization. And the evidence required is based on comparisons that would hardly be possible to perform effectively without standardized security measures. Or the evidence is hardly possible to compare, which would make it much more difficult to make an objective decision between different offers.

Summary: User organizations expect reduced costs and complexity from using ICT services from external parties. Users also demand a higher quality including an adequate level of security. The ICT Service Providers can only meet these expectations through rigorous standardization and by utilizing economies of scale. Economies of scale require an industrialized organization of IT provisioning. This also holds for security. Security managers must reduce the complexity of their security

---

[12]   Eberhard von Faber: In-house standardization of security measures: necessity, benefits and real-world obstructions; in: ISSE 2014 Securing Electronic Business Processes, Highlights of the Information Security Solutions Europe 2014 Conference, Springer Vieweg, Wiesbaden, 2014, ISBN 978-3-658-06707-6, p. 35-48 [46]

business and standardize their concepts, methods and measures as far as possible. Only then securing ICT is a manageable task and feasible at reasonable costs in today's, large-scale and industrialized IT production environments.

1.3 Solutions

Introduction and summary: The ICT Service Provider must deliver secure ICT services to its customers. It has been shown in Sect. 1.2 that more is necessary than just having measures in place that protect the ICT services, to provide for detecting suspicious and hostile action and to prepare for an appropriate reaction. The actual challenges for an ICT Service Provider serving large user organizations were summarized in Sect. 1.1 by means of twelve challenges expressed in terms of questions. This section now summarizes the solutions. The comparison of these solutions with the challenges (Table 1 on page 5) shows what one can expect from the *Enterprise Security Architecture for Reliable ICT Service (ESARIS)* described in this book.

Table 3 shows solutions for the challenges. Note that the solutions for the ICT Service Providers comprise the implementation of numerous concepts, methods and measures of the *Enterprise Security Architecture for Reliable ICT Service (ESARIS)* which fill the rest of this book.

Table 3: Solutions for ICT Service Providers to respond to the challenges

Solutions (compare to challenges in Table 1 on page 5)
1. Reliability/transparency. Using ESARIS, all IT security measures are defined in advance and made available in a central library. The architecture constitutes a classification and organization scheme that allows possible gaps to be immediately identified. The modular nature of the IT security measures allows them to be used for various ICT services and platforms. A selection procedure supports practical application and the tailoring to the specific service for the customer.
2. Industrialization. An extensive architectural approach is required in order to ensure the security of an industrialized IT production with thousands of employees whose work is organized in a large number of highly specialized teams and departments, and who are usually also spread over a large geographical area. ESARIS is designed as a classification and organization scheme for this purpose and combines standardization with flexibility based on modularization. A composition procedure supports the aggregation of components to form secure complex ICT services.

Solutions (compare to challenges in Table 1 on page 5)
3. <u>Work areas</u>. Solutions are developed or improved almost everywhere in an IT company. Traditional models for the life-cycle not go far enough in a large-scale IT production with hundreds of major customers. ESARIS therefore defines work areas based on roles and targets, and takes account of the reality of an IT production and major IT outsourcing undertaking.
4. <u>Interaction with customers</u>. ESARIS explicitly takes account of all phases during IT outsourcing – including sales, contract negotiations, service takeover (transition), service modification (transformation) and regular operation. A personnel and procedural interface is defined for each phase. IT security measures describe exactly how interaction with the customer is to take place.
5. <u>Contract design</u>. ESARIS implements its own set of IT security standards. The IT security measures it contains are sufficiently specific for contractual regulations, yet at the same time implementation-independent and highly modular, with the result that technical enhancements are possible without the need for contract modifications. They are also used with the same text as specifications for safeguarding the ICT services.
6. <u>Standardization</u>. Practically all security documentation is drawn up in the form of security standards, made available centrally and recommended for implementation or defined as being mandatory. Any contradictions or duplications are eliminated beforehand. ESARIS excludes from this standardization only information that is verifiably organization-based or contract-related. The documentation formats are consistently modular; the classification and organization schemes are sufficiently generic.
7. <u>ITIL integration/enabling</u>. ESARIS does not order the IT security measures based on security topics, but based on purely technical factors in IT and along core production processes (ITIL). As a result, the IT security measures relevant in each case can be found by everyone and it is ensured ("secure by definition") that their implementation is part of the company's core or day-to-day business.
8. <u>Efficiency</u>. ESARIS assigns the IT security measures to all technology areas and production processes in a clear manner and integrates them there inherently as a property. As the IT security measures have a modular structure, they can easily be reused. Release procedures with regard to standardization verify that gains in efficiency and quality can be achieved.
9. <u>Hierarchy</u>. ESARIS defines a hierarchy of security standards, in which the IT security measures are progressively refined, increasing the degree of detail and information quantity accordingly. Security standards with higher degrees of detail refer to specifications at the next level up, which is more general. Various forms of dependencies are explicitly documented and recognizable.

Solutions (compare to challenges in Table 1 on page 5)
10. Division of labor. ESARIS takes account of and supports typical models of the division of labor by assigning the IT security measures to technology areas and production processes. A selection procedure allows the measures to be compiled based on the ICT service or product being provided. ESARIS implements its own set of IT security standards structured in such a way that it can be used for contractual agreements and as a specification for the producer. The procedures can be used for internal and external supply chains.
11. Knowledge management. ESARIS is primarily a classification and organization scheme. This includes the documentation that is indispensable for a large-scale IT production. Document IDs are chosen in such a way that the subject and purpose of a document are clear. This also helps users to locate information quickly. A maintenance system ensures that the document is always up-to-date, consistent, well-structured and of a high quality.
12. ISMS integration. ESARIS is a powerful tool for security management in a large-scale IT production. Procedures are therefore defined in particular in order to monitor adherence to standards, manage evidence of compliance and ensure that possible deviations are eliminated.

An Enterprise Security Architecture (ESA) is a systematic approach to protect an enterprise or, if it focuses on information security, the information and ICT being used. It can be built and maintained by any enterprise (user organization) that processes information. This book, however, concentrates on ICT service provisioning. It describes an architecture and its components specifically designed for ICT Service Providers and large IT departments as well.[13] The architecture has the clear goal, purpose and focus of delivering ICT services to user organizations (or business units) with an adequate and verifiable level of security. In order to highlight the difference from other models, the approach is called *Enterprise Security Architecture for Reliable ICT Services (ESARIS)*. It comprises various concepts, models and undertakings that are presented and described in this book.

ESARIS is also helpful for user organizations since it assists in assessing security and in choosing ICT services with the appropriate risk profile. ESARIS is designed to provide transparency mainly for user organizations. It comprises concepts for providing proof that the user's security requirements are met. User organizations acquire an instrument for working with suppliers. The ICT Service Provider acquires a tool that allows the active management of information security and that reduces costs while improving quality. In this way, the architecture addresses all of

---

[13] In the following, the term ICT Service Provider is exclusively used. This shall also cover large IT departments (of user organizations) serving different business units (their customers).

the above objectives expressed in form of twelve challenges and solutions. Note: All concepts and models are real-world ones. The concepts, models and underlying security measures have been developed by a large ICT Service Provider delivering telecommunication and information technology services around the globe. The provider has carried out a large Transformation program to implement ESARIS and its security standards in its large IT production. This program and the experiences gained from the roll-out and use of ESARIS are also a subject of this book.

2   Environment

Introduction and summary: The *Enterprise Security Architecture for Reliable ICT Services (ESARIS)* does not organize all security-related activities in a corporation. For example, all larger corporations including ICT Service Providers require an Information Security Management System (ISMS) for steering the security management by defining the organizational structure and procedures used. Such systems form the so-called *Frameworks for ESARIS* in which ESARIS is embedded (Sect. 2.1). ESARIS concerns only the security of ICT services and not of the corporation as a whole. The two perspectives corporate and ICT service security are discussed in Sect. 2.2 and a general governance model is given further clarifying interdependences with respect of using ESARIS.

Fig. 8 summarizes what ESARIS is about. Note that ESARIS is neither a sole conceptual tool nor a means for planning only. It is a realization of a tool box which provides a classification, organization and standardization schema which will be used by every employee in the company (when it comes to security). It provides a collection of practical security standards designed to meet the needs of a large-scale IT production. It does not only tells what to do, but provides detailed guidance how to do it. The concepts, methods and measures are tried and proven and actually applied in practice.

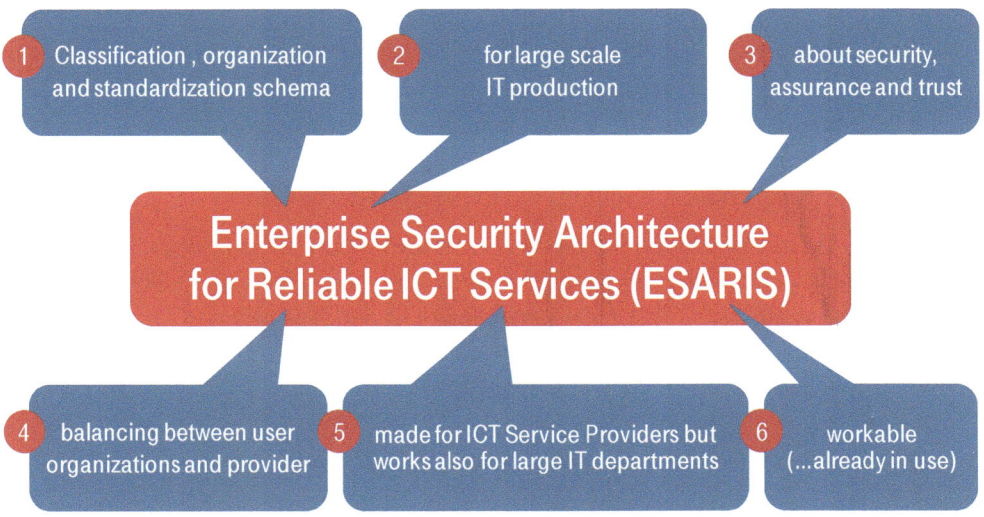

Fig. 8: Characteristics of ESARIS

2.1   Frameworks for ESARIS

Introduction and summary: The ESARIS approach – the subject matter of this book – does not cover all the activities within an enterprise that relate to information security and IT risks. Firstly, a security management organization and processes for it on a corporate level are required. This Information Security Management System (ISMS) build or maintain the so-called *Enablement Framework for ESARIS*. Secondly, one must manage the relations to standards, industry and other best practices. The collection and classification of security measures or controls is the subject of the so-called *Endorsement Framework for ESARIS*. This framework also maintains a mapping between all existing security measures from the different sources as required for the Internal Control Framework of the ICT Service Provider and its customers.

An environment and conditions need to be defined in which the *Enterprise Security Architecture for Reliable ICT Services (ESARIS)* is used. The security-related "set of environmental conditions" is referred to below as the "Framework for ESARIS". Other conditions exist, but only those relating to information security are considered in the following.

The Framework for ESARIS consists of two parts (refer to Fig. 9). The *Enforcement Framework for ESARIS* provides the capabilities whereas the *Endorsement Framework for ESARIS* provides input for ESARIS and manages relations to different sources:

- The *Enforcement Framework for ESARIS* can be considered the *Information Security Management System (ISMS)* of the ICT Service Provider since it provides the organization, the processes and other resources and is built to establish, implement, operate, monitor, review, maintain and improve information security. An ISMS which is largely defined in ISO/IEC 27001 [14] is used by many large organizations and implemented on a corporate level.

- The *Endorsement Framework for ESARIS* builds the part that manages relations of ESARIS to norms, industry standards and best practices as well as legislation and regulation. This framework looks in detail at security implementation standards, namely ISO/IEC 27002 [15] or PCI-DSS [16]. It also comprises a mapping between the security measures defined in ESARIS and the security controls stipulated in the environment.

---

[14] ISO/IEC 27001 – Information technology – Security techniques – Information security management systems – Requirements, 2013 [5]

[15] ISO/IEC 27002 – Information technology – Security techniques – Code of practice for information security management, 2013 [6]

[16] PCI Standards Council: PCI DSS (PCI Data Security Standard); Version 3.2 as of 2016 [13]

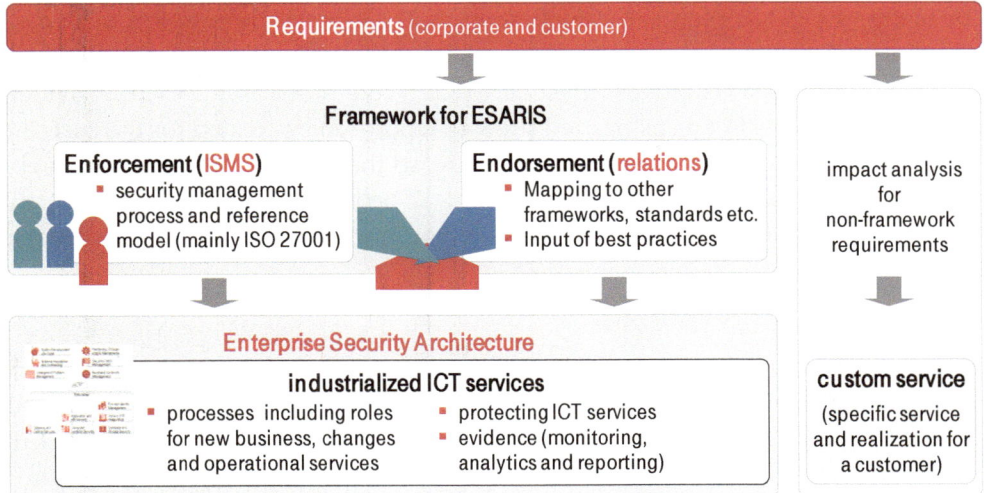

Fig. 9: Role and content of the Framework for ESARIS

The *Endorsement Framework for ESARIS* comprises participating in standardization boards (such as ISO), industry associations (such as the Information Security Forum, ISF, and the Cloud Security Alliance, CSA). It also deals with the analysis of legislation and regulation. As a result, it delivers material for the development of ESARIS and its security standards.

ESARIS is built to fulfill corporate and customer security requirements using predefined controls. It may be, however, that some specific customer requirements cannot be met by controls which are foreseen and selected beforehand. Those requirements are called "non-framework requirements" (right in Fig. 9). In such cases, a business impact analysis is performed in order to decide the following:

- the existing security will be advanced so that the "non-framework requirements" will no longer be "non-framework" ones,

- the customer's request will be rejected,

- a customer specific service will be built.

The modification of the ESARIS security standards will result in an improvement which can be used for subsequent businesses with other customers (case 1). The alternatives are a "no-go decision" (case 2) and a full-custom solution (case 3). Note that a custom solution may or may not balance between security level and costs. However, such a decision can affect the provider's business as a whole. Hence, an impact analysis is necessary and the decision is taken on a rather corporate or board level (refer to Fig. 9).

Though custom solutions are out of the scope of ESARIS, they should be built, as far as possible, using elements taken from the industrialized ESARIS services. A "no-go decision" is not the preferred choice for the customer or the provider. Often there are other ways to solve the problem if special customer requirements cannot be met by an ESARIS control in the first place. The following example may demonstrate this: The customer requests access to firewall management systems to control specific activities. This request must be rejected due to the ICT Service Provider's policy restrictions. But a customized firewall report can be created for the customer as an alternative and compensating response, so that the user organization is able to get the necessary information about firewall activities. In this case it may turn out that this alternative solution is already covered by ESARIS so that no custom solution has to be built and maintained.

Enforcement Framework for ESARIS

The *Enforcement Framework for ESARIS* is defined, controlled and maintained by the Security Management of the ICT Service Provider on a corporate level. As already mentioned, ISO/IEC 27001 [17] is often used as a basis. This standard defines the same requirements for security management in enterprises of all types and sizes.

The development of the ISMS and its activities can be planned along the "Plan-Do-Check-Act" cycle (PDCA) though such an approach is not described in the standard. Furthermore, this framework ensures that activities are supported through the central provisioning of processes, tools and methods. It provides a foundation for the achievement of an appropriate security level of the enterprise and defines and standardizes activities throughout all departments and units of the enterprise. An example for grouping the activities is shown in Fig. 10.

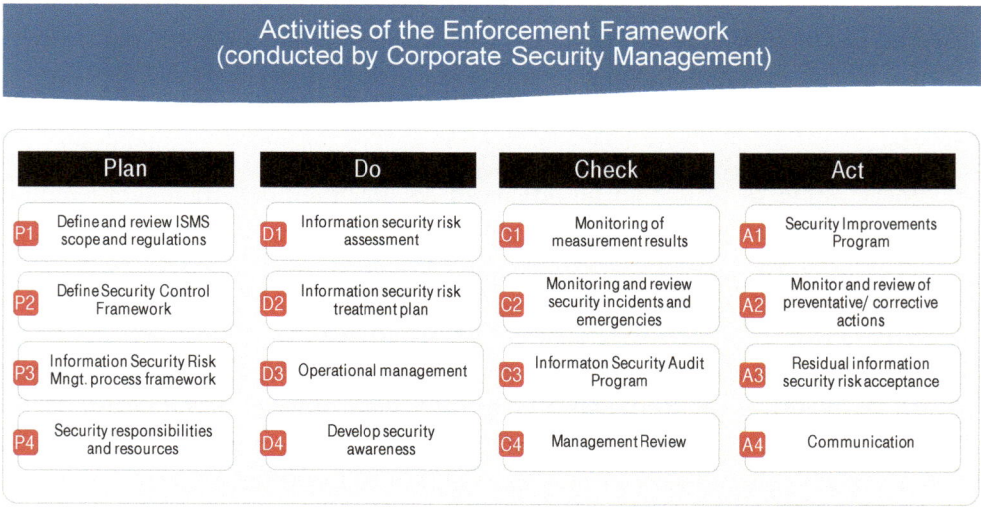

Fig. 10: Activities within the Enforcement Framework for ESARIS

Although most activities are intended to enable the ICT Service Provider to meet security requirements, some activities can also be considered a control. For in-

---

[17] ISO/IEC 27001 – Information technology – Security techniques – Information security management systems – Requirements, 2013 [5]

stance, "developing security awareness (D4)" can enable persons (make them capable) or cause them to act (being a measure).

Endorsement Framework for ESARIS

The framework comprises

- consideration of norms, industry standards and best practices as well as legislation and regulation, and

- mappings between the security measures defined in ESARIS and the security controls stipulated in the environment.

The main sources for best practices are security implementation standards from the ISO (e.g. ISO/IEC 27002 [18]), the ISF (e.g. the SOGP[19]), ENISA (e.g. about cloud computing[20]), the Federal Office for Information Security (BSI, Germany, e.g. IT-Grundschutz[21]), the Cloud Security Alliance (e.g. security guidance[22]), the NIST (e.g. the handbook for managers[23]) and the PCI Security Standards Council.[24] In addition, organizations must adhere to legislation and consider regulation. Moreover, an ICT Service Provider regularly learns from its customers. All these sources are collected and classified as shown in the upper half of Fig. 11. The sources (represented by the braces in the figure) define single security measures (represented by the grey bricks below them). These measures may exist also in other sources whereas specific security measures may be unique to one source.

A main function of the *Endorsement Framework for ESARIS* is to maintain a mapping between all security measures just mentioned (upper half in Fig. 11) with the security measures laid down in ESARIS security standards (lower half in Fig. 11). Such mappings are required for the Internal Control Framework of the ICT Service Provider. The ICT Service Provider can also use the mappings when providing evidence to the customers that their security requirements are met.

---

[18] ISO/IEC 27002 – Information technology – Security techniques – Code of practice for information security management, 2013 [6]

[19] Information Security Forum (ISF): The Standard of Good Practice for Information Security 2016 [25]

[20] European Network and Information Security Agency (ENISA): Cloud Computing Information Assurance Framework; November 2009 [22]

[21] Federal Office for Information Security (BSI): IT-Grundschutz-catalogues; Version 13, 2013 [24]

[22] Cloud Security Alliance (CSA): Security Guidance; Version 3.0, Nov. 2011 [31]

[23] Pauline Bowen, Joan Hash and Mark Wilson: Information Security Handbook: A Guide for Managers, Recommendations of the National Institute of Standards and Technology; NIST Special Publication 800-100, October 2006 (updated 2007) [15]

[24] PCI Standards Council: PCI DSS (PCI Data Security Standard); Version 3.2 as of 2016 [13] (PCI: Payment Card Industry)

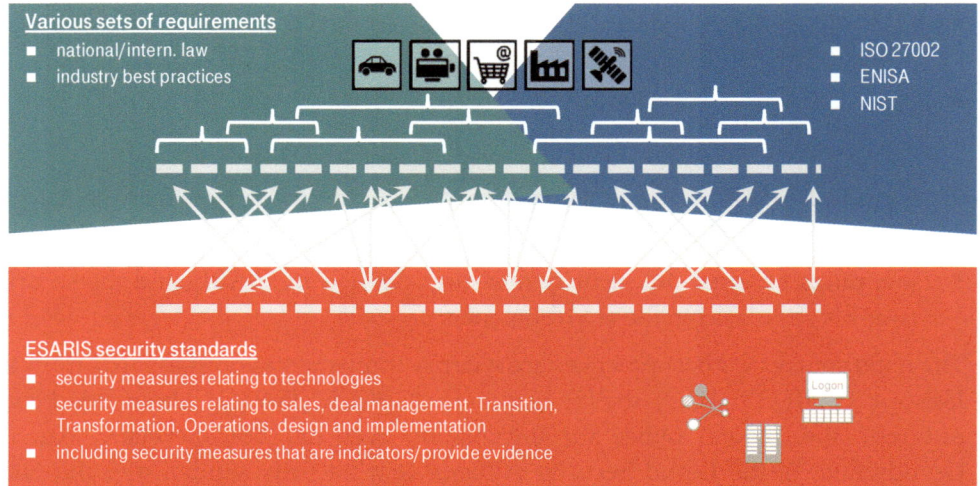

Fig. 11: Endorsement Framework as the mediator from requirements to controls

2.2   Perspectives: corporate versus product security

Introduction and summary: Information security is a discipline that affects many other realms. At a large ICT Service Provider, almost all departments, business processes and the technologies and tools used could have an impact on the achieved level of security and are affected by requirements that relate to information security. Hence, there are several departments and roles that are responsible for reducing risks that arise through the use of ICT. This section looks at two perspectives and distinguishes between the corporate and product perspective, resulting in a Corporate and a Product Security Management. This distinction is necessary since ESARIS focuses on the ICT service or product security only whereas the risk management of the ICT Service Provider must consider product security as one but important element of corporate security.

Leading ICT Service Providers are far too large and complex for strategy and goals to be easy and obvious. They have different departments and the division of labor is very distinct. This makes an organization very powerful, but requires the coordination of different interests. In terms of security, there are two possible perspectives:

- Corporate Security Management
  - which is responsible for the overall security of the enterprise
  - including information security for which an Information Security Management System (ISMS) is operated,
- Product Security Management
  - which is responsible for ensuring that the enterprise's products (and services) are secure and meet the customers' requirements

- using rules and methods from Corporate Security Management as well as those specifically defined for securing products/services.

The situation is shown in Fig. 12.

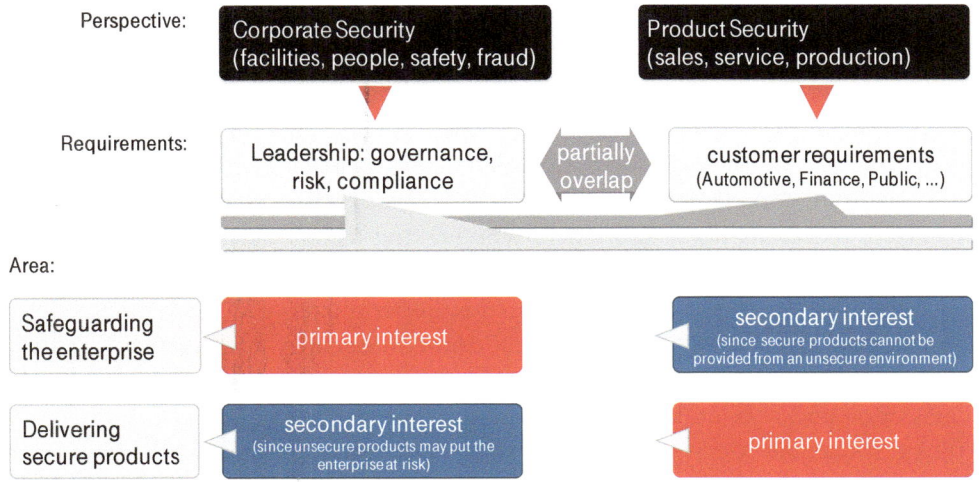

Fig. 12: Two interwoven security perspectives

Corporate Security Management must ensure reliable and efficient leadership and control through the implementation and maintenance of a system for control and regulation as well as corporate organization and processes (Governance). Corporate Security Management must also ensure the systematic identification and assessment of the risks which the enterprise is exposed to and the realization and control of counteracting measures (risk management). Furthermore, Corporate Security Management must ensure adherence to legal and other requirements as well as internal policies and contractual duties (compliance). This task includes the identification, definition and update of regulations as well as their enforcement and control.

Thus, Corporate Security Management is primarily addressing the protection of the enterprise as a whole. Of course, unsecure products or services that are delivered to customers may also put the enterprise at risk and such products or services may lead to noncompliance. Refer to Fig. 12.

An enterprise has several organizational units that are responsible for delivering products or services to customers. The delivery of products and services is the main purpose and mission of an enterprise. Hence, the enterprise must also care for secure delivery and for the security of products and services. The corresponding requirements are considered as those of the customers since they are driven by the business objectives and the market.

Thus, Product Security Management primarily focuses on making products (and services) secure in order to meet market requirements. Of course, weaknesses in the enterprise, e.g. in the way of working in processes, in the organization and in the tools and other methods that are used, may not allow delivery of secure products (and services). Hence, Product Security Management is also interested in the security of the enterprise as a whole. Refer again to Fig. 12.

The necessity and existence of the two perspectives as well as their interwoven way of working is called *ESARIS Duplex Security Management Concept*. Note that the two perspectives are not distinct from each other. They do overlap.

Fig. 13 shows this situation once again. The left-hand side shows the GRC ("Governance, Risk and Compliance") approach and interests. The business with Product Security Management adheres to the corresponding requirements but must meet the requirements of customers while taking technological and business constraints into account. The right-hand side shows the genuine tasks of the business including the sales, service and production departments, which are responsible to secure product and service delivery. Corporate Security Management generally overrules Product Security Management. Examples are compliance issues (e.g. legislation and regulation). In other cases, conditions and constraints shown in the figure may count: Corporate security requirements may only overrule others if this is possible from a business point of view (e.g. strategy, investment, operating costs, margins).

This principle is called the *ESARIS Governance Model*. The ICT Service Provider's Security Management organization must consider these facts.

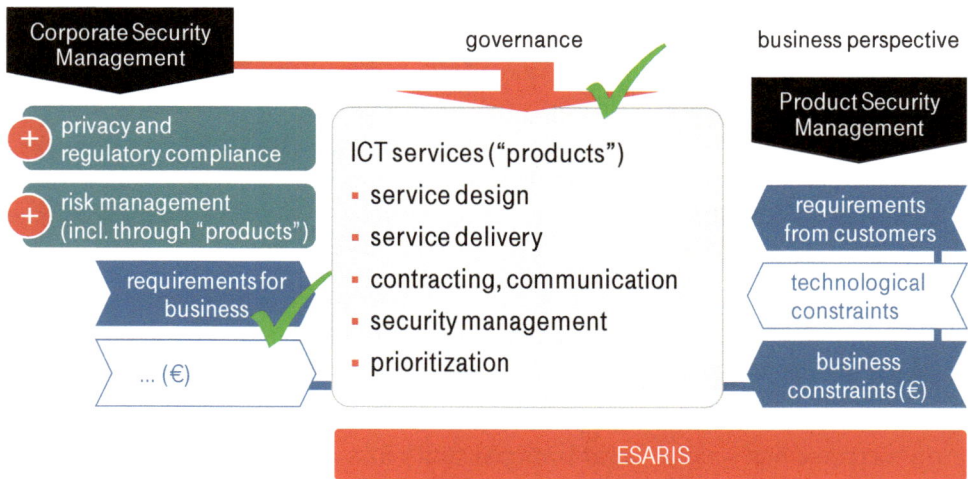

Fig. 13: ESARIS Governance Model

The majority of security measures maintained by an ICT Service Provider are defined, enforced, controlled, improved and maintained for Product Security. Product or service security management is the main focus of ESARIS.

3   Main building blocks and general set-up

Introduction and summary: ESARIS spans three dimensions: work areas, roles and collaboration, as well as security standards. Each is described in detail in the following chapter. Sect. 3.2 explains the three work areas and thereby shows that the architecture considers planning phases up until a customer contract is implemented, operating phases where the ICT service is delivered to the customer, as well as all types of preparations and integration of security measures into technology and related processes. Sect. 3.3 introduces the *ESARIS Collaboration Model* and describes the roles and responsibilities in all three work areas and their interaction. Sect. 3.4 brings in the security issues by defining a *Hierarchy of Security Standards* and its content. This hierarchy again reflects the two perspectives of security management (corporate and product), where the product security perspective is the one that is elaborated and specified in precise detail within ESARIS. Sect. 3.5 describes a concept that is fundamental for ESARIS and its use and may ultimately be the reason why this book actually exists: It is essential that the same documentation is used for implementation (provider's side) and for demonstration of assurance and achievement of requirements (customers' side).

3.1   ESARIS Dimensions

Introduction and summary: ESARIS is an architecture providing for classification and organization. This section splits the subject into three dimensions: work areas, roles and collaboration, as well as security standards. The work areas are an important element and outlined at the end of this section.

The *Enterprise Security Architecture for Reliable ICT Services (ESARIS)* is developed as the sole reference used to ensure that ICT services meet security-related requirements. It comprises the technological, organizational and procedural means required to secure ICT services and to provide dedicated security services as well.

ESARIS spans three dimensions and thereby answers three questions:

- What? ESARIS comprises all components that are needed to deliver secure ICT services (and dedicated security services to customers as well).

- Who? ESARIS comprises definitions of roles and responsibilities as well as of processes and practices that these roles are using.

- How? ESARIS comprises a collection of specific security standards showing how security is "achieved" and allow for "assessing" the level being achieved.

The *ESARIS Dimensions* are shown in Fig. 14.

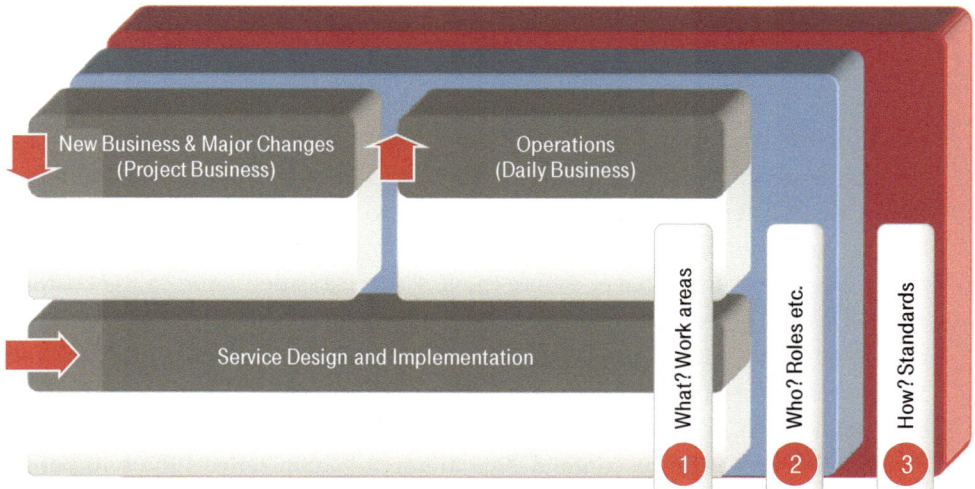

Fig. 14: Dimensions of ESARIS

The above figure shows also that there are three work areas which are covered by ESARIS:

- The area Service Design and Implementation forms the basis for delivering ICT services in a secure way. It comprises all ICT elements that are prepared and available to deliver ICT services in a secure way.

- The preparation of new business and major changes is carried out as part of the ESARIS project business conducted for a specific customer. In these projects, the ICT elements are selected and reused which are basically developed in Service Design and Implementation.

- Operations refer to the daily business whereby security is maintained while ICT services are delivered to user organizations.

It is very important to note that all dimensions fill the same area. In particular, the second and the third dimension are behind all three work areas (first dimension). Thus, security standards (third dimension) are defined for and integrated into all three work areas. Roles and responsibilities (second dimension) are defined for all three work areas and cover their interaction and collaboration.

The three *ESARIS Work Areas* are described in more detail in the following Sect. 3.2. Thereafter in Sect. 3.3, an in-depth look at roles and responsibilities is provided by describing the *ESARIS Collaboration Model*. Finally, Sect. 3.3 introduces the ESARIS security standards and concepts of their overall organization, namely the *Hierarchy of Security Standards* and a few of the implications thereof.

3.2   ESARIS Work Areas

Introduction and summary: Security must be planned, built and maintained. Security must be considered right from the beginning, be subsequently integrated and be continuously reinforced and adapted. ESARIS takes this into account by considering the three work areas of plan-build to obtain and implement a customer contract, run or operations to provide the ICT service in a secure way, as well as all types of preparations in terms of integrating security into technology and related processes following an industrialized approach. The three work areas are different since, for instance, there is project business and continuing business as well. The project business is split into internal business and business for specific customers. The interaction and mutual support of these work areas will become clearer when considering the roles and responsibilities in Sect. 3.3.

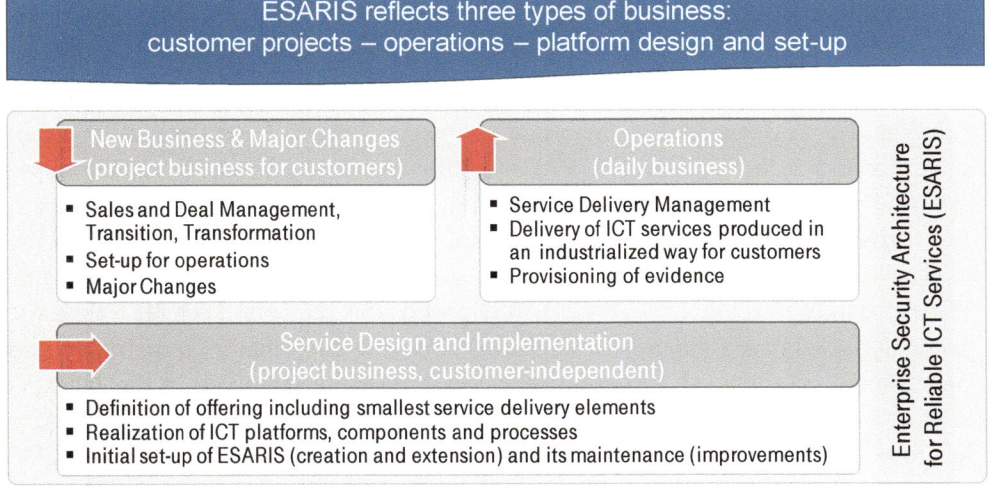

Fig. 15: ESARIS Work Areas

Service Design and Implementation

The ESARIS approach covers different activities or work areas of the ICT Service Provider. The first work area is called Service Design and Implementation (see Fig. 15). It comprises all technology and practices made for service delivery. This work area includes all preparation activities, maintenance and the like conducted independently from any specific customer request or project. As a result, there is a direct link between this work area or core component and the service offering portfolio of the ICT Service Provider and its Service Delivery Elements (SDE). The activities covered here relate to the initial set-up, i.e. the creation and any extension as well as maintenance activities, mostly for improvements. This work area has internal projects with a distinct starting point and a completion time defined in advance, i.e. before starting the project. The work area also comprises activities for major changes to the ICT platforms as long as they are not confined to one or more specific customers but are considered as a general development of future offerings.

In contrast, the two other work areas do have a concrete relation to one or more specific customers. They are performed in the context of specific customer contracts or the preparation thereof. There is a distinction between these two work areas since there is project business for new business and major changes as well as continuing business in operations (refer to Fig. 15).

New Business and Major Changes

The second work area includes design and set-up in the Manage the Deal, Transition and Transformation phases. These activities are performed as projects (with a clear timeline and estimated end point). Refer to Fig. 15. Projects are started for big deals and other new business in order to set up or prepare technology for operations, i.e. delivery of services to customers. A project might also be advantageous if major changes are to be made in technology and practices used for this service delivery.

The provisioning of ICT services for larger user organizations is usually not a "click and use" decision or a "pay and use" process with fixed general terms and conditions. For the ICT Service Provider, this process begins early with market analysis and account planning and covers the management of business opportunities through their phases. These early phases are not considered in ESARIS. However, as soon as the ICT Service Provider starts to promise anything to customers ESARIS comes into play. When a concrete proposal is made and sent to a customer, security aspects are relevant for decisions since the customer's (security) requirements must be analyzed and assessed. Thus, ESARIS is involved in the sales process no later than in the so-called Manage the Deal phase. After this, preparations are to be made to provide the ICT service to the customer. This may involve ICT components being taken over by the ICT Service Provider or data of the user organization is being transferred to the ICT Service Provider. This phase is called *Transition*. In larger deals, changes are often made early on in order to make improvements. This transfers the existing ICT (which was located at the user organization's site or at the site of the former ICT Service Provider) from the so-called Current Mode of Operation (CMO) to an improved one called CMO+. The details are not that important and may differ between ICT Service Providers.

Then the phase of normal *Operations* starts, which is part of the third work area. If the ICT Service Provider took over ICT systems, further improvements and optimizations may be necessary and therefore contractually agreed. Such changes are the subject of the so-called *Transformation* phase which takes the ICT from the CMO+ to the so-called Future Mode of Operation (FMO). The changes are performed as part of a project with a clear starting point and an estimated end point. Hence they belong to the New Business and Major Changes work area. The reality is slightly more complicated, something which will become apparent when considering the roles and collaboration model.

Operations

Most importantly, the third work area is *Operations,* where services are delivered to customers according to the contract. All three areas are different in nature and require a specific organizational structure and processes in which different people do different things in different business roles and responsibilities. This will be described in more detail in Sect. 3.3 below. Operations (nature: daily business) is controlled by the Service Delivery Management of the ICT Service Provider. Industrialized as well as customer-specific ICT services are produced. This includes monitoring, analytics and reporting to customers, i.e. providing evidence that security requirements are met and that the agreed service levels are complied with.

3.3   ESARIS Collaboration Model

Introduction and summary: Having identified the work areas, people with roles and responsibilities are needed to perform the activities in those areas. Hence, roles are defined and responsibilities are assigned in order to organize the development, integration, provisioning and maintenance of security measures. A collaboration model describes how these roles interact and cooperate in order to ensure security throughout the whole process from the Manage the Deal phase to Operations while considering all preparatory work in Service Design and Implementation. The main roles are the *Security Manager*, who takes responsibility for New Business and Major Changes, and the *Customer Security Manager*, who is responsible for security during Operations. The Security Management has a governance role and mediates between different interests.

Large ICT Service Providers have organized their business along the plan – build – run cycle, specifically using the core areas described in ITIL. Fig. 16 shows the principle adapted to IT outsourcing since ITIL does not consider the interfaces to the user organization (customer) as already described in Sect. 1.2.2. A typical sequence of actions is as follows. The ITIL core area Service Strategy and Service Design (1) comprises the development of ICT platforms and components. The ICT platforms and components are realized and the processes are implemented in the next ITIL core area Service Implementation (2). Both ITIL core areas are part of the *ESARIS Work Area* Service Design and Implementation. The work is performed in form of customer-independent projects. The next activities belong to the *ESARIS Work Area* New Business and Major Changes. Sales activities and the management of new customer deals (3) are obviously performed in form of customer-related projects. Note that such activities are not covered by ITIL. After contract closure, the ICT services need to be prepared for delivery. This usually comprise taking over data from the customer but may additionally mean to take over the customer's ICT. Then, it can be necessary to apply modifications to this ICT from the customer. These extensions for customers relate to the ITIL core area Service Implementation (4) which is referred to again (see Fig. 16). These activities are the subject of the IT outsourcing phases Transition and Transformation. After this, project business is transferred to day-to-day business (*ESARIS Work Area* Operations). This continuous business is covered by the ITIL core area Service Operations (5). The ITIL core area Continual Service Improvement (6) is also assigned to this work area.

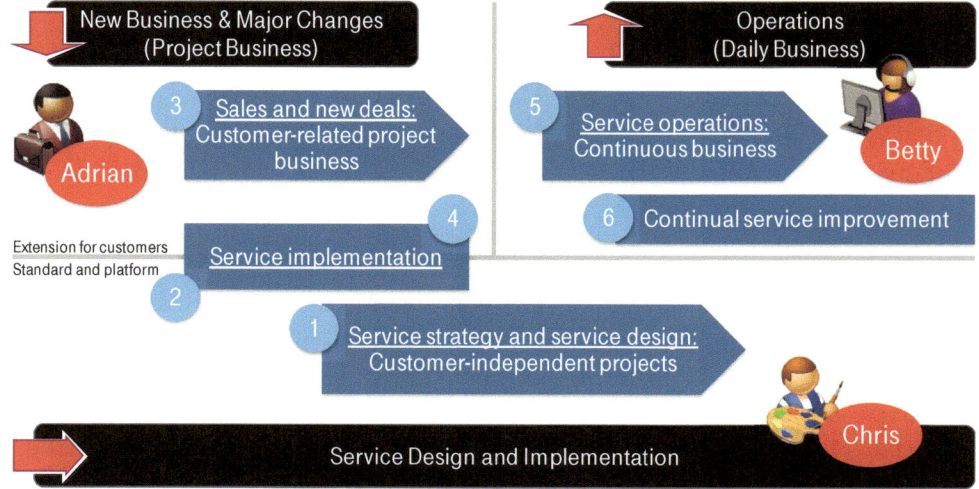

Fig. 16: Major roles in ESARIS

This sequence of actions and the organization into work areas seem complicated for many employees. Therefore, the personas Adrian, Betty and Chris are introduced representing the three *ESARIS Work Areas* and the ITIL core areas behind them.

This process is used to describe the roles and responsibilities with respect to ESARIS. The collaboration model is developed especially for big customer deals. But it is also used for other business as appropriate.

Roles for New Business and Major Changes

This work area is controlled by the sales and deal management. Refer to Fig. 17. There are two major security roles which are important in the ESARIS project business (New Business and Major Changes). The *Security Manager* ensures that security requirements are appropriately considered from the Manage the Deal phase through contract implementation and Transition to the Transformation phase. The role *Security Manager* also supports during the solution design (in the deal phase) and implementation (build or Transition and Transformation) phases. The people acting as *Security Managers* may centrally be organized in a security experts department and must have close relations with the IT production departments.

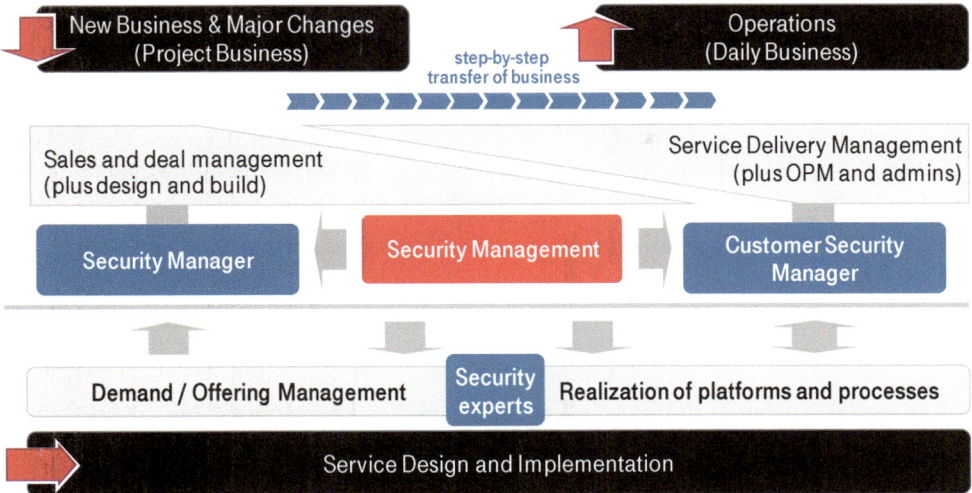

Fig. 17: Interaction of roles and key responsibilities

The *Security Manager* shall reuse the standardized ICT platforms, services and processes as defined in Service Design and Implementation. Deviations from the corporate standards should be avoided and re-engineering should be reduced to the absolute minimum required.

The *Security Management* is the ICT Service Provider's authority mandated to ensure that security requirements are taken into account. This unit ensures that a common level of security is guaranteed throughout all customer projects. This includes the development of work instructions and the verification of their application. Though the sales and deal management is given the overall responsibility, the *Security Management* shall additionally ensure that security aspects are appropriately being considered and not overruled by short-term considerations such as implementation costs. Note that the *Security Management* may not be directly involved in every deal with customers. The role is to steer security in this *ESARIS Work Area* and verify if the security-related requirements of the corporation are fulfilled in customer projects.

In the Transformation phase, ICT services are already being operated. The *Security Manager*, Solution Designers and other technical personnel conduct projects which are organized in a similar way as in the Manage the Deal or Transition phase. They are not responsible for managing the service delivery. Refer to Fig. 17.

Roles for Operations

The genuine Operations phase is controlled by the Service Delivery Management. The ICT Service Provider delivers the ICT services, which includes the management of the relationship with the user organization or customer of the ICT Service Provider. The active management of the relationship with the customer is very important since new threats may appear, new vulnerabilities arise, risks may be rated differently, and the security requirements may change due to changes in the business or its environment.

Managing a customer relationship basically focuses on steering and monitoring the contracted service delivery and on the intricate interaction between the provider and the customer. The Service Delivery Manager (SDM, refer to Fig. 17) is the central point of contact for all operative service-related issues and requirements. He is responsible for contract fulfillment and has the overall responsibility for managing the service in the required quality, within budget and on time. The Service Delivery Manager regularly communicates with the customer. Security issues during Operations are also considered and dealt with by the Service Delivery Management.

The *Customer Security Manager* supports the Service Delivery Management in the field of security. This role is in charge of security-related aspects regarding the customer. *Operations Managers (OPM)* and other technical personnel including administrators are responsible for the realization. Refer to Fig. 17. The *Customer Security Manager* is a role which is staffed in accordance with the complexity of the services being delivered. He is the main point of contact for customers regarding specific security issues during Operations. There is no need for customers to contact service operations personnel directly.

The *Customer Security Manager* is consulted when new business is set up and major changes are made, and during the migration of ICT elements and data from the user organization to the ICT Service Provider. The *Customer Security Manager* should already be involved during Transformation and provide support in case of major extensions to existing services.

Roles for Service Design and Implementation

This work area is controlled by the Portfolio and Offering Management process. The *Enterprise Security Architecture for Reliable ICT Services (ESARIS)* is used and considered in the design of the offering portfolio. A very general Offering Management process is shown in Fig. 18. There are different stakeholders in this business. The process begins with managing demands. The most important role is the Offering Manager (refer also to Fig. 17). This role is responsible for the development and timely availability of the ICT service, including all characteristics usually defined in a service specification or in Service Level Agreements (SLA). The Realization Management is responsible for the implementation. In general, security aspects or security characteristics of the ICT service are the features which are to be managed by the Offering Manager. It is one of the main goals of ESARIS to support this. *Security experts* should be consulted to support the appropriate consideration of security features and the adherence to ESARIS security standards.

Some security characteristics of an ICT service may be achieved by combining a basic ICT service with an ICT security service that is also offered by the ICT Service

Provider as a dedicated security service. These dedicated security services are part of the offering portfolio.

Fig. 18: Offering Management is relevant for Service Design and Implementation

Synopsis

The division of labor and the responsibilities are made clearer in Fig. 17 which summarizes the *ESARIS Collaboration Model*.

The development of the ICT services is steered by the Portfolio and Offering Management. The realization and actual integration of ICT platforms is carried out by the engineering. Engineering combines the service definitions (provided by the Offering Managers) and the standardized practices of operations. *Security experts support the design of ICT services and the correct integration of the ESARIS security standards.*

Sales and deal management are responsible for establishing new business with customers. The *Security Manager* is heading the management of security aspects in the Plan – Build phases, whereas the *Customer Security Manager* does this in the Run business (Operations) both in Current Mode of Operation (CMO) and in Future Mode of Operation (FMO). Both roles respond to customer requirements. The Security Management also brings in overarching and corporate requirements and is in charge of governance and control.

At any time, either the *Security Manager* or the *Customer Security Manager* is responsible for security performance where the *Security Manager* transfers this responsibility to the *Customer Security Manager* when the business is taken over by the latter. Refer to Fig. 17.

The *Operations Manager* is responsible for delivering the ICT services according to the agreed service levels. The *Service Delivery Management* is the responsible interface to the user organization (customer). The *Customer Security Manager* supports the *Service Delivery Management* with respect to security. This role should already be involved in the Transition phase. This ensures that the security process requirements are considered, prepared and established so that the project results can be seamlessly transferred to service operation.

The exact details must be defined in the process and operating manuals of the ICT Service Provider. In large-scale, industrialized ICT service production in particular, it is important that all roles, responsibilities and collaboration models are clearly defined. Otherwise, it is difficult for the ICT Service Provider to provide any ICT service efficiently and secure.

3.4   Hierarchy of Security Standards

Introduction and summary: Information security is a question of needs. It cannot be taken for granted. The top-level management has to provide directives and set policies and rules. System administrators, on the other hand, need extremely specific and detailed instructions on how to secure ICT elements and systems. Hence, security requirements and measures do exist on very different levels of abstraction. Thus, they must be arranged in a hierarchy in order to achieve a consistent whole, to foster mutual support of individual measures and to avoid inconsistencies in requirements and interference to actions. A *Hierarchy of Security Standards* is presented as an example. Its structure is essential and will be used for later concepts of ESARIS.

3.4.1   Overview

Security requirements and measures vary and may come in the form of a policy, objective, requirement or measure. Sometimes it is not easy to distinguish between demands (something that requires a response) and measures (something that provides the response). A policy, for example, can be a demand if it causes people to do something. It can also be a measure if it can be assumed that people can and will adhere to the procedure expressed with the policy. This problem will be put to one side for the time-being. Instead, all the commitment or regulation which finally results in information security can be summed up as "standards".[25]

Larger enterprises including ICT Service Providers maintain a *Hierarchy of Security Standards* which must be used in the company. An example is shown in Fig. 19. The levels of abstraction in this hierarchy are numbered from Level 1 down to Level 5 to provide better orientation. In the following, this model is used as the basis together with its numbering, though the reality may differ in companies.

The two perspectives, corporate and product security, which are typical for an ICT Service Provider are described in Sect. 2.2. They should be taken into account when considering the *Hierarchy of Security Standards*. Standards on a corporate level are valid for the whole organization. They are located in Level 1 and Level 2 as Corporate Security Policy (Level 1) and Corporate Security Rules (Level 2). The other perspective is product security. The *Enterprise Security Architecture for Reliable ICT*

---

[25]   Strictly speaking, those in the Enablement Framework for ESARIS are not incorporated here. The Endorsement Framework for ESARIS only provides material on the one hand and means to integrate this material into the Hierarchy of Security Standards on the other. Regarding these Frameworks refer to Section 2.1.

Services (ESARIS) is built to secure the ICT services being delivered by an ICT Service Provider. Hence, the next levels exclusively refer to the ICT services. The names that are used are ICT Security Principles (Level 3), *ICT Security Standards* (Level 4) and *ICT Security Baselines* (Level 5).

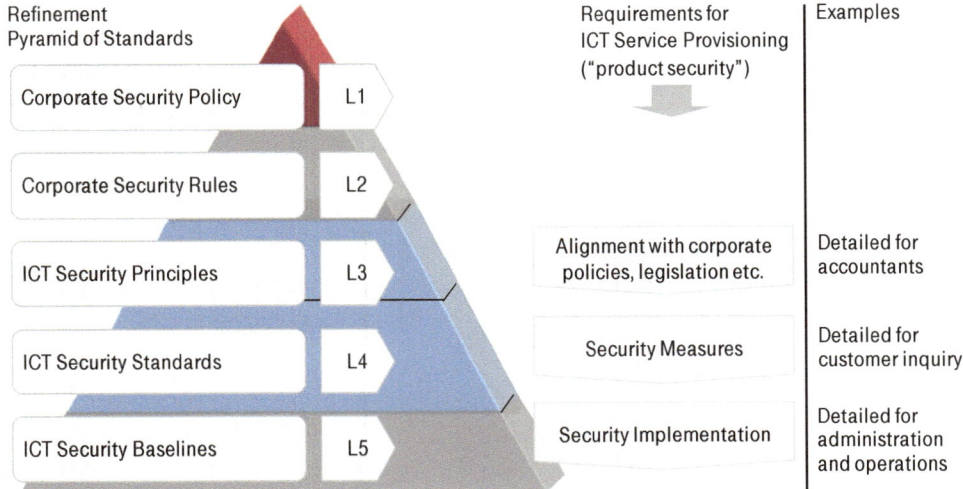

Fig. 19: Hierarchy of Security Standards

The different levels of abstraction or detail can be understood by means of Table 4.

Table 4: Why three levels are needed to specify ICT security

Level 3: ICT Security Principles	<ul><li>Alignment with corporate policies</li><li>Alignment with international frameworks, industry standards etc.</li><li>Overall security principles that apply to all ICT services and technology and process areas</li></ul>
Level 4: *ICT Security Standards*	<ul><li>Implementation independent specification of security (e.g. independent from product version, product, manufacturer)</li><li>Communicating, negotiating and agreeing security issues with customers</li><li>Synopsis of all security aspects relevant in IT production; level that allows to verify completeness and dependencies and provisioning of an integrated mutually supporting whole</li></ul>
Level 5: *ICT Security Baselines*	<ul><li>Instruct people how to implement the security measures</li><li>Instruct people how to act (during development, implementation and operations)</li><li>Ensure correct implementation and maintenance of the security measures.</li></ul>

Level 4 and the so-called *ICT Security Standards* that are assigned to it in this hierarchy play a distinctive role. The *ICT Security Standards* and their security measures are the appropriate tools for communicating, negotiating and agreeing security issues between a user organization and an ICT Service Provider.

3.4.2   Level 1: Corporate Security Policy

A corporate security policy is the top-level and most general "security standard". It explicitly shows the commitment of the board of management to its responsibilities for the company's security and applies to the whole enterprise. It sets binding requirements to ensure a sufficiently high level of security within the enterprise. The policy is directed at all employees and persons working in a functionally equivalent position, such as trainees, temporary workers, or consultants, for whom it serves as a constitution of security and data protection culture as well as providing guidance for security-conscious and data protection-conscious conduct. It also provides general information to customers and shareholders. For them it is a testimony to the enterprise's commitment to security and transparency.

A typical approach to or the content of a corporate security policy may be as follows. It states that the employees are committed to a value-oriented security and data protection culture. The policy may explain that security is on the one hand an obligation to meet statutory and regulatory requirements, but on the other hand also a promise of quality and a testimony to a customer-oriented approach. The policy refers to general rules of conduct, culture and behavior and points out the responsibility for safety, protection of assets including intellectual property, for competitiveness and value creation.

3.4.3   Level 2: Corporate Security Rules

The next level, the corporate security rules, supplements the corporate security policy and defines specific requirements for different areas. It outlines protection goals, principles of security management, the regulation hierarchy, the responsibilities, the risk-oriented approach in business, and provides guidance for security awareness and training as well as measures and reports. The rules are directed at all employees and persons working for the enterprise.

The areas covered can be organized differently. An example for organization and content is shown below.

- Security organization: This part outlines the principal organization of security management including major departments, roles and responsibilities.

- Information security and data protection: The corporate security rules define standards for the whole enterprise to ensure an adequate level of information protection and privacy.

- Office security: The document provides standardized security requirements for adequate protection of workplace computers and other systems that are used by the employees in their work.

- Operating continuity and safety: This realm includes all measures that are taken to ensure continued operation, availability and efficiency of production systems as well as those used for supporting the enterprise's business processes.

- Physical security: This section of the corporate security rules provides security requirements for building security, site rules, storage of documents and goods, and transportation security.

- Human resources security: These requirements are designed to ensure that before, during, and upon termination of an employment or business contract, all measures required to achieve an appropriate level of security are taken without compromising the individual right to privacy of the parties concerned.

- Emergency handling: This part comprises all the measures required to protect people from any injury and from risk to life and limb due to fire, flood, attacks or other disaster. The measures comprise those which are intended to avert such an attack or disaster and others which mitigate their impact.

- Control and investigations: This section provides security requirements for methods that control that other measures are effective, for tracking and for analyzing possible violations of policies and for the prosecution and other counteraction.

Note that all the above areas provide general requirements that are easy to understand for all employees and may typically not exceed 5-10 pages. The scope is still the whole company with all its divisions and businesses.

3.4.4 Level 3: ICT Security Principles

The ICT security principles are more detailed, and the scope has changed. Both Level 1 and Level 2 are orientated towards corporate security; they are directed at all employees and persons working for the enterprise. Level 3 and below relate to product security, more precisely to the ICT services being delivered to the market. ESARIS is built for and maintained by ICT Service Providers. Thus, the scope of the ICT security principles is all employees, departments and even suppliers that are directly or indirectly involved in the design, production and delivery of ICT services for user organizations that are customers of the ICT Service Provider.

The aim of the ICT security principles is to ensure the authenticity, integrity, availability and confidentiality of information being processed by ICT services. The ICT services are generally very different and encompass a wealth of different solutions. All ICT services are secured using security measures realized in technology, processes and organization as well as combinations thereof.

The ICT security principles describe the fundamental structural, technical, and organizational measures and procedures which safeguard the aforementioned protection objectives of authenticity, integrity, availability, and confidentiality. The documentation of the ICT security principles is released to customers.

3.4.5   Level 4: ICT Security Standards

The *ICT Security Standards* are the most detailed ESARIS standards which are intended to be communicated to customers. Refer to the *Hierarchy of Security Standards* (Fig. 19). Individual measures contained therein are split into those for standard security and those for optional security, depending on whether they are always being implemented or can be realized as an option (Sect. 6.2).

The set of all *ICT Security Standards* (or the security measures they describe) is qualified to respond to the security-related requirements that originate from both the ICT Service Provider and the user organization (customer).

The *ICT Security Standards* (Level 4) are described in great detail in Sect. 4.3 and Chapter 12.

3.4.6   Level 5: ICT Security Baselines

The ICT security baselines are the most detailed standards within the *Hierarchy of Security Standards*. They comprise for instance

- security concepts,
- network diagrams,
- architecture and detailed design documents,
- bill of materials,
- installation manuals,
- configuration lists including hardening guidelines,
- security testing documentation and reports,
- operating procedures and manuals,
- work instructions for e.g. *Security Managers* and *Customer Security Managers*,
- work instructions for conducting design, implementation and maintenance activities,
- checklists e.g. for quality gates and for testing, and
- other documents.

These documents support and direct the technical implementation of the Level 4 security measures for a specific ICT service, system, application or device. Many documents are product or at least product family-specific. The content depends on the type of standard. Configuration lists usually provide the following information: identification, the task, parameters, requirement description, comment, primary responsibility and an indication of the source of or reason for the action. This level may not be standardized. It contains intellectual property of the ICT Service Provider.

3.5   ESARIS Concept of Double Direction Standards

Introduction and summary: ESARIS aims to standardize the security measures and to provide information, transparency and evidence to customers that security is actually being achieved. In order to ensure unambiguity, Level 4 of the *Hierarchy of Security Standards* is chosen to provide information to customers and simultaneously to provide directives for ICT service delivery and production. The *ESARIS Concept of Double Direction Standards* stipulates that the same text is used for both purposes. The security measures of Level 4 therefore address a concrete security issue and respond to a question or concern that is of interest for customers. The context, purpose and effect become clear from studying the security measure. The security measures, moreover, provide directions for implementation, formulated as clearly and specifically as required in order to ensure that security objectives are achieved.

It is common practice for ICT Service Providers to develop their own internal security specifications, which are considered intellectual property and are for "internal use only". Essentially, this means that the ICT Service Provider's design and process documentation is kept confidential and not made available to customers. There are good reasons for keeping security concepts confidential; they may contain a security analysis with security issues that are not or not thoroughly being addressed, or provide information that may reduce the effort required for a successful attack. None of these arguments really works with customers who must fully trust the ICT Service Provider. The reason is that user organizations do not require all the details. Checking all the details would mean doing the provider's job. However, user organizations do require details in order to assess risks to their own business. Hence, ICT Service Providers are starting to develop specific documentation for customers. There is a great danger, however, that this documentation will differ from reality. There are many reasons for this. First, the customer documentation is written to win the deal. Second, the IT production and its practices will continue to develop. The customer documentation will at some point become outdated, and the documentation may not be updated as required. One final reason is that customer-specific documentation is designed with a certain intention in mind, and in response to the customer's current concerns. It is not manageable to maintain the consistency of the internal comprehensive documentation and the customer documentation in a long-term relationship where new issues are discussed and raised e.g. due to new developments.

As a consequence, the *ESARIS Concept of Double Direction Standards* stipulates that there is (defined as Level 4 in the hierarchy) one documentation layer that has dual use. It is shown in Fig. 20. On the one hand, this documentation of security measures is used as directive for the ICT Service Provider. The description is used as the basis for the implementation of security measures in technology, processes and organization. On the other hand, the same documentation and the identical description are used to provide information to customers to allow the assessment and comparison of ICT services and to provide evidence that requirements are really met. The content of Level 4 builds the *ESARIS Orchestration Layer*.

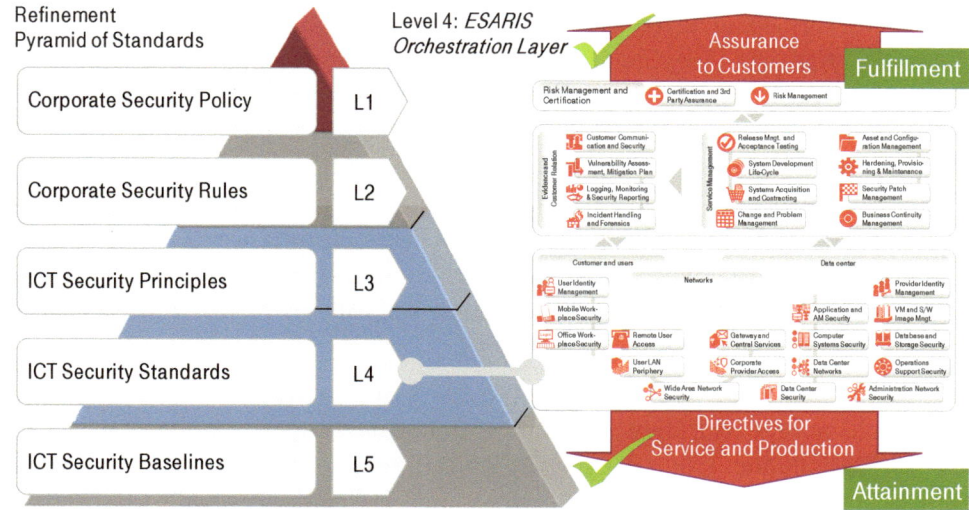

Fig. 20: ESARIS Concept of Double Direction Standards

This concept is considered to be fundamental. The realization thereof is a challenge in a large organization and it may raise several questions. One question which requires an immediate answer is the level of detail that such documentation features. The level of detail is determined using criteria in order to avoid any bias. The level of detail or abstraction can be chosen in a way that the *ESARIS Concept of Double Direction Standards* is feasible and acceptable both for the user organization and for the ICT Service Provider.

Security measures may feature very different levels of detail and thereby cover areas of very different sizes, and provide a different scope or field of application. Security measures range from general policies for employees' behavior through to specific settings of particular software.

Predefined criteria are developed to determine the level of detail of Level 4 (*ICT Security Standards*) or its security measures, respectively. The criteria are provided in Table 5.

Table 5: Criteria to define the level of abstraction of Level 4 (*ESARIS Orchestration Layer*)

Criteria	Description
Criterion 1: specific, informative and unambiguous	In Level 4, a security measure will address a concrete security issue which is actually being raised. It responds to a question or concern that is of interest. The context, purpose and effect become clear from studying the security measure.
Criterion 2: largely implementation-independent	In Level 4, a security measure will be formulated in order to provide as much freedom as possible for implementation. It is largely implementation-independent in order to allow industrialized production and continued technical progress. Documentation may not need to be changed if, e.g. new versions of software or new product components emerge.
Criterion 3: comprehensive and intelligible	In Level 4, the documentation of the security measures will facilitate the provisioning of evidence of coverage and completeness. The *ICT Security Standards* of ESARIS cover all relevant aspects across all technical disciplines and throughout the entire life-cycle. The level of detail chosen is just high enough to allow provisioning of the evidence of coverage and completeness.

The *ICT Security Standards* and their security measures provide a means of communicating with customers and analyzing whether their requirements are met. In fact, the ICT Service Provider starts higher in the hierarchy using more general information: ICT Service Providers observe the markets and define strategic topics and identify developments based on the megatrends that they think will shape the future of economy and society. Examples are net-centric sourcing (with cloud computing), collaboration (with business and social platforms) and mobility (with smart devices and networks). Across all areas, information and communication technology (ICT) will play a pivotal part in resolving the challenges faced by both businesses and public-sector organizations. Security and governance can be considered as one central overarching element that enables all other major developments or megatrends. Security can be considered as the glue that holds together all the individual parts.

ICT Service Providers develop a portfolio of ICT services that respond to customer demands including these trends and developments. The service and production is organized along with this ICT service offering portfolio and its standard offering elements. Security is an integral component of all ICT services. ESARIS provides a means of accomplishing compliance with the customer and other security requirements. This results in the definition of the *ICT Security Standards* (Level 4) and its security measures which provide informative and comprehensive information about securing ICT services.

On the one hand, the *ICT Security Standards* and their security measures are used as the ICT Service Provider's directives for the implementation and operation of ICT services. This is called "Attainment" in Fig. 20 and will be described in great detail in Chapter 7. They are refined by a large number of documents on Level 5.

On the other hand, the *ICT Security Standards* and their security measures are used as the appropriate tool for communicating, negotiating and agreeing security issues between a user organization and an ICT Service Provider. This is called "Fulfillment" in Fig. 20 and will be described in great detail in Chapter 8. The business relation between the two parties constitutes a division of labor. Many security issues are solved by the provider. This removes this burden from the user organization. While doing so, the user organization has less direct control and ad hoc knowledge about the outsourced ICT service delivery and its underlying technology and methods.[26] However, the user organization maintains the risks associated with using the outsourced ICT services. Hence, assurance must be provided that the ICT services perform as required in order to allow the user organization to appropriately manage its remaining risks. The *ICT Security Standards* are the main source for this assurance. Note that a detailed discussion on a very technical level would eliminate many of the benefits of outsourcing. This is particularly true for cloud computing. In addition, it would remove a great deal of freedom regarding implementation and thereby drive up costs and reduce flexibility.

---

[26] refer to Eberhard von Faber and Michael Pauly: User Risk Management Strategies and Models – Adaption for Cloud Computing; in: N. Pohlmann, H. Reimer, W. Schneider (Editors): Securing Electronic Business Processes, Vieweg (2010), ISBN-10: 3834814385, p. 80 – 90 [41]

4   ESARIS Security Taxonomy

Introduction and summary: Level 4 in the *Hierarchy of Security Standards* plays an important role since it serves both as a source of directives for IT production and delivery (provider's side) and as a source of information for the user organization (customer's side). This level comprises all security aspects that are relevant for the security of ICT services. Both the ICT services and the security aspects are diverse. A classification and organization schema is required and the individual security measures are assigned to separate *ICT Security Standards* in order to allow the efficient extraction of information required by user organizations. Such a structure or classification schema, referred to below as taxonomy, is also required to enable the ICT Service Provider to produce and maintain the documentation of security measures. There are several conditions or requirements to be met by the taxonomy. These are identified and analyzed first (Sect. 4.1). Then the taxonomy is presented and explained step by step; first by explaining the three groups in the whole map, then by dividing up the whole map into six clusters (Sect. 4.2) and, finally, by briefly defining each *ICT Security Standard* in the context of its cluster (Sect. 4.3). A brief summary of the procedure and result is provided (Sect. 4.4). Not all standards are relevant for each contract, ICT service, component or activity. Hence, a methodology, called *Provider Scope of Control* (Sect. 4.5), is required to select the relevant ones. It plays an important role in relations with customers and with suppliers and partners.

4.1   Design criteria for the ESARIS Security Taxonomy

Introduction and summary: The *ICT Security Standards* describe all security measures that contribute to the security of ICT services being provided to customers. This complex issue requires a structure that is called taxonomy. The taxonomy helps to find the required information; whereas a monolithic documentation would not allow appropriate use of its contents. The taxonomy is also required in order to develop the security measures. Before setting up the taxonomy, criteria are designed and analyzed in order to understand the requirements that the structure must meet. The taxonomy is developed in Sect. 4.2 based on these requirements or conditions being derived.

It is essential to decide on a structure of standards (logic) and decide which security topics, themes or areas are to be described with a standard. This is called *ESARIS Security Taxonomy*. The areas will be described in different *ICT Security Standards* so that the taxonomy is also the *Taxonomy of ICT Security Standards*.

It is worth noting that, for example, the structure of ISO/IEC 27002 does not meet the requirements: The main point is that the structure of this standard does not correspond to ICT service provisioning and its business organization. Here is an example for ISO/IEC 27002 not meeting the criteria. ISO/IEC 27002 defines controls regarding "network security management" in <u>one</u> area.[27] For an ICT Service Provider the answer is diverse. There are networks at its customers' site which may be set up and managed by the provider. There are networks that are used to offer a communication service to customers, for example to connect the customers with the provider's ICT services (e.g. over the Internet). There are also networks within the provider's data centers as well as between them. The latter are used to increase the availability or performance of ICT services. Moreover, there are networks that connect administrators with ICT elements in order to allow active management. As a result, there are up to <u>five</u> different kinds of networks each with different technology and security levels. The ICT Service Provider must split the security descriptions into these parts since its customers do not necessarily use all the services and available infrastructures. The split is also necessary in order to specify adequate security measures which suits for the technology and security level.

Table 6 provides an overview of the criteria which are described in more detail in this section.

Table 6: Criteria for the ESARIS Security Taxonomy

Criteria	Description
Criterion 1-3: Work with the level of abstraction of Level 4	Refer to the three criteria described in Table 5 (page 49).
Criterion 4: Usable to structure Level 4 downwards	The Taxonomy shall be used as a structure for all lower levels in the gradual refinement of security standards (*Hierarchy of Security Standards*).
Criterion 5: Modularity supporting division of labor	The Taxonomy shall support the organization of and the division of labor within the ICT Service Provider and the division of labor between the provider and its suppliers and partners.
Criterion 6: Modularity supporting standardization	The Taxonomy shall support the application of the security measures in all ICT services that belong to the service offering portfolio of the ICT Service Provider.

---

[27] Network security management is the objective 13.1 of ISO/IEC 27002 – Information technology – Security techniques – Code of practice for information security management, 2013 [6]

Criteria	Description
Criterion 7: Character and number of areas	The Taxonomy shall consist of several areas that together cover all relevant aspects (technology and IT service management). The number of areas shall be limited in order to guarantee ease of use.
Criterion 8: Supports Double direction principle	The Taxonomy shall work with the *ESARIS Concept of Double Direction Standards* and comply with the requirements of using it.

Criteria 1-3 are not detailed here. Refer to Table 5 (page 49). The three criteria will be part of the summary provided at the end of this section.

Criterion 4: The gradual refinement of security requirements is very important and part of the concept *Hierarchy of Security Standards* (Sect. 3.4). The Taxonomy must ensure that this feature is maintained and still usable in Level 4 and Level 5. Note that these levels are characterized by their level of detail (or abstraction). Refer e.g. to Table 4 on page 43.

Criterion 5: Modularity is required since the division of labor in the IT industry shall be taken into account and supported. The division of labor varies and is different for different businesses and depends on the parties being involved. Level 4 provides hundreds of security measures. On the one hand, the security measures act as "requirements specification" for the supplying party. On the other hand, the consuming party (the next party in the supply chain) must be able to verify the security of what they receive. Hence, the security measures must be organized in a way that they can easily be assigned to a department or team within the ICT Service Provider in order to support division of labor and specialization. The Taxonomy must also support the assignment of the security measures to external suppliers of the ICT Service Provider in the supplier network. The Taxonomy must be aligned with IT production and organized in realms that match with production units. In order to allow the security measures (Level 4) to be systematically refined step-by-step, Level 5 shall also be organized along the *ESARIS Security Taxonomy*.

Criterion 6: Modularity is required for being able to reuse security measures for different ICT services. This is in turn required to support standardization and to raise the efficiency. The Taxonomy shall support the application of the security measures in all ICT services that belong to the service offering portfolio of the ICT Service Provider. To this end, it must be organized accordingly. Hence, the Taxonomy must be organized in realms that represent a typical service or component or a collection thereof that suit to each other. The separation shall reflect technical aspects in ICT ("stack" and architecture) as well as the organization of the IT service management services (in development, integration and operations; that is ITIL in case of this Taxonomy). The latter is required to support different service models such as "unmanaged" versus "managed services".

Criterion 7: The number of areas in the Taxonomy shall be limited to fit on one page and should be understandable by IT personnel and not only by educated security experts. Each area has to be detailed by a specific security standard denoted as *ICT Security Standard* (Level 4). Other criteria need to be defined to characterize their content and structure. The Taxonomy shall cover all relevant aspects (technology and IT service management).

Criterion 8: The Taxonomy shall be used as a means to manage information security in a supplier-customer-relationship, i.e. between parties in a supplier network and even between different specialized organizations of the ICT Service Provider. Refer to Criterion 5. This means that the *ICT Security Standards* organized by the Taxonomy must support the *ESARIS Concept of Double Direction Standards* described in Sect. 3.5. In particular the following is required. The *ICT Security Standards* can be used as requirements documents or as directions for the supplying party. They can be used as the basis for defining a sales promise and the security specification for the customer (consuming party). This requires standardizing the language and structure of security specifications.

Summary: Level 4 plays an important role and is also called *ESARIS Orchestration Layer*. If the above criteria 1 through 8 (summarized in Table 5 and Table 6) for the structure of the *ESARIS Security Taxonomy* and the content of each area (and its related *ICT Security Standard*) are considered, the *ICT Security Standards* (Level 4) (each one or all of them as a whole, respectively) will

- respond to customers' questions and concerns and provide clear and understandable answers,
- provide directions / guidance to the supplying party (company or department) for the implementation of security measures
  - in a way that is concrete enough to avoid errors,
  - but flexible enough to allow for technical progress and improvements, also regarding security,
  - allow the implementation and maintenance in accordance with the supplying company's internal organization, processes and practices (such as the organization into different specialized production departments),
- be suitable for any ICT service designed for being delivered to a user organization (end of the supply chain) and thereby align with the service portfolio offering of a company supplying such a market,
- be comprehensive and complete as a set on secure ICT service provisioning.

Note, that *ICT Security Standards* may not provide many instructions for others. Instead, each one will have its own scope of control without referring to the specific content of other standards. For that reason, malware protection, for example, has not been chosen as an individual standard. Services such as malware protection are required on different systems (such as desktops and servers). Thus, this issue is addressed, e.g. in the desktop security standard and in the server security standard. Other services, however, are central services (and general practices) in the provider's IT production and service provisioning. Such services constitute an individual *ICT Security Standard*. The security measures described in such a standard provide support for several security elements (such as the desktop and the server). For example, security patches are applied to all systems and software that are used and provided by the ICT Service Provider. Overall principles are expected here. Therefore, patch management is addressed in a separate *ICT Security Standard*, though it may contain differentiations or descriptions of specific practices in different areas (potentially for desktops and servers to use that example again).

4.2   Structure of the ESARIS Security Taxonomy

Introduction and summary: The *ESARIS Security Taxonomy* comprises 31 areas or parts that are organized in different clusters. Thus, there are a total of 31 *ICT Security Standards*. Roughly half of the areas (each one described in one standard) are associated with ICT services and their functionality, whereas the others are assigned to general IT management services. The structure meets the conditions or requirements developed in Sect. 4.1. The structure has therefore been designed to serve three goals: Customers shall obtain answers on how their requirements are addressed. Secondly, the individual departments and teams of the ICT Service Provider (as well as external suppliers) easily find the guidance relevant for them. Thirdly, the *ICT Security Standards* shall cover all relevant aspects, i.e. "the whole world of IT security" with all details and variants across all technical disciplines and throughout the entire life-cycle.

ESARIS is totally modular and structured. This is true for the definition of security measures in particular. Otherwise, the whole issue could not be maintained with an acceptable effort. Modularity is also required to manage the information and to provide clarity and structure. Firstly, the *ICT Security Standards* of ESARIS provide transparency to customers by explaining how the ICT Service Provider accomplishes and guarantees security. They are used to show whether the individual requirements and demands are appropriately addressed. The security measures had been distributed amongst several *ICT Security Standards* since both the ICT services and the security requirements are manifold. Customers use only those *ICT Security Standards* which are relevant for them. Secondly, the *ICT Security Standards* are directives for all activities of the ICT Service Provider. The structure of the *ICT Security Standards* has therefore been designed so that the supplying parties (department, team, company) can easily find the guidance relevant for them. Thirdly, the *ICT Security Standards* of ESARIS cover all relevant aspects with all the details and variants, across all technical disciplines and throughout the entire life-cycle.

The structure of the standards is called *ESARIS Security Taxonomy*. The taxonomy is an essential element of the *Enterprise Security Architecture for Reliable ICT Services (ESARIS)* and shown in Fig. 21. There are 31 smaller rounded rectangles each representing one area or one *ICT Security Standard*. The Taxonomy is described in the following. ESARIS and its standards in the Taxonomy are totally modular and structured.

The Taxonomy is explained by considering modules in different levels of magnification. There is

- 1 map of the *ICT Security Standards*, which comprises
- 3 groups of *ICT Security Standards* or
- 6 clusters of *ICT Security Standards*, which in turn comprise in total
- 31 *ICT Security Standards* that provide
- a considerable number of security measures.

The 31 standards are outlined in Sect. 4.3. The map with groups and clusters is described below.

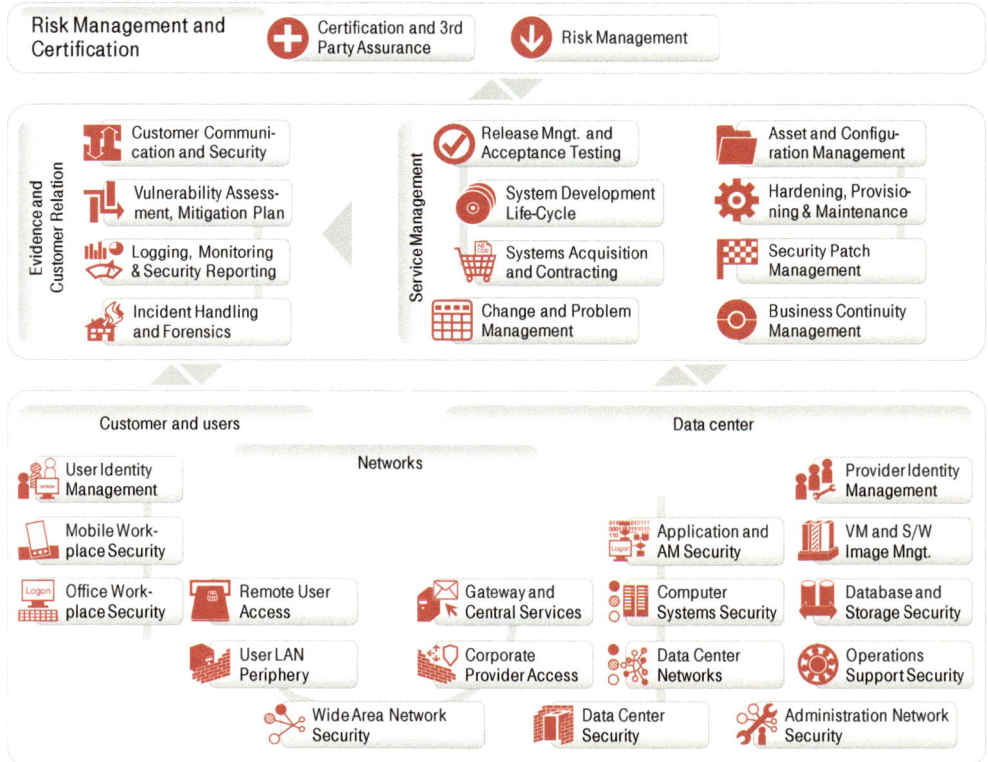

Fig. 21: Map of the ICT Security Standards (Level 4)

There are three groups of standards associated with

A) genuine ICT services, i.e. ICT functions generated by hardware and software,

B) IT service management services that produce and maintain those genuine ICT services, and

C) overarching practices concerning the other two groups.

In other words, Group A relates to the primary ICT services for users, Group B for the secondary IT management services, and Group C to overarching aspects.

These three groups can be seen in the Taxonomy as follows:

- Group A (associated with ICT services and their functionality)
  - This group (lowest in Fig. 21) comprises 17 standard areas. This Group A and the *ICT Security Standards* it contains are associated with ICT services and their functionality.
  - ESARIS addresses the security of ICT services that are provided to customers. There is a variety of ICT services comprising desktop services, network services as well as computing services. Therefore, one half of the *ICT Security Standards* is organized so that they can be assigned to individual ICT services. (Customers who buy desktops are provided with the Desktop Standard.)

- Group B (associated with general IT management services)
  - This group is formed by the long rounded rectangle in the middle and comprises 12 standard areas. This group and the ICT Security Standards it contains are associated with general IT management services common to several ICT services (Group A).
  - This group spans several individual ICT services and is of a general nature. The security measures have therefore been "centralized" since aspects such as availability, system maintenance and troubleshooting have to be managed in a general way. The ICT Service Provider must perform such activities in a standardized manner throughout the IT production and for all ICT services being delivered. Therefore, such security issues are separated from the areas of Group A.

- Group C (associated with all standards of Group A and B)
  - This group with the overarching practices (at the top of Fig. 21) is formed by the long rounded rectangle and comprises two standard areas (small rounded rectangles). This group and the *ICT Security Standards* it contains are associated with all standards of the other two groups A and B.
  - This group contains two very general standards. The first one describes the general approach of the ICT Service Provider to certifications and how third-party assurance is planned, conducted and integrated into the provider's business strategy and communication. The second one describes the provider's approach to risk management or more specifically, its procedure of making decisions on implementations of security measures.

The separation of technical standards (Group A) on the one hand and IT service management standards on the other (Group B) is a major requirement for using the Taxonomy in the context of an industrialized IT production. All ICT services and technical components shall be developed, implemented and managed according to the same unique processes and practices. This forms Feature #1 of the Taxonomy supplementing the criteria for it described in Sect. 4.1.

The relation to common practices of IT service management (ITIL[28], ISO 20000[29]) is made apparent although the Taxonomy only deals with aspects of information security. Note that this Taxonomy and its exemplification/execution by related security standards –for the first time- really integrates *IT security management* and *IT service management*. This is one of the major new ideas behind this Taxonomy. Though ITIL has a security management process, there is no real integration with other processes and activities. Security standards such as the ISO 27000-series are not considering the organization of novel, larger-scale IT (production). This forms Feature #2 of the Taxonomy supplementing the criteria for it described in Sect. 4.1.

Clusters of standards

The Taxonomy appears clearly structured and understandable for any IT-aware person. This is why IT related terms are preferably used. Moreover, the lower half of the Taxonomy (Group A) is based on simple principles of IT architecture. It uses a model formerly called "client-server-model": The users' equipment is shown on the left; the IT components residing in data centers are shown on the right-hand side, and the network elements are in between. The more complex data center infrastructure is organized into elements of a primary IT stack and a second supporting one. Boundaries (especially the interface of the data center to the outer networks) are important in terms of security and therefore defined as extra areas. Note that the lower half contains four areas for four different types of networks because their nature and protection requirements are quite different. The upper half of the Taxonomy (Group B) shows the supporting activities. There is a generalized life-cycle with four areas in the middle. Four more technical disciplines are – due to their importance for IT security – on the right-hand side. Another four disciplines – primarily related to IT security – are on the left-hand side. Note that there are two important areas: one concerning the interface to the customer and the other concerning the relation to suppliers. This forms Feature #3 of the Taxonomy supplementing the criteria for it described in Sect. 4.1.

---

[28]   Ahmad K. Shuja: ITIL: Service Management Implementation and Operation; Auerbach Publications, 2010 [35]

[29]   ISO/IEC 20000 – Information technology – Service management – Part 1: Service management system requirements, Part 2: Guidance on the application of service management systems; 2012 [2]

Clusters build the next level of magnification to look onto the map of *ICT Security Standards* in order to understand the *ESARIS Security Taxonomy*. Two versions of clustering are shown. Firstly, the *ICT Security Standards* are clustered as follows (refer to Fig. 22):

- Risk Management and Certification (⬤),
- Evidence and Customer Relation (⬤),
- Service Management (⬤), and
- ICT Service Provisioning with the clusters
    - Customer and Users (⬤)
    - Networks (⬤), and
    - Data Center (⬤).

This organization is more service-oriented. It will be used below in Sect. 4.3 in which all 31 *ICT Security Standards* are briefly explained.

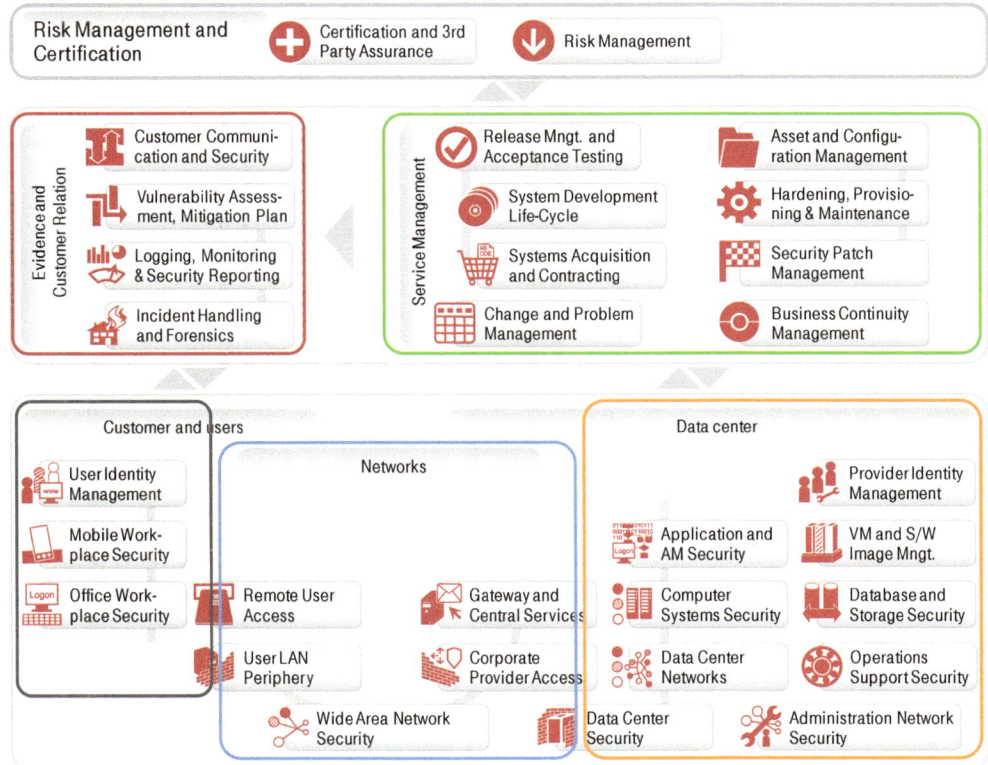

Fig. 22: Clusters of ICT Security Standards (1/2)

Note: The interface to the customer does not actually exist in ITIL and in security standards such as ISO/IEC 27001/27002 or ISO/IEC 27017 as understood here. For instance, sales, deal management, migration activities and provider-customer relationships in Service Delivery Management during Operations do not exist in ITIL. The ISO security standards do not offer guidance for managing a customer-provider relationship in these phases. Refer to below for more detail. This forms Feature #4 of the Taxonomy supplementing the criteria for it described in Sect. 4.1.

Other types of clustering are possible which provide different perspectives. Another organization of the 31 *ICT Security Standards* is shown in Fig. 23. This organization of the *ICT Security Standards* has no overlap and is strictly oriented by purpose. It will not be used subsequently.

- Evidence and Presentation (●),
- Design and Management (●),
- Workplace and User LAN (●),
- Network and DC Access (●), and
- Computing Services (●).

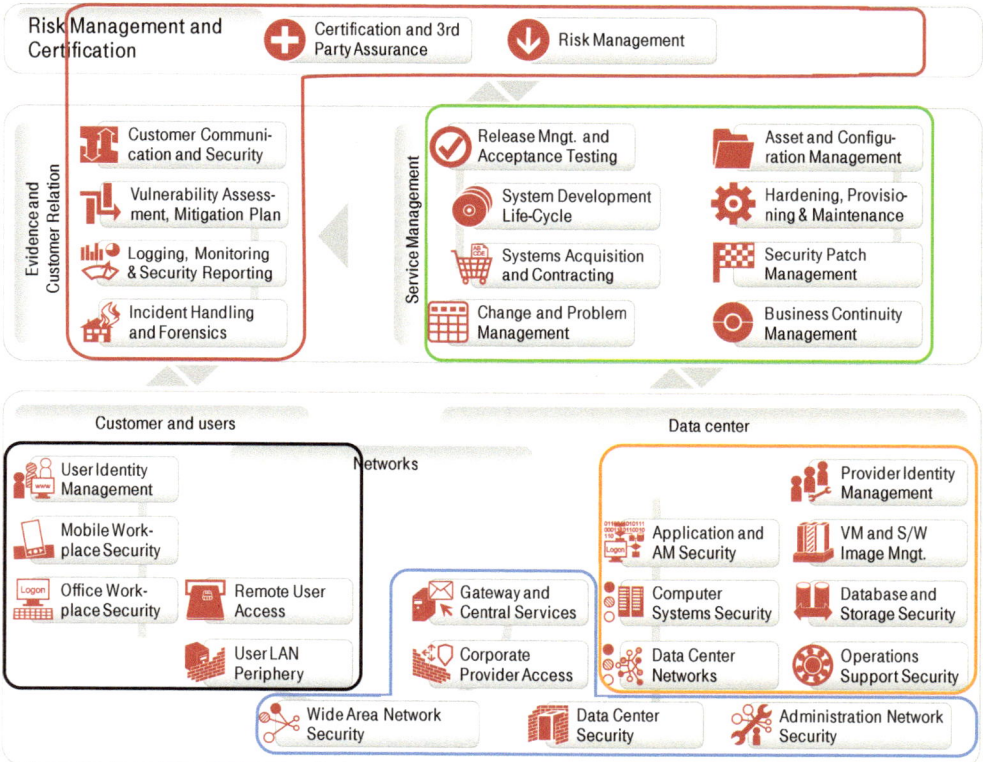

Fig. 23: Clusters of ICT Security Standards (2/2)

These examples of clusters and their explanation emphasize another principle of the Taxonomy. Areas which are related to each other are close together; if areas are fare from each other in a group they are more independent from each other. This forms Feature #5 of the Taxonomy supplementing the criteria for it described in Sect. 4.1. Each *ICT Security Standard* provides great detail about the security in a specific area. Typically, each standard specifies security aspects by means of 10-20 security measures. Fig. 24 provides an overview of topics addressed by security measures in the cluster "Computing Services". Details are provided later.

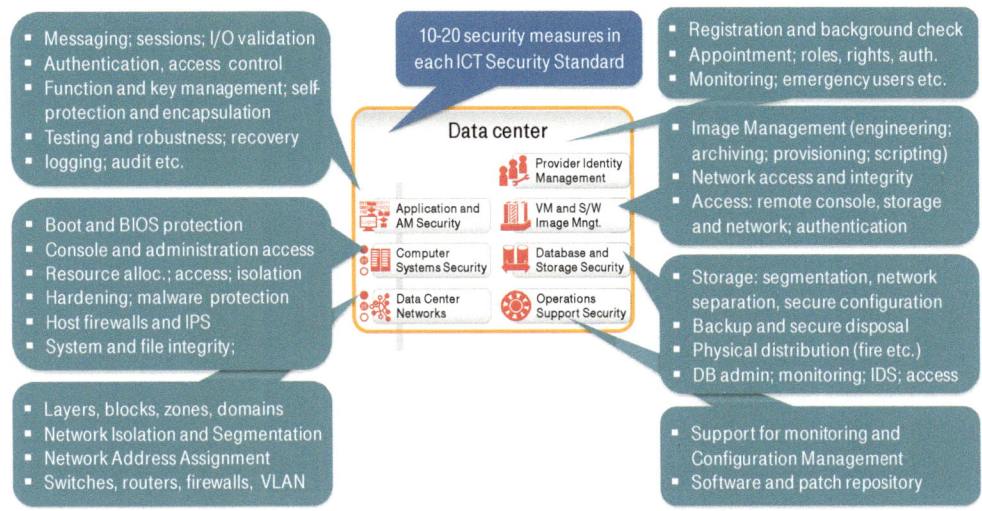

Fig. 24: Details for the areas in the cluster Computing Services (example)

Fig. 25: Taxonomy with 31 areas detailed by 31 *ICT Security Standards*

4.3 Areas and the ICT Security Standards at a glance

Introduction and summary: Level 4 within the *Hierarchy of Security Standards* comprises 31 areas which are each described in a single document called *ICT Security Standard*. Now more details are provided by briefly looking at each *ICT Security Standard*. All 31 areas and their relation to each other are outlined here. Then the key constituents of each area are specified. At the same time, the names of the *ICT Security Standards*, along with an abbreviation and an icon are introduced. The abbreviation and icon are used to facilitate access to the relevant information and to record any dependencies between them, for example. Note that a separate Chapter 12 is provided for a full understanding of the standards.

Each area of the *ESARIS Security Taxonomy* is detailed by means of one *ICT Security Standard*. This is shown in Fig. 25. This should be kept in mind in the following when each area is outlined in more detail.

4.3.1   Networks

All *ICT Security Standards* that belong to the "Networks" cluster are specified and briefly characterized in this section. Networks connect users (or user organizations) with ICT services from the ICT Service Provider. Hence, *Wide Area Network Security* is the first standard. *Corporate Provider Access* comprises all network and IT elements required to protect the provider's computing periphery and to provide VPN capabilities. The customers connect from their side. *User LAN Periphery* comprises the corresponding ICT security solutions such as firewalls and VPNs, if provided by the ICT Service Provider. The customers (and other third parties) may also connect via *Remote User Access*. The standard *Gateway and Central Services* (on the provider's side) comprises elements above the sole connection such as e-mail security services.

For more details, refer to Table 7 below. The table provides the name of the standard, its icon and abbreviation. It provides a short summary and definition of the standard with the ICT components or other major elements which are covered.

Table 7: Cluster "networks" and its *ICT Security Standards*

Networks	Communication of users (from their LAN or remote) to consume ICT services centrally produced (in a data center)	
Standard	**Abbr.**	**ICT components and major areas**
Wide Area Network Security	WAN	All means used to transport data between users and between users and IT systems in data centers including direct network links, Internet access, bandwidth, MPLS.
Corporate Provider Access	CPA	All ICT equipment between the WAN and the data center LAN, i.e., the communication periphery of the data center. This includes packet filter firewalls, switches and routers, VPN gateways and intrusion detection/prevention (IDS/IPS) solutions.
		"Transportation level" only: application-related ICT equipment comes under Gateway and Central Services (GCS).

Networks		Communication of users (from their LAN or remote) to consume ICT services centrally produced (in a data center)
Standard	**Abbr.**	**ICT components and major areas**
Gateway and Central Services	GCS	All ICT equipment that is centrally provided for specific communication such as e-mail and for user authentication. This includes e-mail security and archiving, other communication services, file sharing as well as directory services, LDAP, other authentication servers, web SSO and identity federation services, application level gateways including proxies and reverse proxies and web application firewalls (WAF).
		"Application level" only: purely transport-oriented "gateways" come under Corporate Provider Access, CPA.
User LAN Periphery	ULP	All ICT equipment that is located between the user LAN and the WAN, i.e. the users' central communication periphery. This includes site-to-site gateways, firewalls, intrusion detection / prevention (IDS/IPS) solutions and domain services.
Remote User Access	RUA	All client components that are used to securely communicate via the WAN or the Administration Network, or to securely connect to ICT services that are centrally produced (in a data center). That includes VPN clients, authentication tokens and other such tools.
		"Transportation level" only: other equipment comes under Office Workplace Security (OWS) and Mobile Workplace Security (MWS).

4.3.2   Data center

All *ICT Security Standards* that belong to the "Data center" cluster are specified and briefly characterized in this section. ICT services are produced in data centers (of the ICT Service Provider). Therefore, *Data Center Security* is important comprising all aspects of physical and environmental security aspects relating to the data center as a whole. Management of the ICT is performed remotely from operations centers. *Administration Network Security* defines security requirements for such administrative access. There are *Data Center Networks* within the data centers which connect physical computer systems to each other, these computer systems to storage and administrators to both computers and storage systems. *Operations Support Security* concerns all security aspects of procedures, tool sets and utilities needed for data center operations. *Computer Systems Security* comprises computer hardware and operating systems as a minimum. *Database and Storage Security* is considered as an extra discipline. Applications are executed on top. Thus, *Application and Application Management Security* is a further issue. In dynamic computing environments, hypervisors and such means of virtualization are part of the computer systems. *Virtual Machine and Software Image Management* addresses the security issues relating to the engineering (creation and configuration) of software images, their handling and deployment to machines as well as moves and other management activities including the management systems required for this. Access by operations personnel (administrators) to these and other critical systems or systems functions needs to be controlled with care. The related security issues are summarized in *Provider Identity Management*.

For more details, refer to Table 8 below. The table provides the name of the standard, its icon and abbreviation. It provides a short summary and definition of the standard with the ICT components or other major elements which are covered.

Table 8: Cluster "data center" and its *ICT Security Standards*

Data Center	Equipment and resources for the production of central ICT services (location: data center)	
Standard	**Abbr.**	**ICT components and major areas**
Data Center Security	DCS	All physical and environmental security aspects of a data center. It does not include ICT security equipment except for that relating to entrance control etc.
Data Center Networks	DCN	All networks and network equipment within the data center that is used to connect Computer Systems (to each other, to the data center's external interface, and with Storage) as well as to connect operations personnel (administrators) to Computer Systems, Storage and Operations Support equipment.
		Note that all that network and network equipment is "inside the firewall". Connectivity between data centers of the ICT Service Provider is also included.

Data Center		Equipment and resources for the production of central ICT services (location: data center)
Standard	**Abbr.**	**ICT components and major areas**
Computer Systems Security	CSS	All parts of the IT stack except user applications, centralized storage and middleware including runtime environments and data bases. Computer Systems comprise physical computers with operating systems and system virtualization software such as hypervisors.
Database and Storage Security	DSS	All centralized storage equipment and software (accessed by Computer Systems via Data Center Networks) plus Data Base Management Systems even if they run on individual Computer Systems. It also contains all resources for backup and disaster recovery.
Operations Support Security	OSS	All procedures, tool sets and utilities that are used by operations personnel (administrators) for basic data center operations. This includes software for systems management, ICT asset and life-cycle management, ICT service management as well as for service availability and performance management.
Application and Application Management Security	AMS	All software that produces the primary ICT services for users. It does not include platforms and infrastructure services. Applications sit on top of Computer Systems. Middleware such as runtime environments (e.g. .NET) is also included except for Data Base Management Systems.
Virtual Machine and Software Image Management	VMM	All procedures, tool sets and utilities that are used by operations personnel (administrators) to deploy, start, stop, move and otherwise manage Virtual Machines that run on Computer Systems. All procedures, tool sets and utilities that are used to generate and configure software images (engineering of images) and for archiving as well as the inventory of these images. Software images comprise those for operating systems and those for applications.

Data Center		Equipment and resources for the production of central ICT services (location: data center)
Standard	**Abbr.**	**ICT components and major areas**
Administration Network Security	ANS	All networks and other equipment that allow operations personnel (administrators) to connect to the data center and its components remotely in order to perform management and maintenance tasks. This includes network security plus jump servers and centrally provided services such as authentication services. Note that the use of such equipment is confined to administrators only.
Provider Identity Management	PIM	All procedures and regulations, systems and services that are used to create and manage the digital identities including rights and other attributes for operations personnel (administrators).

4.3.3   Customer and users

All *ICT Security Standards* that belong to the "Customer and Users" cluster are specified and briefly characterized in this section. The user organization requires an Identity and Access Management solution in order to manage users, equipment and their access to ICT components and services. If provided by the ICT Service Provider, the management of digital identities is described in *User Identity Management*. Users use their workplace to access ICT services that are provided remotely. *Office Workplace Security* and *Mobile Workplace Security* address the corresponding security issues of protecting these workplaces and the information and applications being used and processed with them.

For more details refer to Table 9 below. The table provides the name of the standard, its icon and abbreviation. It provides a short summary and definition of the standard with the ICT components or other major elements which are covered.

Table 9: Cluster "customer and users" and its *ICT Security Standards*

Customer and users		Equipment and resources used by customers and users (location: user's premises or mobile)
Standard	**Abbr.**	**ICT components and major areas**
User Identity Management	UIM	All procedures and regulations, systems and services that are used to create and manage the digital identities including rights and other attributes for users. The digital identities of a person are described as "personalized identity objects" which are assigned to other identity objects like location, organization, legal entity, etc. These identities are managed in the so-called Identity Management Life-cycle. The Identity Management service is the basis for real-time access management.

Note that authentication services are mostly provided as a central service (refer to Gateway and Central Services (GCS)). All client components for authentication and secure networking are covered under Remote User Access (RUA). |
| Office Workplace Security | OWS | All software and equipment that is used to protect desktop computers and the data and software stored and processed there.

Note that Office Workplaces may also be provided in a virtualized way and hosted as an "application" in the data center. |
| Mobile Workplace Security | MWS | All software and equipment that is used to protect mobile computers and the data and software stored and processed on these. This includes notebook computers and different types of smartphones.

Note that mobile workplaces may also be provided in a virtualized way and hosted as "application" in the data center. |

4.3.4   Evidence and Customer Relation

All *ICT Security Standards* that belong to the "Evidence and Customer Relation" cluster are specified and briefly characterized in this section. The *Customer Communication and Security* standard provides more details on how the ICT Service Provider works, interacts and communicates with customers. *Vulnerability Assessment and Mitigation Planning* refers to all related activities like security testing, regular scanning, CERT services, evaluation of impact and planning of corrective actions. *Logging, Monitoring and Security Reporting* concerns log management and analysis, monitoring of systems, measurement and information provisioning to customers. In *Incident Handling and Forensics*, practices are described to handle (security) incidents in IT production and potentially together with the customer. It also describes investigations of log data and systems to find evidence of suspicious, malicious and fraudulent action.

For more details, refer to Table 10 below. The table provides the name of the standard, its icon and abbreviation. It provides a short summary and definition of the standard with the ICT components or other major elements which are covered.

Table 10: Cluster "evidence and customer relation" and its *ICT Security Standards*

Evidence and Customer Relation	Management of vulnerabilities, security information, events and incidents as well as secure communication with customers	
Standard	**Abbr.**	**ICT components and major areas**
Customer Communication and Security	CCS	All procedures which establish the communication with customers and all means used to secure this electronic communication. This includes non-disclosure agreements and encryption technology for e-mails.
Vulnerability Assessment and Mitigation Planning	VAM	All activities relating to regular security testing and scanning of systems software and their configuration, CERT services, evaluation of impact and planning of corrective actions.
Logging, Monitoring and Security Reporting	LMR	All activities and tools used for central log management and analysis, monitoring of systems, measurement and information provisioning to customers. It includes Security Information Management (SIM) with log management, data collection, analysis and reporting of log data, privileged user and resource access monitoring as well as Security Event Management (SEM) with real time log and event data processing, correlation and analysis of events.

Evidence and Cus-tomer Relation	Management of vulnerabilities, security information, events and incidents as well as secure communication with customers

Standard	Abbr.	ICT components and major areas
Incident Handling and Forensics	IHF	All procedures and means used to handle and respond to security-related circumstances that may have a significant impact and require a timely resolution by implementation of workarounds or by removing the root cause.

4.3.5 Service Management

All *ICT Security Standards* that belong to the "Service Management" cluster are specified and briefly characterized in this section. These *ICT Security Standards* relate to life-cycle issues and general aspects of operations security. The *Release Management and Acceptance Testing* standard describes the corresponding security-related activities that are conducted in the plan–build phases, which are typically planning, design, implementation as well as end-of-life management. Security testing is also part of the acceptance procedures. *System Development Life-Cycle* describes requirements for software being developed by the provider and used for ICT service provisioning in particular. *Systems Acquisition and Contracting* describes specific requirements for systems and services being purchased from vendors for the purpose of ICT service provisioning. The *Change and Problem Management* standard describes how new requirements are met and realized and how possible problems are managed, possibly in cooperation with the customer. Changes may be initiated by customers or may be required as the result of vulnerabilities being identified or security incidents that have occurred. The four remaining standards refer to general aspects of operations security: *Asset and Configuration Management, Hardening, Provisioning and Maintenance, Security Patch Management* and *Business Continuity Management*.

For more details, refer to Table 11 below. The table provides the name of the standard, its icon and abbreviation. It provides a short summary and definition of the standard with the ICT components or other major elements which are covered.

Table 11: Cluster "service management" and its *ICT Security Standards*

Service Management	Life-cycle issues and general aspects of operations security	
Standard	**Abbr.**	**ICT components and major areas**
Release Management and Acceptance Testing	RMA	Release Management plans, tests, communicates, implements and monitors the implementation of a release into the ICT service environment and ensures that all technical and nontechnical aspects are considered.
		A release is considered as a set of pre-approved changes of the ICT service environment (i.e. ICT systems and components used by the ICT Service Provider to provide ICT services).
System Development Life-Cycle	SDL	The System Development Life-Cycle is a process for developing demonstrably reliable and secure ICT systems. It includes activities performed with the goal that ICT systems respond to needs by providing the required functionality correctly and nothing more. This means that requirements are implemented correctly without introducing vulnerabilities.
Systems Acquisition and Contracting	SAC	Selecting the right supplier is critical when purchasing ICT systems and components (or even services) that are reliable, secure, etc.
		Properties and other characteristics, the possibility of corrections and the process to achieve them are all examples of things which need to be fixed in a contract. Otherwise, it may be difficult to have any of these activities carried out.
Change and Problem Management	CPM	Changes are alterations to ICT components which are requested mainly due to incidents or problems. Change Management is the life-cycle process from request and analysis to implementation and final verification.
		Problems are the cause of any failure of or incidents in ICT service delivery. Problem management is the life-cycle process from occurrence, notification, analysis and identification of causes to the planning of workarounds and changes.

Service Management	Life-cycle issues and general aspects of operations security	
Standard	**Abbr.**	**ICT components and major areas**
Asset and Configuration Management	ACM	Asset Management is the process responsible for tracking and reporting the value and ownership of ICT systems and components throughout their life-cycle. Configuration Management is the process responsible for maintaining information about any component required to deliver an ICT Service, including their relationships.
Hardening, Provisioning and Maintenance	HPM	Hardening comprises all methods applied to ICT systems, software and components that reduce the possibility of vulnerabilities and susceptibility to attacks. Provisioning comprises all methods of deployment and activation of ICT service including conception, installation, configuration, and approval. Maintenance comprises technical support to ensure continued operation and actuality, including the help desk.
Security Patch Management	SPM	Security Patch Management is the process responsible for the consolidated proactive update of ICT systems for which new potential vulnerabilities are discovered and their fixes are available. It is applicable to all ICT systems, both customer specific installations and general infrastructure.
Business Continuity Management	BCM	Business Continuity Management provides precautions that minimize the impact of possible disruptions to ICT service provisioning or of loss of data, which includes a timely and full recovery of service and data.

4.3.6 Risk Management and Certification

All *ICT Security Standards* that belong to the "Risk Management and Certification" cluster are specified and briefly characterized in this section. *Certification and 3rd Party Assurance* describes the general approach of the ICT Service Provider to certifications and how third-party assurance, gained through audits and assessments, is planned, conducted and integrated into the provider's business strategy and communication. The *Risk Management* standard describes the procedures of making decisions on the implementation of security measures.

For more details, refer to Table 12 below. The table provides the name of the standard, its icon and abbreviation. It provides a short summary and definition of the standard with the ICT components or other major elements which are covered.

Table 12: Cluster "Risk Management and Certification" and its *ICT Security Standards*

Risk Management and Certification	Top-level security issues	
Standard	**Abbr.**	**ICT components and major areas**
Certification and 3rd Party Assurance	CTP	Third-party assessment and validation may provide a greater level of independence and acceptance in a wider market. Utilization of security practices from industry standards provides benefits since expertise and experience from a wider market is used.
Risk Management	RMP	Security and compliance can be compromised by different circumstances. Risk Management comprises the identification of risks, the analysis and categorization of risks, and the determination of countermeasures to reduce the risks to an acceptable level.

4.4   Summary of standards and taxonomy

ESARIS describes security measures in a structured and totally modular way. The security measures were distributed amongst several *ICT Security Standards* since both the ICT services and the security requirements are manifold. The *ICT Security Standards* provide transparency to customers by explaining how the ICT Service Provider achieves and guarantees security. They are also directives for Production and Service Delivery. The structure of the *ICT Security Standards* has therefore been designed to serve three goals: Customers shall obtain answers to how their requirements are addressed. Secondly, the supplying party shall easily find the guidance relevant for them. Thirdly, the *ICT Security Standards* shall cover all relevant aspects, i.e. "the whole world of ICT security" with all the details and variants across all technical disciplines and throughout the entire life-cycle. The *ICT Security Standards* are located on Level 4 which is called the *ESARIS Orchestration Layer*.

In order to achieve these goals efficiently, the *ESARIS Security Taxonomy* has been designed. The map of all *ICT Security Standards* consists of three groups. The first group is primarily oriented towards individual ICT services and their functionality. The second group of standards comprises all standards that are associated with general IT management services common to several ICT services. The third group provides the standards that are associated with the other two groups.

The standards can be organized into so-called clusters. There are different versions. The clusters are a further means to understand the purpose and intent of the *ICT Security Standards* contained therein.

Each *ICT Security Standard* is given a unique name, an abbreviation and an icon. The explanations and the short summary and definition of the standards provide further understanding of the *ESARIS Security Taxonomy*. The description of the standards is continued in the next chapter. All *ICT Security Standards* are structured in the same way. There are templates and guidance documents for authors, which ensure the quality, usability und uniqueness of the documentation.

The *ESARIS Security Taxonomy* is complex since the summary of all its constituents is designed to cover all the security aspects of the ICT services being provided to customers. The taxonomy helps to find the information required; whereas monolithic documentation would not allow appropriate use of its contents. The taxonomy is also required in order to draw up the security measures. The taxonomy has been developed using predefined criteria that are analyzed to understand the requirements which the structure must meet.

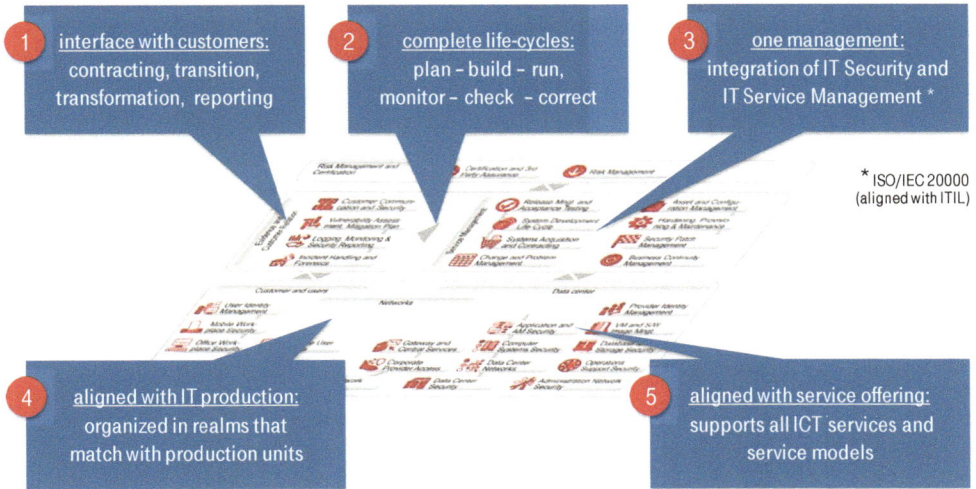

Fig. 26: Unique features of the *ESARIS Security Taxonomy*

Fig. 26 highlights five unique features of the *ESARIS Security Taxonomy*. They are reasons why ESARIS has been developed as a new approach for securing large-scale ICT service provisioning. The Taxonomy introduces and details the interface to user organizations (customer) and to suppliers. Of course, it covers security aspects along the whole life-cycle. However, it does not only focus on development and implementation. Instead it also covers all phases of IT outsourcing and of modern IT production. A major goal of ESARIS is the integration of *IT security management* and *IT service management*. This ensures that security guidelines are actually adhered to. ESARIS and its Taxonomy are aligned with industrialized IT production which is necessary for all production units to find their security requirements easily. It is also an important factor to support the division of labor which enables specialization and finally raises efficiency. The Taxonomy and its security measures are modular. This enables the alignment with a complex service offering portfolio of a large ICT Service Provider and, in consequence, is the precondition for re-using security measures for different ICT services which in turn is the basis for standardization.

4.5   Provider Scope of Control

Introduction and summary: On the one hand, the *ICT Security Standards* are used as the source of information for customers. On the other hand, they are used as directives for parties providing ICT services and parts of them. In case one, it must be proven to customers that their requirements are met and how. This requires selecting the relevant information from the ESARIS documentation in the first place. In case two, the ICT Service Provider or its suppliers require security requirements relevant for the ICT service or other deliverable they are responsible for. This requires the relevant standards to be selected. The concept developed for this selection is called *Provider Scope of Control* and described in this section.

ESARIS is comprehensive and provides information regarding all aspects of securing ICT services. However, not all ESARIS standards are relevant in every context. ESARIS defines a method for selecting the right information for a customer. The ICT Service Provider's delivery units use the same method to locate the security information they have to adhere to. This method is called *Provider Scope of Control*. It is also used to manage suppliers and the services or components they are providing. The *Provider Scope of Control* is the methodology to manage the division of labor within the ICT Service Provider as well as in the relationship with customers and with suppliers.

Only a few customers of the ICT Service Provider consume all available ICT services (in the areas of desktop, networks, computing) and buy them from one provider altogether. Therefore, they are not interested in all *ICT Security Standards*. The latter cover all possible ICT services and describe general aspects such as availability, system maintenance and troubleshooting as well. If a customer uses the desktop service, for example, then the Office Workplace Standard is relevant as well as general standards about service management and security management as far as the ICT Service Provider delivers such services for the desktop service. This is shown in Fig. 27. First, the contracted service is examined. The ICT service and their functionality determine the relevant areas from the lower half of the *ESARIS*

Security Taxonomy. In the figure, workplace computers and equipment for remote access is relevant. Second, the IT management services are identified which are a subject of the contract. In the example, maintenance and patch management services are relevant. The ICT service delivered to the customer comprises third-party components. The customer is interested that also these components meet the ESARIS security standards. – The same method is used for the contract between the ICT Service Provider and its supplier.

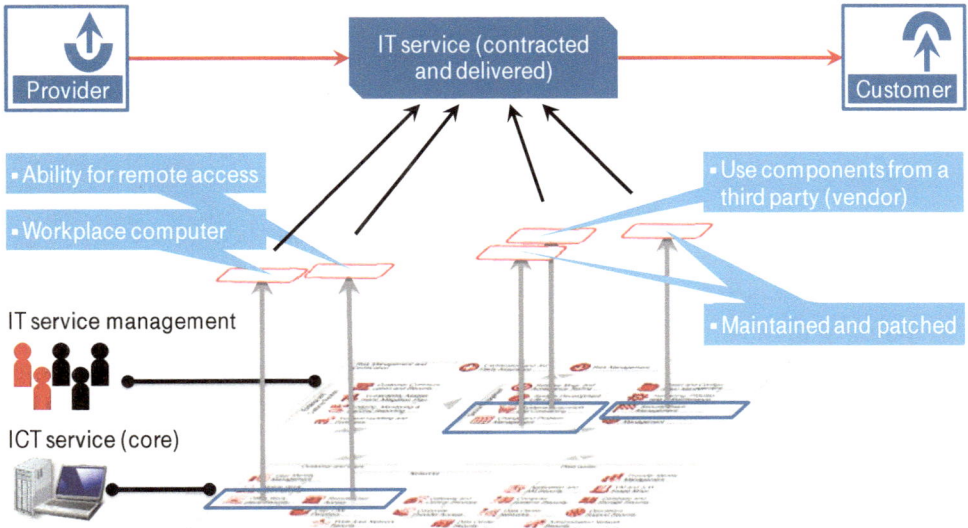

Fig. 27: Example for the application of Provider Scope of Control

The selection process is now explained in more detail where the involved parties are called supplying party and consuming party. Supplying party refers to suppliers and internal departments and teams of the ICT Service Provider. Consuming parties are internal departments and teams of the ICT Service Provider and the customer of the ICT Service Provider. The description is exemplified by the specific customer service request "Managed Desktop with a Smart Card". Refer to Fig. 28.

Ⓐ The ICT elements are identified by inspecting the offering or ICT service being delivered or planned to be delivered to the consuming party. In this step, the focus is on ICT services and their functionality. The relevant *ICT Security Standards* (from the lower half of the *ESARIS Security Taxonomy*) are selected. Refer to Fig. 28. If desktop services are to be delivered to the customer, the standard *Office Workplace Security (OWS)* is selected. Notebooks, for example, may be equipped with a VPN solution so that the standard *Remote User Access (RUA)* is selected as well. *User Identity Management (UIM)* is also selected since this service requires the management of digital identities for using the two functions.

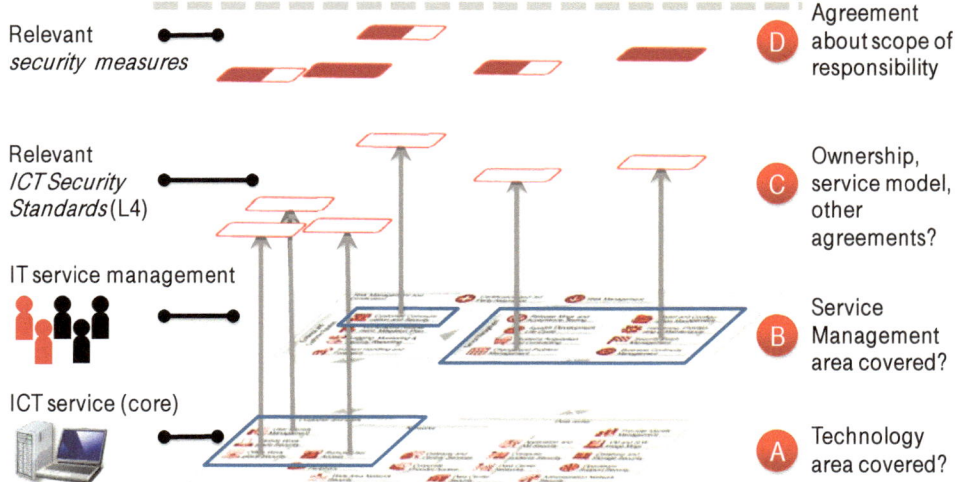

Fig. 28: Provider Scope of Control

B Now the associated IT management services are identified by inspecting the offering or service being delivered or planned to be delivered again. In this step, the focus is on operations and maintenance and the division of labor with respect to IT management activities. In the example, the desktop is managed. Hence, the *Change and Problem Management (CPM)* and the *Security Patch Management (SPM)* standard are selected. The management of the interface to the consuming party is also important so that the standard *Customer Communication and Security (CCS)* is selected too. Refer to Fig. 28.

C Then it is analyzed if the supplying party is actually responsible for the corresponding security elements. This includes answering the question as to whether or not the supplying party actually possesses, owns or delivers the ICT elements. In the example, the notebooks are equipped with a VPN solution using a smart card. The card is maybe delivered but the associated identity management is conducted by the consuming party. Therefore, the *User Identity Management (UIM)* standard is not relevant in this specific case. The same check is performed for the areas relating to IT service management.

D A further step may be necessary in order to take contractual details into account. The ICT elements, possession or ownership, service types, service models, modes of production and other circumstances such as the location need to be analyzed in more detail. The contract may include or exclude specific services and define further rules that determine the selection of standards or of security measures within these standards. As an example, Problem Management is not supported, functions available for workplaces are not ordered, and one set of measures is reduced since the contract is renewed only. Refer to the three areas in Fig. 28 which are not completely filled red.

It is important to note that it is definitely not sufficient and adequate to work with the titles of the *ICT Security Standards* only. The *ESARIS Security Taxonomy* is developed to ease the process of selecting security measures and to determine the *Provider Scope of Control*. Nevertheless, each *ICT Security Standard* provides a detailed description of its "Scope and Coverage" which needs to be checked in many cases.

The *Taxonomy of Service Models* is shown in Fig. 29.[30] It considerably helps defining the *Provider Scope of Control* especially in complex IT outsourcing situations. It is built to differentiate between different service models using three major characteristics. Seven (typical) service delivery models are listed on the left-hand side of the diagram shown in Fig. 29. From bottom to top, these are monitoring and support, managed services, hosting, infrastructure-as-a-service, platform-as-a-service and software-as-a-service. Cloud computing resides on top but is connected to the "as-a-service" models to indicate that cloud computing is a production method for these service models.

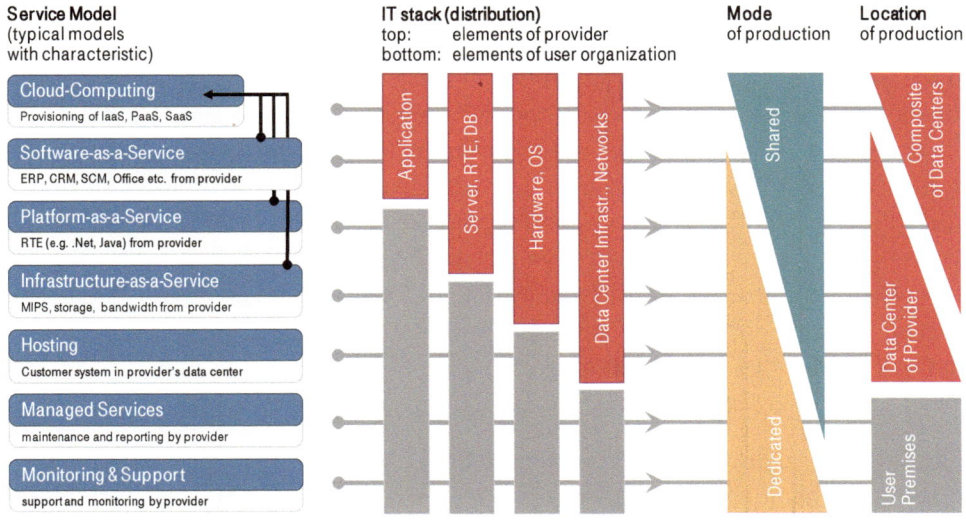

Fig. 29: Taxonomy of Service Models and the origin of specific risks

These seven service delivery models relate to different models of the division of labor between the ICT Service Provider and its customer or, more general between the supplying and the consuming party. The division of labor and responsibility, as well as the associated implications, can be analyzed using, for example, three

---

[30] This model was originally published by one of the authors, for instance in Eberhard von Faber and Michael Pauly: User Risk Management Strategies and Models – Adaption for Cloud Computing; in: N. Pohlmann, H. Reimer, W. Schneider (Editors): Securing Electronic Business Processes, Vieweg (2010), ISBN-10: 3834814385, p. 80 – 90.

characteristics that are shown in the three columns on the right-hand side of the figure, entitled

- IT stack distribution,
- mode of production, and
- location of production.

Others may be added.

A rough illustration of the "IT stack" is shown in the center of Fig. 29, divided into

- data center infrastructure and networks (right),
- hardware and operating system,
- server, run-time environment and data bases, and
- application (left).

Each service delivery model utilizes the whole IT stack (row). Note the arrows that go from left to the right. There are two basic possibilities when building the IT stack. Refer to the "mode of production" column. Dedicated technology can be set up for the user organization (dedicated), or the ICT service is being produced on a platform that is shared with other organizations (shared). This is important for the determination of risks. The last characteristic in this figure is the "location of production". In the first two service models, the ICT is located at the user organization's premises. In all other cases, the ICT service is produced by the ICT Service Provider (data center of provider). However, large providers may have a huge infrastructure with dozens of interconnected data centers distributed around the globe (composite of data centers). Both parameters are important since the provider has different security measures and practices for dedicated and for shared environments. The security measures may also differ between subsidiaries and, possibly, data centers. Note that also the social and political environment may be different in the countries they are located in.

The seven service models are briefly characterized below:

Monitoring and Support: All elements of the IT stack are owned by the user organization. All elements of the IT stack are shown in gray in that row (see Fig. 29). There are no other user organizations. As a result, the systems are dedicated ones (specific to the user organization, refer to Mode of Production in the figure). The technology is located in the premises of the user organization (data center, refer to Location of Production in the figure). The ICT Service Provider only monitors the systems and provides reports about performance and incidents. The provider is typically also responsible for ICT support.

Managed Services: This service model comprises all services from the first model. However, the ICT Service Provider actively manages the ICT of the user organization. Examples are software updates and possibly also configuration.

Hosting: This is the first model where the data center of the ICT Service Provider is used (refer to Location of Production). However, most elements of the IT stack are still dedicated and used by one user organization only. They are shown in gray in the figure and are usually owned by the user organization. However, different user organizations do share the data center infrastructure and networks. This is sometimes forgotten.[31] Virtualization and sharing of infrastructures started long before cloud computing was developed. Hosting can be dedicated or already use hardware and operating systems owned by the ICT Service Provider. In the latter case, this element of the IT stack would be red and not gray. Refer to this row in the figure.

Infrastructure-as-a-Service: More and more elements of the IT stack are now shared by different user organizations. In this model (formerly also "utility-computing"), user organizations share computer systems.

Platform-as-a-Service: In this model, only applications are user organization-specific ("dedicated"). All other elements of the IT stack are used by several user organizations simultaneously ("shared").

Software-as-a-Service: Here many user organizations are provided with one software. In fact, there are different versions (not shown in the figure) depending on the realization of access, software construction and data management.

Cloud computing: Cloud computing provides ICT "as-a-service" (refer to Fig. 29) where potentially all elements are shared and the production is located at the provider's data center or a grid of these data centers.

The *Taxonomy of Service Models* or a similar model is helpful for the determination of the *Provider Scope of Control* (which uses the *ESARIS Security Taxonomy*). The *Provider Scope of Control* is important in understanding the responsibilities of the ICT Service Provider in detail. It is then clear which *ICT Security Standards* and which security measures (possibly with limitations or modifications) are valid and describe the ICT service being purchased by the user organization.

---

[31] Note that in almost all cases the wide area network infrastructure is already shared between user organizations. Fixed lines dedicated to one user organization are more expensive and used exceptionally.

5 Secured by definition – integration with core business (ITSM)

Introduction and summary: The starting point is the question, why IT security management and IT service management (ITSM) must be integrated at all? Reasons are provided and discussed. ITIL defines practices for the ITSM and is used as a reference. Fourteen ITIL core areas and processes are summarized and assigned to the ESARIS areas in order to provide a sound basis (Sect. 5.1). ITIL is security-aware and comprises a dedicated Information Security Management process. It is shown that more is required. The role of the Security Management organization requires a change. Based on this division of labor between Security Management and IT business departments a staged model for integrating IT security in IT service management activities is presented (Sect. 5.2). Two examples are used to show how the integration of IT security management on the one hand and IT service management (ITIL) on the other should actually be done. New activities need to be added to the ITIL processes or even to the process map in order to make sure that the specific requirements of managing security are met. The ITIL processes dominate the industrialized IT production. In this environment, processes are important elements that exactly specify all steps in advance which need to be carried out by employees. Security activities need to be integrated. The discussion of the two examples shows how this is accomplished in practice (Sect. 5.3).

5.1 ITSM processes and why security must be integrated into them

Introduction and summary: The characteristics of industrialized IT production are recapped. Then five reasons are provided and discussed why security must be integrated into the IT service management processes (as described e.g. in ITIL). It is necessary to understand how ITIL works: Therefore, fourteen ITIL core areas and processes are summarized in brief. They build the skeleton of IT service management according to ITIL. They are matched with the areas and *ICT Security Standards* in the *ESARIS Security Taxonomy* which provides further insight about the consideration of IT service management in ESARIS.

IT personnel are often heard saying that security is not their business but security experts should care for security instead. However, it is also observed that security experts are involved very, very late. Why? They are supposed to cause delay. If the IT personnel are asked why delay is expected, they may answer that the security experts are not sufficiently familiar with the IT stuff (technology, processes or other). Moreover, the security experts are not expected having predefined solutions at hand. Security experts may not be involved at all since they seem to mainly ask questions and come along with additional requirements. As a result, delegating IT security to security experts may not be easy. Note that often security experts are not available and can therefore not be involved since there are not so many of them. There are actually much more IT-related activities than security experts. Hence, it is not possible to delegate IT security to a dedicated group of security people only.

If the limited number of security experts is not able to care for IT security alone, then every IT employee must care for it. But what is required to enable and motivate them to do so. Here are two more questions:

- Do you think that a major part of the employees will continuously make considerable investments (time, money) which are not in the scope of the corporation's core business?

- Do you think that a major part of the employees will keep pursuing costly activities though this is not described in the work instructions they are primarily forced to follow?

The questions are almost identical because companies tend to specify in written instructions what is really important for them. If at least one of the answers is "No", it seems worth discussing about the integration of IT security management on the one hand and IT service management on the other hand.

Larger organizations organize their IT production along IT service management processes as described in ITIL[32] and ISO/IEC 20000.[33] In the following, it is described why and how IT security is integrated into such processes used to organize the core businesses of ICT Service Providers. ITIL is owned by Axelos (refer to www.axelos.com). In the following, the IT service management processes are taken for granted and not described in detail. They are only characterized briefly in order to provide sufficient background information necessary to understand how IT security is to be integrated into such an environment according to ESARIS. Different naming conventions and differences in coverage and scope of single processes do not matter much in this context. For the sake of simplicity, "ITIL" will be referred to as a synonym for "IT service management processes" although even larger IT organizations may primarily use ISO/IEC 20000 or similar definitions.

Fig. 30 shows characteristics of today's, large-scale ICT on the left-hand side and reasons for integrating security management with IT service management on the right. Modern large-scale IT production has already been described. But a few

---

[32] ITIL: Information Technology Infrastructure Library

[33] ISO/IEC 20000 – Information technology – Service management – Part 1: Service management system requirements, Part 2: Guidance on the application of service management systems; 2012 [2]

things are worth to be highlighted again. The business is distributed amongst many highly specialized teams and departments. This results in a high demand for coordination which cannot be managed using direct contacts between people. Written instructions need to exist which are exact and precise enough to ensure achieving quality constantly. Note that this is not security specific. Today, the IT production is no longer organized into silos (vertical organization). The industrialized way of production is mainly organized horizontally by means of core business processes (though a vertical steering for customers or products may exist in addition).

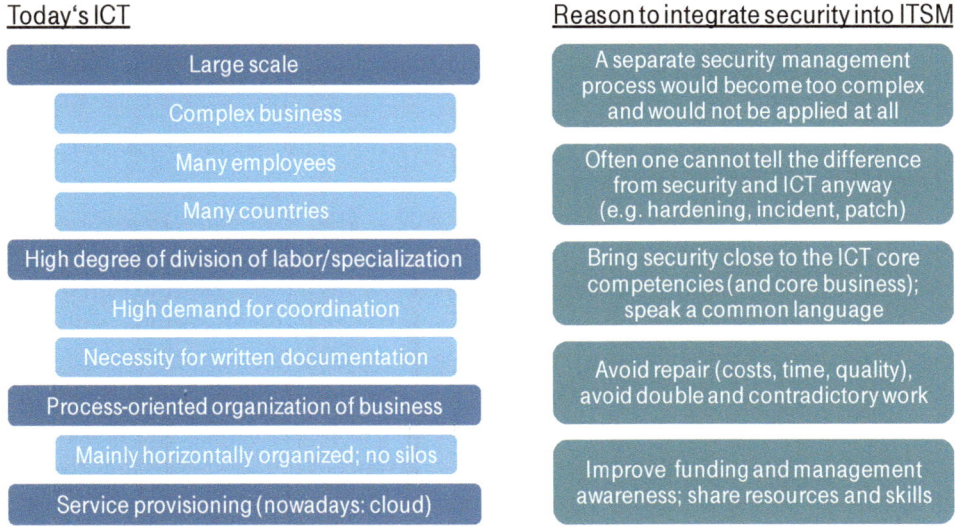

Fig. 30: Today's large-scale ICT and reasons for integrating security with ITSM processes

The right-hand side in Fig. 30 is much more interesting. It summarizes reasons for actually integrating IT security management with IT service management. *Firstly*, the main goal of this integration is to ensure that security is actually implemented. The ICT services are designed, implemented and operated according to IT service management processes defined by the rather complex framework ITIL and ISO/IEC 20000. IT security is also a complex matter. Why are processes used at all? The activities must be repeatable. Therefore, all steps that need to be carried out have to be defined in advance. If one would try to specify all required security activities in one security management process the result would either be very general only or too complex to be used at all.[34] This means that it would either describe only general security management principles that cannot directly be applied by the employees or nobody would study this comprehensive work. The result is the

---

[34] Consider that such a separate security management process would have to refer to every important ITIL process, sub-process and activity and then specify what is required with respect to security.

same: only some heroes would care for security whereas the majority wouldn't care. Note that ESARIS pursues another model. Level 3 and Level 4 are mainly used by the Security Management organization and security experts. The *ICT Security Baselines* (Level 5), however, are designed to provide practical, hands-on guidance for almost every member of the IT staff which tells them how to take action in order to provide for security or avoid endangering it. These instructions are dedicated to specific people (roles) performing very specific activities in managing ICT on a day-to-day basis. This includes incident agents, change approvers, quality managers, people from the procurements department, testers and administrators with numerous responsibilities just to name a few.

Secondly, often one cannot separate security from ICT. When a technician configures an IT component he or she adjusts several settings. In many cases one cannot differentiate if the setting is for providing a usual function or for security. It is even difficult to put this fact into words. One cannot actually separate hardening and security hardening. If an incident occurs such as the breakdown of a server it is not clear if it was hacked or simply malfunctioning. The same with patches; though vendors denominate some patches as security patches, this is merely done to say that this does not alter the primary functionality. Repairing the functionality can also have an effect on security since malfunction can result in a vulnerability that put data at risk. The *third* argument for integrating security with the core processes is that it brings security close to the core competencies of the ICT Service Provider. Technicians who care for the IT functionality including all characteristics are very experienced and familiar with the technology. Hence, it makes sense that they care for security too. They can most probably do it better than others. *Fourth,* a parallel stream of security activities does not make sense at all. This would result in extra work because everything must be touched twice. *Fifth,* budgets for security are limited as others are. If security is cared for in an extra security management process and maybe by extra people, this must be funded from the security budget. What happens if the budget is exhausting? What happens if this budget is cut? Security managers all over the world know such situations. A way out can be as follows: Do not feel responsible for the implementation of security! That's it. It is the IT business unit that is responsible for providing the ICT service including all its characteristics! Treating security like all other characteristics means to make the best with the limited security budget.

If there is a separate security management process that is actually responsible for the implementation of security measures, the equation is simple: extra process means extra costs and this also means that it's somebody else's business. Extra costs result in a situation that the IT business reduces security in order to produce competitive ICT services. Somebody else's business means that eventually nobody cares for security. The Security Management organization will definitely be pushed too hard. Budgets will never be sufficient. And one may look at the numbers: There are maybe thousands of IT experts. How many IT security experts are required or available to work after each IT employee? Security was often treated as a patch attached after completing ICT that turned out to be imperfect with respect to security. This does not work.

As a matter of fact, IT security management and IT service management (ITIL) need to be integrated. It is, however, also true that ESARIS is the first approach that systematically pursued this integration.

It is outlined in the following how this integration is done: ITIL processes are mapped with the areas of the *ESARIS Security Taxonomy*, especially with the *ICT Security Standards* from Group B associated with general IT management services because ITIL is about IT service management. This mapping shall provide an overview only. The details of the integration are explained near the end of the book in Chapter 12. The matching that follows also provides a good overview of ITIL for readers which are not familiar with it.

The mapping is organized in two parts. First the core ITIL processes are considered:

Service Design (ITIL) comprises the activities which are necessary to set up or significantly modify an ICT service ready for subsequent release (including deployment). This process is not described in detail within the core ITIL publications. In ESARIS this is described in the *ICT Security Standard – Systems Development Life-Cycle (SDL)*.

Supplier Management (ITIL): This process ensures that the hardware, software, system or ICT services obtained from third parties have the necessary characteristics such as functionality and quality. It also ensures that contracts are agreed and met by the supplier. In ESARIS this is covered by the *ICT Security Standard – Systems Acquisition and Contracting (SAC)*.

Release Management (ITIL): A Release comprises one or typically many Changes to be applied on hardware, software, documentation, processes or components. The Release Management process coordinates the planning and steers implementation, testing and deployment including handover to Operations. In ESARIS this is described in the *ICT Security Standard – Release Management and Acceptance Testing (RMA)*.

Service Catalog Management (ITIL) delivers and maintains service catalogs which contain all information about customer-facing ICT service and supporting services. In ESARIS this is a subject of the *ESARIS Attainment Model*.

Service Portfolio Management (ITIL): The service offering portfolio comprises all ICT services of the ICT Service Provider. The Service Portfolio Management process develops and maintains the portfolio and ensures that all ICT services meet defined market requirements and deliver the business value as expected. In ESARIS the link is created by the *ICT Security Standard – Release Management and Acceptance Testing (RMA)*. The activities themselves are the subject of the *ESARIS Attainment Model*.

Event Management (ITIL): An event is a change of state in ICT that has or may have significance for the management of the ICT service. Security events are covered by the *ICT Security Standard – Logging, Monitoring and Security Reporting (LMR)*. Security events are events that are security-related or security-relevant. They are recorded in form of log data or are generated as an alert.

Incident Management (ITIL): This process is triggered through the occurrence of an incident which is an unplanned interruption or a reduction of the quality of an ICT service. The Incident Management process aims at normal service operation is restored as soon as possible and that impacts on the business are minimized. In ESARIS the *ICT Security Standard – Incident Handling and Forensics (IHF)* covers this.

Problem Management (ITIL): In this process, the root causes have to be found that caused incidents. A solution must be found too in order to avoid subsequent incidents and/or to minimize their impact on the business. In ESARIS this is part of the *ICT Security Standard – Change and Problem Management (CPM)*. However, due to the complexity of this area, the *ICT Security Standard – Vulnerability Assessment and Mitigation Planning (VAM)* also plays an important role here.

Change Management (ITIL): This process is triggered by a Change Request (CR). The process coordinates the execution of changes in a way that their impact (especially disruption of ICT services) is minimized and risks are confined to an acceptable level. Changes are addition, modification or removal of anything which is part of or affects an ICT service. In ESARIS this is part of the *ICT Security Standard – Change and Problem Management (CPM)*.

Service Asset and Configuration Management (ITIL): This process ensures that appropriate and reliable information is available about hardware, software and other objects ("assets") that are used to deliver ICT services. The information being managed includes information about the configuration of the assets and their relationship. In ESARIS this is covered by the *ICT Security Standard – Asset and Configuration Management (ACM)*.

A summary of this mapping is shown in Fig. 31.

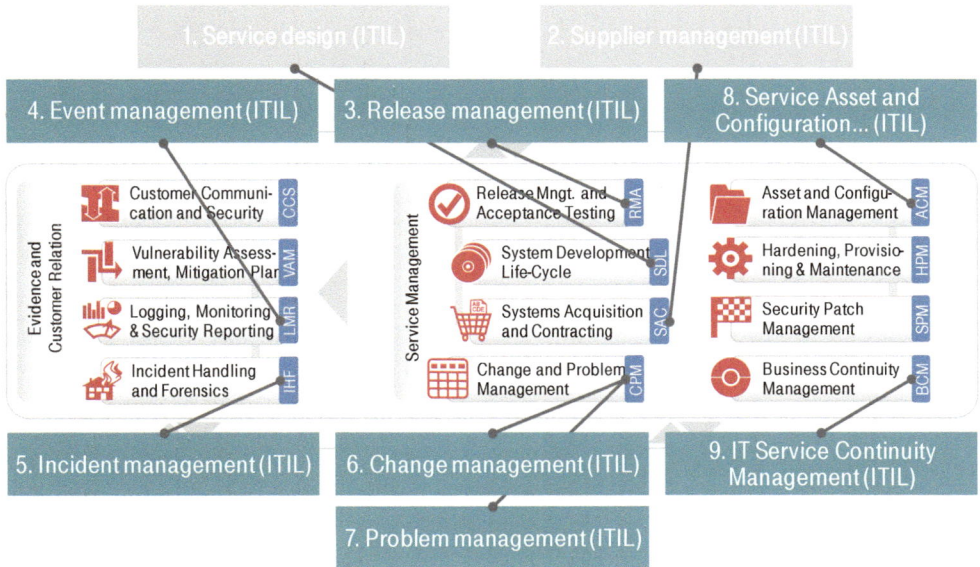

Fig. 31: Core ITIL processes versus areas in the ESARIS Security Taxonomy

In this overview some processes were left out that nevertheless are worth mentioning in the context of discussing how ESARIS areas consider ITIL processes. The following forms the second part of the matching.

Demand Management (ITIL): In this process the requirements and expectations of the customer (users and user organization) are collected, understood, analyzed, judged and communicated internally so that they are considered especially during design. In ESARIS this is partly covered by the *ICT Security Standard – Customer Communication and Security (CCS)* and a subject of the *ESARIS Fulfillment Model* too.

Access Management (ITIL): This process ensures that only authorized users have the ability to make use of ICT services and to modify them. In ESARIS this plays an important role and is therefore distributed amongst different standards. The *ICT Security Standard – Provider Identity Management (PIM)* is about managing digital identities (including credentials and rights) for privileged users (administrators). The *ICT Security Standard – User Identity Management (UIM)* does the same for normal users usually not working for the ICT Service Provider but for the user organization or even being a customer of the user organization. The technical realization of granting access depends on the technology and is therefore a subject of the individual *ICT Security Standard*. General infrastructures such as authentication services are usually described in *ICT Security Standard – Gateway and Central Services (GCS), ICT Security Standard – Operations Support Security (OSS)* and others like *ICT Security Standard – User LAN Periphery (ULP)*. The access infrastructure for privileged users (administrators) is a subject of the *ICT Security Standard – Administration Network Security (ANS)*.

IT Service Continuity Management (ITIL) shall minimize the impact of possible disruptions of the ICT services or of a loss of data which includes a timely and complete recovery of services and data. In ESARIS this is covered by the *ICT Security Standard – Business Continuity Management (BCM)*. Note that the term business relates to ICT services since ICT service provisioning is the business of the ICT Service Provider.

Information Security Management (ITIL): ESARIS provides concepts, methods and means for managing information security in a large-scale IT production.

There is only one *ICT Security Standard* from Group B missing in the above list. Group B in the *ESARIS Security Taxonomy* comprises all areas associated with general IT management services. The missing standard is the *ICT Security Standard – Security Patch Management (SPM)*. There is a simple reason for this. Surprisingly, ITIL does not talk about patching. With respect to security, however, patching is so important that a separate *ICT Security Standard* was created. The relations to vulnerability management, problem management, change management and incident management are described later.

5.2   Division of labor between IT and IT security

Introduction and summary: ITIL is security-aware and a dedicated process is defined for this. In practice, however, this receives little attention from practitioners. A different approach is required. In this section the advantages and disadvantages of using the ITIL Information Security Management process are discussed. It is shown that security needs to be treated differently. The different role of the Security Management organization and a staged model for integrating IT security in IT service management activities is presented.

There is actually an ITIL process not yet described in any detail. It is the Information Security Management process quite arbitrarily assigned to Service Design. The ITIL process shall ensure that overarching objectives are considered and processes and objectives are coordinated. Why is this process not used? Actually, it is used. There is the so-called *Enforcement Framework for ESARIS* (Sect. 2.1) with the Information Security Management System (ISMS). The ITIL process as well as the ISMS ensures that defined processes are in place for the security organization to take care for security which includes the definition of corporate security policies and their implementation. The problem is that the ITIL Information Security Management process is automatically assigned to the Security Management organization and the people working in this field.

More critical, extra process could be understood as extra charge. This is the opposite from "inherent security" or the ESARIS objective "secured by definition". It is a fundamental principle of ITIL to define everything service-based. It is recommended to develop and offer a catalog of security services that can be consumed by other departments of the company. Although security features of ICT services must be described in the ICT Service Provider's services catalog, these features cannot be delivered by anybody else than the one who delivers the functionality that needs to be secured.

The role of the IT business and Security Management organization and the division of labor between them is shown in Fig. 32. There are two things which need to be centralized and coordinated from a central point: the production of security standards and guidance (requirements engineering and setting) and the verification if the security standards and guidance are correctly applied. There is one thing which can neither be centralized nor delegated to certain individuals: the implementation and use of the security standards. It is up to the IT business to deliver secure ICT. This includes all the features necessary to gain business value from using the ICT services. Obviously, security or mitigation of associated risks to an accepted level is one of these features.

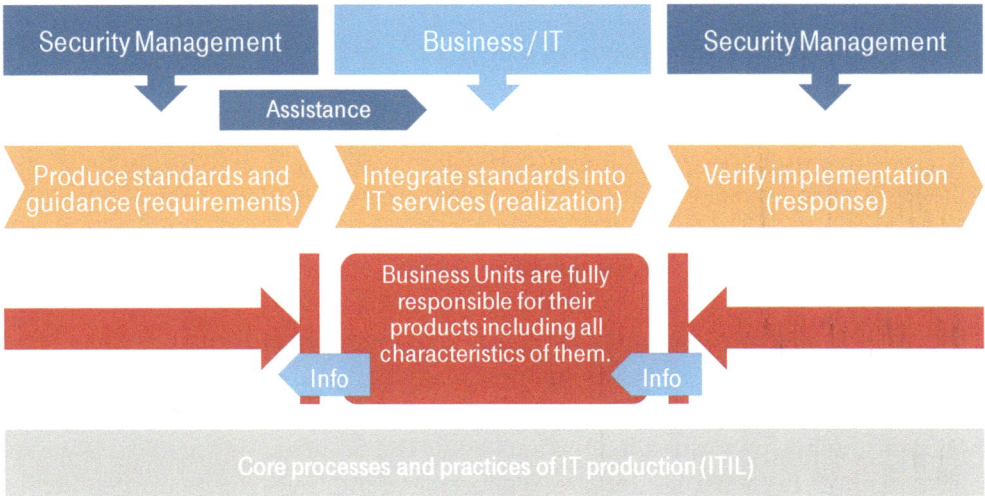

Fig. 32: Role of the IT business and Security Management organization

There is one major lesson learnt for managing security in the past. People start acting if they are affected by the negative result of their own activities. Making security features part of the ICT specification is one step. Making the IT teams and departments responsible for securing their deliverables is consequently the second step. Security programs must be built around the people whose impact is greatest. The Security Management organization is not responsible for the security of the ICT services. It is responsible for providing best support for securing them and for ensuring that inappropriate security is made apparent and evident so that the business is able to take sound decisions whether to improve the security or treat the risk differently.

A large-scale IT business is organized along the ITIL processes. This means that the security management activities have to be integrated into them. Fig. 33 shows four steps in this integration each being characterized by a higher maturity.

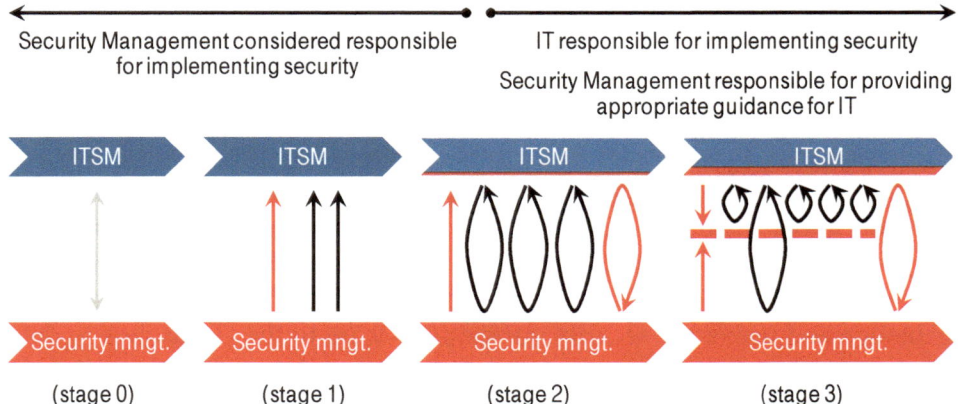

Fig. 33: Four stages of integrating security with IT service management activities

In stage 0 there is almost no integration though both sets of processes and activities exchange information. This ensures that security requirements may or may not be considered. In stage 1 the Security Management organization takes over the mandate to care for security of the ICT services. It defines requirements for securing the ICT services (red arrow in the figure) but also feels responsible for implementing the security measures to a great extent (black arrows). In stage 3 the IT businesses get aware that securing the ICT services is their job. They use the requirements defined by the Security Management organization and implement the security measures by their own. However, considerable assistance is required from the Security Management organization (black looping arrows) for two reasons. First, the security guidance is not as mature, ready for use and fit for purpose as it should be. Second, the IT staff is not familiar enough to actually care for security on their own using written instructions only. The Security Management organization monitors the activities, receives feedback and improves the security guidelines continuously (red looping arrow in the figure). Note that at this stage the IT teams actually take the responsibility for securing the ICT services they are responsible for. The Security Management organization is mainly responsible for providing appropriate guidance for the IT. This may result in approaching stage 3 in which the IT teams and departments become more and more involved in security. Refer to Fig. 33. They not only use security guidelines, they participate in their development. They may take over their development so that the Security Management organization mainly approves what they have defined (two red arrows). Assistance during the application of the security guidelines is provided by security experts not necessarily belonging to the Security Management organization (arrows that loop closely). The IT departments have their own (who of course work along the policies and requirements set-up by the Security Management organization;

red bricks in the middle). Sometimes however, central support may still be required (large black looping arrow). The Security Management organization is still responsible to verify compliance and to provide evidence if and to what extent the security measures have been implemented in technology and activities.

5.3 How the integration looks like and actually works

Introduction and summary: Two examples show how the integration of IT security management on the one hand and IT service management (ITIL) on the other should actually be done. New activities need to be added to the ITIL processes or even to the process map in order to make sure that the specific requirements of managing security are met. The ITIL processes dominate the industrialized IT production characterized by rigorous division of labor and by a high degree of specialization and standardization. In this environment, processes are important elements that exactly specify all steps in advance which need to be carried out by employees. Security activities need to be integrated.

It is now assumed that security standards exist which are fit for purpose and used. Then the Security Management organization must work on improvements including corrections. There are three types of instances that should cause the ICT Service Provider to become active with respect to security:

- First, an actual policy violation is observed. Some employee may have actually seen that something went wrong. The inspection and analysis of log data may have revealed a hostile action (like hacking) or any other event that turns out to be not in line with the security policies. Or, a technical audit or any other audit or self-assessment brought something like this to light. These are just examples.

- Second, a deviation from the ESARIS security standards is revealed. Here are examples for this. The inspection of design information or of evaluations of the design have shown that some security measures were not or not appropriately been implemented. Vulnerability or compliance monitoring (scanners) showed that an ICT element was not patched or not correctly been configured. Penetrating and other testing have shown that there are differences between standard and actual implementation.

- Third, a gap or an error in the security standards is revealed. This may also cause a security issue since the correct implementation of the deficient security standard would lead to a vulnerability.

These three triggers are also shown in Fig. 34. The follow-up activities are discussed now showing how security activities are conducted as part of core ITIL processes. While doing this, it becomes clearer why ITIL integration is quite compulsory though for the first time the integration is elaborated explicitly with ESARIS.

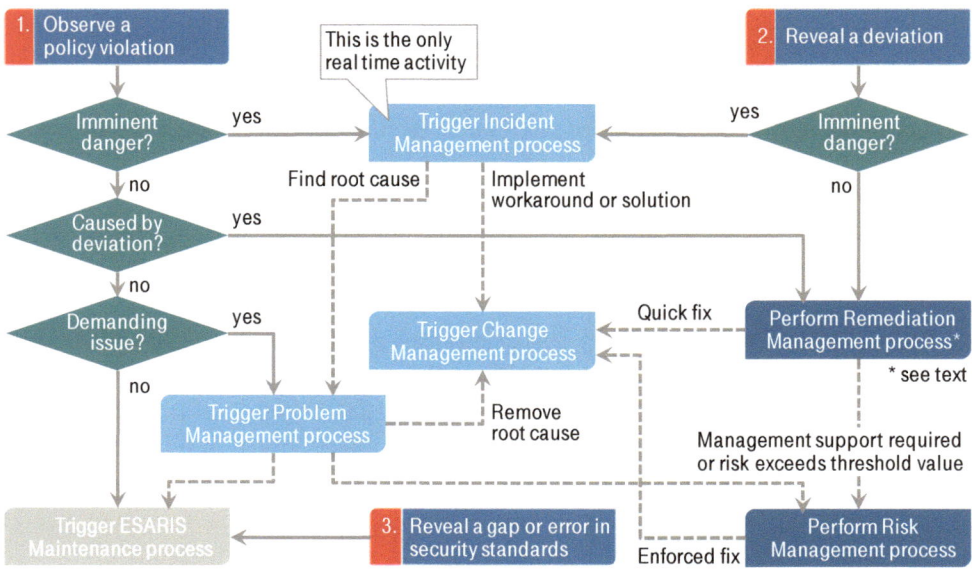

Fig. 34: ITIL integration - activity triggers and follow-ups

The *first trigger* is the observation of a policy violation. In this context it is of no interest how this was observed. The source of information doesn't matter here; the focus is on discussing follow-up activities. Three core ITIL processes are considered: Incident Management, Change Management and Problem Management (light blue boxes in Fig. 34). A Risk Management process (lower right in the figure) is added as an extension of the security management to ensure that information security risks are explicitly treated. The other two boxes will be explained little later. When a violation of a security policy was observed, the next step is determined by the nature of the case: As a general rule, the Incident Management process (ITIL) must be triggered if the violation entails an imminent danger. For instance, the hacker is still active and in the system. Note that Incident Management is the only process which really works "real-time". Each activity is executed right after having finished the preceding one. Everything is done immediately if possible. The Incident Management process (ITIL) must therefore become capable of managing security incidents. More about this comes later. If a solution is known it is implemented; if there is no solution available a work around is implemented and the Problem Management process is triggered (ITIL). The Problem Management process must find a way to find a final solution. The implementation of both a work around and a real solution is coordinated by the Change Management process (ITIL). It might be necessary to record a risk while the problem is being managed. This can be necessary if the ICT Service Provider or its customer is exposed to a considerable risk despite of having implemented a work around. That's why Fig. 34 branches also to the Risk Management process (lower right in the figure). A new solution or fix may also be required to be described in an ESARIS security standard. That's why the Problem Management process branches to a box entitled

"ESARIS Maintenance process". This part is responsible for the update of ESARIS security documentation. Though the Change Management process (ITIL) could also be used for updating documentation it is not realistic to use it for all ESARIS documentation. As a result, an extra maintenance system or document management process is introduced. Details are given in Chapter 10.

The next case is that the "violation of a security policy" does not entail an imminent danger (as it would be in case of an ongoing attack). If it is apparent and for certain that the issue is caused by a deviation from ESARIS security standards, this needs to be fixed. The required change can be initiated directly by triggering the Change Management process (ITIL). This case is not shown in the figure. In many cases it is necessary that some experts do some analysis and take care that the remediation of the security deviation actually takes place. That's why a remediation management process is shown in Fig. 34. This process should be an intermediate solution only, which is required until the organization is mature enough to repair security deviations without assistance (reminders and exerting pressure). The remediation management process also triggers the Change Management process (ITIL) to implement the repair. In case of risk exposure (above a certain threshold) the Risk Management process is triggered. Also the latter can initiate the change, e.g. in case that the general management had released the necessary budget or given order to fix the issue.

Now the "violation of a security policy" is neither entailing an "imminent danger" nor related to a "deviation from security standards". Then one may ask if the issue is really demanding. Further activities can be initiated by the Problem Management process or by the ESARIS Maintenance process which simply performs an update of ESARIS security documentation. It could happen that a policy was simply wrong or that an update of a guideline will for example prevent that the violation can happen again.

The *second trigger* and the *third trigger* are easier to understand. Almost all facts are already described. In the second case, it has been observed that implementation or activity on the one hand and ESARIS security standards on the other deviate. Such deviations are revealed for example by inspecting design information, from vulnerability or compliance monitoring (scanners) or by means of penetrating and other testing. The Incident Management process (ITIL) must be triggered if the deviation entails an imminent danger. This is, for instance, the case if the deviation causes a critical vulnerability that can easily be exploited which would in turn result in a considerable impact. The next steps are as described above. In case that there is no imminent danger, the remediation management process can be triggered. Note that this extra process (refer to Fig. 34) should be an intermediate solution which is, as already mentioned, only required until the organization is mature enough to repair security deviations without assistance (reminders and constant pressing).

The *third trigger* is the simplest: an error in the ESARIS security standards is discovered. This should directly be fixed through the ESARIS Maintenance process. A possible detour via the Incident Management process (ITIL) may not actually speed up the process in case of an imminent danger (not shown in Fig. 34). However, this can be necessary if, for instance, customers need to be informed. If no support from this process is required the course of actions can directly proceed with updating the security documentation.

The length of this description shows two things:

■   The matter of integrating IT security management and IT service management is complex and difficult. The complexity does not come from the integration, it is due to the fact that IT service management and managing security of ICT services is a complex matter in a large-scale IT production environment.

■   One should not expect that this can be specified in one or two chapters in a security management document. Consequently, the *Enterprise Security Architecture for Reliable ICT Services (ESARIS)* uses Level 3 and Level 4 (with the *ICT Security Standards*) for these orchestration activities and reserves the Level 5 (with the *ICT Security Baselines*) for numerous guidelines each for specific activities of specialized people in the supply chain.

In the following example, it is explained why the *ESARIS Security Taxonomy* also comprises the two areas *Vulnerability Assessment and Mitigation Planning (VAM)* and *Security Patch Management (SPM)*. Fig. 31 shows these two areas in addition to genuine IT service management process areas. The next Fig. 35 illustrates how vulnerability and patch management are dealt with in ESARIS. The explanation below underlines what was said in the last two bullets. It will also be apparent that it is absolute necessary to exactly specify all steps in advance that need to be carried out by the employees.

Surprisingly, patching is not explicitly mentioned in ITIL. There is no description about this, although it is very clear that patches as well as all other changes are coordinated by the Change Management process (ITIL) triggered by a Change request. Changes are additions, modifications or removals of anything which is part of or affects an ICT service.

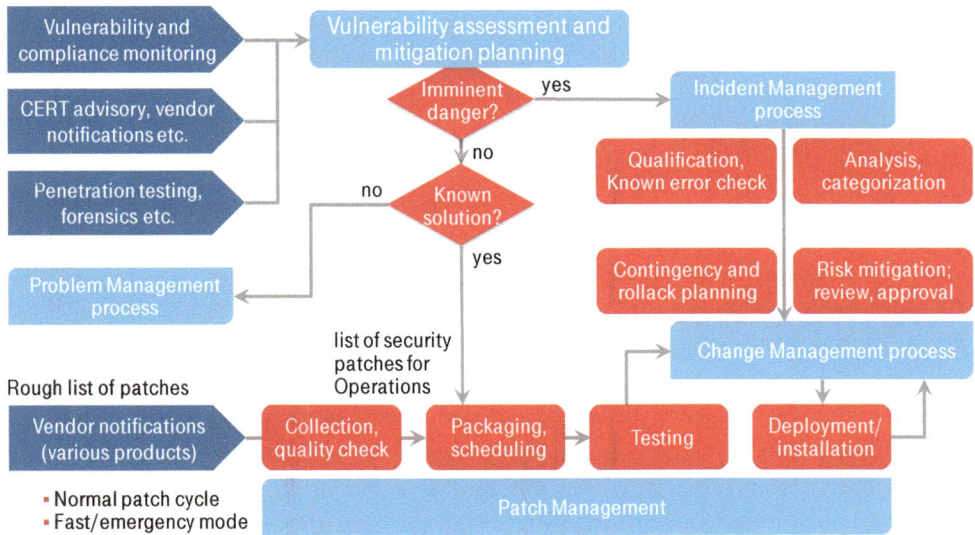

Fig. 35: ITIL integration – security patching and vulnerability management

The Change Management process (ITIL) is shown as a light blue box on the right-hand side of Fig. 35. Contingency and rollback planning as well as risk mitigation and review and approval of changes are major tasks of this process. The Incident Management process (ITIL) has also been already described shown above the Change Management process in the figure. What triggers the cause of actions initially? A patch is provided by the manufacturer of the software. The manufacturer (vendor) notifies if a patch is available. Refer to the lower left in the figure. That's where patch management starts. There are many vendors and different software. The process starts with collecting and checking the notifications and the software patches. Usually the ICT Service Provider has defined at least one normal patch cycle and one fast or emergency mode for patching. Before any patch is applied they are packed and it is scheduled when the patches to be applied. Refer to the figure. They need to be tested and a Change is requested so that the Change Management process (ITIL) is triggered. This also holds for security patches. The actual deployment or installation of the patches can be regarded as being part of the patch management process (not explicitly described in ITIL). This is a standard procedure for patches where security experts or security services are not required and not necessarily involved.

Vulnerability management, CERT services and the like are an important element of security management. In ESARIS all such activities around revealing vulnerabilities, their analysis and planning of mitigation activities are put into one area of the *ESARIS Security Taxonomy*. The related *ICT Security Standard* is called *Vulnerability Assessment and Mitigation Planning (VAM)*. How does the ICT Service Provider get aware of vulnerabilities? There are several sources of information. Refer to the upper left in Fig. 35. Vulnerability and compliance monitoring (using scanners) can for example provide the information that software is not current. The ICT Service

Provider has subscribed to receive so-called CERT advisories or CERT notifications which also contain information about available patches. But also penetration testing can show that software is not kept up-to-date. (Misconfiguration is not considered here for the sake of simplicity.) All such vulnerabilities are collected, assessed and it is planned how and when to fix them. Before any actual change is made, it must be understood if the vulnerability entails an imminent danger. If so, the Incident Management process (ITIL) needs to be triggered since this is the only "real-time" process as discussed above. The Incident Management process (ITIL) finally triggers the Change Management process (ITIL) which in turn involves activities from the patch management as just described. In case if there is no imminent danger, one has to ask if a solution exists for fixing the vulnerability. If not, the Problem Management process (ITIL) is triggered since a solution must be found. Refer to the figure. Note that this is a rhetoric question only since only patches are discussed here. Other types of vulnerabilities like misconfiguration are not described. The result is handed over to the patch management process. This means that the latter receives something similar to the vendor's list of patches. The vulnerability management process has perhaps collected different or additional information. The patch management receives this information together with concrete advice how to deal with the vulnerability and the patch. There are a lot more relations that could not all be discussed. For instance, the Asset and Configuration Management process provides information about the components that need to be patched; it is also used to document the new configuration.

The starting point was very simple. Software is required to be updated (patched). It is neither possible nor appropriate to separate functional patching from security patching. Both processes must be melt together (integrated). However, it turns out that security vulnerabilities require specific care and analysis which can only be conducted by security experts. Hence, an area called *Vulnerability Assessment and Mitigation Planning (VAM)* exists. In this area also other sources of information are used. The analysis and the mitigation planning may also deviate from managing weaknesses and errors in functionality.

This results in an enhanced map of ITIL-related processes. New activities are added in order to make sure that the specific requirements of managing security are met. Existing processes are enhanced in order to interact with them and to ensure that the complete picture actually works in an industrialized IT production characterized by rigorous division of labor and by a high degree of specialization and standardization. In such a production environment, processes are important elements that exactly specify all steps in advance which need to be carried out by employees. The ITIL processes dominate IT production. Security activities need to be integrated. More details are provided in Sect. 12.2.

Part 2: Core activities

Fig. 36 shows the program of this second part of the book. The customer-to-customer-process starts with considerations about standardization (denoted by requirements engineering and document management described in detail in Part 3), implementation of the ESARIS security standards including a verification of compliance, and the contracting including the comparison with the customer's security requirements. The management of suppliers is discussed in the last chapter of this Part 2.

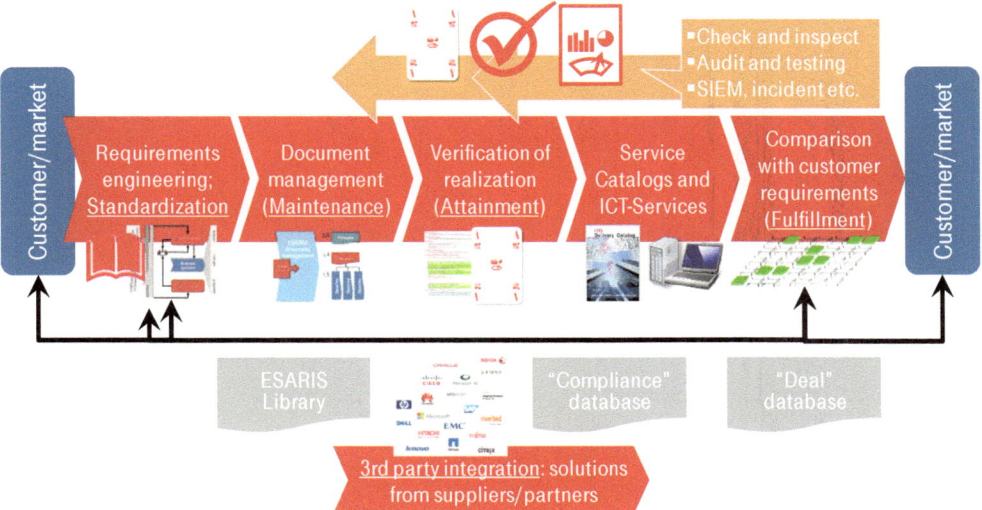

Fig. 36: ESARIS as a customer-to-customer process

6 Standardization – ensuring quality and efficiency

Introduction and summary: The business demands cost reduction, flexible sourcing and customary quality when it comes to getting ICT services. Internal and external ICT Service Providers must therefore industrialize their IT production. Industrialization in turn requires standardization of all components in modern IT production. This includes standardizing the security measures that are used to protect the ICT service provisioning. Necessity and benefits are discussed (Sect. 6.1). The *ESARIS Industrialization Concept* explains how requirements from different sources are treated, structured and used and how standardized elements are combined in order to create tailored ICT services and to meet various security requirements (Sect. 6.2). The *ESARIS Security Specification Concept* provides guidance to structure the ESARIS security standards in order to guarantee modularity, to support standardization and to ease the use of the documentation in practice (Sect. 6.3). There are obstacles in the way towards standardization of security. These are discussed and practical advice is provided to support the standardization in a larger corporation (Sect. 6.4).

Editorial note: This section (except Sect. 6.2 and 6.3) is based on one of the author's earlier publications.[35]

6.1 Understanding standardization, its necessity and benefits

Introduction and summary: The origin of "in-house standardization" and the motivation to use standards in general is analyzed. The topic is further narrowed down by briefly discussing the possible nature of the standards. The term "standard" is defined which is needed in order to discuss benefits later.

Many people associate with a standard that they must use it or adhere to it. This understanding leads into the wrong direction. Standards, as being understood here, are not a "must" – they are not a "law":

- Standards (as used here) primarily provide benefits such as competitive advantages that should motivate to use them.

- If this motivation is not sufficient, enterprises may enforce their use and punish ignorance. No external enforcement, pressure or influence is assumed.

This is shown on the right-hand side in Fig. 37. There are different motivations for standardization such as legislation, regulation or technical reasons which are,

---

[35] Eberhard von Faber: In-house standardization of security measures: necessity, benefits and real-world obstructions; in: ISSE 2014 Securing Electronic Business Processes, Highlights of the Information Security Solutions Europe 2014 Conference, Springer Vieweg, Wiesbaden, 2014, ISBN 978-3-658-06707-6, p. 35-48 [46]

however, not in focus here. It is assumed that the corporation has an intrinsic interest in standardization of security (raise "competitive advantages"). As a result, standardization means "in-house standardization". The term (in-house) standard is defined on the right-hand side in Fig. 37. Such standards are based on agreement driven by the corporation on its own. It is not assumed that the standards are agreed upon or recommended by market players (industry standards) or issued by a standard's organization, the government or any other such authority. However, the origin of standardized measures does not count. It is sufficient to distinguish between "standardized" and "not standardized" (or custom) as long as the motivation is intrinsic.

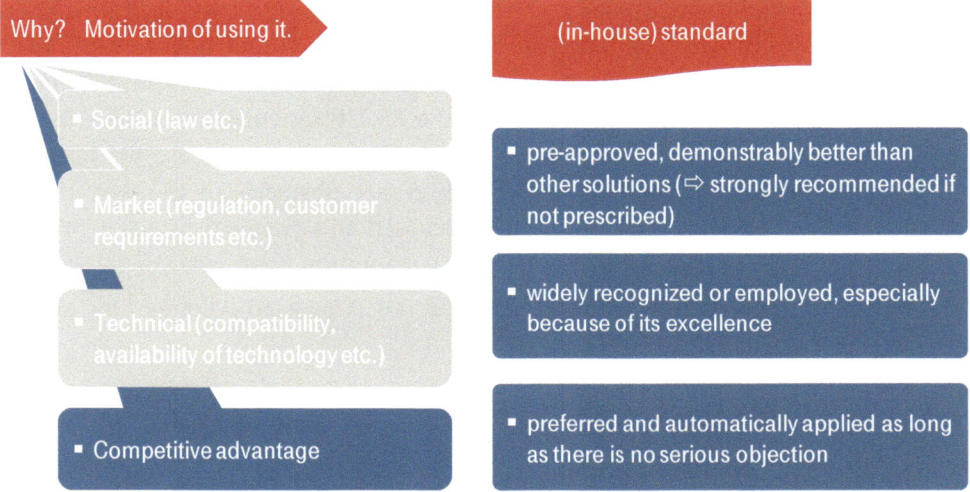

Fig. 37: Motivation for standardization and definition of in-house standards

The above consideration is now applied to standardization of security in an industrialized IT production. It is first described why standards need to be applied in IT production (refer to the upper left in Fig. 38). Then general outcomes of standardization are discussed (upper right in the figure). Finally, specific benefits for security professionals, most notably the CISO,[36] are provided. Note that all three parts are important for the CISO since he does his business in a given corporate environment where all the usual business rules and mechanisms apply.

---

[36] CISO: Chief Information Security Officer; head of security in a corporation

IT service provisioning

Standards:
- basis for division of labor and specialization of people,
- basis for the effective provisioning of different ICT services,
- required to reduce complexity and to make information security manageable.

Qualities and costs

Standards:
- provide the same level of security around the world,
- reduce costs,
- improve quality,
- allow faster provisioning,
- reduce complexity.

CISO specifics

Standards:
- Higher assurance,
- Increase level of security,
- Improve control,
- Security effort and costs can be charged to other budgets

Fig. 38: Necessity and benefits for standardizing security (in-house)

<u>Necessity relating to ICT service provisioning:</u> The provisioning of ICT services (in an industrial fashion) is of complex nature and characterized by a high degree of division of labor and by the distribution of activities throughout the organization. As a result, many organizational units and business roles have to contribute to protecting the ICT services. ICT service provisioning on a large scale ("production") requires the standardization of security for the following reasons:

- Industrial production is characterized by a high degree of division of labor and high specialization of people. Industrial production uses defined processes where procedures need to be clearly defined too. This very structured approach requires many elements described in terms of modules (that can often be reused). Such modules or patterns are the result of standardization. (Perspective: outside-in.)

- ICT Service Providers mostly maintain a comprehensive portfolio of various ICT services including desktop services, communication services, and computing services. The service models (i.e. the division of labor between ICT Service Provider and user organization) may also differ. (Perspective: inside-out.) Producing these services in an industrial way also requires the modules or patterns from standardization as demanded in the previous bullet.

- Reduction of complexity is required in order to make information security manageable. This is required both to understand and to sell/buy the ICT services (perspective: outside-in) and to secure the ICT services (perspective: inside-out).

<u>Benefits relating to quality and cost improvements:</u> The definition of "standard" directly leads to benefits that are produced by standardization. Refer to Fig. 38. The same level of security is required around the world (important for customers with

global business; no. 1 on the upper right in Fig. 38). Enterprises are working on a global basis so that they need to use ICT services on different continents and in different countries. Though there are local differences in legislation and in industry regulation, global enterprises like to streamline their business as much as possible. This also holds for consuming ICT services and for managing IT security risks associated with this. But moreover ICT services can be obtained on a global basis. This is a result of deregulation, the rise of global providers and made possible through the development of communication networks and IT.

The reduction of costs (no. 2 on the upper right in Fig. 38) is the result of re-use which reduces the expenditure or the effort. In modern IT production scaling effects play an important role. They can only be realized if platforms are identical which in turn requires the implementation of standards.

Improved quality and faster provisioning (no. 3 and 4 in Fig. 38) are also straightforward to understand. Quality is increased since more time and effort can be spent to develop and prove the solution. More experience is available from using it. Faster provisioning is an extra benefit which is very important for the fast-moving information technology and its market. Note that quality is in turn directly correlated to security. Reduction of complexity (no. 5) considerably improves security since complex things are hard to understand and to manage. Simplicity helps to meet the security target.

Benefits relating to CISO specifics: The standardization of security has further benefits that are essential for the Security Management department and the people steering the security of the ICT services, foremost the Chief Information Security Officer. There are at least four benefits or advantages (refer to the lower part in Fig. 38). Standardization of security leads to higher assurance (no. 1 of the CISO specifics in Fig. 38). Nowadays, user organizations are facing problems obtaining detailed information when investigating the market in order to find third-party ICT services with the appropriate security or risk profile. They need reliable information about security in order to be able to estimate and manage associated risks. Hence, the ICT Service Providers must deliver appropriate assurance together with their ICT services. This is made easier or is even enabled through standardization that is as complete as possible.

But more straightforward, standardization increases the level of security (no. 2 in Fig. 38). If there are no security standards, the consideration of security maybe left to people with their respective personal opinions and priorities. If using security standards (as security patterns) it is more likely that security is considered at all. Standards also improve the availability of information about the "security". This in turn helps to identify gaps and vulnerabilities. Transparency is essential for an effective security management. Without standards, transparency is hard to achieve in a complex IT production.

Improved control (no. 3) is very similar. The Security Management department can concentrate on the standards. The available resources are usually far from being sufficient to control security in a largely heterogeneous environment. In this way, standardization of security also helps to live with the limited resources the CISO may have available.

Good news for the CISO (no. 4). The security standardization is also a way to integrate security into the day-to-day IT business. This can help the security organization to safe money since the costs are transferred from the security budget to other corporate budgets:

- It is a main principle of ESARIS that IT security management is integrated with IT service management. One result is that some dedicated security costs become inherent IT costs. Another main principle is: security is everybody's responsibility. This reduces the work load of security professionals.

- However, the main effect of standardizing security is reduced costs for development and maintenance of security measures. The standardization leads to a harmonization of the IT environment which reduces all efforts that are associated with the management of information security.

But security experts should not expect money to be left. Increasing demands will eat up this money. Security experts must standardize security in order to be able to do their job with reasonable quality.

6.2   ESARIS Industrialization Concept

Introduction and summary: The design, production and marketing of ICT services incur considerable costs. There are two ways to reduce these costs compared to traditional computing: economies of scale and standardization. Smaller IT departments and providers can standardize, whereas their ability to generate economies of scale and distribute costs through different services and users is limited. Especially large ICT Service Providers require a concept of industrialization in order to reduce costs. Generally, such a concept comprises dealing with the various requirements (Sect. 6.2.1) and the composition of the service using predefined, standardized elements (Sect. 6.2.2). Both issues are dealt with below.

6.2.1   Dealing with requirements

Fig. 39 illustrates the process from the identification of requirements (first row), through their consolidation (second row) to the conception and integration of ICT solutions (third row) and the operation and maintenance of them (fourth row).

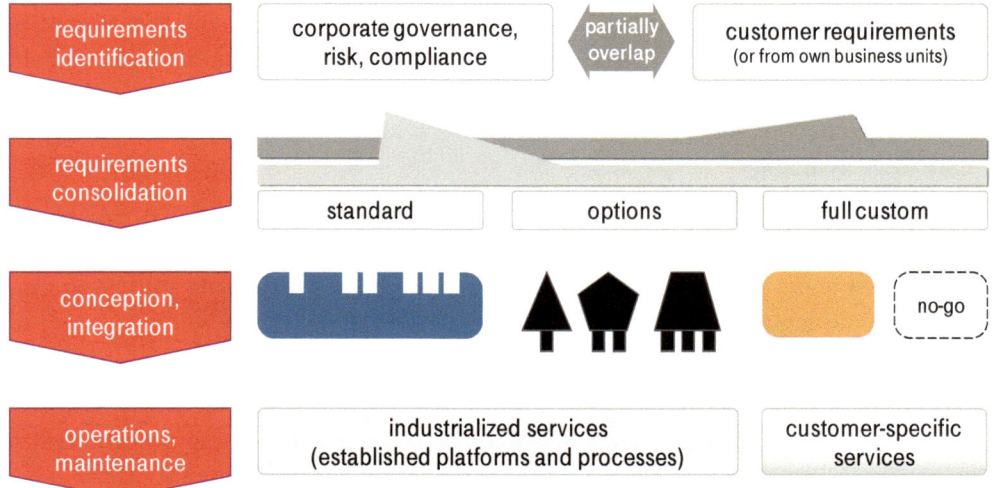

Fig. 39: From requirements to services

Security-related requirements originate from both the ICT Service Provider (corporate) and the user organizations (customers):

- The ICT Service Provider maintains its business in a legal, social and economic environment. As a result, there are requirements from the imperatives Governance, Risk (management) and Compliance – more specifically those relating to ICT usage and provisioning.

- The ICT Service Provider provides ICT services for customers. The customer in turn maintains its business in a legal, social and economic environment and therefore has specific security concerns which need to be considered in the ICT services it consumes from the ICT Service Provider.

Note that both sets of requirements may partially overlap.

In order to meet all the different requirements, the ICT Service Provider needs to organize and assess them. It is one rule of ESARIS that requirements are categorized as follows:

- Standard requirements: these will constitute and correspond to a "baseline security"; no service will come with "lower" security (unless an exception is required and overrules this baseline);

- Options: such requirements are not common to all services and customers; they are, however, important for several customers, thus they are considered and addressed in the (standardized) offering portfolio of the ICT Service Provider;

- Full custom: the ICT Service Provider is not prepared to meet such requirements with out-of-the-box services; it may be decided to develop a specific (i.e. custom) solution to meet such special requirements.

It is important that requirements fall into one of these categories. It is also important that the first group covers a considerable part, and that the first two groups cover the vast majority. Otherwise, the ICT Service Provider cannot sufficiently realize economies of scale.

These three sets of requirements result in three types of service categories. Similar to the requirements, there are

- the "baseline security services" (in line with industry standards) which can be considered as a "foundation" and

- the "optional security services" which can be added.

Both are used to deliver industrialized services using established platforms and processes.

- Full custom requirements can be met by providing "customer-specific security services" which may or should also take advantage of what already exists.

Note that meeting "exotic" requirements and the provisioning of corresponding services may not be in line with the strategy of the ICT Service Provider. Therefore, the company may decide not to serve the customer.

6.2.2   Composition of services

The *Enterprise Security Architecture for Reliable ICT Services (ESARIS)* comprises technological, organizational and procedural means required to secure ICT services and to provide dedicated security services as well. ESARIS implements and maintains security.

The main emphasis is on supporting the core business (ICT) of the ICT Service Provider. The ICT Service Provider must develop a modular approach in providing ICT services. This is shown in Fig. 40. An ICT service consists of a "core service" where "options" may be added. The same approach is used for security. There are the "baseline security services" where "optional security services" can be added.

ICT services incorporate security services as shown in Fig. 40. In the first example, the customer consumes the "pure" ICT service with the "baseline security services". However, there are ICT service options (black plugs in Fig. 40) as well as "optional security services" (red plugs) which are not used in this example. In the second example, the customer uses ICT service options (one black plug) as well as "optional security services" (two red plugs), even though there are still unused options.

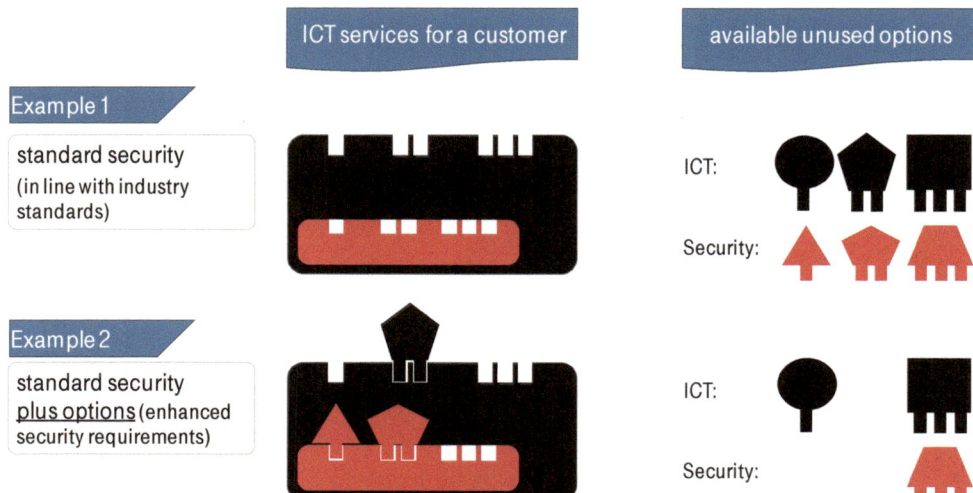

Fig. 40: Provisioning of ICT services

Most security services (the red plugs on the right-hand side of Fig. 40) are required to secure ICT services. Some security services, however, may also be provided as dedicated or stand-alone security services. The offering portfolio of large ICT Service Providers also includes dedicated security services both to complete the overall offering portfolio and to strengthen their ability to secure other ICT services.

6.3   ESARIS Security Specification Concept

Introduction and summary: The *ICT Security Standards* describe security measures that are in place to protect the ICT services delivered by the ICT Service Provider. The level of abstraction of the standards, more precisely of their security measures, was already determined. The *ESARIS Security Taxonomy* has been developed that determines the structure and organization of topics, realms, areas or aspects and that distributes the corresponding security measures amongst 31 *ICT Security Standards*. In this section, the internal structure of the *ICT Security Standards* is defined. All standards are structured in exactly the same way. They provide a definition of a security target and specify the solution in terms of security measures. With this approach modularity and standardization is consequently pursued.

The *Enterprise Security Architecture for Reliable ICT Services (ESARIS)* is strictly modular and will appear as a hierarchy. Refer to Fig. 41.

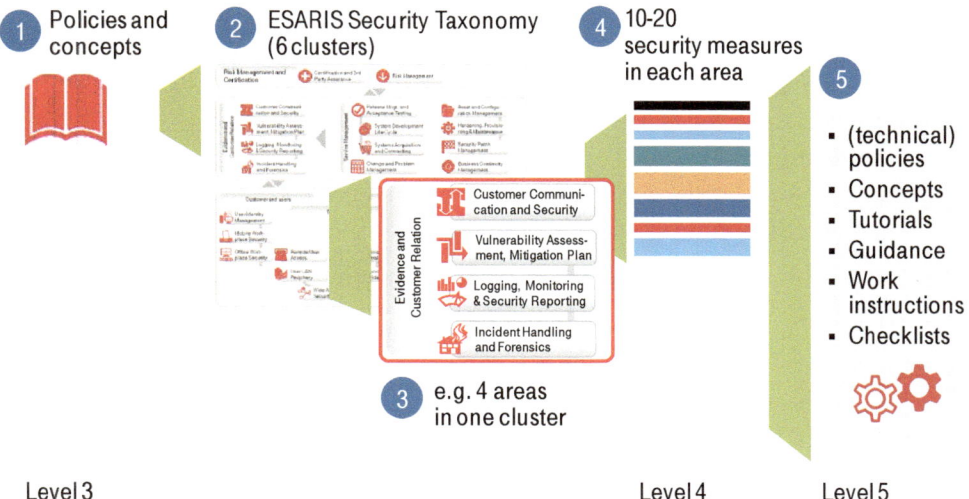

Fig. 41: General structure of the ESARIS security standards

In order to support this and guarantee its realization, the following is stipulated regarding the *ICT Security Standards* (Level 4):

- All *ICT Security Standards* have exactly the same structure. This greatly facilitates the use of the complex material, since information can better be found and readers can more easily be acquainted with the standards after having studied the first one. The unique structure also guarantees that the required content actually exists in all standards.

- A mandatory document template has to be provided to every author. In practice, a unique structure for all standards cannot be accomplished without providing a template that is mandatory and must not be changed by the authors of the standards. Usage of templates and style sheets for the office programs being used also has the benefit of improving the quality and the efficiency of drawing up and maintaining documents.

- A guidance document has to be provided to every author which explains the purpose and expected content of each section in the document.

- The standards are structured as security concepts or security targets [37] even though they mainly define the security measures that are being implemented.

This methodology

- helps to ensure that all standards contain the required information, and

- facilitates the handling of the standards; in particular, required information can be found more easily.

---

[37] Refer to: ISO/IEC 15408 – Information technology — Security techniques — Evaluation criteria for IT security — Part 1: Introduction and general model; 2009 [9]

Each *ICT Security Standard* is organized as follows:

- security problem definition,
- security objective identification,
- scope and coverage clarification,
- identification of external support (dependencies with other standards),
- definition of security measures with implementation guidance and rationale,
- responsibilities and possible deviations.

The structure of the *ICT Security Standards* is shown in Fig. 42.

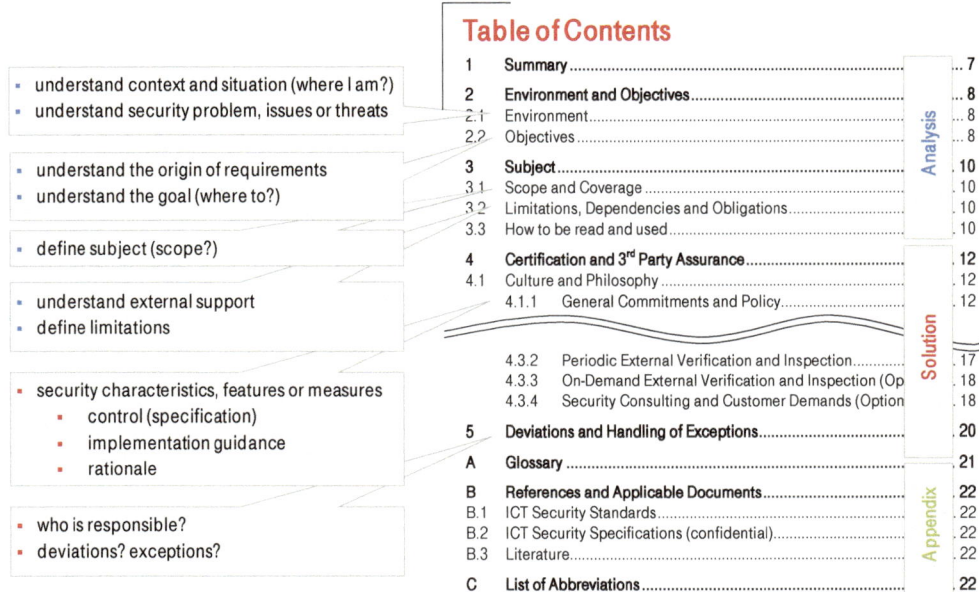

Fig. 42: Structure of the ICT Security Standards

Together with the regulations mentioned before, this structure and related guidance constitutes the so-called *ESARIS Security Specification Concept*; which is explained in more detail below.

Note that in the remaining part of this section, all references to chapters and sections are made to the content of an *ICT Security Standard* (Fig. 42) and not to chapters and sections within this book.

The security measures only describe the solution. Strictly speaking, they cannot be understood if their context is not also provided. This context is described in detail in the Chapters 2 and 3 of each *ICT Security Standard* (see Fig. 42). The scope or concrete field of application is not evident from the title of the *ICT Security Standard*. The world of ICT is far too complex to allow this. Moreover, it is best practice to derive requirements and measures, respectively. If technology changes (e.g. emergence of a new operating system), measures need to be adapted. Where security objectives have not been defined, this adaptation may lead to a reduction in the security achieved, even if the new technology looks better and is more state-of-the-art. Furthermore, it is not possible from studying the security measures alone to determine whether or not they are adequate and complete. This can only be managed if they are mapped to security objectives in the context of a well-defined scope. Finally, adequate security objectives can only be formulated if the problem has been analyzed appropriately and understood.

This concept is borrowed from the security target specification defined in the Common Criteria.[38] In Common Criteria, a security target is an implementation-independent specification of security needs. This is what is exactly needed here. Common Criteria sets standards for security evaluations. After such an evaluation, a security target "serves as a basis for an agreement between the developer or reseller of the TOE and the potential consumer of the TOE".[39] The abbreviation TOE means "Target of Evaluation" and should be translated into "ICT service" in the ESARIS context. All relevant security standards together make the ICT service secure that is provided by the "developer or reseller" (ICT Service Provider) and used by the "potential consumer" (user organization).

All *ICT Security Standards* are organized in exactly the same way. Firstly, the environment is described in Sect. 2.1 ("Environment"). It comprises the identification of ICT elements, important processes or tasks as well as other conditions or constraints that are necessary or relevant to understand the situation. At the same time, this section addresses primary security concerns or challenges. To summarize, this section contains a minimal risk analysis. The guidance document states that the following have to be described and observed:

Facts that are determined to be relevant in order to understand the context

This section contains a description of the "environment" which includes *conditions or constraints necessary to understand the situation*. This may comprise the information and communication technology (ICT) being used, organization and important processes, laws, contractual dependencies as well as expertise or knowledge or operations personnel.

Minimum analysis of threats and risks

This section addresses major *security concerns, threats, risks or problems* that are relevant in order to understand the security measures being proposed and specified in the standard. *Critical assets* may also be mentioned which require specific protection. *Major assumptions* may be added which are to be met by the

---

[38] ISO/IEC 15408 – Information technology — Security techniques — Evaluation criteria for IT security — Part 1: Introduction and general model; 2009 [9]. In 1999, the Common Criteria were published as the International Standard ISO/IEC 15408.

[39] Ibid.

organization in order for the system to be considered secure. This may comprise specific security policies or framework conditions.

The security objectives are derived and described in Sect. 2.2 ("Objectives"). The description starts with some kind of demand analysis. The section may provide information about sources for specific requirements and policies that need to be observed. Then the security objectives are described, which explain the situation to be achieved. They are used to derive the security measures which later build the main part of the security standard. The guidance document states:

Facts required to understand the origin of requirements

This section outlines the *origin of requirements* in order to address security concerns or counter threats. This information is helpful to identify the stakeholder or *understand motivation and the business case*. This section is intended to inform the reader about specific sources for requirements such as specific protection requirements according to PCI-DSS [40] in the event that credit card payment data are processed. If there are no such specific sources of requirements, this section can be used to provide general guidance, e.g. for the mapping to ISO/IEC 27002,[41] or may be left blank.

Minimum description of objectives and goals

This section also outlines the *purpose of the security measures* being specified in the standard. Note that this is different to the analysis of threats and risks in Sect. 2.1 since the focus here is on the *situation to be achieved*. This description should be consistent with the "environment" stated in Sect. 2.1. Note that the information to be given in this section is important and must not be left out. Instead, a precise description of objectives and goals should be given which aids the understanding of the result of the security expenses and costs associated with this security standard.

Chapter 3 ("Subject") is also important. Sect. 3.1 ("Scope and Coverage") contains information about the specific field of application or the scope. This includes the boundaries and possible interfaces. Here one can learn how the security standard is embedded into the overall architecture (*ESARIS Security Taxonomy*) and the business of the ICT Service Provider. The guidance document states:

What is in scope – what will be covered?

This section describes *all the elements which are subject to security measures*. It therefore describes the elements which are in scope and therefore covered by the security standard. Such a description can outline the information and telecommunication technology (ICT), its architecture or construction. It can also

---

[40] PCI Standards Council: PCI DSS (PCI Data Security Standard); Version 3.2 as of 2016 [13]

[41] ISO/IEC 27002 – Information technology – Security techniques – Code of practice for information security management, 2013 [6]

describe usage scenarios and thereby mention the elements being used. If the security standard is about service management, the processes and procedures are outlined. The *boundaries* can also be described. All the details should be added here in order to allow ICT minded people to understand the subject which needs to be controlled.

Sect. 3.2 ("Limitations, Dependencies and Obligations") contains limitations and describes dependencies. Here one can also learn how the *ICT Security Standard* and its security measures interact with other areas. The guidance document states:

What is out of scope – what is not covered?

In order to enhance clarity it might be helpful to list *elements which are not considered* and out of scope. Providing this information here and not in the "Scope and Coverage" section makes the latter easier to read. It may also be important that *specific exceptions* are prominently listed here early in the document. For instance, one can state here that "Release 5.7" is excluded and does not provide the features described in the document. This can be useful if "Release 5.7" is used in exceptional circumstances.

What are the dependencies – what are others needed to do?

The security measures do not stand alone; they often need support from other measures. Prominent examples are procedural and organizational measures to support technical means. It is considered helpful if *supporting functions that are not under the control of the standard* in particular are identified early in the document, even though details about them can be provided later and their effect can also be understood only after having read the main body of the document. The *ICT Security Standard* will or may require direct support from other security measures which are the subject of another *ICT Security Standard*. These other *ICT Security Standards* will be listed and may be referred to as *assisting ICT Security Standards*. These references to major support and primary needs should be limited since all security standards are binding; all standards and security measures are needed and contribute to overall, comprehensive security.

Dependencies should also be mentioned here if the security measures have an impact on other security standards. For instance, a system requires central support for log management. Such relations to other security standards can also be mentioned here. Note that only the direct and "most important" dependencies are to be described here: There is no need to explain the world of information security – all security measures work together in the sense that they all come together to make ICT services appropriately secure. From this perspective, they all depend on each other.

One further type of dependency to be described here is *obligations for other people to cooperate (especially customer's obligations)*. This does not refer to issues which are usually addressed by user manuals. However, if for example another department or even the customer takes responsibility for a part of a system or a process, then this should be mentioned here. Normally, such issues are the subject of contracts. For instance, they are listed as disclaimers in such contracts.

Chapter 4 provides the description of the security measures. This is the main body of an *ICT Security Standard*. Each description comprises three parts: the authoritative description, the Implementation Guidance and the Rationale (see Fig. 43).

Security Measure: Malware and Spam Protection

Protection against viruses, malware or spam is a central issue. Therefore, effort is taken to protect the Office Workplace against such threats on different levels. Malware scanners are implemented on an operating system level protecting the handling of files and on a communication level protecting e-mail and Internet access using a browser. Another component ensures that the patterns for scanning and filtering are regularly updated and kept up-to-date.

Implementation guidance:
- Lorem ipsum dolor sit amet, consectetur adipiscing elit. Vivamus tempus nisi sed metus viverra eget eleifend augue posuere. Proin consequat nunc vitae metus gravida at ornare velit rutrum. Curabitur facilisis tortor ut erat consectetur sit amet sollicitudin est tristique. Maecenas nec turpis at sapien sodales dapibus a vitae urna. Pellentesque.

Rationale:
Lorem ipsum dolor sit amet, consectetur adipiscing elit. Vivamus tempus nisi sed metus viverra eget eleifend augue posuere. Proin consequat nunc vitae metus gravida at ornare velit rutrum. Curabitur facilisis tortor ut erat consectetur sit amet sollicitudin est tristique. Maecenas nec turpis at sapien sodales dapibus a vitae urna. Pellentesque.

Fig. 43: How a security measure description looks like

The definition or description of each security measure is highlighted in a box and is relatively concise in order to fulfill the following three criteria for security measures that are explained in Table 5 (of this book on page 49):

- Criterion 1: specific, informative and unambiguous,
- Criterion 2: largely implementation-independent,
- Criterion 3: comprehensive and intelligible.

The so-called "Implementation Guidance" provides further details and substantiation with examples of implementation or technical detail. Technically-oriented readers in particular are therefore helped to associate the security measure with their own practical experience and knowledge. Finally, the Rationale provides justification and additional information about the purpose and benefit of the security measure. The Rationale feeds back to the security analysis and to the definition of security objectives which are part of Chapters 2 and 3 of each standard. The guidance document states among other things:

> In this chapter the *main security characteristics, features or measures* are described. Note that this is not a comprehensive, thorough specification which is detailed enough for implementation. Instead, consider this description as some kind of

high-level design documentation. Design documentation means that it identifies and states "security-related facts". Security measures are the conclusion or consequence of a risk analysis. Security measures are formulated for the subject of the security standard (ICT or process/procedure).

Chapter 5 provides additional information. The guidance document states:

Service design and delivery

The information provided here first of all is the identification of the *departments responsible* for the realization of the security measures, including design and/or delivery and/or compliance. Additional information can be added. For instance, in the case that there are questions or demands for further information, it is helpful to know who is responsible for the results stated in this document. In some cases, it may also be helpful for the reader if some explanation is given about the *role and the mission of the corresponding department or team*.

Deviations

This section also enables some *specifics such as deviations* to be described– or even the provision of *compliance statements*. Why? – because there might be *frequently asked questions* (FAQ) or concerns from auditors or customers. In this case, there is room to actively address them. One might claim compliance but provide information about restrictions (if any) or explain why the intention of specific requirements is met but do not match word for word because other means are used to achieve the same requirements.

Exceptions

Standards are to be followed – they are valid. However, there might be exceptions for some reason. This section provides an opportunity to *give information on such exceptions and provide guidance* on how to deal with them.

Due to their exclusive role the *ICT Security Standards* (Level 4, *ESARIS Orchestration Layer*) are specifically standardized. They refine the principles from Level 3. It may not be appropriate to standardize the *ICT Security Baselines* (Level 5) as rigorous as the *ICT Security Standards* (Level 4) and the security measures they describe. However, the whole structure of documents is standardized. On Level 5 also document types and a basic structure of their content is predefined. This is described in detail in Chapter 10 which deals with the maintenance of the documentation which includes assignment of document IDs according to the *Hierarchy of Security Standards* and the *ESARIS Security Taxonomy*, as well as many other methodologies that relate to standardization and ease the use of security standards.

6.4   Obstacles towards standardization and solutions

Introduction and summary: There are obstacles in the way towards standardization of security. These are discussed in this section. The obstacles or problems are organized into those which are business related, related to security concerns and those which are related to humans. Solutions are provided for each type of obstacle.

Business issues may hinder standardization of security, human behavior may hinder standardization of security, but also the aim to increase the security may provide reasons against the standardization of security. Refer to Fig. 44.

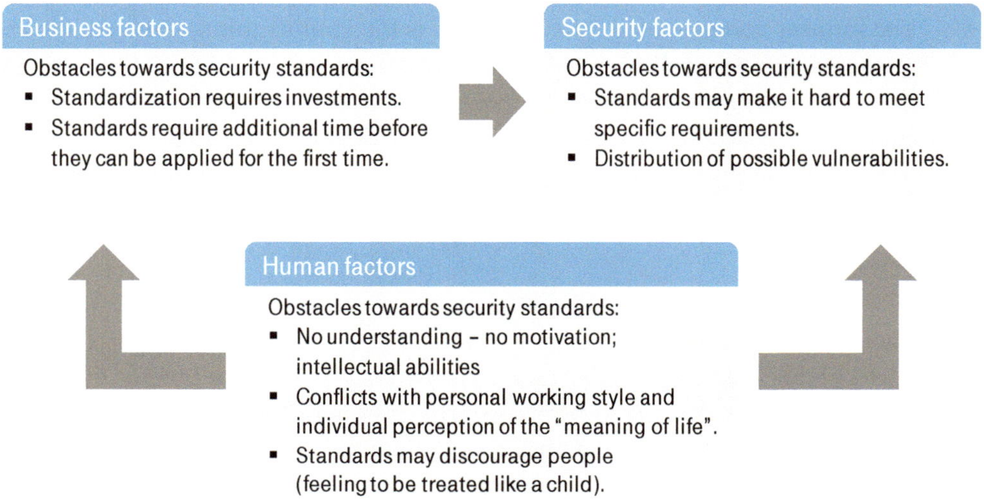

Business factors	Security factors
Obstacles towards security standards: • Standardization requires investments. • Standards require additional time before they can be applied for the first time.	Obstacles towards security standards: • Standards may make it hard to meet specific requirements. • Distribution of possible vulnerabilities.

Human factors
Obstacles towards security standards: • No understanding – no motivation; intellectual abilities • Conflicts with personal working style and individual perception of the "meaning of life". • Standards may discourage people (feeling to be treated like a child).

Fig. 44: Obstacles and problems towards standardization of security

Business factors

Standardization of security requires investments. There are fixed costs before any economies of scale or any other improvement becomes visible. In many cases it is not easy to justify the investments. Everybody seems to know that there is no other way but the go-ahead for the investment in standardization requires a well calculated business case where often only numbers count. In practice, too many people hesitate to develop the business case and some managers are reluctant to make the only reasonable decision. Even more critical, the standardization also means delay. The standards need to be developed and approved before they can be used. This takes time. Ad hoc implementations are much faster. People tend to prefer fast ad hoc solutions and the management mostly demands fast completion of projects. Standardization only takes place if the corporation is lucky enough to have an informed management that is also willing to make a decision.

The situation with the business is shown in Fig. 45 (schematically only). The figure shows the function of the total effort spent over the elapsed time. There are two cases: Without standardization the effort decreases only slightly over time. The decrease is due to practice. – Now standardization is considered. The effort is initially higher. But after having elaborated the standards, the effort is lower than in the first curve. The area between the two curves indicates the investment and the savings, respectively. These simple graphs show the following:

- Firstly, the CISO can try to prolong its planning horizon beyond the break-even. If the planning horizon is shorter, no standardization will take place.

- Secondly, the investment costs. No problem if the CISO's budget is increased so that it also covers the extra investments for standardization. But in most cases this will not happen. The only way to master the standardization is a budget shift: Reserve 10% of the total budget or so for standardization. This means stop about 10% of other activities and live with the security chaos (that will not occur). Alternatively, oblige every security project and longer lasting security activity to produce about 15-20% results that can be reused as standards.

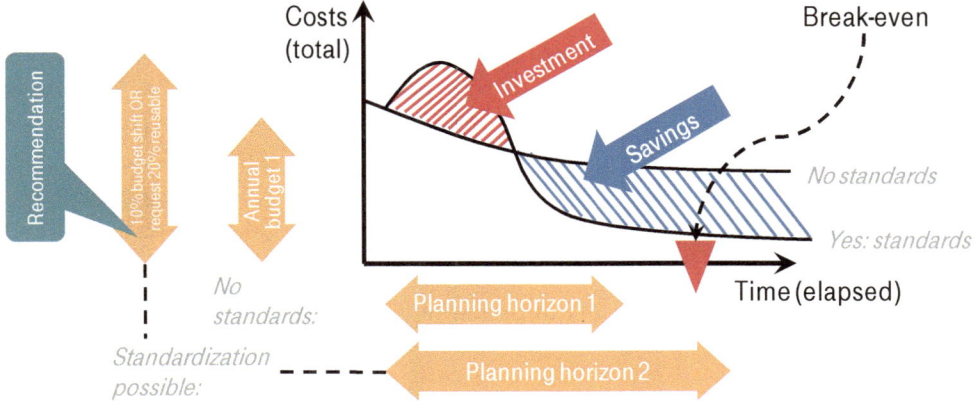

Fig. 45: Standardization as investment and how to circumvent an obstacle

Security factors

Security concerns may also hinder the standardization of security. The very first and most frequent objection is the lack of flexibility and the belief that requirements cannot be met. To make it short, this is not true. In the 1990ies, user organizations may have insisted that their ideas are exactly realized and their requirements are exactly used as the basis. Time has changed. Cost cutting etc. has led to a situation where even complex applications are moved to cloud computing environments that are highly standardized and do not provide many options. Optional security measures can be used to meet specific (uncommon) requirements. These optional security measures are added to the standardized environment as described in Sect. 6.2.2. It's worth noting that these optional security measures are also predefined and standardized. That's why the objection is not correct.

In terms of security, standardization is double-edged. On the one hand it raises the quality and strength of a mechanism if it is widely investigated and proven. On the other hand, it is best practice not to put all eggs into one basket. Standardization means using the same technology. If there is, for example, a vulnerability in the technology, the ICT Service Provider gets more vulnerable if the measure is distributed through its IT infrastructure by applying standards. Not without reason, there is the rule to better combine technology or solutions of different manufacturers in order to get a good result. If one fails the other(s) can maintain the security. Note that, however, a standard can exactly define the use of different technologies.

But in fact, the level of security can be decreased when the degree of standardization becomes too high. Fig. 46 (schematically only) shows the degree of standardization and its effect on quality and security. The quality raises with the degree of standardization. But there is a saturation at high values. The "level of security" does not follow this curve directly. There is a delay instead since many things are interwoven in security and need to be fixed altogether. If the degree of standardization becomes high, the security decreases since flexibility and attention will decrease and measures will no longer be up-to-date and state-of-the-art:

- This means that the real conflict between a high degree of standardization and security is a lack of speed in modernization and adaptation. But long before this point is reached, standardization raises the quality with positive effects to the level of security. The CISO shall drive standardization and focus on the most stable aspects. He should also consider the 80:20 rule and stop before the standardization has provided its maximum effect and the curve has reached its maximum value.

- Another solution is to work with predefined (also standardized) optional security measures that may be added if required. This combines standardization with flexibility.

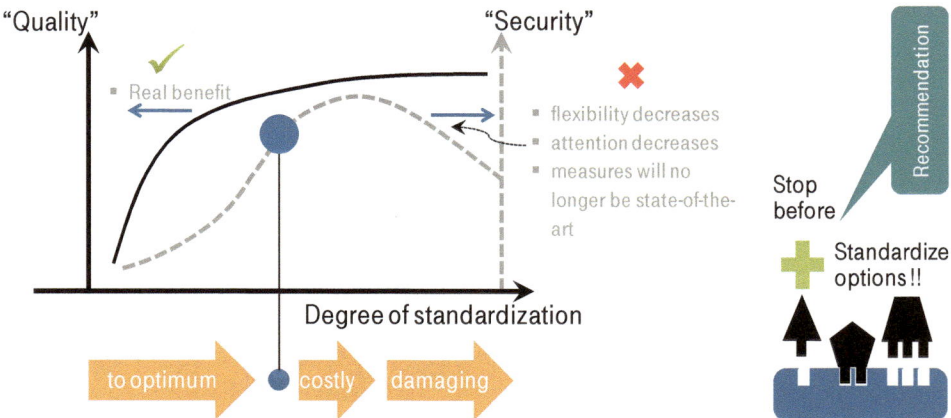

Fig. 46: Quality and security versus degree of standardization

Human factors

This third area is the most critical one. People are different and their motivation is different. Some characters tend to move towards standardization but many are reluctant and hesitate to do so. Their background is maybe illustrated with the following. There are highly skilled, multi-purpose experts (Type 1): These individuals do not have any problem with standardization and will support such programs since they are firmly convinced to do the right. Unfortunately, it seems that only about 5% of a large enterprise's staff belong to this group. There are also experienced experts who worked in one specific topic for long (Type 2). They may be reluctant to adopt standards since they become less important and perhaps they fear that they can be replaced. However, they understand the value of standardization and know that it is useful. Less experienced and less skilled persons (Type 3) often don't understand the approach and dislike standardization at all. Maybe they fear that they can be replaced. Then there are the "firemen" (Type 4) who are very important since they regularly help out in critical security situations. As a result they have a high reputation. Nonetheless, they often don't think in a strategic and corporate way. Instead, they act very pragmatic. The "fireman" dislikes standardization since their working style is situational, event-driven and often disordered. Perhaps they also intuitively feel that they become less important since critical situations would become more seldom if security measures are standardized.

Finally, there are the managers (Type 5) who understand their role as "moderator", "admin employee", "preserver" or "executor" only. Many managers are aiming at short-term objectives only. Standardization requires managers who think strategically and act tactical accordingly.

The study of such characters may provide less than half of the truth. The other half should be filled with real analysis. This may provide the common denominator. Here are some reasons why people may have problems to adopt standardization:

- Standards describe how people should work. The "how" is often subject to the personal working style which people don't want to have addressed. Standards also affect or try to change an individual's attitude to work. This causes resistance.

- Standards replace some of the work ("what"). The standardized part appears to be done already. This may impose a restriction on people's creativity. But moreover, the definition of parts of the workers' result may also discourage them. Some people may also fear to lose their job.

Such problems may vanish if an industry gets mature and reaches a high level of industrialization. In other words, the problems just stated may be less critical in other industries and work areas than IT. The CISO may sometimes publically talk about working methods in such mature industries in order to push employees towards standardization.

Security professionals, especially the CISO, must know how to overcome the barriers. There are several ways towards this. Refer to Fig. 47 for an overview of possible solutions. The advices on the right-hand side are mapped to existing practices in order to make the issue more clear.

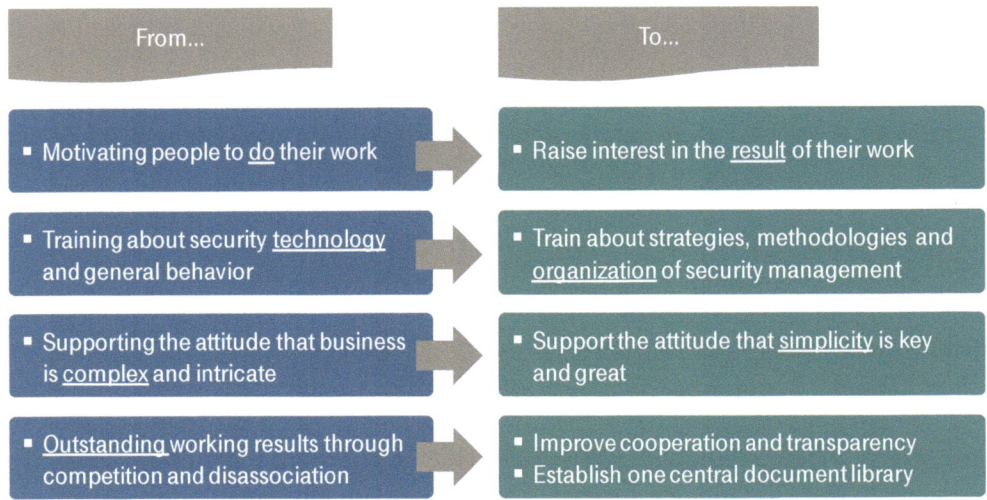

Fig. 47: Possible strategies to unleash standardization of security

Standards add conditions and constraints to day-to-day work. This causes resistance by the staff. Notwithstanding, standardization leads to an improvement of the final result of the work. Therefore, one may not solely focus on motivating people to do their work! Instead one must support that people are interested in the result of their work. Only then they will also be motivated to use and adhere to standards.

The second advice is to change the security trainings held in the corporation accordingly. Often they are designed according to the principle "the more actionable detail the better". To support standardization it must be explained that results and quality are important and why. So, strategies and methodologies should be explained. The "actionable detail" should be about "Who does what in the chain?" and "Why does our success solely rely on all links in the chain?"

It is a fashion to consider IT as complex. Compared to other disciplines like producing airplanes it is not. So, stop repeating that the IT and security business is complex and intricate. Instead support the attitude that simplicity and transparency is great and support the willingness to reduce complexity and to make things easier whenever possible.

Motivation is key in every corporation. Hence the management provides incentives for individuals who have done extraordinary things. This is right. But one should be cautious not to support the opinion that only "hero performance" counts. Most people cannot be heroes and cannot provide outstanding performance. They may be discouraged. Instead, improve the cooperation and the spirit necessary for this. Honor teams and their team leaders. Real "heroes" are those who brought the business to a smooth mode of operation, who supported simplicity and transparency and who increased the degree of security standardization.

Competition between organizational units and the disassociations of them may be natural and maybe necessary in today's business. But this must not lead to fencing and protecting intellectual property within the corporation since this adds another serious barrier to standardization. The CISO should support cooperation and transparency.

It is strongly recommended to establish one central library for security documents that is the mandatory place to store relevant security material. This provides the necessary transparency and forces all organizational units and experts to open their material for other departments. In this way contradicting specifications become apparent and will be standardized. Best practices are better distributed so that they can replace others.

Encourage people to open their knowledge and material. They must not fear corporate-wide criticism. Instead they shall internally publish their material with the attitude: "It's not mine, it belongs to the company anyhow." – And my manager says "It's better to give than to receive."

7 Attainment – achieving compliance with ESARIS standards

Introduction and summary: The *ESARIS Attainment Model* (or: *ESARIS Compliance Attainment Model*) relates to activities ensuring that the ESARIS security standards are actually implemented and comprise methods for verifying this (Sect. 7.1). In the first place, the ESARIS security standards have to be developed by starting with requirements engineering as the basis (Sect. 7.2). The "Attainment" is organized into five *ESARIS Attainment Levels* which relate to the achievement of milestones in delivering ICT services according to the methods, procedures, and standards of ESARIS. The first three levels are related to more technical activities (IT engineering, implementation), the set-up for delivery (operations) and include methods for measuring the compliance (Sect. 7.3). The other two levels relate to the integration into portfolio and service catalogs. The portfolio development and the consideration of security in service catalogs (Sect. 7.4) are important for user organizations or even the next party in the internal supply chain of the ICT Service Provider.

7.1 Foundation

Introduction and summary: The *ESARIS Attainment Model* is an important means for an active security management. It ensures that appropriate security standards are maintained and used. It also provides information if and to what extent the ESARIS security standards are actually implemented. But the information relating to the compliance with ESARIS security standards is moreover important when making any business with user organizations (customers).

The *ESARIS Attainment Model* describes how security is integrated in the ICT services using ESARIS. This comprises the phase where the ESARIS security standards are being developed as "security design patterns" and the phase where they are applied. In the second phase it is measured if and to what extent an ICT service meets the security standards stipulated in ESARIS. The result is called the *ESARIS Attainment Statement* and provided in form of so-called Aces. This measurement is a snapshot that measures a current outcome. If practices are still adhered to, the ICT services maintain the quality that has been attained.

The basis for ESARIS attainment assessments are the ESARIS security standards, mainly the *ICT Security Standards* (Level 4) with the security measures described therein. The *ICT Security Baselines* (Level 5) provide information on an implementation level including detailed work instructions etc. Refer to Fig. 48.

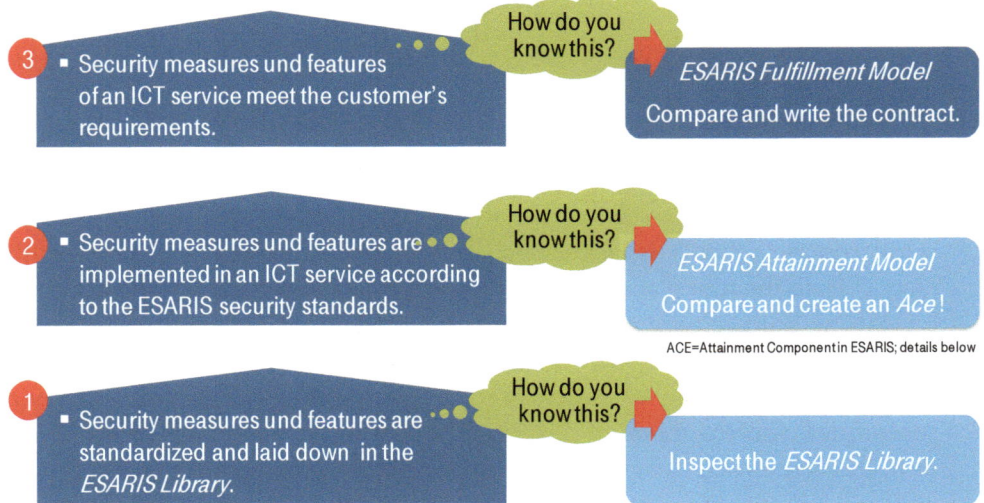

Fig. 48: Role of ESARIS Attainment and the Aces

(1) The standards are used to develop and implement ICT services including their basic constituents such as components and activities. They also provide the design patterns which shall be used to achieve the "secure by design" goal. The ICT Service Provider files the ESARIS security standards in a central *ESARIS Library*. Refer to the figure.

(2) The design and its implementation are compared with the ESARIS security standards from the *ESARIS Library* (step 1). The result is the *ESARIS Attainment Statement* called Ace (see below) which states compliance with and potential deviations from ESARIS security standards. The integration of ICT services and their security features into the service catalogs is also covered by Attainment.

On the one hand, the *ESARIS Attainment Statements* form the basis for an operative security management which identifies possible vulnerabilities and organizes their remediation. Refer to Fig. 48.

On the other hand, the *ESARIS Attainment Statements* provide information about the security features actually being built-in. This information plays an important role in the relationship with user organizations.

(3) When preparing new business with customers it is necessary to verify if the customer's security requirements are fulfilled. Refer to Fig. 48. To this end, one must know if the ICT service being subject of the contract is compliant with the ESARIS security standards. The *ESARIS Attainment Statements* (in form of Aces) provide the information about the built-in security features and possible deviations from the ESARIS security standards (step 2). Hence, the verification of "attainment" is the basis for a sales promise to customers and for contracting ("Fulfillment", see Chapter 8).

7.2   Requirements engineering and elaboration and application of ESARIS standards

Introduction and summary: Any verification of compliance with ESARIS security standards assumes that the latter exist and that they are high quality and fit for purpose. The development of security standards starts with requirements collection, analysis and acceptance. It must consider constraints of industrialized IT production. Development of security standards and design of ICT services are often interwoven.

The overall process of implementing security standards comprises three steps.

- Requirements engineering (Step A): The ICT business starts with the identification of relevant requirements and their analysis.

- Provisioning of guidelines (Step B): Then security standards are developed based on the identified requirements. The security standards provide re-usable design patterns for IT production in an industrialized fashion.

- Application of security standards (Step C): The security standards are used for the design of technology and processes and implemented accordingly. Security features become part of the ICT services specification and are used during operations.

Requirements engineering (Step A)

Fig. 49 illustrates the process from the identification of requirements (left) to their consolidation (middle).

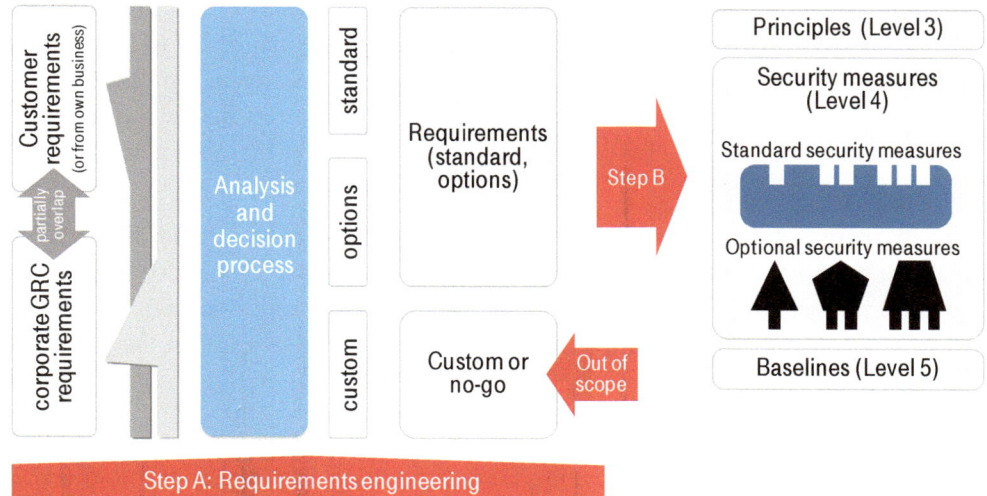

Fig. 49: Requirements engineering (Step A)

Basically, Fig. 49 shows the *ESARIS Industrialization Concept* (Sect. 6.2). There are two sources of security-related requirements: corporate and market requirements. Note that the two types of requirements do overlap. The focus in this section is on customer-independent developments. Customer requirements are requirements that are seen in the market and articulated by actual and potential customers. Corporate requirements are mostly defined to mitigate risks for the ICT Service Provider.

It is important here that the requirements are analyzed with respect to their significance and grouped into

- Standard requirements,
- Optional requirements, and
- Custom requirements.

Standard requirements are accepted as state-of-the-art so that they shall be met on a global basis by all ICT services. Optional requirements need to be met in many cases. But it is too costly to implement the corresponding security measures in every ICT service regardless of whom it is delivered to. For both types of requirements security measures are developed in Step B. Finally, there are requirements that are very specific and only relevant for one customer or a specific group of them. In this case it may not be economic to develop related solutions in advance and to include them into the standard catalog. Such custom security requirements may be realized in customer projects. Consequently, they are out of scope here. Examples are legacy and very high security requirements.

Security requirements differ in scope and relate to different level of abstraction. Hence, the analysis also considers this fact. Refer to Fig. 49.

The security management organization is responsible for the requirements engineering (Step A). However, employees, especially if engaged in deals and in service design, must support this process by identifying security requirements that are not met yet or where standards need to be modified in order to increase the level of standardization or for the sake of general improvements. It might be necessary to identify today's custom requirements which may become optional or standard requirements in the future if they are requested by more and more customers.

The Security Management organization uses the same process, boards, and roles that are used for the management of security documents. This process covers request, analysis, planning, and approval and is part of the so-called *Maintenance System for ESARIS* (Chapter 10) which is mainly designed to support the provisioning of guidelines.

Provisioning of guidelines (Step B)

The next step comprises the development of security documents and is therefore also straightforward to understand. Refer to Fig. 50.

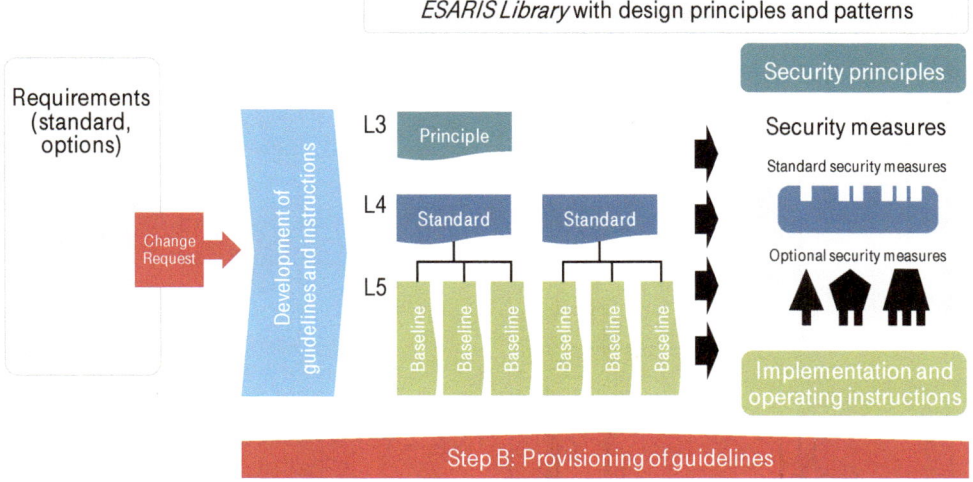

Fig. 50: Provisioning of guidelines (Step B)

New or modified requirements (from Step A) result in a formal Change Request that describes what has to be added or modified and where. Then the security standards are developed or modified, respectively. This process results in having security documents that are approved and mandatory. The *Hierarchy of Security Standards* has three levels in which security standards are provided for ICT service on a different level of abstraction (refer to Sect. 3.4).

All security documents are filed in one *ESARIS Library* and made available throughout the ICT Service Provider in this way. Otherwise standardization may not take place.

The business units are responsible to develop and maintain all security documentation which they require for developing, implementing and operating ICT services in an industrialized fashion. This especially covers the *ICT Security Baselines* (Level 5) they are requiring or use. *ICT Security Standards* (Level 4) should also be considered since the security measures stipulated in there are the base for the detailed implementation and operating instructions (Level 5). The Security Management organization supports the development and maintenance of all security documents. But their main responsibility is requirements engineering, approval of security standards, as well as steering and control that the security standards are used and adhered to.

Application of security standards (Step C)

The application of security standards covers
- Development (design),
- Implementation (realization), and
- Operations (delivery)

of ICT services. The development, implementation and operations processes are not security-specific and follow the standard processes of the ICT Service Provider.

Fig. 51 shows the application of the ESARIS security standards. All information about implementation and operations should be covered by the design which either provides explicit descriptions or refers to standards. Especially Operations should follow general processes and procedures which are not specific to an ICT service. For the sake of simplicity implementation and operations are not shown in the figure. In terms of security the *ESARIS Library* provides all information that has been agreed in advance and is therefore standardized. In order to provide ICT services in an industrialized fashion these security standards shall be reused as design patterns.

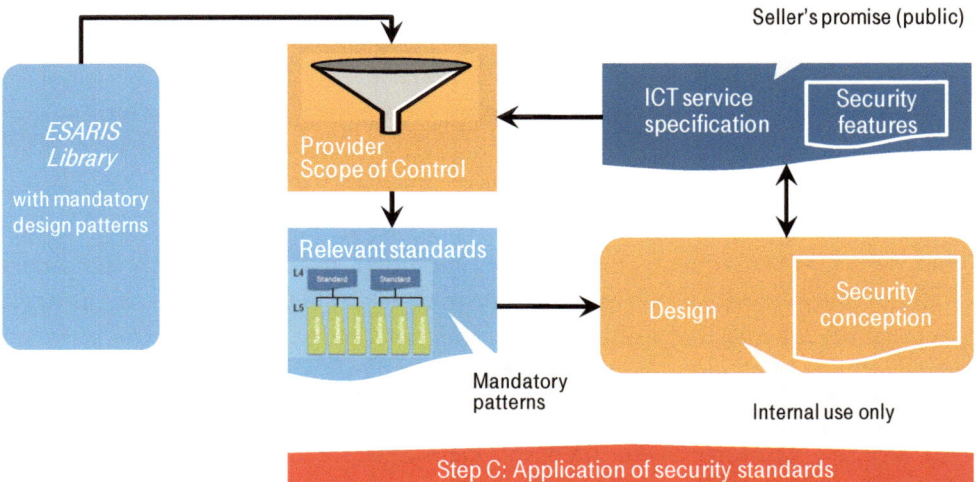

Fig. 51: Application of security standards (Step C)

Not all security standards have to be used for a specific ICT service since some information is obviously not relevant. For instance, computing service does not include user workstations such as notebooks. Hence, the relevant standards need to be identified. This is done using the method called *Provider Scope of Control* described in Sect. 4.5.[42] In short, the ICT service specification is analyzed in order to identify all areas where the ICT Service Provider is responsible for. Implemented technologies are identified and it is analyzed how the ICT service is developed and managed. Based on this information the relevant *ICT Security Standards* (and security measures) are selected. The funnel in Fig. 51 represents this. The *ESARIS Security Taxonomy* as a basic element considerably helps to identify the relevant areas. In specific cases, it may additionally be required to verify if all security measures stipulated in a standard actually apply to the ICT service under consideration. The

---

[42] This method is not only used for "attainment". It will be used again when verifying compliance with customer requirements in contracts ("fulfillment", Chapter 8) and when managing supplier networks ("3rd party integration", Chapter 9). The *Provider Scope of Control* methodology is a fundamental principle of ESARIS.

result of this analysis is a set of relevant standards (refer to Fig. 51). The relevant standards are mandatory. If not being used, the degree of standardization is decreased which has an impact on industrialized ICT service provisioning. However, it is possible to step out and decide to use other solutions than specified. This step-out process is risk-based and requires a business case. The decision needs to be documented.

The mandatory security standards or patterns are the input for the "design" together with a bunch of other material that is not related to security aspects. The "design" incorporates a security conception. Important features from the design are reflected in the "ICT service description" as used in service catalogs. This also holds for security so that the "ICT service description" is expected to also describe security features. Refer to Fig. 51. The "ICT service description" must contain information about security if this is important for the next party using the ICT service (customer or next unit of the ICT Service Provider in the supply chain).

Note that there is a cycle in the relation shown in Fig. 51. If the "design" for some reason leads to a change of the "ICT service" and its "ICT service description", it may be required to analyze again what standards are actually relevant. This may in turn lead to a changed set of mandatory standards which can have an effect on the design.

The business units are responsible to develop and implement an ICT service. This means that they are also responsible to develop and maintain all design documentation (including those about security). The designers can reuse the security measures stipulated in the *ICT Security Standards* (Level 4). The related *ICT Security Baselines* (Level 5) contain further detail which should also be reused. This approach reduces the effort for designing the security part of ICT services. During operations the business benefits from using standards which allows for provisioning ICT services in an industrialized manner.

Summary: The overall process is shown in Fig. 52.

Step A: Internal and external requirements are analyzed and it is decided which of them shall be met by all possible ICT services (standard requirements) and which of them shall be considered as possible additions (optional security requirements).

Step B: Solutions are elaborated. This means that design patterns are developed in form of security standards. They are made available in a central library.

Step C: The security standards can now be used. This covers the phases of development or design, implementation as well as operations. Each activity is based on standards and predefined elements that are reused. All information can be considered to be part of the design. The business units are fully responsible for the provisioning of ICT services which includes all security features.

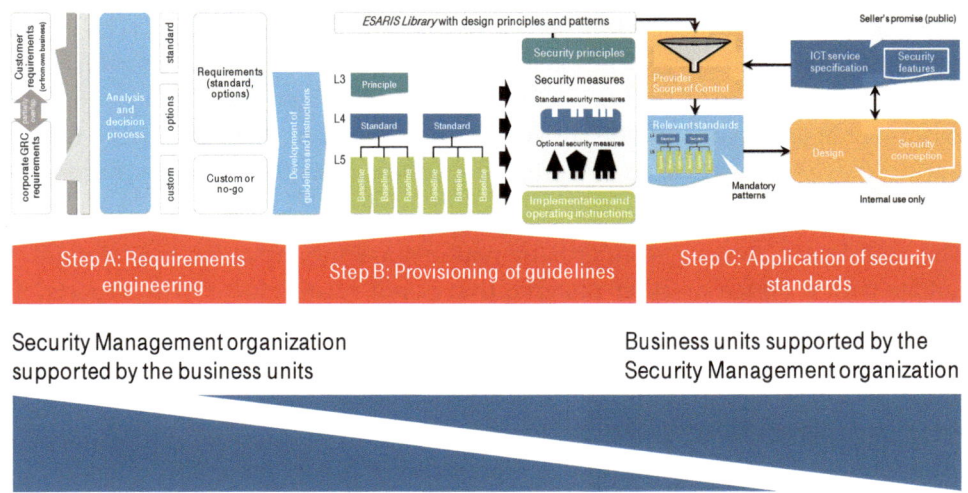

Fig. 52: Overview of the Attainment process

Fig. 52 also shows the responsibilities and the focus of both the Security Management organization and the IT departments (business units).

Step A: The Security Management organization manages the requirements with the help of the business units.

Step B: The Security Management organization manages the provisioning of the security standards. The business units must elaborate the implementation and operating instructions.

Step C: The business units design, implement and operate the ICT services. The Security Management organization provides support and verifies results.

7.3   ESARIS Attainment Levels and verification of compliance

The application of the ESARIS security standards goes along with a "verification process". It is organized into five *ESARIS Attainment Levels* which relate to the achievement of milestones in delivering ICT services according to the methods, procedures, and standards of ESARIS. The first three levels are related to the design and implementation of technology and IT management processes but also include "successfully delivered". The last two stages are related to the management of the service portfolio (called Service Catalog Management in ITIL). The ICT (functionality) and the related IT service management activities shall comply with the ESARIS security standards. The *ESARIS Attainment Model* (or: *ESARIS Compliance Attainment Model*) comprises a method to formally verify if and to what extent an ICT service, component or activity complies with the ESARIS security standards. The result is documented in form of an *Ace* which also contains the *ESARIS Attainment Statement*.

In order to ensure that the ESARIS security standards are actually used, a verification mechanism is required that checks if and to what extent an ICT service, a component or a activity complies with the relevant security standards. The verification mechanism is an important element of the *ESARIS Attainment Model* and organized in stages each associated with achieving an *ESARIS Attainment Level*. The first three stages are related to more technical tasks (engineering and implementation). The last two stages are related to the management of the service portfolio. The *ESARIS Attainment Levels* are shown in Fig. 53.

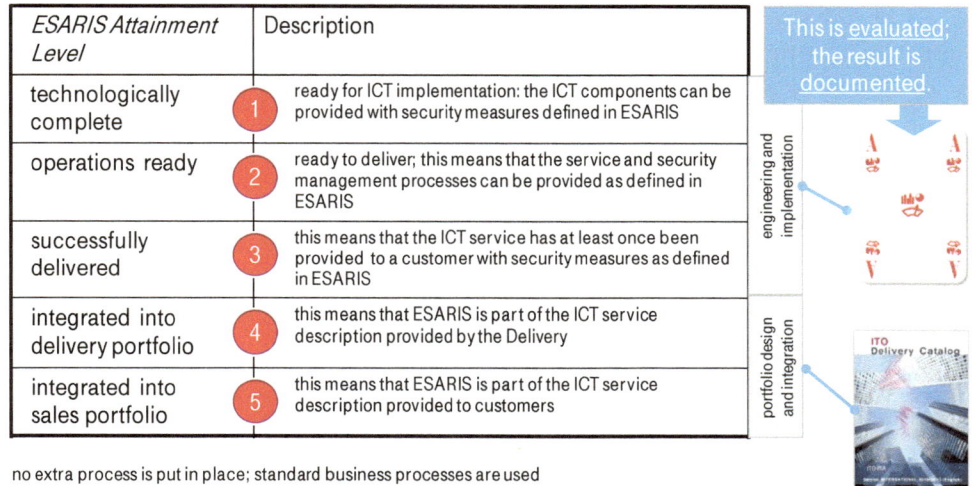

Fig. 53: ESARIS Attainment Levels

The *ESARIS Attainment Levels* are as follows:

- Engineering and implementation
    - Level 1 – Technologically complete (ready to "run"; this means that the ICT is build and functional; the components integrate the security measures defined in the lower half of the *ESARIS Security Taxonomy*),
    - Level 2 – Operations ready (ready to "deliver"; this means that the service and IT security management processes are in place; the IT service management activities are enhanced as described by the security measures from the upper half of the *ESARIS Security Taxonomy*),
    - Level 3 – Successfully delivered (this means that the ICT service has at least once been provided to a customer with ESARIS security measures in place),
- portfolio design and integration
    - Level 4 – Integrated into delivery portfolio (this means that service catalogs for internal use describe relevant security features explicitly or by referring to ESARIS security standards),

- Level 5 – Integrated into sales portfolio (this means that service catalogs which describe ICT services for customers also describe their relevant security features).

A core ICT service with its functionality achieves the *ESARIS Attainment Level 1* ("technologically complete") if the security measures from the lower half of the *ESARIS Security Taxonomy* are applied. A comparison must also exist which shows possible deviations from the ESARIS security standards.

An ICT service (functionality and included IT service management) achieves the *ESARIS Attainment Level 2* ("operations ready") if the security measures from the upper half of the *ESARIS Security Taxonomy* are applied. This means that all relevant IT service management processes are in place and can be applied to the core ICT service. A comparison must also exist which shows possible deviations from the ESARIS security standards.

An ICT service can reach the *ESARIS Attainment Level 3* as soon as it has been successfully delivered to a customer. This level is seen as a reality check since the real business of ICT service provisioning is expected to provide extra knowledge which can be used to review and proof the information gathered for the levels 1 and 2.

While the first three *ESARIS Attainment Levels* focus on service design and implementation as well as on operations based on standardized processes in the delivery units, the ESARIS Attainment Levels 4 and 5 are related to the organization of sales processes and of the internal supply chain. In general, the ICT Service Provider's service catalogs cover two types of ICT service: customer-facing ICT services that are to be purchased by the customers and supporting ICT services that are required to deliver customer-facing services. The service catalogs are developed and maintained according to the Portfolio Management process usually by people specialized in this job. In fact, three categories of ICT service exist: those in the pipeline (proposed or in development), those which are currently "for sale" (live or available for deployment), and retired ICT services as well.

An ICT service achieves the *ESARIS Attainment Level 4* if appropriate information material about security features (including an appropriate *ESARIS Attainment Statement*) is integrated in the ICT service description reproduced or referred to in a service catalog for internal use. Obviously, design and operating documentation must also contain such security-related information.

An ICT service achieves the *ESARIS Attainment Level 5* if the same is achieved with respect to a service catalog used to sell and deliver ICT services to user organizations (customers of the ICT Service Provider). Highly standardized ICT services may be sold, purchased and deployed over the Internet (user self-provisioning). In such a case, the necessary preparations are subject of this attainment phase.

Both parts as well as the stages may be started or run simultaneously. However, the attainment of ESARIS compliance follows a bottom-up approach. The foundation is built first with ICT and process implementation. The stage "successfully delivered" demonstrates that the implementation works. Portfolio design and integration is put at the end which does not mean that the development process should not follow a top-down approach. It is put at the end here, since the message "ready to deliver" assumes the foundation in technology and IT service management.

The major goal of "attainment" is to ensure that the ESARIS security standards are adhered to through the correct implementation of the design patterns provided by the ESARIS security standards. This needs to be verified. Fig. 54 shows how the compliance with ESARIS security standards is verified. The comparison between "reality" (left in the figure) and "standards in paper" (right-hand side) results in a document called Ace which includes the *ESARIS Attainment Statement* as a summary.[43] Compliance with ESARIS security standards is documented by means of Aces. An Ace is created for an entity which can be an ICT service, a component, or a activity. Such entities (and their Aces) can be reused when building composite ICT services. Aces are the basis for an operative security management since they contain information about deviations which are to be dealt with.

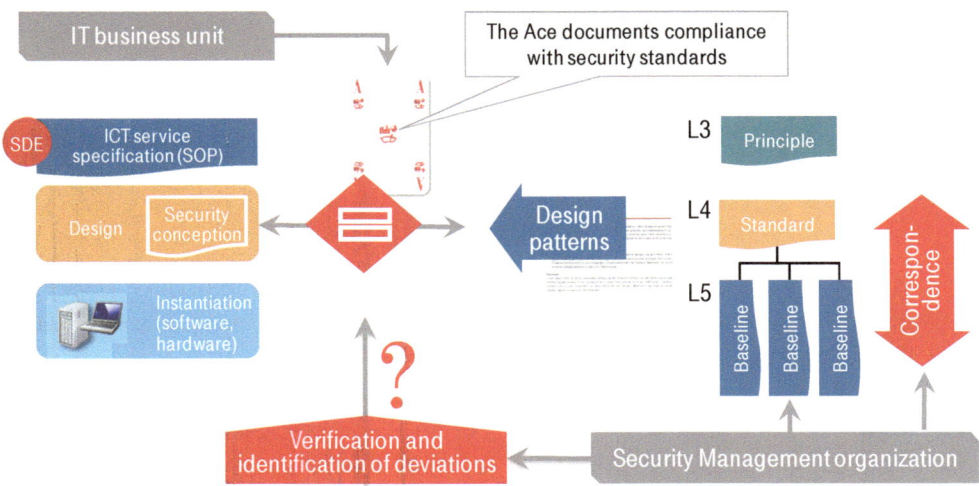

Fig. 54: Verification of compliance with ESARIS security standards and Aces

The attainment verification is performed for all relevant areas in the *ESARIS Security Taxonomy*. Hence, the relevant *ICT Security Standards* (Level 4) need to be identified first. Perhaps, it is necessary to analyze if specific security measures are relevant or not. This selection of standards and measures is done using the method called *Provider Scope of Control* described in Sect. 4.5.

---

[43] "Ace" is an abbreviation which stands for "Attainment component in ESARIS". However, the name was mainly chosen to draw the attention of stakeholders to this important instrument and raise the motivation to elaborate one. "Do you have an Ace up in your sleeve?"

The Ace is created during development and provided by the Business Unit ("service owner") responsible for the ICT service design, realization, and provisioning. This approach ensures that the designers are applying the ESARIS security standards and that caring for security is everybody's obligation and not restricted to the Security Management organization. The finalized Aces are approved by the Security Management organization. The Aces are then centrally stored for future reference and re-use.

An Ace documents the level of compliance with *ICT Security Standards* and *ICT Security Baselines* and thus serves as *ESARIS Attainment Statement*. An Ace for an ICT service, component, or activity consists of a frame document which contains several attachments. The following information is collected in the documents:

- Ace summary:
  - Identification and characterization of the ICT service, component, or activity including its supplier and the intended areas of application,
  - Identification of the relevant ESARIS areas (*ICT Security Standards*) together with an indication of the depth in which the verification or comparison was performed (on Level 4 only or including Level 5).
  - Summary of compliance levels with the security measures from the applicable ESARIS areas and description of major exceptions.
- Detailed ESARIS Statement of Compliance document (attachment): Evaluation of compliance with security measures defined in the *ICT Security Standards* for each of the relevant ESARIS areas. Any deviation from security measures is identified and forwarded to the evaluation of potential risks implied by this noncompliance.

- List of related *ICT Security Baselines* (Level 5) which actually have been incorporated in the design and therefore been considered in the Attainment evaluation (attachment).
- List of referenced Ace(s) of sub-components in case of a composite Ace (attachment). A composite Ace relates to an ICT service, component or activity which is composed of other ICT services, components or activities already evaluated so that Aces exist.

It is worth to note two things. First, the business is responsible for the comparison of reality with standards and the evaluation of compliance. Templates exist. Though, security experts may do the work and consult the Security Management organization too, the business manager ("service owner") is responsible for the result. The Ace is signed by him or her. This also holds if the Ace is elaborated under the auspices of the Security Management organization or initiated by it. Second, deviations from ESARIS security standards are possible for several reasons. Some may be tolerated. However, deviations which result in exposing the ICT Service Provider or the user organization (customer) to a significant risk are tracked and require treatment according to common risk management practices.

Modularization is important for an industrialized IT production. As a consequence, ICT Service Providers follow a modular approach in providing ICT services. The service offering portfolio is hierarchical and modular which supports combining different elements. The composition is based on a set of building blocks and uses a hierarchy of standardized ICT delivery components as illustrated in Fig. 55. This needs to be taken into account when considering the management of *ESARIS Attainment Statements* (Aces) since all yellow elements in the figure may have an associated Ace.

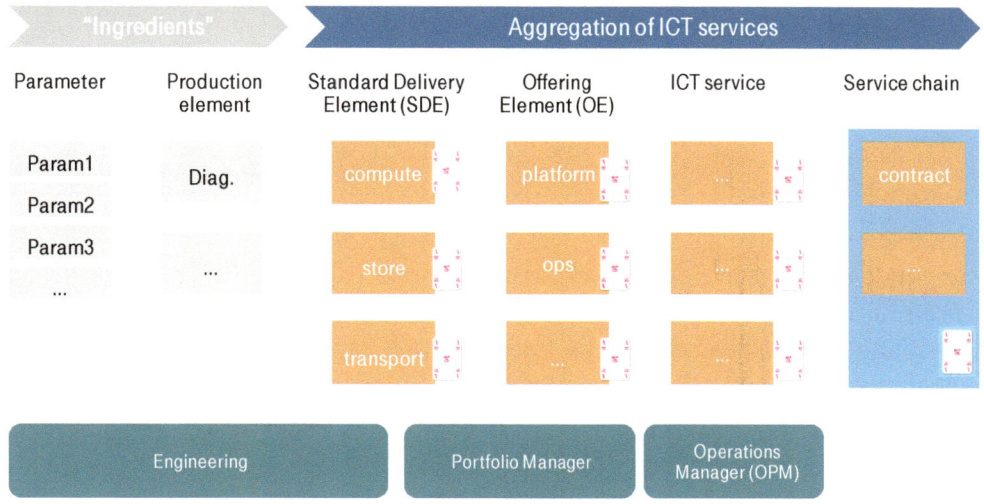

Fig. 55: Structure of an offering portfolio (principle only)

An industrialized IT production uses a composition schema in which ICT services are combined with options and are aggregated to ever more complex ICT services. This means that "production elements" are used to build Standard Delivery Elements (SDE), the SDE are used to build ICT services, and the ICT services can be used to build "service chains".

Fig. 56 shows the aggregation of ICT services again. Each ICT service has an ICT service specification and a design. The design comprises a security conception which in turn provides information about compliance with the ESARIS security standards in terms of the *ESARIS Attainment Statement* in the form of an Ace. If the ICT Service Provider works on the next level of aggregation it is not necessary to analyze compliance with ESARIS from scratch. Instead the Aces from the reused ICT services can be reused where available. This is shown in Fig. 56. If Aces are not yet available, they need to be requested from the service owner in a recursive process to get all required Aces. Of course, the attainment statements are not only collected and summed up. They are aggregated requiring a step where the integration is being analyzed.

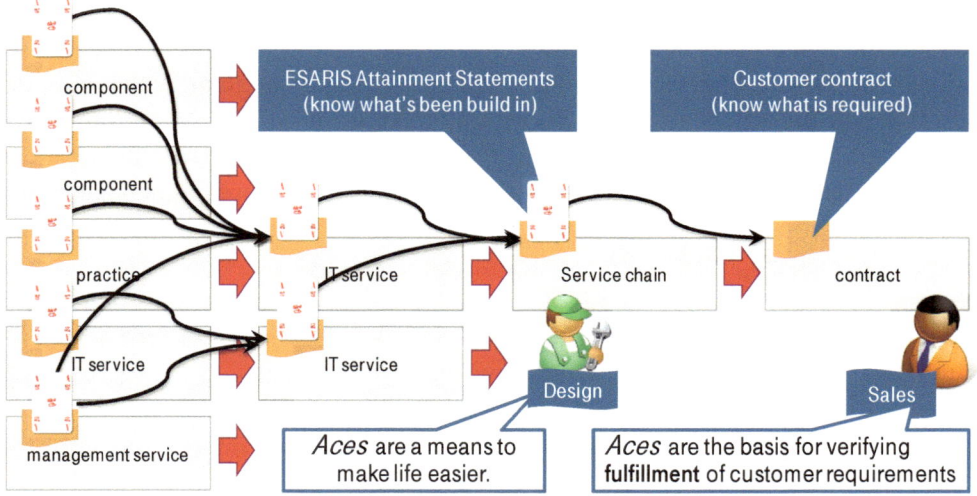

Fig. 56: Composition of ICT services and aggregation of Aces

In order to avoid multiple checks and verifications of *ESARIS Attainment State-ments*, it is usually only required to step down to the next lower level of the com-position hierarchy and refer to the Aces available at that level. In case that further detailed information needs to be reviewed, the references to underlying *ICT Securi-ty Baselines* (Level 5) or additional Aces on even lower composition levels can be retrieved from the information collected within the Aces.

7.4　Service offering portfolio integration

> **Introduction and summary:** The collection of available ICT services and their specification together form the so-called service offering portfolio of an ICT Ser-vice Provider. The security measures specified in ESARIS security standards must be implemented in the ICT services. Their service specifications must re-flect this fact and also describe relevant security features. In this way, security is one element in service catalogs. The latter are an important instrument for man-aging the relationships along the complete supply chain. The structure of the ESARIS security standards is the perfect input for the service portfolio manage-ment and the elaboration of service catalogs. This relates to the achievement of the *ESARIS Attainment Levels 4* and *5*.

The Service Portfolio Management (or Service Offering Portfolio Management) is a complicated process interwoven with several other processes. For example, almost all ITIL processes are directly affected, including Service Strategy (SS), Service De-sign (SD), and Service Transition (ST). Continual Service Improvement (CSI) and Service Operation (SO) are involved rather indirectly. Merely the result of the pro-cess is therefore shown in the following instead of describing all the necessary steps in the standard Portfolio and Offering Management process.

It has been mentioned, that the ICT Service Provider's service catalogs cover two types of ICT service: customer-facing ICT services that are to be purchased by the customers and supporting ICT services that are required to deliver customer-facing services. It has also been mentioned, that two types of service catalogs exist relating to two types of portfolio. There are service catalogs that describe the delivery and are used by the ICT Service Provider only internally to organize the internal supply chain. And there are service catalogs which are given to the customers and describe the sales portfolio with the corresponding ICT services. Both types of service catalogs may contain both customer-facing services and supporting services. Note that supporting services may optionally supplement customer-facing services and require an order from customers in this case. This means, that the portfolio (and service catalog) integration relates to the achievement of both *ESARIS Attainment Levels 4* and *5*. Service catalogs (and offering portfolios) are structured in a modular way which corresponds to and is necessary for an industrialized IT production. In the following, no distinction is made between delivery and sales portfolio because the differences are not essential in the context given.[44]

The offering portfolio consists of individual, predefined ICT services each being described by a service specification. Security is one characteristic or feature among others and must therefore also be part of the service description. The principle is shown in Fig. 57 using a simple example of a managed workplace service.

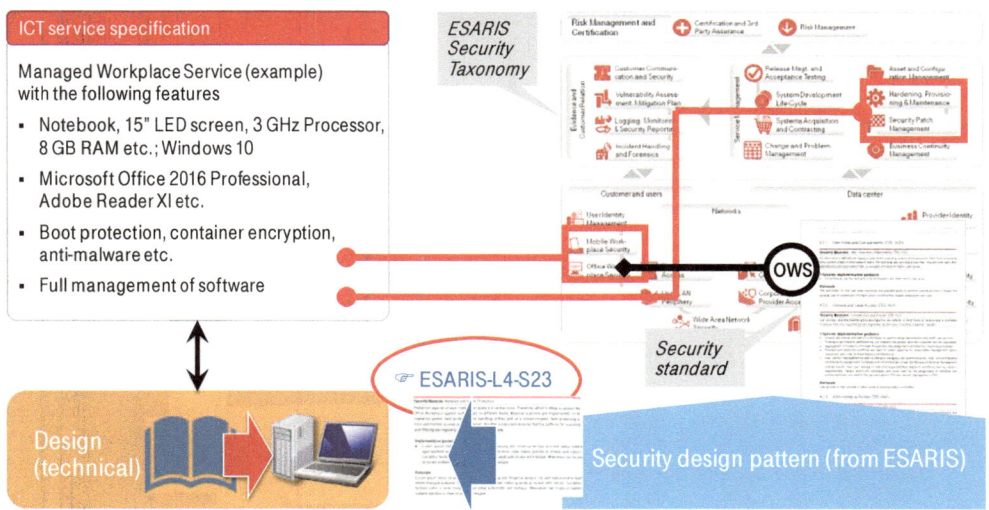

Fig. 57: ICT service specification (workplace) versus ESARIS security standards

The service specification (upper left) is examined by possible customers and their buying decision depends on its contents. In this example, the hardware features are not security relevant, but the software and the management services are. The

---

44   ITIL moreover distinguishes between pipeline (planned ICT services), catalog (ICT services that are currently delivered), and retired ICT services (delivered in the past).

ESARIS security standards (right in the figure) provide the pattern both for the design (lower left) and the service specification (upper left). In the example, the workplace is equipped with appropriate means for boot protection, container-encryption and malware protection. And the software is fully managed. IT service management includes the maintenance of the software based on a secure initial set-up of the machines (using a software image). Both types of security aspects are covered by *ICT Security Standards* (Level 4, *ESARIS Orchestration Layer*). This is visualized by two red boxes in Fig. 57 that frame specific *ICT Security Standards* which specify the security measures in detail. In the above example, the *Office Workplace* (OWS) standard is providing the re-usable patterns for the service speci-fication and the high-level design (Level 4). The underlying *ICT Security Baselines* (Level 5) are used for the low-level design. Note that the service specification in the service catalog directly reflects the description of the security measures stipulated in the relevant *ICT Security Standards*. Utilizing the underlying *ICT Security Base-lines* (Level 5) ensures that the security measures are correctly implemented result-ing in reliable service catalogs. The same is done regarding the aspects of IT service management.

In an industrialized IT production environment, IT service management and other services are defined and set up once and then used for almost all ICT services. This results in a modular service offering portfolio and, more important, in higher qual-ity and lower costs. Two examples are discussed in the following.

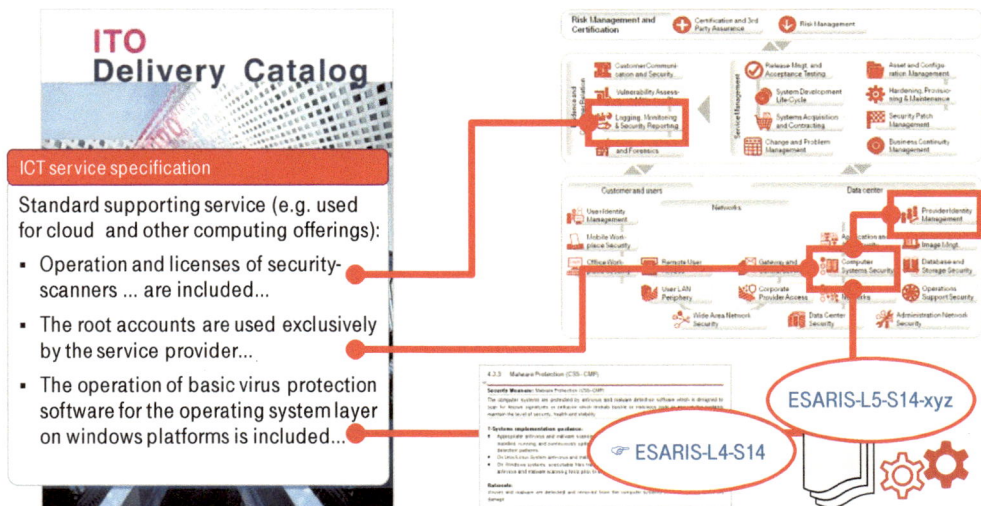

Fig. 58: ICT service specification (standard support) versus ESARIS security standards

The first example is shown in Fig. 58. The ICT Service Provider has standardized the security support for cloud and other computing services. Three aspects are shown on the left-hand side of the figure: security scanners, use of root accounts and a basic virus protection. All three have their equivalent in ESARIS security standards shown on the right-hand side. The figure shows more detail for the last aspect: The text in the ICT service specification (left) is a copy or a shortened version of the text specifying the security measure in the *ICT Security Standard* about computer systems in data centers. The document ID (ESARIS-L4-S14) is indicated but explained later in Chapter 10. There is a complete set of design patterns specifying how this virus protection is implemented. The document ID "ESARIS-L5-S14-xyz" refers to these *ICT Security Baselines*.

The second example is shown in Fig. 59. Most large companies are organized along business processes though people still belong to legal entities. These business processes are a mixture of processes from general business administration (or Enterprise Resource Planning, ERP), typical business processes and others relating to the life-cycle of the products or services offered by the company. A diagram with such a process map is shown in the upper left of Fig. 59. The upper half of the *ESARIS Security Taxonomy* (upper right in the figure) relates to the life-cycle activities of the ICT services, more specifically to the IT service management activities.

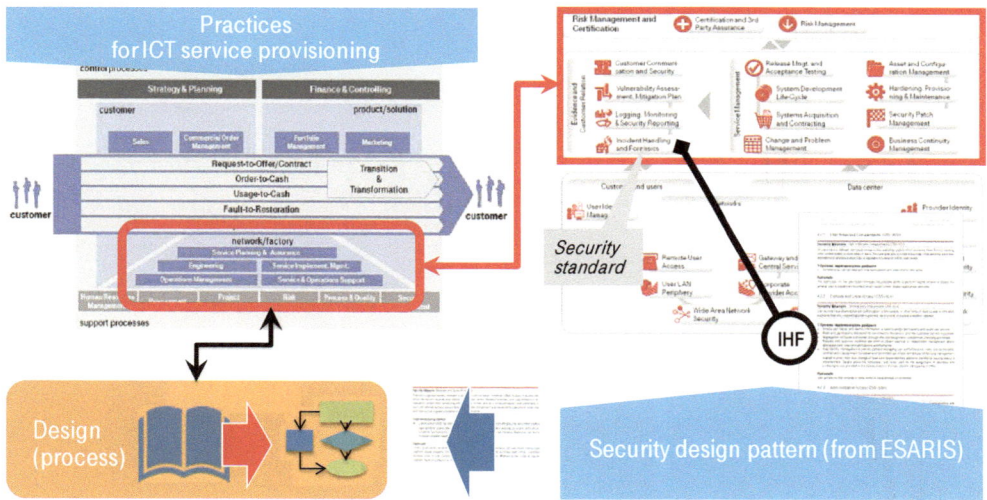

Fig. 59: Set-up of processes and practices versus ESARIS security standards

The ESARIS security standards provide design patterns (lower right in Fig. 59) that are to be reused. If new processes are designed or existing ones are modified (lower left in the figure), the ESARIS security standards must reflect these additions or changes and vice versa.

There are several reasons for, on the one hand, having security integrated in the portfolio and the process landscape and for explicitly specifying security in ESARIS security standards. First, managing security in a complex environment requires having one defined set of documents which can be looked at and analyzed. Gaps cannot be found if the information is distributed amongst an undefined series of documents which may also be updated or revoked quite independently. That's why the ESARIS security standards, namely the *ICT Security Standards* (Level 4), are required even if the same contents would also be part of process documents. Second, the ESARIS security measures need to be implemented. Therefore, the security aspects need to be described or referred to in the primary process documents. IT personnel will expect all relevant information to be provided by the primary work instructions they are using, either in form of directly workable instructions or as a reference to other such material (e.g. *ICT Security Baselines* (Level 5)). Third, customers need to be informed and to be provided with a complete picture about all relevant security measures in place. Contracts need to have a common basis. Hence, descriptions of security measures are required that are unique, not ambiguous and not providing room for interpretation. This can only be achieved by having one centrally managed set of ESARIS security standards. Note that for the same reason, ICT service specifications are centralized and made available by means of service catalogs. Both the security standards on Level 4 and the service catalogs are highly modular, well-structured and provided in a formalized form.

8   Fulfillment – meeting customer demands

Introduction and summary: User organizations are strongly dependent on using secure ICT services. But ICT Service Providers must do more than just implementing suitable security measures. They must actively manage the relationship with their actual and possible customers (Sect. 8.1). The importance of transparency as well as of having interfaces and room for interaction has already been stressed. This is now made specific by considering big IT outsourcing deals, their phases and the activities in each phase in detail. Consideration of contracting provides advice for the user organization and the ICT Service Provider to fill the contract with security agreements appropriately (Sect. 8.2). User organizations require evidence that their requirements are met when purchasing ICT services from a third party. They need such information for their own risk management and as evidence for their own customers and auditors. Contractual evidence is only one element of the assurance required. The provider must demonstrate fulfillment of the requirements also at run time. This is called operational evidence here. These aspects are also covered by the *ESARIS Fulfillment Model* (Sect. 8.3).

8.1   Foundation

Introduction and summary: ESARIS takes operational requirements into account and focuses on user requirements, thus facing the reality in the market economy. Obviously, the ICT Service Provider must meet the expectations and requirements of its customer, a user organization. Otherwise the latter would not buy. This section emphasizes that "meeting customer requirements" is more than just implementing the right security technology. Transparency, interfaces and interaction as well as standardization are the keywords. By providing some more insight about these topics, the scene is set for a comprehensive consideration of "Fulfillment" in subsequent sections.

Enterprises continue to intensify the use of third-party ICT services and reduce or give up internal IT production. Though ICT services can almost completely be taken over by ICT Service Providers, the risks associated with using these ICT services cannot. Nowadays, IT risks put business at risk. Those risks cannot be "outsourced". User organizations can buy the design, integration and operation of ICT from specialized service providers, but they are still responsible for information security. This means that users have to have the ability and the resources for corporate IT risk management. They have to define their general security and compliance requirements and need to make the comparison with the ICT services provided from the external.

Large enterprises in particular take a comprehensive risk-oriented approach. They have different requirements due to the fact that their business differs. Hence, it is important to verify if the customer's security requirements are actually met by the ICT services delivered or planned to be delivered by the ICT Service Provider. This chapter is about the comparison between demands on the one hand and promise and reality on the other.

Such a comparison is the subject of the *ESARIS Fulfillment Model* (or: *ESARIS Customer Fulfillment Model*). It measures if an ICT service is compliant with the user organization's security requirements. Note that in ESARIS, compliance refers to two different areas. 1) The *ESARIS Compliance Attainment Model* (Chapter 7) measures if the ICT services are compliant with the relevant ESARIS security standards. It is verified if the security features are correctly implemented in technology and processes used for delivering the ICT service. The result is documented in form of an Ace. 2) The *ESARIS Customer Fulfillment Model* (this chapter) compares the security measures of real ICT services with the security requirements of a specific user organization (customer). This duality is also the subject of the so-called *ESARIS Concept of Double Direction Standards* (Sect. 3.5).

But more is required to satisfy user organizations. Already at the very beginning of this book (Sect. 1.2)
- Transparency,
- Interfaces and interaction, as well as
- Standardization
were described as the main focus for user organizations when it comes to security.

User organizations (consuming parties) require <u>transparency</u>, i.e. meaningful information about the security of the ICT services. This information is required to feed the user organization's risk management and to verify compliance as e.g. demanded by auditing companies.

Cloud computing services are inherently non-transparent for the user organization. Users will not see how the ICT service is produced. This constitutes the security dilemma with cloud computing. But less transparency and control are not specific to cloud computing. The more tasks are outsourced and the more technology is at the providers' side, the more the users lack ad hoc knowledge and direct control. Notwithstanding, user organizations require transparency and knowledge of implementation details for their risk management. From the ICT Service Provider's perspective, transparency is the basis for a successful business relation with customers.

What does ESARIS define for supporting transparency? ESARIS is a structured approach helping to understand how secure ICT services are produced and delivered. ESARIS is designed to support transparency in an appropriate way. The ESARIS security standards are organized in a *Hierarchy of Security Standards*. Level 4 (*ESARIS Orchestration Layer*) is introduced and used for communicating, negotiating and agreeing security issues with customers. It is important to know that Level 4 shall also provide a synopsis of all security aspects relevant in IT production. It allows verifying completeness and dependencies and provisioning of an integrated mutually supporting whole.

The exchange of information between the two parties requires having <u>interfaces</u> in all phases of the business (from sales all the way to Operations). Security requires the ability to make changes and to directly control and check. Hence, <u>interaction</u> is required. There is one fact in IT outsourcing which makes such interfaces more important on the one hand and more complicated to implement and maintain on the other. Compared with buying from an internal IT department, the user organization cannot directly intervene in a third-party IT production. People belong to another legal organization and there is no common boss directing them if required. No one has the authority to issue directions to both parties. Note that the separation of the user organization on the one hand and the ICT Service Provider on the other was one of the reasons to develop ESARIS since the separation generates a new situation which has a radical impact. Existing models and processes need to be adapted.[45] However, it is worth noting that the same situation may arise in case that an internal IT department becomes really huge. Then internal ways become long, interests appear to be very different and specialization demands a price. That's why ESARIS is also designed for large IT departments.

A specific form of interaction is contracting which also includes verification of contract fulfillment. That's where the term *ESARIS Fulfillment Model* comes from. Details will be provided later in this chapter. It is explained how contractual evidence is gained and how operational evidence is provided using security measures that have been contractually agreed.

The last aspect is <u>standardization</u>. It has already been mentioned that standardization is a consequence of an industrialized IT production or the other way around. Industrialization in turn is the means to decrease the costs while improving quality. ICT service provisioning on a large scale ("production") requires the standardization of security since industrial production is characterized by a high degree of division of labor and high specialization of people. This results in a higher quality at lower costs. This is what customers want. Standardization is a must-have for producing competitive ICT services. Refer to Chapter 6 for more detail. Standardization meets customer requirements and provides benefits for them.

---

[45] Eberhard von Faber and Michael Pauly: User Risk Management Strategies and Models – Adaption for Cloud Computing; in: N. Pohlmann, H. Reimer, W. Schneider (Editors): Securing Electronic Business Processes, Vieweg (2010), ISBN-10: 3834814385, p. 80 – 90 [41].

8.2   IT outsourcing

Introduction and summary: User organizations strongly depend on getting reliable ICT services reliably. The importance of transparency as well as of having interfaces and room for interaction has already been stressed. Now this is applied to real situations. The reality of big IT outsourcing deals is considered. IT outsourcing is organized along phases. The activities in each phase are explained. The interfaces and ways for interaction are different in those phases. All important security aspects shall be specified in the contract. Its structure is unique for big IT outsourcing undertakings. It is a challenge for the user organization and the ICT Service Provider to fill the contract with appropriate security agreements appropriately.

Nowadays, IT is used almost everywhere in industry, commerce and administration. It seems that no business, governmental or public administration process can be executed without the help of some software. The use of IT speeds up processes and reduces costs. IT is the fuel and the lubricant of today's society. The other side of the coin:

- User organizations are strongly dependent on the reliability of the ICT services they are using.
- The IT must carefully be planned and maintained since it is the IT being a major factor to achieve competitive advantages.
- Hostile or mistaken activity can cause considerable damage to the business if the ICT services are not sufficiently protected.

This still holds if ICT services are outsourced.

Consequently, ICT Service Providers invest much in organizing the relationship with their large customers accordingly. ESARIS is one example for this. However, security managers and experts do not always understand the environment and complexity of IT outsourcing, the sequence of actions and the reason why they exist, and how this affects the security they are responsible for. That's why ESARIS has also been introduced.

Fig. 60 shows the IT outsourcing phases with indication of interfaces and interaction. "IT outsourcing" needs to be initiated, implemented and executed; hence, it has its own life-cycle schematically shown in top of the figure. The figure also shows that different teams or businesses are involved in each stage. These are shown as interfaces because IT outsourcing is about managing the relationship between provider and user organization. Finally, the figure shows examples for the interaction which takes place throughout the sequence of actions. Examples are shown only.

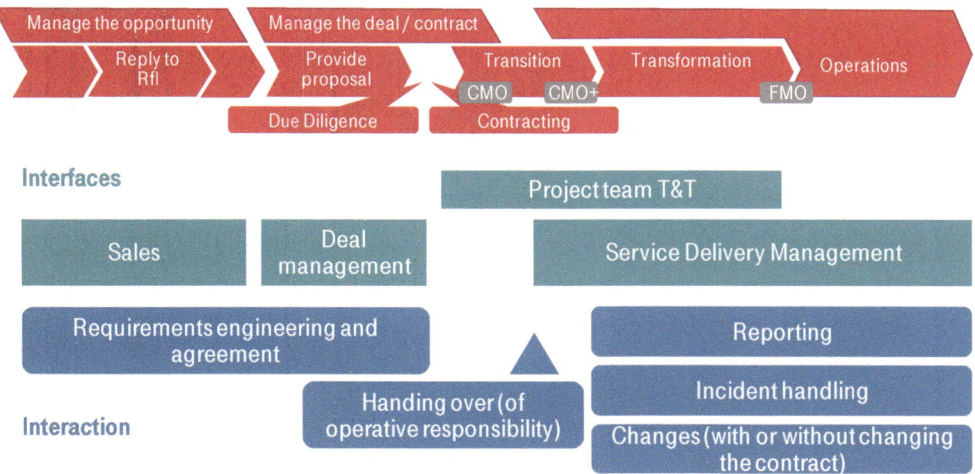

Fig. 60: IT outsourcing phases with indication of interfaces and interaction

Why is this so complicated? Often the IT outsourcing contracts have really high volume ranging for instance from millions to hundreds of millions of Euro. The ICT is very complex and often it needs to be modernized. IT outsourcing is not like purchasing a product, it means purchasing a service. There is a big difference between a product like a computer and a service like getting an application running and maintained. The product is purchased as-is. Perhaps some services are added including repair and software updates in case that the manufacturer made mistakes. Nevertheless, the product (including some services) is well-defined from the very beginning. An ICT service is different if it is more complex than using e.g. cloud storage. Here are the reasons: An ICT service cannot be specified in all detail since the environment may and will change in the future. New business requirements need to be met which requires changes in software. Capacity and access need to be modified due to different use cases or user habits. Performance needs to be adjusted since the use of ICT services is about to change. Technology had changed and some components are no longer available or maintained by the vendor. Errors causing e.g. malfunction as well as vulnerabilities are discovered and require repair. The threat landscape has changed since there are new players; they have different tools and opportunities; targets and motivation changed, or even the possibility to generate money has turned a pure theoretical scenario into a real opportunity for attackers.

The phases of IT outsourcing are as follows (mainly from the provider's perspective). It is assumed that the user organization has performed some planning, has analyzed the current situation and identified the needs, has examined economic circumstances and developed a business case, and knows about commercial and business risks. Then the user organization can analyze the market and look for possible providers. Often they contact possible providers by sending a so-called Request for Information (RfI) to collect written information about the capabilities of various providers. In other cases, possible providers are directly contacted, or the user organization is contacted by providers e.g. they know that an IT outsourcing contract is to be renewed. Despite these details, the ICT Service Provider starts managing a business opportunity (refer to Fig. 60). Often such contacts have a long history and the provider's sales departments and representatives of the user organization have met several time and exchanged information about requirements and possible solutions.

After this it is getting more concrete. The user organization sends out a Request for Proposal (RfP) (also called Request for Tender, RfT, or Request for Quotation, RfQ). ICT Service Providers which are on the "long-list" of the user organization receive this RfP. If interested in the matter, they are working towards a "deal" and elaborate a proposal. Refer to Fig. 60. This requires analyzing the user organization's requirements and developing a solution for it. If there is mention of "solution design" in this phase, in an industrialized environment mostly the arrangement of standardized, predefined elements is meant. This can be complicated and time-consuming, and sometimes customer-specific elements need to be developed in addition. On the provider's side, the Deal management is responsible. The proposal is sent out and then studied by the user organization. Proposals are checked if they meet the minimum requirements. Here, the user organization uses lists of criteria which were defined before the RfP was sent out. Several workshops are performed by both parties in order to obtain more information and to clarify open issues. The ICT Service Providers can present their proposals or offers. The user organization often visits the ICT Service Providers' premises including data centers. This is the basis for the user organization to finally assess the proposals and to decide with whom to continue. The list of possible providers is reduced and a so-called "short-list" is created.

The so-called due diligence is executed with the ICT Service Providers on the short-list. This means that further audits are planned and conducted; several rounds of negotiations take place each concentrating on a specific topic; the handing over of the ICT service provisioning (called Transition) is planned and discussed, and last but not least both parties and their representatives become more acquainted with each other which is necessary because they may have to closely work together in the following years.

The contract is signed. Before, the user organization assessed all available information and discussed possible alternatives and effects of their proposed decision. Based on this the ICT Service Provider is selected. Of course, the general management takes this final decision not only the IT department. Refer to Fig. 60.

Now the selected ICT Service Provider starts managing the deal or contract in a different direction. ICT services, hardware and software are taken over from the customer and/or existing ICT is allocated to the customer. Sometimes, whole data centers and personnel are taken over. Usually, at least data needs to be migrated to the provider's premises. This is a critical period with respect to security because neither the existing security measures (old location) nor the new ones (target location) are in place during the "transport". When taking over ICT, the provider already starts to apply changes towards meeting the contractual expectations and the provider's internal standards. This brings the ICT from the Current Mode of Operation (CMO) to the CMO+ which means that changes were applied. Of course, this phase called Transition (Fig. 60) needs to be carefully planned and executed. The planning includes fall-back scenarios etc. since usually the ICT services are taken over while being used. Note that the representatives have changed on both sides. The "Deal management" has done its job which is now taken over by a "project team" which implements the ICT services and applies the changes according to the plan. But also the provider's Service Delivery Management (SDM) becomes active since ICT services are up and running and the ICT Service Provider took over the responsibility for Operations which is no longer project business. But further adaptations may follow in order to run the ICT services according to the provider's standards (and according to final agreements) which is often called Future Mode of Operation (FMO). Refer to Fig. 60.

As soon as the ICT services are operated under the responsibility of the ICT Service Provider, the Service Delivery Management (SDM) gets involved and the organization of the business changes. It is no longer project-related but built for continuous business though major changes may be performed in the future in form of projects embedded into the continuous Operations business. The ICT Service Provider must continue to provide transparency to the user organization. This includes reporting e.g. about security. Incidents (including security incidents) must be managed, in case of major incidents mostly in cooperation with the user organization. Finally, changes may be required as mentioned and explained above. Such changes may require changing the contract too. Other changes are covered by the contract. They are conducted according to the IT service management processes and practices and the Service Level Agreements (SLA) agreed upon in the original contract.

The structure of a typical IT outsourcing contract is shown in Fig. 61. It is essential that contracts define the ICT service including all maintenance activities as exact as possible despite the general problem of specifying an ICT service to be delivered in an "unknown" future environment which may come up with new circumstances, conditions, requirements, scenarios and the like.

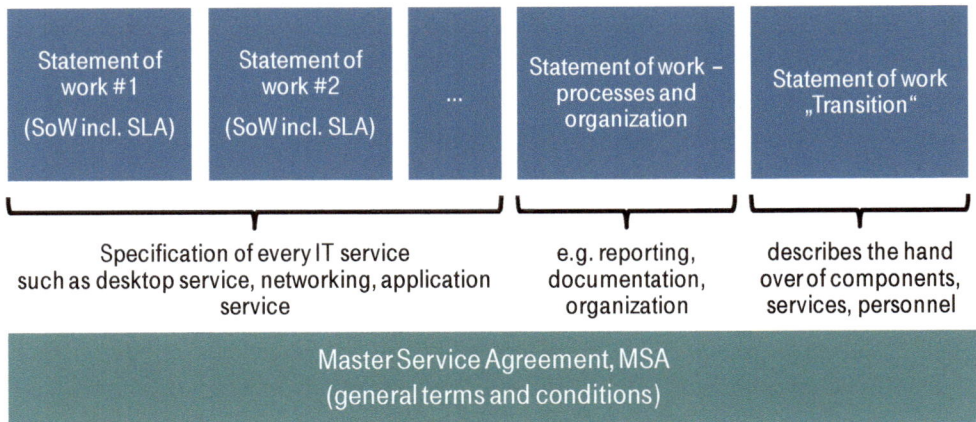

Fig. 61: Structure of large IT outsourcing contracts

An IT outsourcing contract can have hundreds of pages and more. Therefore, a structure is needed. Primarily, the ICT services need to be specified. If several different ICT services are purchased by the user organization, then the contract will comprise more than one part called "Statement of Work". Refer to Fig. 61. Each of these parts describes the core ICT service (functionality) but does also contain the related Service Level Agreement (SLA). The SLA specifies quality, availability and responsibilities. In most cases, common practices are applied e.g. for the IT service management. Also organizational issues such as contacts are common to all ICT services covered by the contract and specified in a Statement of Work. Hence, it makes sense to specify ICT-related common practices such as processes and organizational issues in one central Statement of Work. Refer to the figure. There is one specific work which is done only once: this is the Transition or migration of the ICT services from the current provider to the new provider. The work and its characteristics (quality etc.) are also specified in a separate Statement of Work as shown in the figure. Finally, there are general terms and conditions which are related to commercial matters such as reimbursement, rules for subcontracting etc. These clauses are incorporated into the so-called Master Service Agreement (MSA). All other clauses which not seem to fit into any Statement of Work are also put into the MSA.

The contract must also specify security. How is this managed? Refer to Fig. 62. The security requirements of the user organization must be collected, analyzed and clarified. They can be distributed amongst all sections of the contract. Note that such a complex document is developed by many people each specialized in a specific topic. There are procurement people involved, pure IT staff, compliance managers, IT managers, process and application managers, business units (the users' representatives) just to name a few. Some of them are aware to express their security requirements now. They choose the chapter they are responsible for. That's why security issues are usually distributed throughout all parts of the contract and perhaps also contained in documents that are only referred to as being contract-relevant. This is shown on the right-hand side in Fig. 62. Not only this, also legislation etc. is relevant with respect to security.

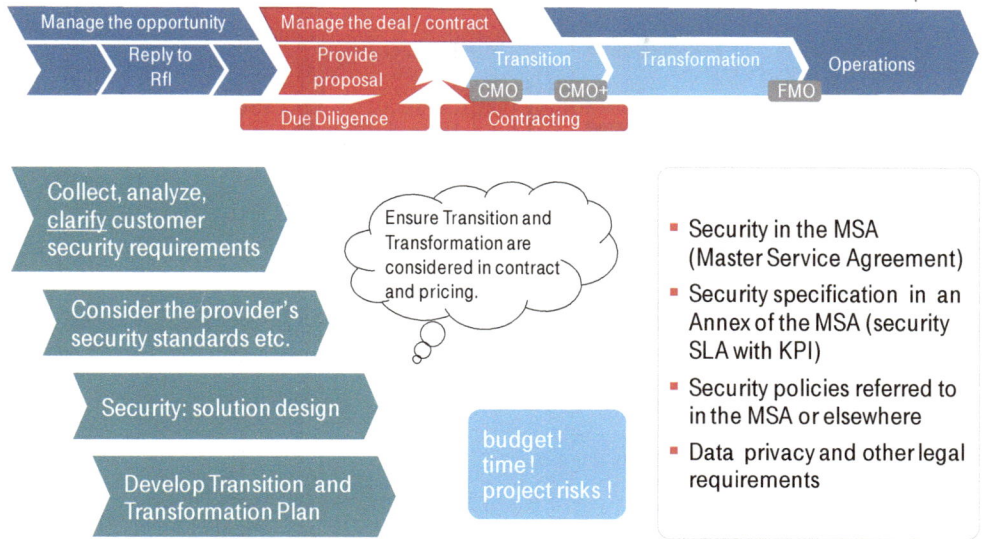

Fig. 62: Contract design and review during the phase Manage the deal

The ICT Service Provider must ensure that the provider's own security standards are considered. At least all specifications must go hand in hand with them. Based on both the user organization's security requirements and the provider's security standards, solutions are developed and specified. Refer to Fig. 62. The ICT services must be migrated into the hand of the ICT Service Provider and adaptations are required in most cases. This is the subject of the phases Transition and Transformation which start after signing the contract. The ICT Service Provider must plan all these activities and consider all costs related to these activities. A real challenge, especially for the security experts, is shown in two light blue rounded rectangles in the figure: Managing the deal cannot last long. There are costs for managing the deal because people are kept busy. And it's not clear for the ICT Service Provider that the contract is signed while working on it. Time is another criterion. There are fixed times and the next project is knocking on the door. Risks are number three. Usually project risks are considered more important than security risks later in Operations. Losing the deal appears more serious than having a few security incidents or a longer discussion some month from now. This makes it hard to ensure that the contract is, also with respect to security, neither vague nor ambiguous but very specific and the provider is able to fulfill it.

Well-structured and well-designed security specifications (such as the ESARIS security measures) help to achieve this. But a method for verifying the fulfillment of the user's requirements is required. This is described in the next section.

8.3   Assurance for customers

Introduction and summary: User organizations require evidence that their requirements are fulfilled when purchasing ICT services from a third party. They need such information for their own risk management and as evidence for their own customers and auditors. However, the security measures protecting the ICT services are implemented by the ICT Service Provider. In large IT outsourcing situations, user organizations use tendering for getting information about the ICT services and their security. It is up to the ICT Service Provider to provide assurance and demonstrate that the user's security requirements are met. The contractual evidence is only one element of the assurance required. The provider must demonstrate fulfillment of the requirements also at run time. This is called operational evidence here. Both aspects are covered by the *ESARIS Fulfillment Model* and described in detail in the following.

8.3.1   Contractual evidence

The *ESARIS Fulfillment Model* (or: *ESARIS Customer Fulfillment Model*) describes a method to demonstrate that the customer's security requirements are met and how. Though the method or procedure looks very straightforward and may be simple, it is important to formalize it: The assessment of customer requirements and the mapping to existing security measures is the most important issue in terms of security in the relation between the user organization and its ICT Service Provider. Moreover, it is not easy to perform this method or procedure in big IT outsourcing deals in practice.

Verifying the fulfillment on a contractual level comprises several steps. The process comprises

- the collection of existing material (step 1),
- the identification of relevant ESARIS security measures (step 2), and
- the requirements matching (step 3),
- the treatment of possible differences (step 4).

User organizations (customers) express their security requirements on a different level of detail. More precise, the security requirements have different scope and therefore different level of abstraction and detail. This is shown in Fig. 63. Users provide general policies (case a). In this case, ESARIS concepts may provide the answer provided that the ICT Service Provider follows them. User organizations often refer to security standards or industry guidelines such as ISO/IEC 27002 [46] or guidelines of the Cloud Security Alliance[47] (case b). ICT Service Providers are recommended to develop a comparison between such sets of requirements and their

---

[46] ISO/IEC 27002 – Information technology – Security techniques – Code of practice for information security management, 2013 [6]

[47] Cloud Security Alliance (CSA): Security Guidance; Version 3.0, Nov. 2011 [31]

own ESARIS security standards. Refer to the *Endorsement Framework for ESARIS* described in Sect. 2.1. Then such a mapping can be reused to show the fulfillment. Users also require e.g. the existence of a security incident handling process (case c). In such cases, the reference to an *ICT Security Standard* (Level 4) would be sufficient. Most requirements are more specific (case d). An answer can be given using specific security measures from the *ICT Security Standards* (Level 4).

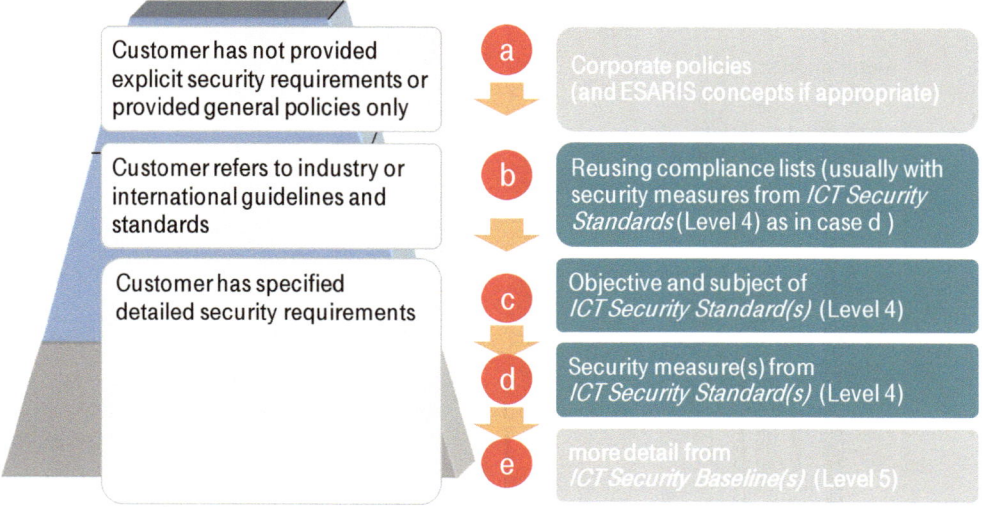

Fig. 63: Security requirements in contracts feature different level of detail

Sometimes even more detailed requirements find their way into the contract draft (case e). In the following it is assumed that user organization's requirements are expressed with a level of detail that corresponds to the ESARIS security measures stipulated in the *ICT Security Standards*. If not, the second step is modified and other types of ESARIS security standards are brought in.[48]

Step 1: The collection of existing material is the starting point and shown in Fig. 64 above. The available material to be collected comprises:

- The customer's requirements Ⓐ are analyzed first. They need to be collected, reviewed and documented. In Fig. 64 these requirements are schematically represented by R1 through R5 and red arrows. They point to a chess board or matrix that will later be used to verify if appropriate measures (C1 – C7) are in place that are suitable to meet the customer's requirements.

- Then there are the security measures in 31 *ICT Security Standards* Ⓑ. These standards (Level 4) are organized in the *ESARIS Security Taxonomy* which is also shown in the figure. The *ICT Security Baselines* Ⓒ may also be required selectively. They refine the security measures in the *ICT Security Standards* (Lev-

---

[48] Important: Note that this model is developed for complex ICT services and high volume contracts. Other cases might be treated less formal.

el 4). The *ICT Security Baselines* (Level 5) instruct people how to implement the security measures (from Level 4) and how to act during development, implementation and operations. They may provide helpful background if required.

- The last important input is the specification ⒟ of the ICT service that is under consideration. The nature and scope of the ICT service determines which ESARIS security standards are relevant.

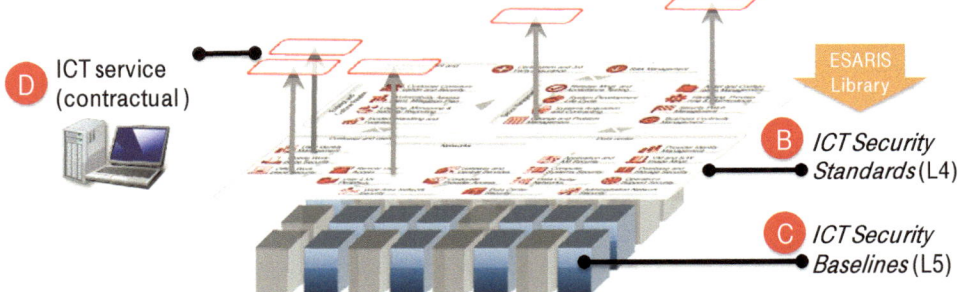

Fig. 64: ESARIS Fulfillment Model, collection and analysis of material

This inventory is important and builds the basis for the next steps.

Step 2: The identification of relevant ESARIS security measures is also shown in Fig. 64. The *ESARIS Security Taxonomy* (and its *ICT Security Standards* ⒝) are matched to the ICT service ⒟. A security standard is relevant if the ICT Service Provider is responsible for this part. The concept called *Provider Scope of Control* is used for the selection. The tasks are already described in Sect. 4.5 but summarized here for the sake of convenience:

- The ICT service (being delivered or planned to be delivered to the customer) is analyzed. Based on the ICT service specification the relevant *ICT Security Standards* are identified. In many cases it is sufficient to work with the *ESARIS Security Taxonomy* only. An *ICT Security Standard* is selected if the ICT Service Provider is responsible for the corresponding technology or IT service management activities.

- Then the division of labor between the provider and the customer is analyzed in more detail. In order to provide final clarity it can be necessary to take more contractual details into account. It may then be necessary to remove single security measures from the list because the customer is responsible for them.

The resulting set of relevant security measures (Ⓔ in Fig. 65) is used in the next step.

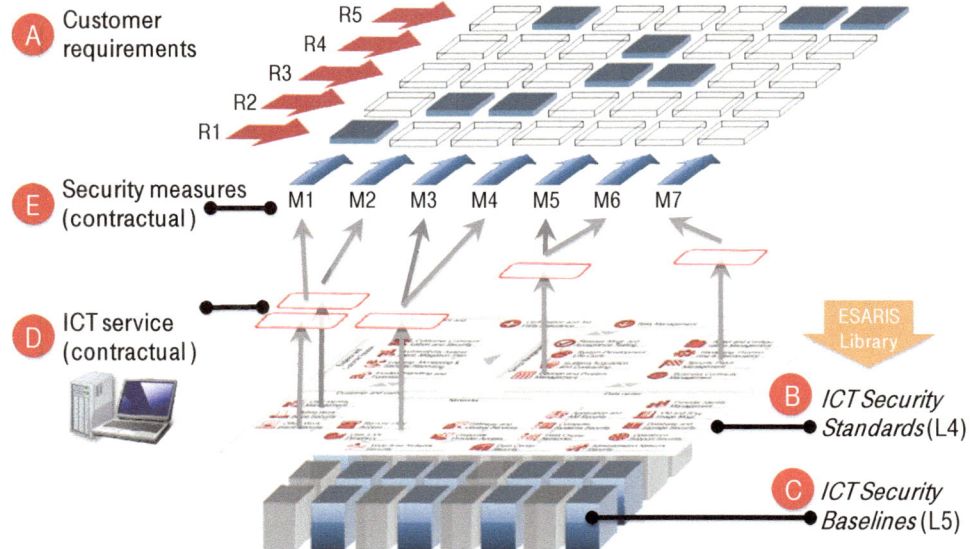

Fig. 65: ESARIS Fulfillment Model, selection of security measures and matching

Step 3: Now the security measures (Ⓔ) from the ESARIS security standards are assigned to the customer's requirements Ⓐ. Refer to Fig. 65. Then it is verified if the latter are actually met. This runs as follows:

- The customer's security requirements are analyzed one after the other. For each of them one or more relevant security measures (M1 through M7 in the figure) are identified which are suitable to meet the customer's requirements. (Security measures that do not have any counterpart on the requirement's side may be left out at this point or later.)

- It may be required to have more than one security measure to meet one requirement (for instance M2 and M3 to meet R2). In can also happen that a security measure (for instance M4) serves two requirements (R3 and R4 in Fig. 65).

- It is checked if the security measures are actually implemented. This is done by inspecting the internal *ESARIS Attainment Statements* (provided in form of Aces). Aces are the result of the "Attainment" process. Refer to the next Fig. 66 which shows the Aces.

- The result Ⓕ is specified. Three results are possible: accordance, difference and no counterpart found.

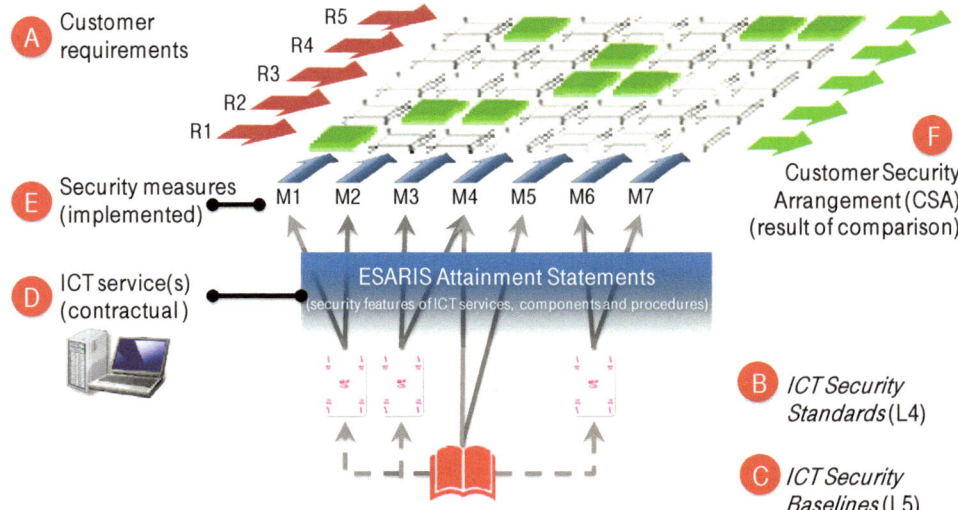

Fig. 66: ESARIS Fulfillment Model, verification of matching

Step 4: The treatment of possible differences and open issues is the last step:

- In case that not all customer requirements are fulfilled, the following solutions are considered: a) minor extensions, additions or modifications to existing security measures or b) specification of new or considerably modified security measures. c) The customer may also realize that the provider's security measures provide appropriate protection so that no further action is needed. In case of changes, the resulting security measures need to be verified again to see if the open issues have been resolved.

- If the customized solution or the new solution is (expected to be) required for multiple customers or contracts, its specification may become a part of an updated *ICT Security Standard* (Level 4) or *ICT Security Baseline* (Level 5). The change may be initiated through a formal change request.

- In the last step, the result is summarized. This requires performing a synopsis. The result of the analysis (including solutions for possible differences) is provided in form of a so-called *Customer Security Arrangement (CSA)* (often also called customer security concept).

The *Customer Security Arrangement (CSA)* is a major outcome of this analysis. The CSA will be developed by the ICT Service Provider but should be reviewed and accepted by the user organization. Moreover, a CSA can be used as a contractual document and signed by security officials of both parties. The first version of the *Customer Security Arrangement (CSA)* is developed when the proposal or draft contract is developed. It can be updated during Transition and Transformation. Further changes during Operations should also be documented in form of the CSA. The identification of possible differences between the user organization's security requirements and the security measures of the ICT Service Provider should, however, already take place in the "Manage the Deal" phase to spot open requirements as early as possible. The *Customer Security Arrangement (CSA)* can then also be used to track the remediation of gaps.

8.3.2 Operational evidence

The above method of comparing requirements from customers with implemented ESARIS security measures may flatter to deceive that this is about design only. It is not. The ESARIS security measures are designed in a way that they cover the verification if security features are still correctly effective and corrections are made if necessary. To this end, they additionally ensure that the necessary information is being generated and used.

The term operational evidence shall summarize all means which ensure that security measures are not only designed in an appropriate way but also implemented, used, maintained and repaired during Operations. The ESARIS security measures are designed in a way that this is also covered

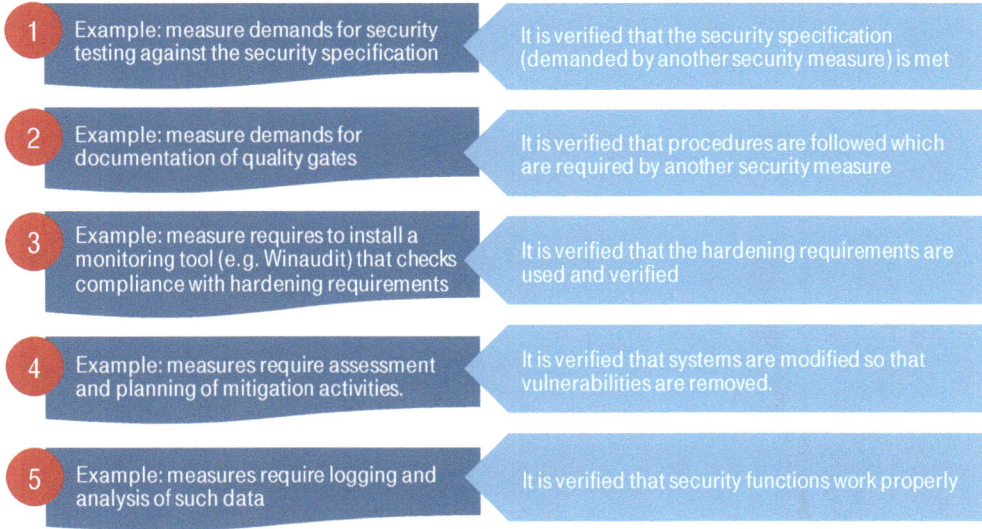

Fig. 67: Measures provide evidence about implementation of others (examples)

Fig. 67 shows the principle using five more general examples:

- ESARIS security measures require security testing. This directly provides operational evidence about the correct operation of other security measures which are tested. The same is achieved by performing audits, evaluations etc.

- ESARIS security measures provide instructions for people to implement ESARIS security measures as well as instructions for others to verify that the implementation is correct. Quality gates are examples which provide operational evidence, e.g. in the form of records.

- ESARIS security measures require IT components to be checked in order to identify vulnerabilities caused by using outdated or unpatched software versions and by wrong configurations. The operational evidence that such vulnerabilities do not exist is provided by using appropriate monitoring tools such as system scanners. The scanners additionally demonstrate if for example provisioning, hardening and patching were correctly carried out.

- ESARIS security measures require the assessment and planning of mitigation activities. They are performed by means of changes organized through the Change Management process. The latter requires planning including a specification of the change as well as verification of the correct execution. In this way operational evidence is given that the target was actually modified so that mitigation has successfully been performed and vulnerabilities are removed.

- ESARIS security measures require logging and the analysis of such data. Log data provide operational evidence whether security functions work properly.

Fig. 68 shows again Level 4 and Level 5 of the ESARIS security standards. The important point here is that there are two types of ESARIS security measures (Level 4, *ESARIS Orchestration Layer*).

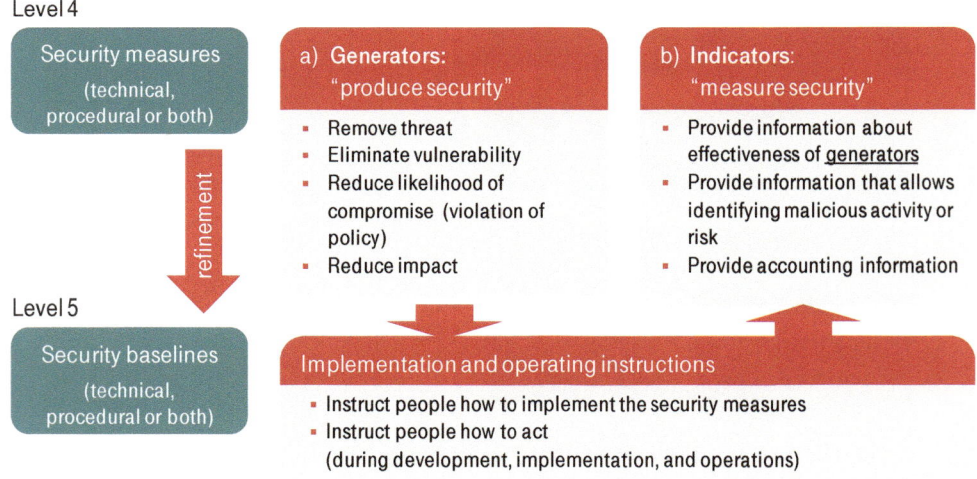

Fig. 68: Measures provide evidence about implementation of others (indicators)

The "generators" actually "produce security" by actively hindering or preventing a compromise of security policies. They are lowering a risk by
- removing a threat (e.g. the technical architecture eliminates a threat scenario),
- eliminating a vulnerability (e.g. addition of a security feature),
- reducing the likelihood of a breach (e.g. strengthening of a security feature), or
- reducing the impact (e.g. limit the scope of an attack by separating components).

The "indicators" (Fig. 68) are not hindering or preventing any attack or accidental security breach. They are just "measuring security". They provide the basis for specific "generators" (organizational and technical measures) to work. The "indicators"

- provide information about the effectiveness of "generators",
  (For example, security testing verifies existence and functionality of security functions.)
- provide information in order to identify malicious activity or risk,
  (For example, log data allow to apply corrections.)
- provide accounting information.
  (For example, records about passing quality gates and inspection of log data collect evidence about security-relevant activities.)

It is the goal and methodology of ESARIS to specify all means required to achieve an appropriate level of security in form of ESARIS security measures. The only thing which is assumed and not specified by means of security measures is that the ICT Service Provider is capable of implementing and maintaining the ESARIS security measures. E.g., the company must have a Security Management organization and processes. These means are part of the *ESARIS Enforcement Framework* which comprises the Information Security Management System (ISMS) which is not separately specified in ESARIS. Hence user organizations can thoroughly rely on agreed security measures provided that the "indicators" and their outcome are appropriately used.

The *ESARIS Fulfillment Model* combines contractual evidence and operational evidence. The comparison between the user organization's security requirements and the built-in security measures is conducted by the ICT Service Provider, documented in form of a *Customer Security Arrangement (CSA)* and agreed upon between the two parties. This is embedded in the phases of IT outsourcing while the ICT Service Provider cares for transparency and provides interfaces and possibilities for interaction. The design and structure of the ESARIS security measures shall ensure that all relevant security aspects are covered appropriately.

8.3.3   Contractual and other changes

It has been mentioned that the *Customer Security Arrangement (CSA)* is continuously kept up-to-date so that it reflects the current status of compliance with the user organization's security requirements at any time. Obviously, if the customer changes its security requirements the current CSA is possibly invalidated. But there are two other types of changes which may put a question mark on it:

- Change of ESARIS security standards and
- Change of technology or of process activities related to the contracted ICT service.

It is now examined how these types of changes relate to the CSA and the contract. This examination is performed based on Fig. 69. The figure has three layers: the

ESARIS security standards on the bottom, the ICT service(s) (implementation) above them and the CSA and the contract on the top.

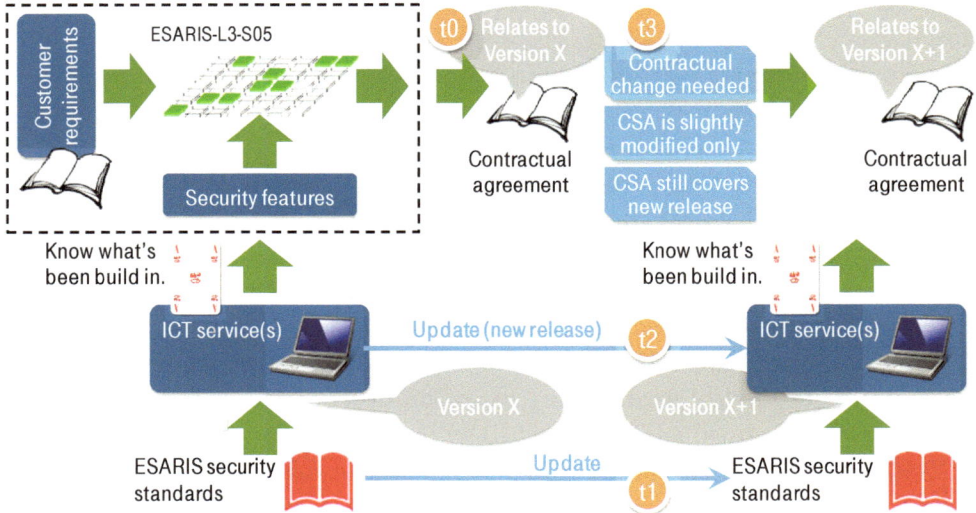

Fig. 69: Contractual agreements and treatment of changes

Now possible changes are tracked and their effect is studied.

- To recap, the ESARIS security standards are used as design pattern for delivering secure ICT services (bottom left of Fig. 69). The standards have a version and the ICT services are considered to be of version X. They are assessed according to the *ESARIS Attainment Model* and an Ace is created which tells if and to what extent the ICT service is compliant with the relevant ESARIS security standards. Then the *ESARIS Fulfillment Model* is applied in a deal with a customer. It is evaluated if the implemented security measures fulfill the customer's security requirements. The result is documented in form of a *Customer Security Arrangement (CSA)* shown as the contractual agreement in the figure. Version X is also assigned to it because all documents and the ICT service in the left column of Fig. 69 belong to the same time period denoted by t0 in the figure.
- Now the time is getting on to t1 and the first change occurs. An ESARIS security standard is changed. Refer to the bottom in the figure. It is important to understand that there is no effect on the customer's business, ICT or level of protection. The current *Customer Security Arrangement (CSA)* still reflects the actual situation since it shows if and to what extent the currently delivered ICT service meets the customer's security requirements.
- In time t2 a new release of the ICT service is deployed which has now version X+1. This is the same version as that of the ESARIS security standard since the most recent version of the latter was used for the new release. The *ESARIS Attainment Statement* in form of the Ace is updated for this new version.

- In time t3 this new release of the ICT service (version X+1) shall now be provided to the customer. As a result the existing *Customer Security Arrangement (CSA)* (Version X) is no longer valid. Three cases are possible leading to three different results.
  - It turns out that the CSA still covers the new release of the ICT service described by the new Ace (version X+1). In this case, the CSA can easily be updated by updating versions only. There is no reason for discussions, contractual negotiations and the like.
  - The CSA must only slightly be modified since the fulfillment of the customer's security requirements is not affected though the security measures of the ICT service were modified or changed. Again there is no reason for discussions, contractual negotiations and the like.
  - In case that a new analysis and a comparison between the customer's security requirements and the security measures of the ICT service (version X+1) reveal new differences, both parties have to discuss possible impacts and solutions. In other words, the process of discussing, negotiating and agreeing starts again. The result is a new *Customer Security Arrangement (CSA)* (Version X+1) and an updated contractual agreement.

This examination showed that no change except the planned deployment of a new ICT release (new version of the ICT service) requires immediate action with respect to the contract. Although, it is common practice that new releases are announced to customers and possible effects on contracts and business are discussed and resolved in advance.

Nevertheless, there is another aspect. The ESARIS security standards are not only used for designs which have an effect on real ICT services later when actually being deployed. ESARIS security standards are also used by IT personnel as guidance for their day-to-day activities. Only exceptionally, they will use different versions of guidance for different versions of ICT services and customer contracts. In general, they are told to use the most recent standard filed in the central repository. This underlines the necessity to keep the security measures used in contractual agreements as stable as possible. As a consequence they should not contain implementation details because the latter tend to change more frequent than the major security achievement. In other words, the implementation should not be the subject-matter of a contract whereas the security achievements (and the implementation independent specification of the security measures) shall. Both parties must have an interest to manage contractual changes only if considerable changes with a real impact need to be considered. Otherwise there are costs at both sides with actually no real gain.

9 Flexibility – managing the supplier network

Introduction and summary: ICT Service Providers deliver ICT services to customers but does not produce all of its parts by themselves. Instead, products and services are purchased from other companies called 3rd parties (Sect. 9.1). These products and services are then integrated and become part of the ICT service delivered to customers. The ICT Service Provider is still responsible for the complete ICT service. Hence, procedures must be put in place to ensure that the ESARIS security standards are met so that the security requirements of the customers can be fulfilled. The *ESARIS Third Party Integration Model* allows managing external suppliers or partners of the ICT Service Provider, more specifically the security of products and services they are providing. It extends ESARIS to the whole supplier network. The link is established by one of the 31 *ICT Security Standards* (namely, *Systems Acquisition and Contracting, SAC*). The *ESARIS Third Party Integration Model* describes how this standard is applied in practice. Thereby the *ESARIS Attainment Model* is used. The *ESARIS Security Taxonomy* is the basis since one of its design principles is "aligned with IT production: organized in realms that match with production units" (Sect. 9.2).

9.1 Roles and types of suppliers

Introduction and summary: It is useful to have some insight in the structure of the IT industry. There are different types of companies each being specialized to provide a specific range of products or services. This forms the basis for understanding the importance of managing security in the supplier network on the one hand and for getting aware of the complexity of such an undertaking on the other hand.

The industrialization of IT is going on and has intensified during the recent years. As a result, the IT industry is highly specialized and characterized by a high degree of division of labor and by intensive networking and interdependencies between companies working together in a global supplier network. Though there are very large IT companies even those are specialized. They are not doing everything; their vertical range of manufacture is limited. Instead, several services and also hardware and software are purchased from other companies and then integrated in order to create an ICT service for the customer. On the left-hand side of Fig. 70 examples for such specialized roles in the supplier network are shown. Obviously, there are manufacturers or vendors of hardware and software. Note that the production of hardware and sometimes of software as well is also distributed amongst many participants (not shown in the figure). Many hardware and software vendors do not sell their products directly but use resellers for this purpose. Then there are system integrators (see figure) which often develop complex software systems but also combine many hardware and software components to complex systems. The term "provider" in the figure primarily relates to companies which actually operate such systems in order to provide ICT services to user organizations or other customers. Currently the market is split in most cases between those companies providing network services (TC) and others providing IT services. This differentiation was not important till now so that the term ICT Service Provider was exclusively used. Finally, there are broker and reseller which concentrate on offering services produced by other companies as well as consulting companies and analysts. This picture is not complete but provides some insight in the division of labor in modern ICT provisioning and the organization of today's supplier networks.

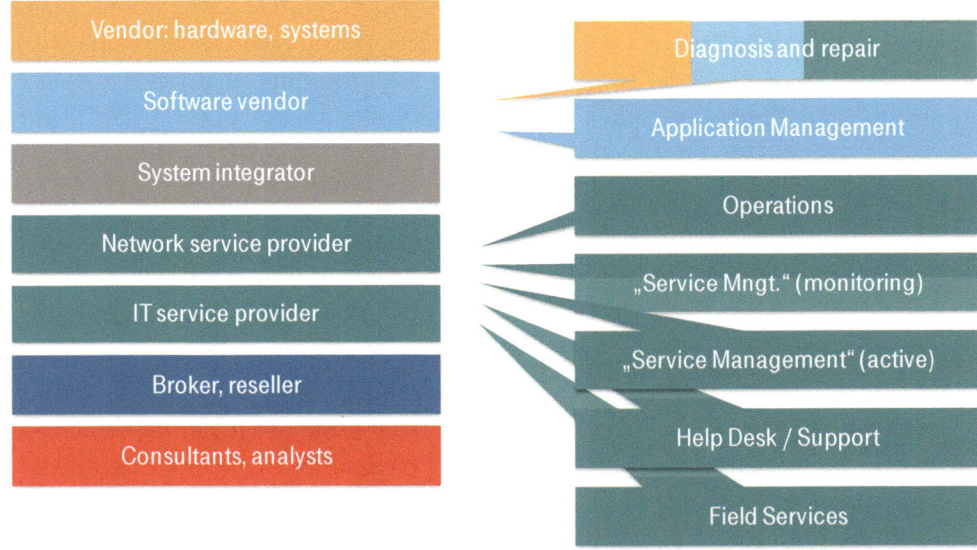

Fig. 70: Participants in supplier networks (left) and selected services (right)

The right-hand side of Fig. 70 shows examples of services being used in this context. Today hardware and some systems are so complex that the ICT Service Provider is not able to manage it. The vendors also learned that they can deliver their systems as a managed service and no longer as a product that is basically managed by the ICT Service Provider though the latter would also fall back upon the vendor in case of issues relating to second or third level support. Storage systems, for example, are often offered "as-a-Service". The ICT Service Provider purchases the "Storage as-a-Service" from the manufacturer that is now fully responsible for many IT service management activities relating to the storage system. Typical examples are diagnosis and repair services. This is quite more than software for which the vendor delivers updates and patches. The supplier has direct access to the storage system in the infrastructure of the ICT Service Provider. The same holds for large networks. Supplier of equipment and services for networks and data center infrastructures belong to the greatest corporations in the IT industry. Another activity which can often not be performed by the ICT Service Provider itself is application management. Application management (or application life-cycle management) covers the definition and update of demands, development, integration, testing, release and the maintenance of the software till its end of life. It also includes adaptation necessary to increase performance in a specific infrastructure and use case and maybe many more. The other activities (or supporting services) mentioned on the right-hand side of Fig. 70 can be conducted by the ICT Service Provider in many cases. Obviously, the ICT Service Provider will not give up Operations because this is its core business. But other services (see figure) may be candidates for being delegated to suppliers.

It is rather impossible to draw a map of a "typical" supply chain in the IT industry that considers most business relations. Nevertheless, Fig. 71 shows a decomposition of computing, workplace and network services (red boxes) into typical services and components which are or may be provided by other companies than the ICT Service Provider being the primary contracting party of the user organization (customer; shown as dark grey box). The figure shall mainly demonstrate that the supply chain is complex and composed of multiple tiers.

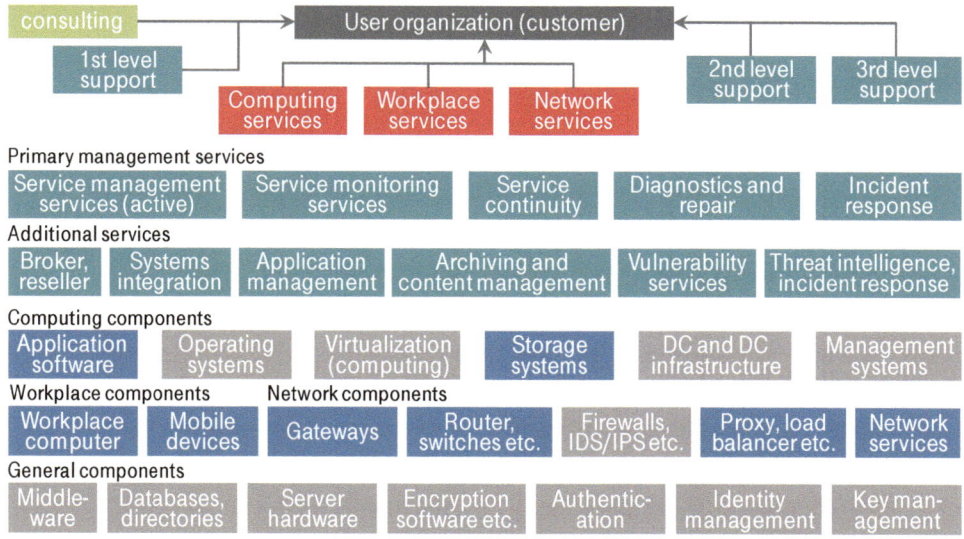

Fig. 71: Services and components of the IT industry (illustrative)

The ICT services primarily used by the user organization (shown as red boxes in Fig. 71) are subject to upkeep and maintenance. Such management services (green boxes) can be performed by the ICT Service Provider or by other service providers (or even by the user organization itself). Moreover, it is possible that the user organization purchases additional management services (also shown in green) which are more likely provided by another company than the primary ICT Service Provider. The lower half of the figure shows several business areas in which many companies provide numerous hardware and software components and systems; often together with related maintenance services. For example, today's storage systems are made available "as-a-Service" which means that the manufacturer also provides IT service management services in addition to diagnostics and repair services. The provisioning of ICT services is characterized by a high degree of division of labor; the IT industry comprises highly specialized companies. There are many interdependencies between them in the supplier network. Hence, it is very important to deal with these relations. Every component, technology or service, may guarantee an appropriate level of security or even have vulnerabilities. The chain is only as strong as its weakest link. Eventually, it is the ICT Service Provider being responsible for all ICT services according to the contract with the user organization regardless if the services and components are produced by the ICT Service Provider or by one of its subcontractors.

9.2   Third party integration model

Introduction and summary: The *ESARIS Third Party Integration Model* allows managing external suppliers or partners of the ICT Service Provider, more specifically the security of products and services they are providing. The *ESARIS Third Party Integration Model* describes how the 31 *ICT Security Standard*s are applied in the relationship between the supplier and the ICT Service Provider. The *ICT Security Standard - Systems Acquisition and Contracting (SAC)* defines the sequence of actions for managing third-party products and services. The modularity of ESARIS and the methodology *Provider Scope of Control* play a major role too. The model also works within a multi-tier supplier network.

Today's IT industry consists of numerous companies each being specialized in a specific manner. Especially ICT Service Providers use products or services from other companies. It is therefore necessary to open the ESARIS models so that suppliers and their products and services are also covered. It is worth mentioning that the ICT Service Provider is the contract partner for the user organization and therefore responsible for the composite ICT services including all its constituents. So, the situation is as follows:

- The ICT Service Provider purchases products and services from 3rd parties (suppliers).
- These third-party products and services are integrated into ICT services of the ICT Service Provider.
- The composite ICT services are delivered to customers.
- The ICT Service Provider is responsible for the composite ICT services including the 3rd party products and services.

This is shown in Fig. 72. It shows how the ESARIS security standards are used and how the *ESARIS Security Taxonomy* supports the decomposition of the ICT service and the security standards. The composition is managed by means of the *ESARIS Attainment Model*.

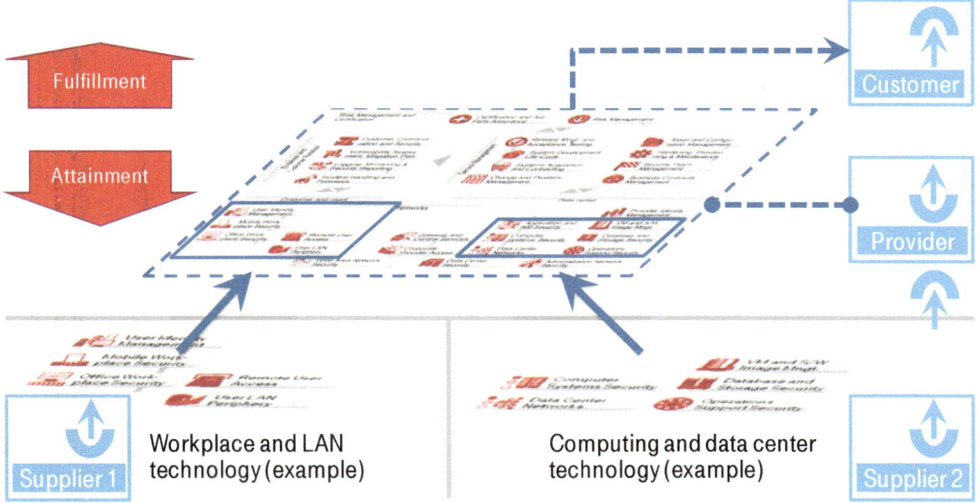

Fig. 72: Supply chain management and division of labor

With respect to security, the ICT Service Provider (central right in Fig. 72) is responsible for all relevant areas in the *ESARIS Security Taxonomy*. But some ICT services relating to specific areas are "outsourced" by the ICT Service Provider to the Supplier 1 and Supplier 2, respectively. Refer to Fig. 72.

To manage the relations between the ICT Service Provider and the two suppliers the following is needed:

▪ The ICT Service Provider must define security requirements for the third-party products and services. To this end, the ESARIS security standards are used.

▪ The ICT Service Provider keeps records that/if the 3rd party products and services are compliant with the relevant ESARIS security standards.

▪ This means that third parties are treated similar to an internal delivery unit except for the fact that they are completely independent companies.

This is detailed in Fig. 73. The required elements of the *ESARIS Third Party Integration Model* are shown on the left-hand side, the sources on the right-hand side.

▪ There is an *ICT Security Standard* (area in the *ESARIS Security* Taxonomy) which defines security measures for managing the relationship with partners/suppliers and the security of the products/services. This standard is named *Systems Acquisition and Contracting (SAC)*.

▪ The *ESARIS Security Taxonomy* is structured in a way that it provides means to recur using the *ESARIS security measures* for 3rd party products and services and not just for the primary ICT Service Provider of the customer.

▪ The ICT Service Provider needs to verify if the third-party products and services are actually compliant with the ESARIS security measures and to document the result. This is achieved by using the *ESARIS Attainment Model* namely the concept of Aces (Chapter 7.3).

- Third-party products and services become part of a composite ICT service which is then delivered to a customer of the ICT Service Provider. A composition model is required for integrating internal and third-party products/services. This is also part of the *ESARIS Attainment Model* which is reused for managing supplier networks.

■ ESARIS security measures for the treatment of partners/suppliers and their products/services	■ Defined in the *ICT Security Standard – Systems Acquisition and Contracting (SAC)* (ESARIS-L4-S26)
■ Means to recur using ESARIS security measures: now for the third party products/services	■ Built in into the *ESARIS Security Taxonomy* (the Taxonomy is aligned with the organization of the supply chain)
■ Method to measure and document compliance with the ESARIS security measures	■ Used from the *ESARIS Attainment Model* (*Aces*)
■ Composition model to integrate internal and 3rd party products/services	■ Used from the *ESARIS Attainment Model*

Fig. 73: Elements of the ESARIS Third Party Integration Model.

It is important that the *ESARIS Third Party Integration Model* supports multiple stages in the supply chain and supports supplier networks as well. This is shown in Fig. 74:

- A cluster of areas in the *ESARIS Security Taxonomy* can be split into smaller sets (decomposition). In the example, the Supplier 1 uses deliverables from both Supplier 2 and Supplier 3 in order to deliver an ICT service to the next in the supply chain (which is the Provider 1 in the figure).

- Not only clusters can be split, *ICT Security Standards* can be assigned individually and sets of ESARIS security measures can also be assigned to a supplier or the service/product being provided. This is possible due to the rigorous modularization in Level 4 of the *Hierarchy of Security Standards*.

- Supplier networks are supported since all suppliers can deliver both to Provider 1 and Provider 2. (The division of labor may differ.) This works well if the same *ESARIS Security Taxonomy* with the same or similar ESARIS security measures is used. Note that the support of supplier networks requires standardization as introduced through ESARIS.

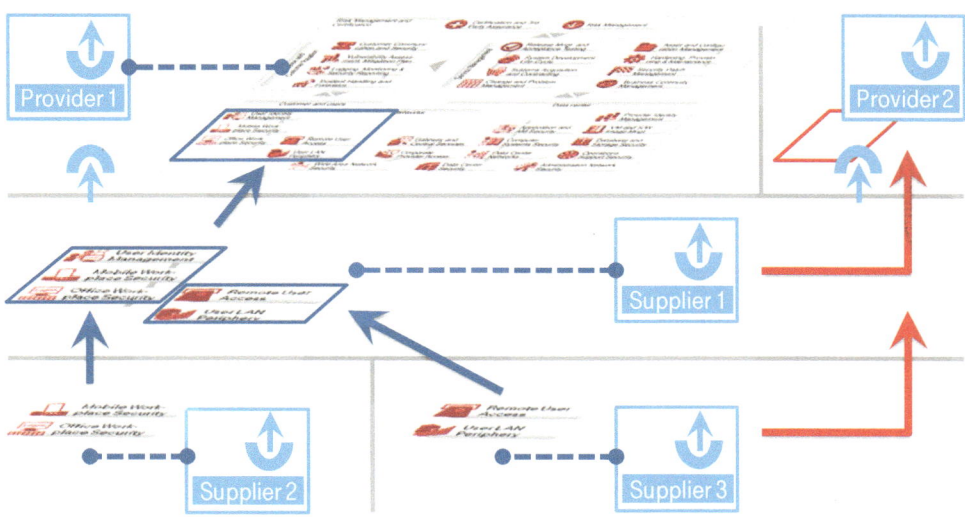

Fig. 74: Supply chain management (multi-staged)

A product or service is provided by a supplier or partner of the ICT Service Provider. The ICT Service Provider integrates them, provides core services and delivers the composite ICT service to the user organization. Reimbursement goes the other way around. The customer pays the ICT Service Provider and the latter pays the supplier. Obviously, the customer sets requirements that need to be fulfilled by the ICT Service Provider. The same happens on the next level. The ICT Service Provider sets the requirements for the product or service bought from the 3rd party product vendor or service provider. Requirements are made explicit and agreed upon in a contract. To this end, the ICT Service Provider (now the customer) must elaborate a list of requirements which need to be met by the product or service from the 3rd party (now the provider). This document is called "Product Requirements Document (PRD)" in the following.

The ICT Service Provider uses ESARIS security standards in order to produce secure ICT services which reduce risks for both the provider and its customers to an acceptable level. Consequently, the ESARIS security standards should also be used when it comes to securing third-party components and services. In both cases, namely the security measures from the *ICT Security Standards* (Level 4) are used as "directives" for the delivering party (refer to Sect. 8.3).

There is a little difference between the usage of ESARIS security standards internally (ICT Service Provider) and for third-party products and services (supplier). The ICT Service Provider has both the *ICT Security Standards* (Level 4) and the *ICT Security Baselines* (Level 5). Whereas the *ICT Security Standards* (Level 4) are communicated, the *ICT Security Baselines* (Level 5) are internal documents that are considered to be intellectual property. Not only that these documents are confidential and not given to external parties, suppliers or partners are independent companies that are fully responsible for the products and services they are producing. The products and services are designed following standards of the supplier. Hence, only the *ICT Security Standards* (Level 4, *ESARIS Orchestration Layer*) which are implementation-independent can be used as "requirements".

The development of the "Product Requirements Document (PRD)" is shown in Fig. 75. There is an *ICT Security Standard* that specifies how an ICT Service Provider should manage suppliers and third-party products and services. This standard, *Systems Acquisition and Contracting (SAC)*, specifies security measures as shown on the upper left in the figure.

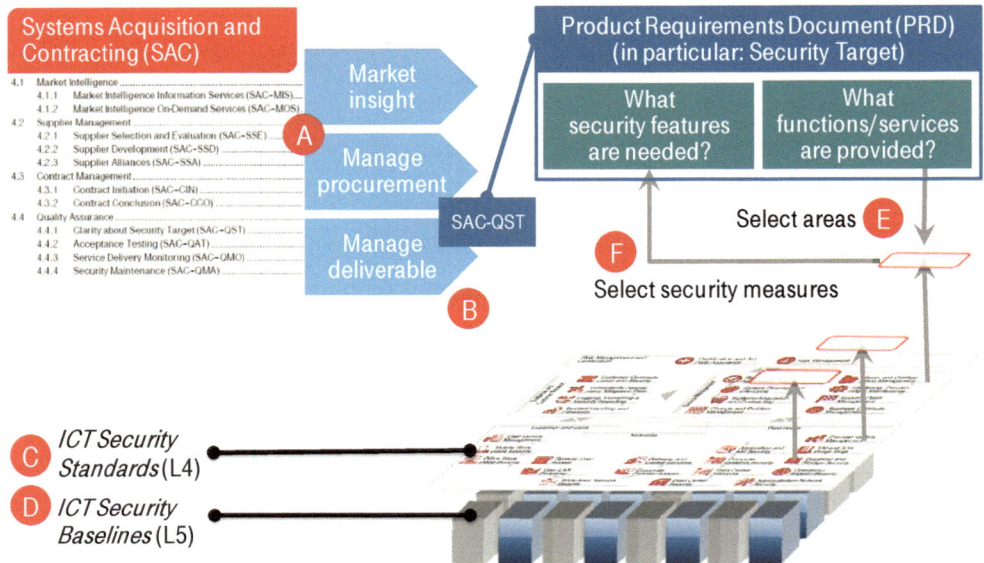

Fig. 75: Development of the Product Requirements Document (PRD)

The security measures described in this standard are independent from the service, system or product being procured. They comprise security measures relating to market analysis as well as supplier and procurement management Ⓐ:

- Preparatory, continuous activities such as market research that includes investigations of demands, technologies, products, and vendors,

- Activities of supplier management which help to evaluate, select and develop suppliers. The latter may include partner programs set up to develop and intensify the cooperation between the ICT Service Provider and the suppliers in order to improve the gain from such a relationship,

- Activities around contracting which includes the preparatory tasks as well as the initiation and the conclusion of contracts. The business relationship is maintained through its life-cycle here.

The security measures defined in this *ICT Security Standard* have to be appropriately considered in all stages of procurement and use of the procured service or product. All security measures are defined to minimize risks for both the ICT Service

Provider and its customers. Uncertainty and ambiguity can leave areas not being considered with care and secured as expected. Managing the relation with suppliers and closing contracts following strict rules does not mean to mistrust. All security measures are safeguards to raise reliability and transparency.

The security standard *Systems Acquisition and Contracting (SAC)* also describes security measures relating to the services and products being purchased or otherwise obtained from a supplier Ⓑ (refer to Fig. 75) including:

- Definition of a Product Requirements Document (PRD) (highlighted with the abbreviation SAC-QST in the figure) as well as

- Activities of quality inspection, in particular in the form of acceptance testing.

The PRD ensures that mandatory security features of the third-party service or product are made explicit. With respect to security, it is the basis for the business between the two parties. Strictly speaking, the specification of security features ("Security Target") is only one part of an overall "Product Requirement Document (PRD)" since security is only one feature amongst others.

But how is such a Product Requirements Document (PRD) being developed? This is very straightforward since all required methodologies have already been described in this book. The definition of the PRD or of the Security Target contained therein shall be based on ESARIS security measures from *ICT Security Standards* Ⓒ (Level 4). As already mentioned *ICT Security Baselines* Ⓓ cannot be used. Now the method *Provider Scope of Control* (Sect. 4.5) is used again in order to identify the security measures relevant for the service or product to be purchased. First of all, the product or service needs to be understood. What are the functions and services being provided? Then the relevant *ICT Security Standards* Ⓔ can be selected. By analyzing the deliverable from the third party in more detail the individual ESARIS security measures Ⓕ are extracted that are to be used for the Security Target specification in the PRD.

Note that this procedure is a little bit more complicated. But in fact it runs very similar to the one described in very detail about managing the internal supply chain with the ICT Service Provider with the *ESARIS Attainment Model* (Sect. 7.3). The contractual relation is managed by means of a Product Requirements Document (PRD) which contains the Security Target specification using ESARIS security measures.[49]

---

[49] Contractual relations are subject to the *ESARIS Fulfillment Model* so that some ideas are borrowed from this model too: The supplier must confirm that the Product Requirements Document (PRD) with the Security Target specification is met. This relates to the "contractual evidence" mentioned in the description of the "fulfillment" method in Section 8.3.1. The ICT Service Provider must also check the deliverable and verify if it actually meets the Product Requirements Document (PRD) containing the Security Target specification. This relates to what was called "operational evidence" in Section 8.3.2

The check of the service or product purchased from a supplier is performed as follows:

- An attestation is required from the supplier that the Security Target specification is fulfilled. In case of complex services, this would correspond to the procedures explained in the last steps of the *ESARIS Fulfillment Model*. Note however that the Product Requirements Document (PRD) and its Security Target specification already contain only relevant ESARIS security measures. No chessboard matching is required. It must only be confirmed if a security measure is fulfilled or not. In case of deviations, the supplier must describe compensating measures or the two parties find another solution for an agreement.

- The attestation should be brought into the form of an Ace. Such *ESARIS Attainment Statements* are the basis for the composition of ICT services by the ICT Service Provider. More details are provided below.

- The ICT Service Provider must verify the quality of the service or products being purchased. More detail is provided by the *ICT Security Standard - Systems Acquisition and Contracting (SAC)* and the *ICT Security Baselines* (Level 5) which refine it. An example is acceptance testing.

The check if the deliverable meets its Security Target shall exist in form of an Ace. Why? This can be understood from Fig. 76.

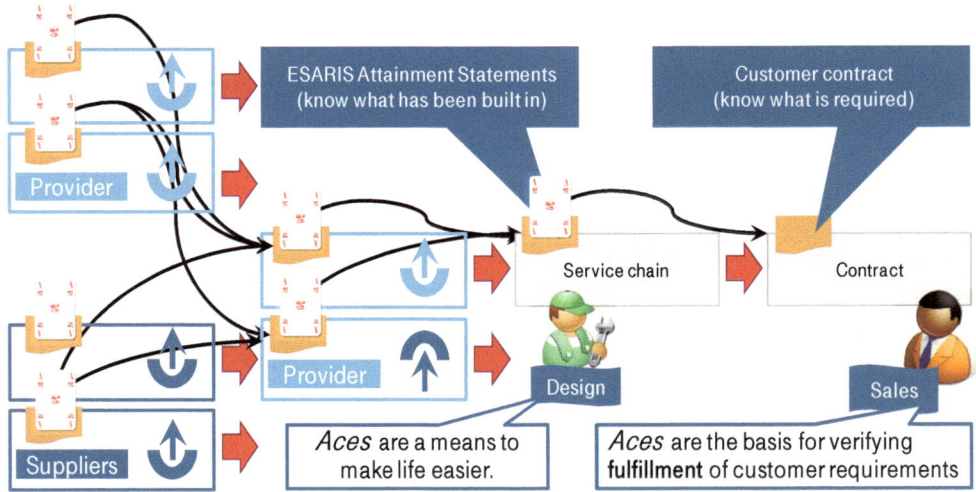

Fig. 76: Compositions of ICT services and the use of Aces in supplier networks

First, the internal business of the ICT Service Provider without external suppliers is briefly considered. An Ace documents compliance with and possible deviations from ESARIS security standards, mainly the ESARIS security measures stipulated

when the relationship between the ICT Service Provider and the user organization was considered.

in *ICT Security Standards* (Level 4). The ICT Service Provider uses the ESARIS security standards to develop, implement and deliver ICT services, components and procedures, i.e. anything which can be covered by an Ace. The standards provide design patterns to achieve the "secure by design" goal. The design and its implementation are compared with the ESARIS security standards according to the *ESARIS Attainment Model*. The result is the Ace which states compliance with and potential deviations from ESARIS security standards and therefore allows identifying built-in security features. In a customer deal, the ICT Service Provider needs to verify if the customer's security requirements are fulfilled. Therefore, one must know if the ICT service being subject of the contract is compliant with the ESARIS security standards. This verification is performed according to the *ESARIS Fulfillment Model*. The verification uses Aces as the basis since the Aces provide the information about the built-in security features and possible deviations from the ESARIS security standards.

Second, the picture is now widened to also cover external suppliers. Refer to Fig. 76. The service or product from the third party is integrated into the ICT Service Provider's ICT service and then delivered to user organizations. Single elements are collected and assembled creating a composite service. Services are combined to build a "service chain" which is the subject of the contract. Such an aggregation of ICT services requires the aggregation of the compliance information provided by Aces. Note that the integration needs to be evaluated in each step to some extent. The information from composing ICT services, components or procedures contained in *ESARIS Attainment Statements* and provided in form of Aces is reused at the level of the composite ICT service to leverage already available information and to avoid performing verification of compliance with ESARIS security standards at a very detailed level over and over again.

Summary: Deliverables from third parties (suppliers, partners) are treated similar to those provided from one internal organizational unit of the ICT Service Provider to another. The details are subject of the *ESARIS Third Party Integration Model* described in this chapter. The model basically extends the *ESARIS Attainment Model* to an external supplier network but borrows also other methods described in this book.

The *ESARIS Security Taxonomy* decomposes the "whole world of security" into areas that relate to and can be assigned to individual businesses (i.e. production units like organizations, departments, teams). In this way, it supports the division of labor. The *ESARIS Third Party Integration Model* applies the *ESARIS Security Taxonomy* and its organization to the external supply chain or supplier network.

The verification of compliance with ESARIS security standards is the subject of the *ESARIS Attainment Model*. The major outcome is a so-called Ace which informs about the level of compliance and possible deviations. The aggregation of single services and components into composite ICT services is also described by the

ESARIS Attainment Model. This method (developed for internal use) is applied in a similar way for managing the supplier network.

Two elements are added in order to manage external relations: First, the *ICT Security Standard – Systems Acquisition and Contracting (SAC)* is applied. This standard is applied by the ICT Service Provider and contains security measures for supplier and contract management. Moreover, it defines security measures that require developing and using a Product Requirement Document (PRD) containing a Security Target specification to ensure that the third-party service or component meets relevant ESARIS security standards. The Security Target is developed using the method *Provider Scope of Control* which helps to apply the *ESARIS Security Taxonomy* and to select the relevant ESARIS security standards and security measures. The PRD and its use represent the second new element.

Part 3: Implementation

The adoption and use of ESARIS start with a management decision shown as "enactment" in Fig. 77 which is not detailed in this part of the book. The improvement, upgrade and revision of the documentation are organized according to the *Maintenance System for EASRIS* which includes a sophisticated identification schema to facilitate the search for and the localization of documents. The introduction of ESARIS in a large organization needs to be carefully planned and executed. This process called *Transformation towards ESARIS* uses a staged approach with maturity and attainment levels. About 100 pages in this book are dedicated to details about the *IT production and its protection in practice*. A wealth of security measures derived from real-world challenges are described in detail. ESARIS changes the *everyday security management*. This is analyzed before a short conclusion is given at the end of this part of the book.

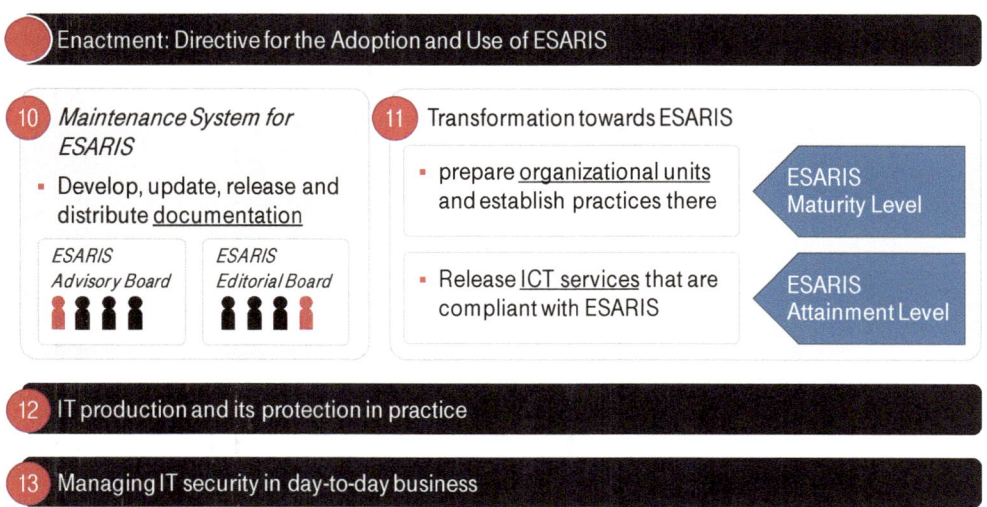

Fig. 77: Adoption and use of ESARIS in practice

10 Maintenance – requirements, documents, improvements

Introduction and summary: Necessary changes and additions in terms of security practices and measures result in updating or extending the ESARIS documentation, respectively. The improvement, upgrade and revision of the documentation are organized according to the *Maintenance System for EASRIS* which is described in the following. Document management is performed according to the relevant process instruction of the ICT Service Provider. However, additions and modifications are required for managing the ESARIS security documents. The documents must be stored and kept accessible for all employees. A documents identification schema is used in order to facilitate the search for and the localization of documents (Sect. 10.1). ESARIS security documents are subject to additions and modifications. The ICT Service Provider requires boards as well as detailed processes and tools to coordinate the activities in the large undertaking of creating and updating hundreds of documents which directly affect the ICT Service Provider's business (Sect. 10.2). All documents must be published in one central library since otherwise standardization will not work. Not only version control is required but also means facilitating to maintain an overview and to help achieving consistency (Sect. 10.3). ESARIS is, amongst other things, a means to communicate, negotiate and agree with customers. But this does not mean that all documents are given to any audience. Rules must be defined to organize the communication of ESARIS documents (Sect. 10.4).

10.1 Document IDs and more

Introduction and summary: The description of ESARIS, including the concepts, rules and standards, must be distributed within the ICT Service Provider and made available to the employees who require access to it. Central storage is required for the sake of consistency and availability. But this is not sufficient since the full documentation comprises a large number of documents. A hierarchy of Document IDs is developed and used in a file naming convention that facilitates finding and organizing documents.

One specific challenge is the storage and availability of documents. However, the large number of documents or files is not easy to handle. For this reason,

- Helping pages are set up in the Intranet which presents an introduction and guides people to access the document repository.

- A document hierarchy is developed and used as prefix in all file names.

All documents that are officially released can be found in a document library of the ICT Service Provider, which is also used to store documentation relating to other topics. The whole library can be organized using the enterprise's process landscape or other methods. The subset of ESARIS documents is called *ESARIS Library* in the following.

A large bundle of documents in particular is often stored in a directory and accessed by means of the operating system (such as Windows) that is installed on the user's workplace computer. In this case, the file managing program (such as Windows Explorer) displays a long and endless list of files. Users can use search functions to facilitate access to these files and to locate the one they want. However, this assumes that the user knows what they want to look at, whereas in fact many users do not. They scroll through the list hoping to find a file that looks promising enough to examine.

With the correct tool, even an alphabetically ordered list of files may provide a clear view. Each file name begins with the Document ID as unique prefix that orders the documents hierarchically and is chosen appropriately. The documents which are most important and are to be read first are automatically placed at the top of the list. The hierarchy of ESARIS is also automatically reproduced in the list. By assigning unique Document IDs that code scope and content document management systems are automatically provided with metadata necessary for greater transparency and instant access.

Fig. 78 shows the general structure of the ESARIS documentation.

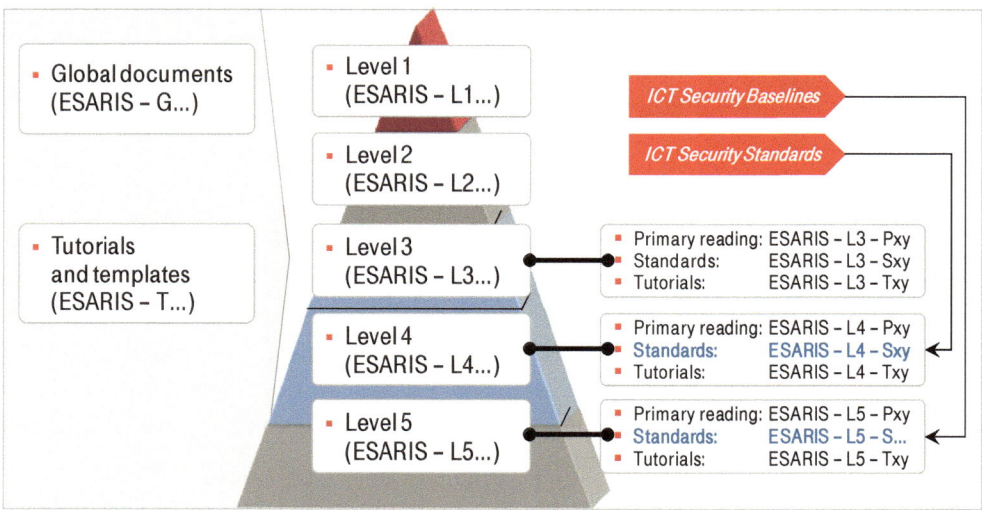

Fig. 78: ESARIS document structure and Document IDs

All documents have a Document ID that starts with "ESARIS–". This string is followed by a letter which codes the type of the document. The entire documentation consists of around three types of documents:

- Concept papers (information as provided in this book) are assigned a Document ID starting with "ESARIS-G",

- Specifications and standards are assigned a Document ID starting with "ESARIS-L". There are five levels in total so that the Document IDs for those documents are "ESARIS-L1" through "ESARIS-L5".

- Tutorials, templates, help documents and presentations are assigned a Document ID starting with "ESARIS-T".

This is the prefix of the Document ID. The *Enterprise Security Architecture for Reliable ICT Services (ESARIS)* is hierarchical and modular, as is its documentation.

The letter "G" stands for "general" or "global". Documents with this letter provide introductions and fundamental information about the architecture. They appear at the top of an alphabetical list. The prefix "ESARIS-G" is followed by a sequence number as suffix so that complete Document IDs are "ESARIS-G1" and "ESARIS-G5".

The same is done for the "T" documents which are tutorials and the like. They exist on the same level as "G" documents within the hierarchy. The prefix "ESARIS-T" is followed by a sequence number as suffix so that complete Document IDs are "ESARIS-T02" and "ESARIS-T03". Tutorials are automatically located at the end of the alphabetically ordered list since ESARIS largely provides standards which are listed between "G" and "T".

The hierarchy of standards has several levels, denoted by the suffixes "L1", "L2", "L3", "L4" and "L5". They are shown after the document with the suffix "G". There are three types of documents

- Overarching documents for primary reading (P) are assigned the Document ID "ESARIS-Ln-Pxy".

- The security standards (S) are assigned the Document ID "ESARIS-Ln-Sxy" or which has this prefix. "S" may also be read as secondary reading.

- Tutorial documents and templates (T) are assigned the Document ID "ESARIS-Ln-Txy".

Here "n" stands for the Level and "xy" is a two digit sequence number.

The result is shown in Fig. 78. Tutorial documents do not provide binding requirements or obligations and the like. They shall be considered as supporting material helping people to adhere to binding requirements or obligations stipulated in other documents. Templates are binding in most cases. "P" documents can have different character. Their content explains how they are to be used.

The *ICT Security Standards* (on Level 4) are an essential part of the ESARIS documentation. Their Document IDs are "ESARIS-L4-Sxy". Each describes one of the 31 areas in the *ESARIS Security Taxonomy*. The sequence number "xy" is chosen accordingly. Refer to the upper part of Fig. 79 where the sequence number "14" is assigned to the *ICT Security Standard – Computer Systems Security (CSS)* which therefore carries the Document ID "ESARIS-L4-S14".

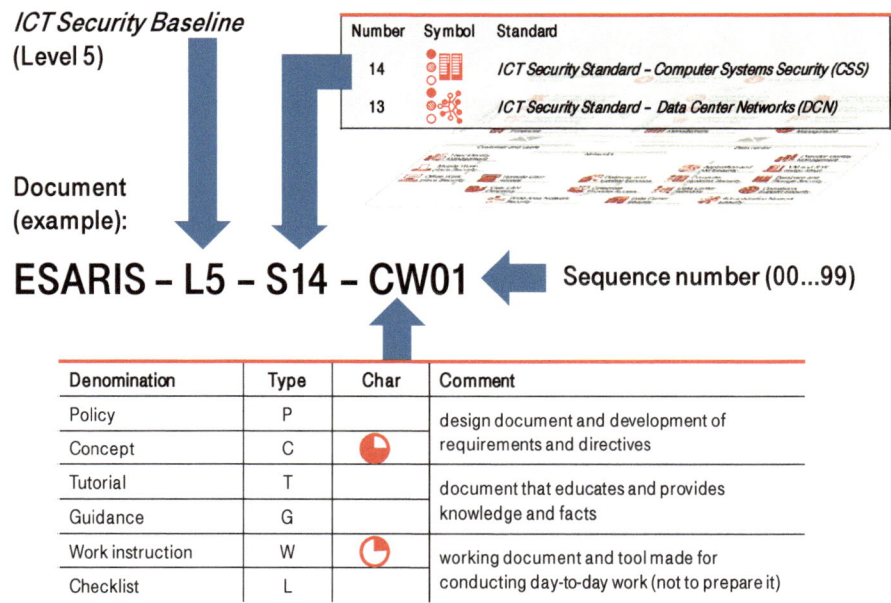

Fig. 79: Document IDs for and types of genuine security standards

The *ICT Security Baselines* (on Level 5) are the other category of genuine security standards. They contain refinements of the *ICT Security Standards* (Level 4). In order to reproduce the hierarchical structure of the standards, the sequence number of the related *ICT Security Standard* (Level 4) is referred to in the Document ID of an *ICT Security Baseline* (Level 5). Refer to Fig. 79.

In the example, the Document ID is "ESARIS-L5-S14-CW01". This document is an *ICT Security Baseline* (Level 5) that refines security measures from the *ICT Security Standard – Computer Systems Security (CSS)* that was assigned the sequence number "14".

Then a further suffix is added which comprises a code for the type of the document ("CW" in the example) and a sequence number ("01" in the example). *ICT Security Baselines* (Level 5) serve different purposes. In order to provide more structure into this large set of documents, the type of the document is coded in the document ID. Refer to the table in the lower half of Fig. 79. The character is doubled (e.g. "PP") for pure documents. In the other case that the document has a mixed character, the two most suitable document types are coded. "GW" is for instance used for material which is a guidance document with a work instruction part.

This concept allows the identification of every single document. References and quotations are made quite easy which is an important feature for indexing and for automated search in a repository. Note that the document title and description in the file name may change but the document remains uniquely identifiable. The concept also ensures that the ESARIS classification schema is maintained as long as the files are listed in alphabetical order (independent from where the files are stored). Such a list of selected ESARIS document files is shown in Table 13.

Table 13: Alphabetical list of some ESARIS documents

Document file name	Document type
ESARIS-G1 – Introduction and Concept	Top level, global document
ESARIS-G2 – Terms and Definitions	Top level, global document
ESARIS-L3-P01 – ESARIS Attainment Model	Level 3, primary to read
ESARIS-L3-P02 – ESARIS Fulfillment Model	Level 3, primary to read
ESARIS-L3-S02 – Security Organization Policy	Level 3, standard
ESARIS-L3-T05 – Template for an Ace	Level 3, template
ESARIS-L4-P01 – Synopsis of ICT Security Standards	Level 4, primary to read
ESARIS-L4-S01 – Certification and 3rd Party Assurance (CTP)	Level 4, standard
ESARIS-L4-S02 – Risk Management (RMP)	Level 4, standard
ESARIS-L4-S31 – Business Continuity Management (BCM)	Level 4, standard
ESARIS-L4-T01 – Template and Guidance for Standards	Level 4, tutorial and template
ESARIS-L5-S14-CW01 –Security setting Windows server…	Level 5, concept with guidance
ESARIS-T01 – Presentation Overview and Concept	Top level, tutorial
ESARIS-T02 – Frequently Asked Questions (FAQ)	Top level, tutorial

This file naming convention has the effect that an alphabetical list reproduces the hierarchy within the documentation. Secondly, it means that by looking at the file name alone, a user can find out if the document provides concepts, standards or tutorials and so on. Moreover, they can obtain a great deal of information about the documents' content and intention from looking at just the file name.

ESARIS comprises 31 *ICT Security Standards*. A large number of documents on Level 5 refine the security measures stipulated in Level 4 in terms of working instructions, checklists, and manuals. Icons are assigned to each *ICT Security Standard* in order to facilitate their use. The small pictures or illustrations are introduced with the *ESARIS Security Taxonomy* in Chapter 4. They are used to easily identify the standards and to highlight dependencies between them. They can also be attached to text in other documents in order to assign an issue to an individual standard. Icons of Level 4 are red so that associated documents on Level 5 can use the same icon in, for example, blue. Other icons can be created for other Levels and other purposes. Here are two examples:

SAC (Level 4)   versus   and SDL (Level 4)   versus

The *ICT Security Standards* define a large number of security measures. It must be possible to refer individual security measures when using e.g. the *ESARIS Customer Fulfillment Model* (refer to Chapter 8). The *ESARIS Fulfillment Model* is used to demonstrate how the customer's requirements are met by the ICT Service Provider. So, a naming convention is required since the organization of a document and the numbering of sections may change.

The following naming convention may be used for the ESARIS security measures:
- The abbreviation of the corresponding *ICT Security Standard* is used as the prefix. The abbreviations (for instance VAM, LHR, IHF or CSS) are introduced in Sect. 4.3 and shown in Table 7 through Table 12. That means, all security measures stipulated in the *ICT Security Standard – Computer Systems Security (CSS)* are assigned an ID beginning with "CSS-".

- The prefix is suffixed with a combination of three letters which may abbreviate the name of the security measure. For example, the security measure which describes the protection of "Administrative Access" is finally assigned the ID "CSS–AAA" for instance. Note that three letters are used in any case.

These IDs are very short names for the security measures. This eases references and quotations. The IDs are very helpful especially in mapping tables. They can easily be used in searches. Of course, the IDs are unique. Moreover, IDs should be modified (i.e., a new one is chosen) if the security measure is considerably modified. This invalidates e.g. mapping tables and alerts users that an update was made.

10.2   Virtual organization, roles and processes

Introduction and summary: ESARIS security documents are subject to additions and modifications. This needs to be organized in a manner that the documents are of high quality and approved to become a global standard. The ICT Service Provider requires at least an editorial board which organizes the document management including approvals. But detailed processes and tools must also exist to coordinate the activities of the participants in the large undertaking of creating and updating hundreds of documents which directly affect the ICT Service Provider's business.

The *Maintenance System for ESARIS* organizes the development, improvement, upgrade and revision of the ESARIS documentation. It consists of

- A virtual organization having a mandate,
- Roles in this virtual organization having dedicated responsibility,
- A process that describes the activities being executed.

General requirements regarding the document management are usually provided by the corresponding process instruction of the ICT Service Provider. They build the basis the *Maintenance System for ESARIS* is established upon.

The virtual organization comprises working groups that bring together people with existing or new roles. Following their mandate, defined activities are conducted according to the defined process. There are two working groups

- the *ESARIS Editorial Board* (maintenance of documents) and
- the *ESARIS Advisory Board* (steering).

The *ESARIS Editorial Board* organizes the practical work with the documents (author guidance and support, proof-reading, content approval, quality assurance). It consists of the ESARIS Chief Editor and a few ESARIS Editors. The *ESARIS Advisory Board* builds a steering committee and is staffed with existing roles. It takes strategic decisions related to ESARIS and its development and supervises the *ESARIS Editorial Board* and its work as well. Main issues that need to be ensured and discussed include a) if requirements and standards are realistic (costs, complexity and enforceability are considered), b) if requirements and standards are effective (objectives are reached, remaining risks are treated), and c) if requirements and standards are consistent (feasibility is examined). The *ESARIS Advisory Board* does not replace the Security Management organization and its major roles. Instead, it can be regarded as a committee of the Security Management organization.

The specific realization of the document management process for ESARIS documents is outlined in Fig. 80. Note that the documents are used and mandatory on a global basis. They have great effects, positive and maybe negative ones. Hence,

- the development and update of documents must involve the subject matter experts and stakeholders,

- approvals are required to ensure that impacts and risks are considered, quality and effectiveness are reviewed, and plans for introducing new practices exist and are agreed.

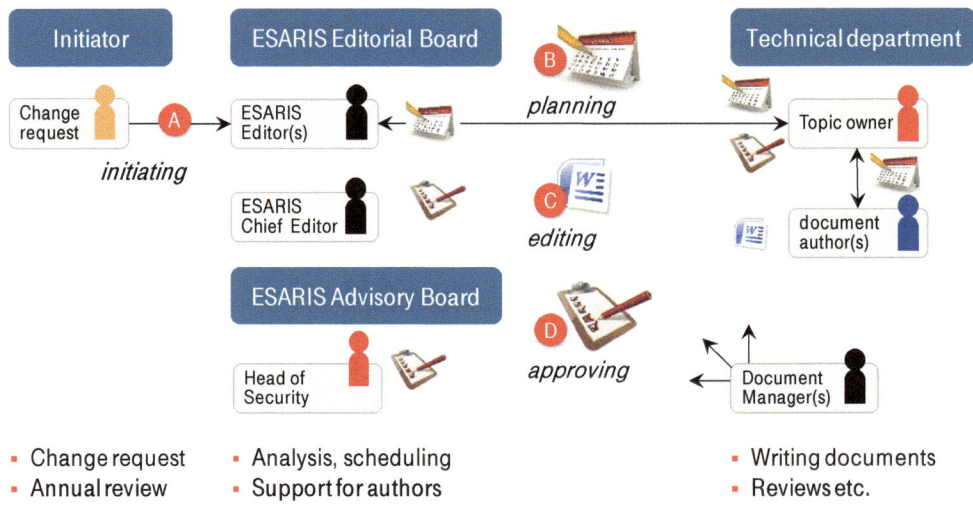

Fig. 80: Process of managing ESARIS documents (simplified)

Four parties are involved in the process outlined in Fig. 80: the requesting party (initiator) which can be any employee, the *ESARIS Editorial Board*, the *ESARIS Advisory Board*, and the technical department ("topic owner" including document owner and authors). Usually, only one representative from the *ESARIS Advisory Board* is required. This is a role entitled "Head of Security" in the figure who provides for final approval. The sequence of actions is as follows:

- A Change Request (CR) is issued. **A** It is registered by the ESARIS Editor and will be tracked by the *ESARIS Editorial Board* until completion.
- Then, the request is analyzed and the realization is planned. **B** Hereby the ESARIS Editor works with the „topic owner". The latter involves at least the author.
- Now the change request is being worked on. **C** A new document is created or an existing one if modified. The author and/or the topic owner involve stakeholders and other subject matter experts if necessary. The *ESARIS Editorial Board* ensures that the right roles are involved. In case that further clarification or a strategic decision is needed, the issue is brought before the *ESARIS Advisory Board*.
- Finally, the result is approved. **D** There are three steps in the approval which starts with the ESARIS Chief Editor, continues with the "topic owner" and concludes with the Head of Security.

The Document Managers support this process. The ESARIS Advisory Board gets involved if there is the need for clarification or decisions.

The approval process is organized in multiple stages. The first check comprises but is not limited to verifying if change requests are considered, if format and structure meets requirements, if relations to other documents are considered and if contents is clear and of high quality. The second check focuses on the correctness and effectiveness of the specification. Moreover, it is verified if costs and other constraints are considered, if corresponding units are prepared and if the solution is ready for production. ESARIS security standards are usually used on a global basis. Hence, it needs to be verified if other units are possibly affected. If so, they have to be involved in order to receive their approval and confirmation if required. At least, they should be aware that they are expected to apply the updated or new practices. In case of major changes or introduction of new practices, it can be necessary to perform an *impact* analysis, with planning of migration and the provisioning of a corresponding documentation. Performing an impact analysis means that it is analyzed if all conditions are fulfilled to release the document as a standard for common practice. It may be necessary to postpone the "document release" if this is not the case yet. A "roll-out planning" can be required too. The migration needs to be planned and documented. Before the document is approved it must be confirmed that the conditions for its application are in place. The concrete sequence of approvals and related activities depend on the "change type" which rates effects of the changes demanded by the updated or new document.

The document management process is organized by tracking individual change requests that are assigned to documents. (The IT uses similar methodologies defined in ITIL.) A tool is used for managing the change requests (tickets) and the management of the documents. The content of such a single ticket is shown in Fig. 81. Each ticket comprises information about the subject in general (dark blue), status and scheduling (red), affected document(s) (black), details (green), involved people (amber), and versions and document files (light blue).

A new entry is created in the list or an existing one is revised when a new change request is received by the *ESARIS Editorial Board*. The status of editing is set to "requested" and changed every time progress is made along the process. The process include all necessary approvals and ends with the publishing of the document in the *ESARIS Library*.

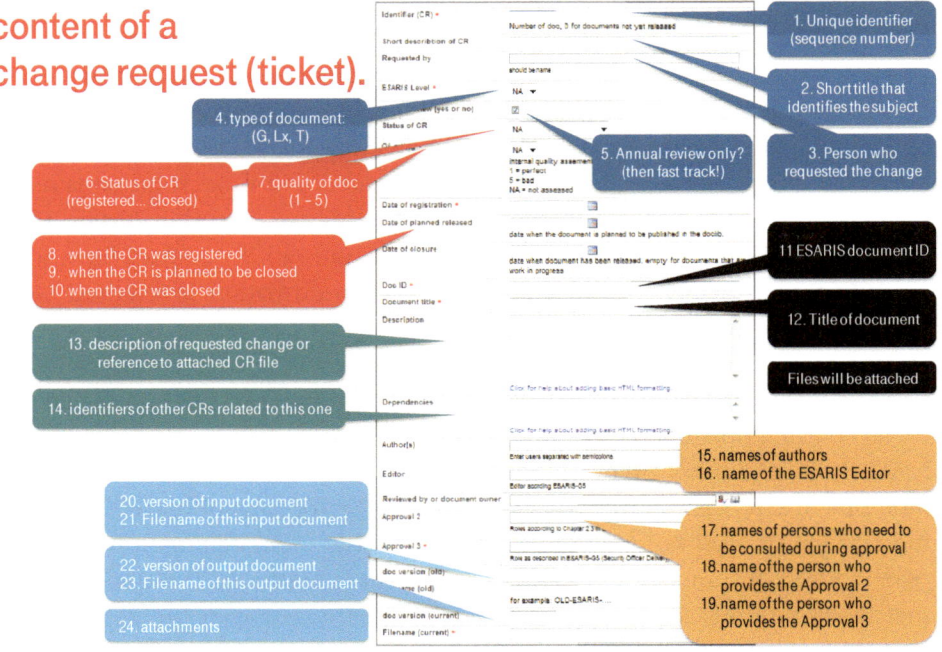

Fig. 81: Ticket (change request) from the Editorial Board Tracking List (EBTL)

10.3   Library, versions and consistency

> **Introduction and summary:** The ESARIS documents must be made available for virtually all employees of the ICT Service Provider. A central library is required for this since otherwise standardization will not work. The existence of hundreds of documents which are regularly reviewed and changed requires rigorous version control but also means facilitating to maintain an overview and to help achieving consistency since documents usually build upon each other so that dependencies exist.

Almost all security facets shall be described in ESARIS documents since this would also mean that the degree of standardization is high. ESARIS documents stipulate security facets that predominantly become global standards of the ICT Service Provider which are mandatory to be observed.

It is absolutely necessary to file all ESARIS documents in one central repository (called *ESARIS Library*). All documents must be available to everybody in the company. Otherwise standardization won't work. Critical (confidential) content can be removed from the document before publishing but the frame document being published must still explain subject, purpose, target group, effect etc. Then people can decide if the document is required for them and initiate to get it. Note that having a central document library is priceless: people see what exist. This avoids that they start reinventing the wheel. They also see documents that are related to their current activity. All this raises the quality and the degree of standardization and therefore reduces costs for security. This used repository must support that people see adjacent and similar documents. It is not sufficient that they find the specific document they are told to read.

Specific organizational units and even projects may also require information (such as lists of contact persons or references to specific inventory) that goes beyond ESARIS. Such information is not for global use. Hence, there are "unit specific documents" too. They provide the unit specific information but may not replace ESARIS documents. They must not copy a significant amount of ESARIS content. Instead these unit specific documents shall make references to ESARIS documents and shall be used together with them. Otherwise consistency problems will occur very likely. Unit specific documents may or may not be filed in the *ESARIS Library*. To make this decision, one should consider if the document can or should be used by a wider audience and therefore be published in the central document library. It is essential that unit specific documents refer to other ESARIS documents. This is important to prevent silos. It is recommended that such documents are assigned a Document ID that is similar to that of ESARIS documents: The prefix „ESARIS –" is replaced by „Oxyz –" where „xyz" stands for a string that identifies the organizational unit. The other part of the Document ID can comply with the ESARIS specification described above.

Customer specific documents (such as statements of compliance or security conceptions) exist too. These customer specific documents shall also make references to ESARIS documents. They may or may not copy text from other ESARIS documents even if they are forwarded to customers. It must, however, be prevented that there are documents with the same content that may evolve differently and diverge at some time. Customer specific documents are not part of the ESARIS documentation. However, they should maintain the ESARIS documentation structure. It is recommended that such documents are assigned a Document ID that is similar to that of ESARIS documents: The prefix „ESARIS-" is replaced by „Uxyz-" where „xyz" stands for a string that identifies the customer or the customer organization. The other part of the Document ID complies with the ESARIS specification. Customer specific documents may also be filed in the *ESARIS Library* because they could play a vital role in standardization. Practices that are unique to one customer today can become a global standard for all customers tomorrow.

Documents are given a unique version and date of release. The documents in ESARIS will be reviewed and updated as required. There will be not one release with all documents having the same version. It is not manageable to bring all relevant documents to a common version. This would require regularly reviewing and updating all documents simultaneously. The amount of work is very large and the interdependencies between the documents make the job very hard to do. The advantage of updating documents on demand is resource efficiency and speed.

Moreover, the document maintenance process can concentrate on the most relevant issues while not spending work on revisions that are formal only.

However, if the documents are updated in that way the question may arise if the documents are consistent with each other and how to achieve and to maintain this consistency.

First of all a "bibliography" (that is a list of all current and released documents) is maintained. The "bibliography" matches with the content of the *ESARIS Library*. It looks similar to the list shown in Table 13 on page 177 though it provides much more detail. In addition, a "library history" is maintained that lists all changes applied to the *ESARIS Library*. The "bibliography" and "library history" are independent from each other. The latter is used to achieve consistency.

The "library history" is shown in Fig. 82.

Version X+1					ESARIS Library History	
No.	Date of recording	Version	Date of release	Change log	Document ID	...
777	2017-02-11	2.00	2017-02-05		ESARIS-L5-S14-CW01	
776	2017-02-11	1.80	2017-01-20		ESARIS-L4-S12	
775	2017-02-11	2.10	2017-01-15		ESARIS-L5-S03-WW07	
774	2017-02-11	1.60	2017-01-11		ESARIS-L5-S07-WC10	
Version X	2017-02-11	1.40	2017-01-08		ESARIS-L5-S20-CW02	
772	2017-01-08	2.20	2017-01-07		ESARIS-L5-S29-CW03	
771	2017-01-08	3.10	2016-12-27		ESARIS-L5-S23-WW01	
770	2017-01-05	1.80	2016-12-12		ESARIS-L5-S05-CW02	
769	2017-01-05	1.00	2016-12-12		ESARIS-L5-S05-CW01	
768	2017-01-05	2.20	2016-12-06		ESARIS-L5-S04-CW06	

Fig. 82: Consistency and the ESARIS Library History

Many documents are developed and updated simultaneously. However, the process of their creation and updating cannot be synchronized. This would require bringing all "document releases" in a timely order that allows an author to become aware of and possibly consider all documents that were released before. This would result in terrible delays and chaos.

Notwithstanding, there is for many documents the need to identify if a certain other document has been considered or not. Documents that were considered are usually listed as a reference. But it is not common to list references in a document that were considered but had no effect. At the end of the day, this would mean to list all existing documents as references just to show that the author was aware of their existence.

The solution which authors may decide to use is as follows.

- The "library history" enumerates all "document releases" in the order of the time of their release. Documents are listed with all necessary bibliographic details (empty right columns in Fig. 82). Each "document release" creates a new entry in the list. The entries are sequentially numbered. One row refers to a creation of a new document, an update of an existing one, or even a revocation of a document. If a document is updated several times, it appears as often as it was updated plus once for its creation.

- Each new item is put onto the top of the list. It is essential that the existing body of the list is never modified and that the list is never reordered.

- Authors can inspect the "library history" in order to identify documents that may be of interest and require consideration.

  - It is assumed that an author has inspected the list published January 5, 2017, i.e. immediately after entry number 770 has been created. Refer to Fig. 82 and the marker "Version X" for the author's document. It is furthermore assumed that all documents that existed on that list were considered by the author.

  - This document of the author (Version X) now passes the approval and is then e.g. published as number 772 on January 8, 2017. The "library history" now contains entries till this date (including 772).

  - After a period of time, after February 11, 2017 in the example, the author again works on his or her document and wants to know if related other documents were changed meanwhile. This can easily be done by inspecting the "library history" which now has 777 entries. Seven changes were completed after the last inspection. Hence, the author must only inspect the entries 771 to 777 were number 772 is his or her own document. Each entry contains a detailed description of the changes applied to each document ("change log" not filled out in Fig. 82). Document IDs and bibliographic details allow inspecting the changed documents in detail. Note that a document's topic is already made clear by the Document ID. With this information the author can create "Version X+1" of his or her document and retains the information of the new marker 777.

  - This document of "Version X+1" (with marker 777) is approved and published. It appears in the "library history" with an entry number greater than 777 (not shown in the figure).

- The author must record this highest sequence number in his document: all document versions below this number were considered. Note that most of the entries are not relevant for the author since the documents are about a totally different subject. It may take seconds to sort them out. The inspection of the "library history" not only shows updates but also new documents. No other version control reveals such information.

- When authors inspect the "library history" it may happen that the same document has been changed more than once since the last inspection of the "library history". Obviously, one has to work with the most recent version only. Notwithstanding all change logs should be inspected.

This document "library history" is an important means towards consistency. Moreover, it is the basis for identifying any change applied to the ESARIS documentation. People can use the "bibliography" in order to browse through the ESARIS Library. This function is very important since people must become aware of documents which are new for them and which relate to the topic they are interested in. The sequence of documents produced by the Document IDs ensures that related documents appear close to each other in the list. The Document IDs reproduce the structure of ESARIS specifically its *Hierarchy of Security Standards* and its *ESARIS Security Taxonomy*.

10.4   Protecting intellectual property

Introduction and summary: ESARIS is, amongst other things, a means to communicate, negotiate and agree with customers. But this does not mean that all documents are given to any audience. The *ICT Security Baselines* (Level 5) in particular will contain information which is intellectual property of the ICT Service Provider and needs therefore be communicated in a restricted way. The distribution of such documents must also be restricted since they may contain information that can facilitate an attack.

In the following, general rules are stated that apply to the forwarding of ESARIS documentation to potential or actual customers of the ICT Service Provider. Such rules are necessary since some documents contain intellectual property of the ICT Service Provider. Their content has to be protected in order to maintain competitive advantages. Other documents will contain information which must be kept confidential for security reasons. Security concepts and detailed design information are examples. This section deals with such documents which are clearly marked as "sensitive", regardless of the reason for restricting the access to them.

The sharing of sensitive, security-relevant information has to balance the protection needs – especially regarding Intellectual Property (IP) - of the ICT Service Provider on the one hand and the valid interest of (potential) customers to gain assurance about professional security management of the provider on the other. The "Need-to-Know" principle tends to describe the problem rather than provide a handy solution. Employees require further assistance. The following rules may provide guidance on what this type of assistance may be.

- The *ICT Security Standards* (Level 4) are used for communicating, negotiating and agreeing upon security. The *ICT Security Baselines* (Level 5) containing the most details are intended for internal use only and usually not given to customers. User organizations that "outsource" IT want to reduce complexity and delegate tasks. They are therefore not usually interested in these "bits and bytes" and are often not even able to understand this documentation because, with the IT outsourcing, they have reduced the corresponding IT competencies. The ESARIS security standards comprise many security measures which ensure that customers are provided with information they requiring, e.g. through security reports.

- Selected parts of the ESARIS documentation (i.e. a couple of *ICT Security Standards* together with some ESARIS-Gx documents) may generally be shown or presented to a (potential) customer, if it is deemed appropriate and promising for a potential deal or simply as part of customer relationship management. Note that this book already provides such information.

- Usually, the ICT Service Provider has to reply to security-specific questions coming from the user organization (customer). It is recommended that these are answered individually and not by providing documents that seem to suitably address the subject. The answers can be given with the help of the relevant and necessary ESARIS security standards. It does not make any sense to handover a bundle of or all *ICT Security Standards* because, among other things, the sheer quantity of the associated information may overload the potential customer.

- Not all documents are relevant for the customer. The set of ESARIS security standards which are relevant and maybe helpful for the customer can be determined by applying the method *Provider Scope of Control* (refer to Sect. 4.5). It always depends on the business with the customer, more specifically the ICT service being provided, which documents could be of interest. Their handover in either format (paper-based or electronically) requires proof of valid interest and a Non-Disclosure Agreement (NDA) signed by the customer. Providing services to customers also means to reduce the amount of information the customer should pay attention to.

These are general rules that are to be applied in an appropriate manner and modified, where required, by authorized personnel. The authorization has to be assigned to roles or even individuals in advance.

The application of confidentiality rules to a well-defined group of documents makes it easier for employees to adhere to confidentiality rules.

11 Transformation – implementing ESARIS sustainably

Introduction and summary: The *Enterprise Security Architecture for Reliable ICT Services (ESARIS)* has been developed for a large ICT Service Provider. This chapter reports real-world experience gained during the "transformation" performed in a global IT organization with business in 20 countries and more than 40,000 employees in total. This also demonstrates that ESARIS is a workable approach and that the concepts and methodologies of ESARIS really work. Security managers are given deep insight into the specific situation and the challenges on the one hand and in the solutions developed to change the security mode of operation sustainably on the other hand. First, it is justified why a program called *Transformation towards ESARIS* is necessary. The description of major goals and achievements rounds this off (Sect. 11.1). The implementation of the concepts, procedures and practices within the ICT Service Provider is complex and must carefully be planned and conducted. It is explained how the project can be organized. A staged approach is used based on the *ESARIS Maturity* Levels. The ESARIS Transformation Master Plan, Key Performance Indicators (KPI) and certifications of organizational units are main instruments for managing the Transformation. Total costs are also estimated (Sect. 11.2). A main challenge is to bring ESARIS into the employees' hearts and minds. Motivation, training and communication are major success factors. A few best practices are presented in this area (Sect. 11.3). The Transformation is not complete if the ICT services of the ICT Service Provider are not affected. Hence, this second "stream" of the Transformation is also considered (Sect. 11.4).

Editorial note: This section is based on one of the author's earlier publications.[50]

11.1 Mission: induce a massive change

Introduction and summary: IT provisioning is undergoing fundamental changes. Technical developments (e.g. cloud) and other changes (e.g. industrialization of IT) require reorganizing the security management of large IT organizations (especially ICT Service Providers acting on the market). ESARIS responds to the challenges. A Transformation program is required for implementing the new methods, procedures and standards. The special character, its scope and achievements are outlined in this section.

---

[50] Eberhard von Faber: Changing the security mode of operation in a global IT organization with 20000+ technical staff; in: ISSE 2015, Highlights of the Information Security Solutions Europe 2015 Conference, Springer Vieweg, ISBN 978-3-658-10934-9, p. 286 – 304 [47]

Why this is not a usual program

A program is required for introducing new methods, procedures and standards in a large global IT organization. This program is *Transformation towards ESARIS* since massive changes are required:

Definition: Transformation is the act of revising or altering into a different form (involving reconsideration and modification). The change (revision or alteration as meant here) has a significant effect so that the starting and the ending point significantly differ in terms of maturity or attainment. The change lasts a period of time and usually has an anticipated ending as projects have. So, the Transformation is not considered to be a continuous process nor it is repeated. The expected changes are massive.

The security mode of operation shall be changed. "Usual programs" mostly have a limited scope and aim at causing limited changes only. There is another difference which makes the Transformation more difficult. In "usual programs", organizational units and employees use to work through predefined material. They execute what has been prepared. In the Transformation the organizational units shall refine on working methods by themselves: They shall identify necessary roles and assign them. They shall identify interfaces to other organizational units (and suppliers and customers as well) and find out what they like to receive and what they have to deliver. They shall understand security in their business and learn how to develop and apply security standards. This means that the organizational units shall take part in shaping the division of labor and in refining the processes.

Cloud computing and industrialization lead to a change of the provisioning processes: The interface between the provider and the user organization changes, and the IT organization must modify and optimize its internal provisioning processes. This results in a situation where "traditional" security management no longer works. Large IT organizations have to change their internal security mode of operation and introduce new methods, procedures and standards. That's why the *Enterprise Security Architecture for Reliable ICT Services (ESARIS)* had been elaborated. The models and standards of ESARIS were developed for large-scale IT production, which is characterized by resolute division of labor and by resolute process orientation. In terms of security, there is the challenge to implement the right division of labor and to shape the processes appropriately.

The three most important changes of the new methodology ESARIS are as follows. Refer to Fig. 83.

- Consequent standardization of security measures including all those in processes and procedures necessary to implement and to maintain technical security measures. Today's technology and provisioning processes are highly standardized. Security can only be ensured if it is also standardized.

- Consequent integration of IT security management (SecMan) and IT service management (ITSM). The IT production is organized according to the ITSM processes as stipulated in ITIL and ISO/IEC 20000.[51] Security can only be ensured if the security management becomes part of the IT service management.

- Modified role and mission of the Security Management organization. This is a direct consequence of the last point. One can no longer solely rely on security experts who care for security. Security can only be ensured if the security measures are applied by the IT staff. The Security Management organization concentrates on setting requirements and on verifying if standards are applied so that the requirements are met. The business units and the IT staff must apply the security standards and implement security measures in technology and processes.

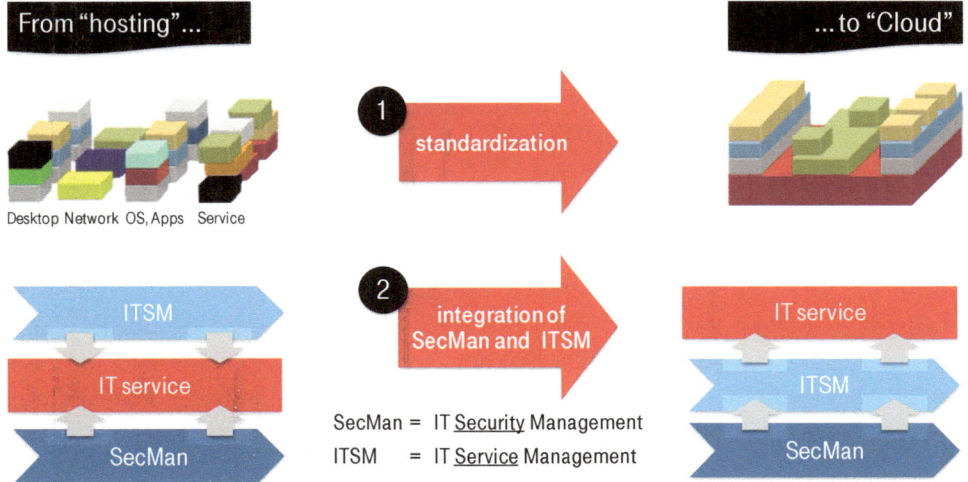

Fig. 83: Fundamental changes requiring reorganizing the security management

This fundamental change is important in our context, since all IT people are now the audience for the "Transformation". They are provided with very detailed material and must learn to care for security autonomously.

What shall be achieved?

Obviously, such fundamental changes need to be actively managed and the introduction of the new guidelines etc. needs to be organized accordingly. Hence, a "Transformation program" needs to be designed, and set-up and progress must be measured continuously.

Fig. 84 summarizes why the "Transformation" is so special and complex. It is not only a common training. The Transformation runs for more than two years and addresses about 40,000 people. The figure (right-hand side) shows what the organ-

---

51   ISO/IEC 20000 – Information technology – Service management – Part 1: Service management system requirements, Part 2: Guidance on the application of service management systems; 2012 [2]

ization (IT business units) must have done in the Transformation autonomously. The left-hand side shows the central support.

Fig. 84: Instruments (left) and results (right) of the Transformation

The program is quite comprehensive and the expectations are challenging. The business units take the responsibility to secure their ICT services and to identify what is required to do so. The IT staff (not primarily security experts from the Security Management organization) applies the security standards that are made centrally available. The business units identify the roles and tasks necessary to do so and assign these roles to teams and individuals. They analyze the supply chain and their own business and organize the collaboration with other units so that security aspects get considered as required. The business units develop their own plan to develop the security methodology and to improve obeying standards. Finally, the ICT services shall be compliant with the security standards and security is considered in the service catalogs (delivery and sales offering portfolio). – This seems to be a perfect world. The Transformation program must, however, deliver accordingly.

As support (left-hand side of Fig. 84) the business units receive guidance in form of a master plan as well as project support from a central office and a competence team. Assessments and audits help them to carry on with the Transformation and to actually work on the right things.

11.2   Approach: ESARIS Maturity Level and master plan

Introduction and summary: The organization of the Transformation covers best practices related to project structure, split into the Transformation of organizational units (people) and the Transformation of ICT services (service delivery), the provisioning of master plans and their use by the organizational units, performance review and KPI as well as tool support and certification. The Transformation of organizational units (people) is organized into five *ESARIS Maturity Levels*. The overall organization is also sketched and costs are estimated for the Transformation.

This chapter reports real-world experience gained while introducing the *Enterprise Security Architecture for Reliable ICT Services (ESARIS)* in a global IT organization with more than 40,000 employees. Several best/proven practices are described. These blueprints help CISOs and other security managers to manage introducing new methods, procedures and standards and to establish a new security mode of operation in a larger IT organization.

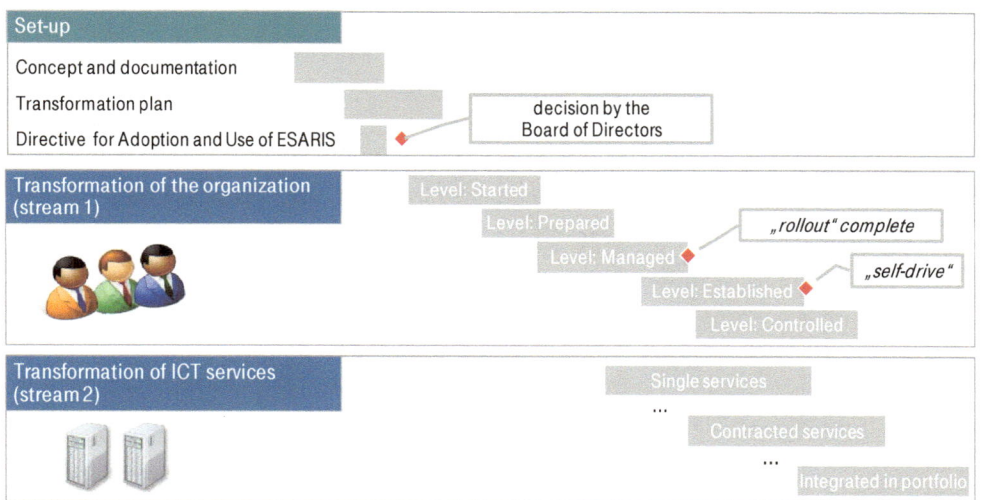

Fig. 85: Structure of the Transformation

Fig. 85 is the overall structure of the Transformation. Three things are required as initial set-up and basis for the genuine Transformation: A) obviously, the new methods, procedures and standards must exist. B) A rough Transformation plan must be elaborated. C) Before getting in touch with all the employees, it is absolutely necessary to have the explicit support from the top management. The ICT Service Provider's Board of Directors issued the "Directive for the Adoption and Use of ESARIS". Hereby the board also formally decided that the organization undergoes the Transformation and that every organizational unit must support the Transformation program which includes provisioning of the required budget and resources as well as the execution of the activities which were predefined to be done.

On the one hand, employees need to be trained and organizational units be enabled to work with ESARIS and to apply the security standards. On the other hand, ESARIS mainly aims at producing ICT services according to the ESARIS security standards which cover all phases of the life-cycle including service strategy, service design, service implementation, service operations and maintenance. As a result, the Transformation is split into two streams. Refer to Fig. 85.

- The preparation of organizational units is seen as prerequisite for "overall ESARIS compliance" and therefore started first. This process (stream 1, called Transformation of organizational units) has to create the necessary conditions for the delivery of secure ICT services according to ESARIS. In this stream, the organization and the people working there learn how to use the methods, procedures and standards of ESARIS in order to produce ICT services that are compliant with the security standards and produced efficiently.

- After having achieved a reasonable maturity level (see below), organizational units can start with stream 2, the Transformation of ICT services. This means that the IT production starts to use ESARIS. Methods, procedures and standards of ESARIS are applied. Note that this needs to be done also step-by-step since during ongoing operations only a few practices can be changed at a time. Hence, the second stream also takes time so that the overall Transformation has two streams both taking considerable time to be completed. Refer to Fig. 85.

Both Transformation processes use a staged approach. There are five levels in each process (or stream). The levels in the Transformation of organizational units (stream 1) are called *ESARIS Maturity Levels*. Refer to Fig. 86. The Transformation of ICT services (stream 2) is organized along the standard *ESARIS Attainment Model* and uses the *ESARIS Attainment Levels* already described in great detail in Chapter 7.3. This simplifies both processes and eases the organization of the overall process. Stream 2 will be taken up in Sect. 11.4.

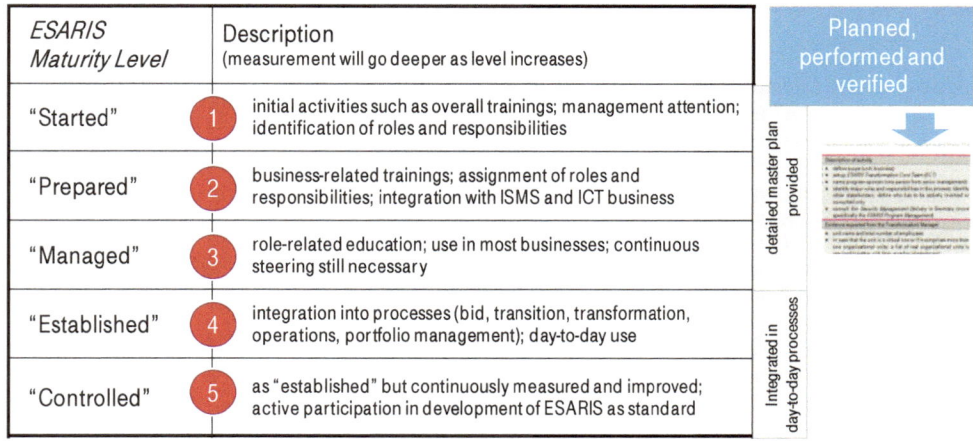

Fig. 86: ESARIS Maturity Level organizing the Transformation towards ESARIS

The *ESARIS Maturity Levels* relate to the achievement of milestones and a defined ranking with five stages: started, prepared, managed, established and controlled (Fig. 86). The levels were developed using input from the Capability Maturity

Model® Integration (CMMI®)[52] and the Systems Security Engineering - Capability Maturity Model® (SSE-CMM®).[53] The CMMI is built to implement and improve processes. Processes coordinate three things: (i) people with their skills and motivation, (ii) tools and equipment they are using, and (iii) procedures and methods that organize and manage individual tasks. The CMMI levels are not used as is. On the one hand, the Transformation towards using ESARIS is not only implementing processes. New working methods are introduced, skills are developed and even the products of the ICT Service Provider are changed. On the other hand, the Transformation towards ESARIS is not a continuous sequence of actions; it is a project having a planned starting time and an anticipated ending.

The whole company is partitioned into many organizational units, departments or teams. This allows starting with smaller entities. After having achieved higher *ESARIS Maturity Levels* the scope is increased so that finally all relevant organizational units are enabled and cooperate efficiently.

Each organizational unit assigns a so-called Transformation Manager who organizes the Transformation in his or her organization. A Sponsor is also assigned for the Transformation of an organizational unit. This ensures the necessary management attention and support. Refer to the left-hand side in Fig. 87. Note that there are hundreds of such entities in a very large company. The execution of the Transformation needs to be organized centrally which requires a central team performing the overall project or program management (right-hand side of Fig. 87).

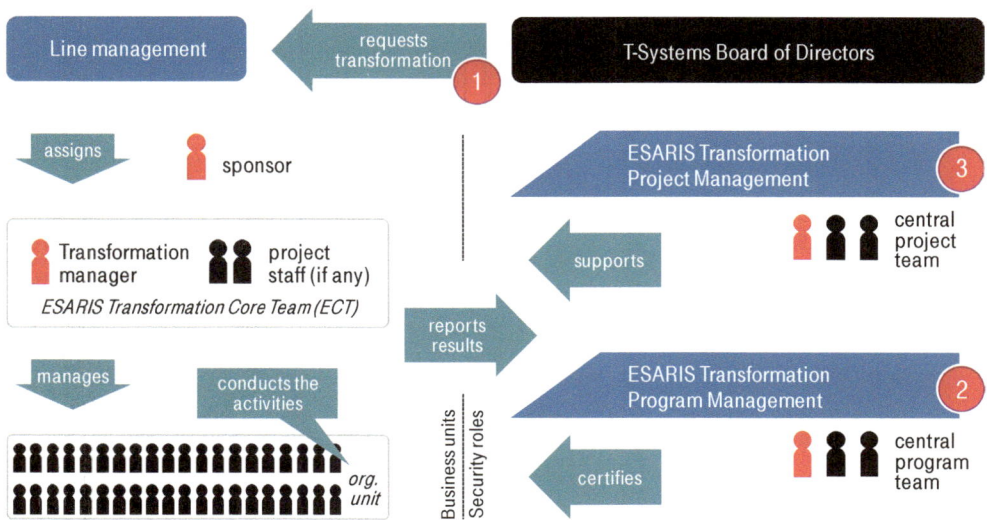

Fig. 87: Organizational structure of the Transformation towards ESARIS

[52] Chrissis, Mary Beth; Mike Konrad and Sandy Shrum: CMMI – Guidelines for Process Integration and Product Improvement; Addison-Wesley, 2003, ISBN 0-321-15496-7 [34]

[53] ISO/IEC 21827 – Information Technology – Systems Security Engineering – Capability Maturity Model (SSE-CMM), 2008 [3]

At this stage we are facing an inconsistency. On the one hand, we want the organization to act autonomously while adopting ESARIS with the new methods, procedures and standards. This is required since the IT staff shall take over tasks that will no longer be conducted by security experts from the Security Management organization. It is also true, that no one can actually anticipate all situations and define the best solution for each of them. On the other hand, it is clear that organizational units require assistance and guidance to step-by-step adopt the new methods, procedures and standards of ESARIS. It was also planned to verify the achievement of milestones and certify the related levels (*ESARIS Maturity Levels*, refer to above). Such a certification also requires the definition of concrete requirements as the basis. One cannot start an assessment without having defined the target.

The way out of this situation turned out to be straightforward but was not easy to go. A so-called *ESARIS Transformation Master Plan (ETMP)* was developed and given to all organizational units in the Transformation. This plan actually comprises five individual plans, one for achieving one *ESARIS Maturity Level*. The levels are reached subsequently; a level must not be skipped. Each plan is organized in different activities or steps and described in one table. Refer to Fig. 88 which shows a small and very simple part of the ETMP. Each activity is given a number and name. Then the major goals are described which shall be achieved. This part also describes the motivation and can be considered as a rationale too. The field "Description of activity" enlists things that are demanded to be done. The field "Further remarks" provides explanations etc.

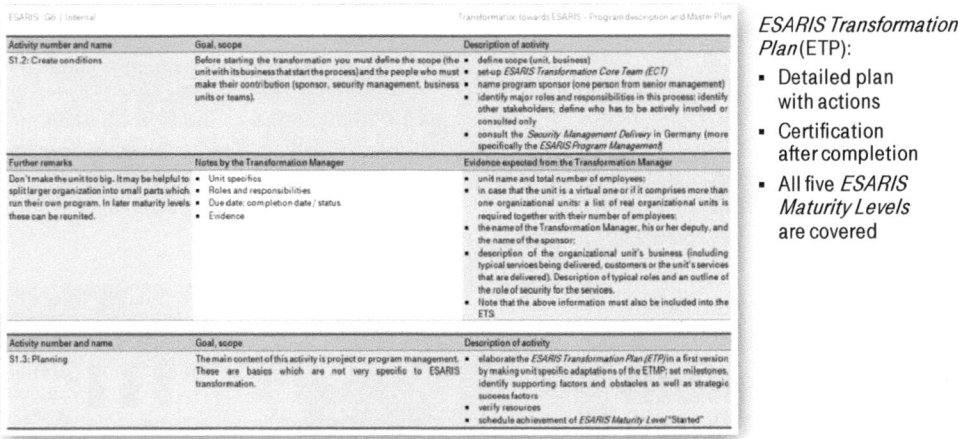

ESARIS Transformation Plan (ETP):

- Detailed plan with actions
- Certification after completion
- All five *ESARIS Maturity Levels* are covered

Fig. 88: Part of the ESARIS Transformation Master Plan (stream 1)

As mentioned above, each organizational unit has its Transformation Manager. This role organizes the Transformation in one organizational unit. A main task for him or her is to create a unit-specific *ESARIS Transformation Plan (ETP)* using the master plan (ETMP) as the basis. The cell describing the information to be added is entitled "Unit specifics". Refer to Fig. 88. This unit-specific information includes for example the following: "Roles and responsibilities" to determine who should do what, "Due date" and "Completion date/status" are for planning to describe the progress made, and "Evidence" refers to things that have to be delivered (documented) by the Transformation Manager in order to complete the *ESARIS Maturity Level* and get certified to have achieved this milestone. The field "Evidence expected from the Transformation Manager" provides the details.

Technically the Transformation of an organizational unit is supported by a well-defined process and central roles. An organizational unit registers for the Transformation process or is asked to do so. Here general information is recorded. The Transformation Manager performs the planning. Hereby he or she uses the *ESARIS Transformation Master Plan (ETMP)* as described above. The Transformation Manager must demonstrate that the activities and sub-activities have successfully been conducted. To this end, he or she must provide evidence. The necessary evidences are also described in the ETMP. Training of employees is e.g. an important part of conducting the Transformation. So, evidence that employees attended the trainings is required. After having performed all activities and sub-activities, the Transformation Manager can request for certification, i.e. formal approval of the achievement of an *ESARIS Maturity Level*. The ETP, specifically the evidences, are checked and verified by the central ESARIS Transformation Program Management. Other people help to organize the overall process: they do normal project management for the Transformation of the whole company and especially take care that the entities keep to the schedule. This team is called ESARIS Transformation Project Management shown in Fig. 87 on page 195.

KPIs are used to manage the overall project where the individual organizational units have to provide key figures. The process described above is supported using tools: there is a workflow tool and electronic filing of all information including the units' plans with the evidences. Also certification reports are filed which are generated using templates with a questionnaire.

How many organizational units must pass how many certifications? This seems to be an easy question but its analysis shows the real challenge. This Transformation program is huge and difficult.

It is really a question if a company can actually manage such a process. In order to find out if this can realistically be managed and how, some estimation is performed. Refer to Fig. 89.

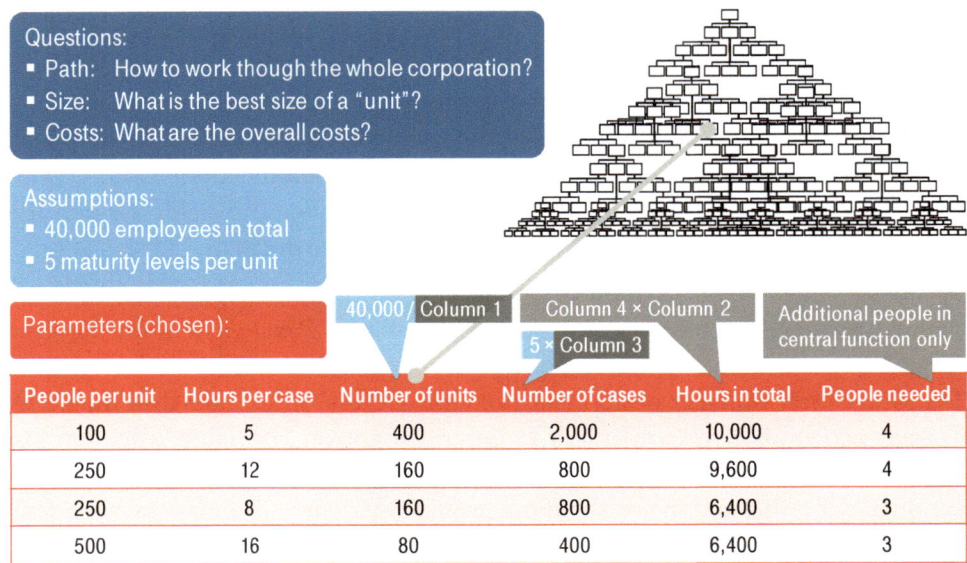

Fig. 89: Four scenarios for which the costs are calculated

Three simple questions guide through the analysis which is necessary for the detailed planning (refer to the dark blue box in Fig. 89):

- Path: How to work through the whole corporation? What are the units to begin with? How to know if the whole organization has actually been covered?

- Size: What is the best or realistic size of an organizational unit that performs the Transformation according to one *ESARIS Transformation Plan (ETP)* as described above? If the units are small, their business is homogeneous which facilitates the process. However, the smaller the units the higher the number of certifications (called cases in Fig. 89).

- Costs: What are the overall costs for the central ESARIS Transformation program/project? Is it realistic at all to perform the Transformation under the given circumstances as planned? Note that one cannot calculate the costs for the business units in detail. Primarily, the extra costs for the central team are estimated. The central team must spent time for kick-off meeting, for support during the Transformation and for the certification process which includes the management of the registration information and of the ETP as well as the evaluation of the ETP and the provisioning of the result.

Fig. 89 (light blue box) shows the assumptions: It is assumed that there are 40,000 employees. There are also five *ESARIS Maturity Levels* so that each unit must go through five processes. The number of cases the central team must manage is "5 × number of units". We assume that one expert can spent 1,400 hours a year and that the Transformation lasts two years.

Fig. 89 (red and grey) shows a specimen calculation. The first parameter is "people per unit" which determines the "size" of a typical organizational unit under consideration. The second parameter is "hours per case" to be spent by the central team for kick-off, support and the certification process.

As an example, three values for the average "size" of a unit are taken for the calculation: 100, 250 and 500 (refer to the lower part in Fig. 89). The "hours per case" which must be spent by the central team are related to the size. It is assumed that the larger the unit the more complex and inhomogeneous its business. As a result, the effort for the central team is higher. We take absolute minimum values: 5 hours only for a rather small unit and only 16 hours for a larger unit with 500 people in average. For the units with 250 people we take the assumption in the specimen calculation that 12 or 8 hours are required for kick-off, support and the certification process.

The results show the challenge. The "number of cases" varies between 2,000 and 400. Note that for each case the unit needs to be registered, the process needs to be started which requires a kick-off meeting (usually using the Web), support during the execution of the Transformation, some project management activities like scheduling and corrective measures in the case of delays, and the evaluation of the *ESARIS Transformation Plan (ETP)* including the certification as well. Hence, 5 to 16 hours per case are not much.

Here are some other numbers:

- Is it realistic to manage 2,000 cases in two years? Or, is even 400 too much? It is advantageous to take smaller units at the beginning, since the process is easier for both the unit and the central team. But the number of cases must be reduced to a minimum.

- The total effort for the central team varies between 10,000 and 6,400 which relates to about four or three extra people. These people only provide project support. The Transformation activities are executed by the people in the organizational units. If every employee would spend two hours a year this would sum up to additional 80,000 hours equivalent to 45 people equivalents (full time).

- Each unit has a Transformation Manager. If we assume that he or she spends only 25% of the time for the Transformation, this sums up to 100 to 20 people equivalents (full time).

Hence, the total costs range approximately between 70 and 150 people equivalents (working full time) which would only work for the Transformation from its start to the end. This does not only mean that the Transformation is complicated It also means that the standardization produced by ESARIS leads to savings in development and operations that are higher than the effort spent for the Transformation. ESARIS is also the basis for the secure ICT service delivery in a industrialized, large-scale IT production. That's why the company introduced ESARIS.

A calculation as the one shown above also provides important information on how to organize the Transformation. There are three things which had to be done to manage the complexity and to reduce the effort:

- Prioritization: A list that helps to choose the right units have been developed. Depending on its business one organizational unit may have higher priority to participate in the Transformation than another. High priority units are "leaders" or "centers of gravity" in a larger organization. Operations management or units that provide infrastructure services may be more important to start with than others.

- Nomination: Finally, ESARIS is used along the whole supply chain. Some "single units" started. Then the scope is increased so that "several units" are involved and reach the same *ESARIS Maturity Level*. Finally, all units that are involved in businesses along the internal supply chain are working with ESARIS. To achieve this, each organizational unit must nominate other organizational units during the Transformation which provide or receive relevant services to or from it. The nomination of "neighbors" helps the unit to apply the ESARIS security standards and to reach a higher *ESARIS Maturity Level*.

- Aggregation: As already mentioned it is best to start with smaller organizational units. The effort for higher *ESARIS Maturity Levels* is higher than for the lower ones. Therefore, the number of certifications (cases) especially in higher levels should be reduced. That's why, only large organizational units are accepted in higher *ESARIS Maturity Levels*.

11.3   Enablement: training and communication

Introduction and summary: The organizational units and the employees should not try to get familiar with ESARIS using the concept papers and security standards alone. Instead, comprehensive training material and training programs are required. This section provides best practices related to target group definition using avatars, video production and distribution, integration of video clips into Office documents, the provisioning of navigators as well as a central repository for leaflets, posters, FAQ etc.

It is a real challenge to distribute the right information to the right people. The difficulties were underestimated at the beginning of the Transformation. For the team that developed the material, it was obvious that a certain information is e.g. for designers or operations personnel. However, in a large organization terms like "design", "engineering", "realization", "implementation", "production", "delivery" or "operations" are not as clear as one might expect. If certain information is e.g. labeled with "design", many employees may ignore it since their unit is not labeled "design" even if they are working in projects where something is designed. Additionally, the internal supply chain is complicated: there are organizational units which perform tasks in different phases of the supply chain. Moreover, experts get involved in tasks which are usually not performed by the unit they belong to. Names and titles also change when the company is reorganized.

Fig. 90: Avatars are introduced to specify the audience

As a result, the material was organized in working areas. The working areas had more or less understandable names. However, it turned out that they were not clear to everybody and maybe they were too long. In addition, people do not necessarily associate a working area with people doing this work independent from the name of their organizational unit. That's why the avatars Adrian, Betty and Chris were introduced representing the three major *ESARIS Work Areas* (refer to Sect. 3.2) as shown in Fig. 90. Each avatar representing a work area / function is then split into three sub-avatars as shown for Adrian in Fig. 90. Short names facilitate communication; the names are gender balanced since Chris may be male or female. The areas are related to the ITIL processes. The employees must only be familiar with these processes since the IT production they are working in is organized along them. The avatars help to recognize activities which originally have complicated and ambiguous names.

Note there is a high volume of information. The organization has to manage a large number of corporate security documents, but due to the high degree of division of labor every team only requires specific security documents although these teams also need to have a complete picture to some extent. There is a huge number of recipients, and the audience is inhomogeneous. The organization has to distribute the content not only to some security experts but to almost all people who are engaged in the design, implementation and delivery of ICT services. Note additionally that in a global organization specific roles and teams with a dedicated deliverable exist many times. The avatars help to get the message actually across.

It is common practice to use multimedia to train people. Companies engage agencies which produce high quality video material based on the specialists' input being provided. The advantages are perfect content and professional performance. The disadvantages are high effort since an external agency needs to be provided with all information and results need to be reviewed in review cycles. Another problem is that the videos get outdated and mistakes cannot easily be fixed.

The solution was that experts use of-the-shelf software that captures the screen and records the voice on a PC. In this way training videos and video instructions are produced. Refer to Fig. 91. External support was only used for specific videos. The training videos (run time 15, 30 or 45 minutes) are stored in a central repository and therefore available to all employees.

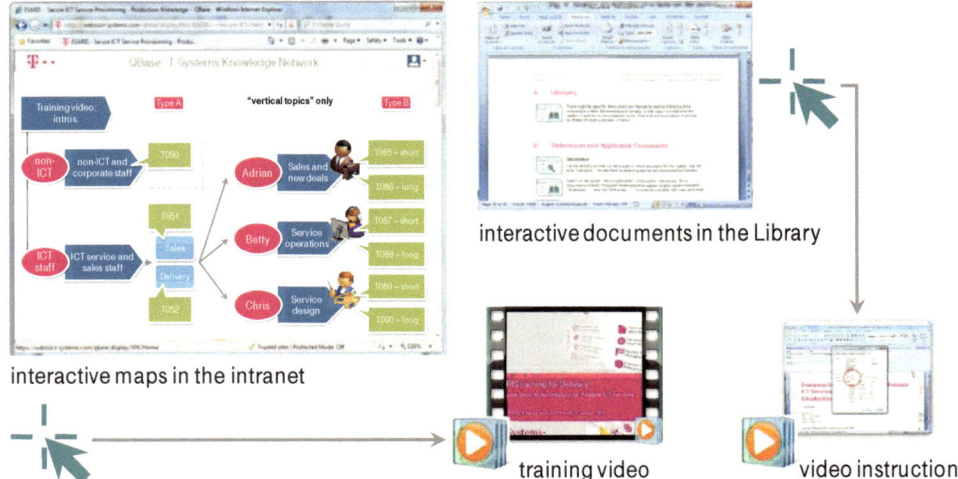

Fig. 91: Interactive content and video material

How do employees know what video to watch? The videos are made available through interactive maps in Intranet sites and the knowledge base. These interactive maps (refer to the upper left in Fig. 91) provide an overview of a specific topic. The interactive maps show the available content and guide employees to the content they are looking for. A click on a graphical element of the map opens a list or directly the video. The interactive maps are called ESARIS Navigators internally. They are created from PowerPoint slides which are converted into HTML5 or Flash using a special software. These formats make it possible to seamlessly integrate the maps into web pages.

Video instructions were also produced which for instance explain how to work with a document. Guidance is given e.g. how to fill in required information. These video instructions are played if one clicks onto a graphical element in the document (right-hand side in Fig. 91). This approach allows employees to get the best support working with ESARIS documents.

In order to ensure sufficient quality, one must develop a training concept. The training concept describes all content on a general level and provides a structure that is necessary to make sure all target groups and all topics are addressed in the right way. Each video is characterized by a few parameters: Of course, all videos are assigned a unique reference number (ID). For each topic a range of reference numbers (IDs) is reserved. Other parameters include length, depth, language, medium, target group and topic code. In addition to these parameters, a short description of the content and of the use case is provided.

One of the big challenges is to ensure that people are able to find and identify documents. ESARIS is a fully hierarchical, structured and modular approach to organize information about how to secure ICT services. Every ESARIS document that is electronically filed for general use throughout the company is assigned a unique document ID. This document ID is composed of letters and numbers which allow identifying

- the nature of the document and location within ESARIS and its hierarchy,
- the topic or area as organized by the *ESARIS Security Taxonomy*,
- the use and purpose of the document.

The details are described in Chapter 10. This facilitates the identification of documents. References to documents can be made with the document ID only. Mixing up is avoided. The document ID also makes it possible to create Navigators as mentioned above. The interactive maps (Navigator) can indicate one document or a group of documents with a specific topic and/or purpose. Document IDs are very space-saving which is important for many multimedia applications.

Not all content can be made available in one repository. The storage media are still optimized to serve specific purposes. Official documents of the company are filed in its Document Library. There is a Knowledge Base to share associated information. A social media platform is optimized for the communication between people and not to store structured content.

One central repository was used for leaflets, posters, FAQ etc., i.e. all information that cannot be stored in the Document Library. However, there are still different sites and people use to start with one of them and may be confused not to see the content they are expecting to see. To this end, each site has been equipped with the same interactive map that provides links to the other sites.

Though this is maybe considered to be common practice, we think it is not. It is complicated to get the message across since people concentrate on the content and there is no time to simultaneously consider why the content is important. However, motivation is important. Hence, three messages were developed (shown in Fig. 92) which were repeated again and again when communicating to the employees. Each message is related to a request since the employees shall act.

What should I remember?

ESARIS can be summarized differently.
Finally, this comes down to: standardize, contribute, and gain benefit.

ESARIS – STANDARDIZATION AND HARMONIZATION OF SECURITY.

We implement security measures as required and reuse pre-defined modules whenever possible.

I know: Utilizing standardized elements helps to improve quality, reduces costs and accelerates processes. Customers expect the same level of security around the globe. That's why I am using the elements from the *ESARIS Library* when it comes to security.
Standardize, now!

ESARIS – SECURITY IS EVERYBODY'S RESPONSIBILITY.

We deliver secure ICT services to our customers since IT risks put the business at risk.

I know that my part is only one single element. But it can be an essential one. Thus everybody in the businesses must take his or her responsibility regarding security. Only then we can safeguard our company and our customers. Success depends on the reliability of our ICT services.
Contribute, now!

ESARIS – SHAPING THE SECURITY OF ICT BUSINESSES.

We integrate security into technology and service management and thus raise our competitiveness.

I know that information security is important – though not always easy to cope with. ESARIS provides a holistic approach and really helps to manage security in our large-scale ICT production. With ESARIS the integration of security can really work. Securing ICT services becomes a manageable task – also for me.
Gain benefit, now!

Fig. 92: Information is linked to one of the three key messages

Finally, the security management itself had to be adapted. Best practices relate to balancing activities

- in the transformation project on the one hand (this Chapter 11)

and those in the day-to-day, continual security management on the other hand. The day-to-day activities cover

- fostering standardization (Chapter 6),
- supporting the "attainment" (including the management of the Aces, Chapter 7),
- watching the "fulfillment" (Chapter 8) as well as
- assessing the management of suppliers (Chapter 9) and
- managing security standards (Chapter 10).

The responsibilities and processes must be (re-)defined accordingly.

ESARIS is introduced to respond to the fundamental changes in IT. The new approach aims at the consequent integration of IT security management and IT service management (ITIL). This has a major effect.

The IT staff (and not only people from the security organization) implements the security measures that are stipulated in the ESARIS standards. The business units are responsible to secure their ICT services. This includes the provisioning of required resources (technology, people etc.). The IT experts shall also participate and strongly support the development and maintenance of the security standards.

This new approach has been summed up with the (elder) slogan "Security is everybody's responsibility". In practice, this is a massive change in roles and responsibilities requiring a quite different mindset of many employees and managers. But also people from the Security Management organizations must learn that standardization alters their way of acting.

As described above, the Transformation is split into two streams. The *Transformation of organizational units* (stream 1) has to establish processes and create the necessary conditions for the delivery of secure ICT services according to ESARIS. In this stream the organization and the people working there learn how to use the methods, procedures and standards of ESARIS in order to produce ICT services that are compliant with the security standards and produced efficiently. After having achieved a reasonable maturity level, organizational units can start with stream 2, the Transformation of ICT services. This means that the IT production starts to deliver ICT services meeting the ESARIS security standards.

The *Transformation of ICT services* (stream 2) is also initiated by the unit's Transformation Manager. The business unit (represented by the "service owner") designs, implements or operates the ICT service and must thereby take the ESARIS standards into account. ESARIS defines a methodology (*ESARIS Attainment Model*) for documenting the level of compliance of an ICT service with the ESARIS security standards. The result is called Ace and produced by the business. This attainment information is collected and then checked and verified by the Security Management organization. They assess the risks associated with deviations and request mitigation if required. In this way, stream 2 of the Transformation initiates a process that will later run in the same way without support from a Transformation Manager.

People from the Security Management organization play also a major role in inspecting the *ESARIS Transformation Plans* (ETP) delivered by organizational units to get certified. The Transformation Manager is required to describe critical success factors as well as obstacles and supporting factors for the use of ESARIS in his or her organizational unit. Obstacles and supporting factors are an important source of information. The Security Management organization can use such information to plan and initiate corrective measures (as a part of Transformation or not). In addition, a quality gate with an extensive audit is scheduled before the work on *ESARIS Maturity Level 4* ("established") actually starts.

11.4   Voyage of ICT services

Introduction and summary: Rome was not built in a day and the transformation of all existing legacy ICT systems and related processes and practices would take a long time and be expensive. Legacy systems may deviate from the security measures stipulated in ESARIS for many reasons. If an ICT Service Provider starts using one unique set of security standards, which means disposing of others, it must analyze effects on existing contracts and on the current business. Consequently, the effects of the Transformation of ICT services (stream 2 of the

Transformation) are studied in little more detail. Note that deviations from *ICT Security Standards* may not be limited to legacy systems.

To recap: The *ESARIS Attainment Levels* relate to the achievement of milestones in delivering ICT services according to the methods, procedures and standards of ESARIS. The first three levels are related to more technical tasks (IT engineering and implementation). Level 1: The technical components integrate the security measures that are stipulated in the ESARIS security standards. Level 2: The IT service management processes also integrate security as defined in the ESARIS security standards. Level 3 is "successfully delivered" which means that the ICT service has at least once been provided to a customer with security measures as defined in the ESARIS security standards. The last two stages are related to the management of the service portfolio (called Service Catalog Management in ITIL). Level 4: integrated into delivery portfolio means that ESARIS is part of the ICT service specification provided by the delivery units. Level 5: integrated into sales portfolio means that ESARIS is part of the ICT service description provided to customers.

The consideration of compliance with *ICT Security Standards* during Transformation requires the consideration of history and the rollout of ESARIS at an ICT Service Provider. The *ICT Security Standards* may not have existed when certain ICT services were implemented or these standards had a different content. The process is shown in Fig. 93. There are several factors which determine if and to what extent a given ICT service actually complies with the relevant *ICT Security Standards*. The letters A through E denote a timeline which is simultaneously a first filter. The *Transformation towards ESARIS* started with letter C. The ESARIS security standards were applied on a voluntary basis (C) and finally became mandatory (E). The letters F and G denote steps for deeper analysis. The judgment is shown on the bottom: not compliant, partly compliant or compliant with ESARIS.

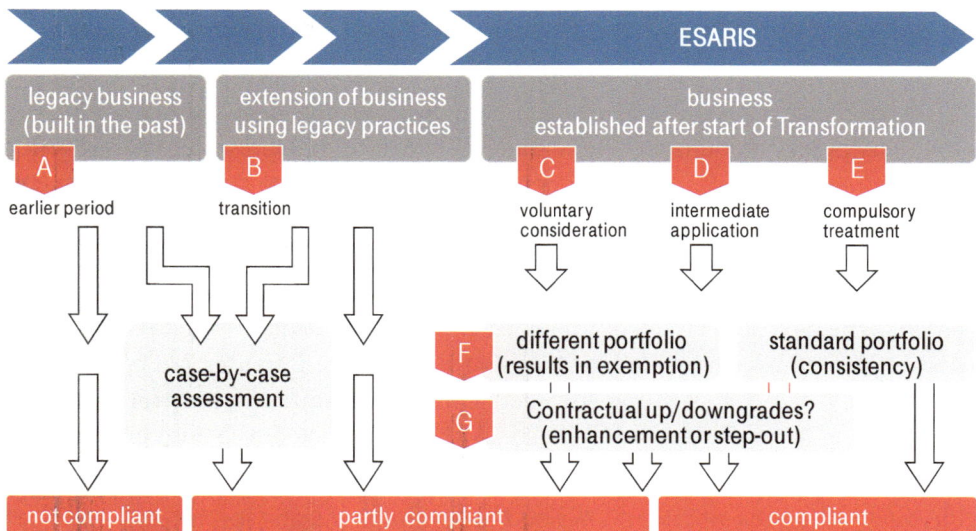

Fig. 93: Time line of the Transformation and effect on ICT services

The time line of the Transformation and the effect on ICT services is now investigated in more detail.

<u>Step A – Earlier period:</u> Providers often stay in the business for a long time. Hence, there are legacy systems as well as services for existing customers which address very different requirements and that therefore have various security measures in place. Legacy does not mean that security has not been adequately considered. However, the security requirements may be different from those in use today. Improvements may also be made later. However, security measures which are defined or consolidated after the deployment of these ICT systems and services may not exist or may not meet the ESARIS specification exactly. The security measures implemented may not match in each case with those being specified as part of ESARIS and its *ICT Security Standards*. As a result, in many cases these legacy systems and services are "not compliant". But even historic systems and services may partly comply with ESARIS measures which can be verified by a case-by-case assessment.

<u>Step B – Transition:</u> An ICT Service Provider may also extend the business using legacy practices. Services are provided using existing platforms or platforms that are simply extended. This means, for instance, that a service is extended by an existing customer (under a new contract). An established and existing platform is used for some reason so that legacy practices have an impact on the security. Hence, this service may still be "not compliant" or "partly compliant" with ESARIS.

The *ICT Security Standards* and their security measures are only applied on entities that are designed and controlled by the ICT Service Provider. As described above, it is determined by the timeline whether or not this is the case. But moreover, it is up to the contracted ICT services and related regulations.

Larger ICT Service Providers continue to take over ICT systems and components from customers, sometimes whole data centers with operations personnel and all the processes established there. When being taken over, the systems are in a status named CMO ("Current Mode of Operation"). It is expected to deviate from the ICT Service Provider's standards. If so, changes and adjustments are made early on in order to achieve the so-called CMO+, which does feature improvements and adaptations. The next step is called Transformation. In this phase, the actual modernization is performed where standards of the ICT Service Provider are introduced in full. Finally, the ICT is in the so-called FMO ("Future Mode of Operation"). ICT systems and services that are CMO or CMO+ are expected to be not or only partly compliant with ESARIS. This must be checked.

Please note that the situation described here is by no means specific to security and also applies to other quality characteristics of the ICT business. Security is not the only area which features gaps between old and new.

Steps C through E – Rollout and treatment: ESARIS is designed and designated to apply to all delivery platforms, locations of production and ICT services in an ICT Service Provider's portfolio. The *Transformation towards ESARIS* is necessary to enable people and organizations to apply the ESARIS methods and security standards step-by-step. Moreover, the providers who have acquired other providers or business from other enterprises in particular are expected to have different ICT offerings and production methods. This applies to ICT services, but is also true for their security. Larger ICT Service Providers require time to implement the same practices and standards in all their subsidiaries and departments. That's why the ESARIS methods and standards are used voluntarily, then from case to case, and finally they are treated mandatorily.

Step F – Portfolio: ICT Service Providers have a well-defined service offering portfolio that describes all the ICT services customers can procure. These ICT services cover the core business of the company. ESARIS defines standards in the field of security for this core business.

The ICT Service Provider may decide to provide custom services that are tailored to a very specific demand of a specific customer. In this case, best practices are adapted and used as far as possible. This applies both to ICT features and to security characteristics. Hence, if the service under consideration deviates from the standard portfolio (refer to Fig. 93) it cannot be expected that the standardized security measures laid down in ESARIS and its *ICT Security Standards* fully apply.

Step H – Contractual up/downgrades: The contractual agreements may also lead to deviations from ESARIS security standards and a "partly compliant" statement (see Fig. 93) even if ESARIS was already made mandatory.

12 Implementation – IT production and its protection in practice

Introduction and summary: The organization, concept and content of the *ICT Security Standards* were described in Chapter 4. This chapter looks behind the scenes and describes the industrialized IT production along with the technology and processes used. Using this portrayal as a basis, security problems, issues or concerns are identified and specified. They need to be addressed. The description of the environment and its analysis is performed step-by-step for each individual realm addressed by an *ICT Security Standard*. Each section is dedicated to one cluster of standards. After characterizing the challenges, the measures are addressed that are intended to counteract the problems and solve the challenges. Thus, information about major security measures is provided for each *ICT Security Standard*. Overall, the chapter offers a comprehensive view about the IT production and protecting it in practice.

12.1 Evidence and Customer Relation

Introduction and summary: This cluster comprises four areas: *Customer Communication and Security* specifies how the ICT Service Provider acts, interacts and communicates with customers. *Vulnerability Assessment and Mitigation Planning* refers to activities such as security testing, regular scanning, CERT services, evaluation of impacts and planning of corrective actions. *Logging, Monitoring and Security Reporting* deals with log management and analysis, monitoring of systems, measurement and information provisioning to customers. In *Incident Handling and Forensics,* practices for handling (security) incidents in IT production are described, possibly, together with the customer. It also describes investigations. This section is split into two types of descriptions. Firstly, the general environment, the scope and major activities are described in each area of the whole cluster. Thus, the context in the ICT service production and delivery is portrayed in order to highlight the security problems, issues or concerns which need to be addressed. Secondly, information about major security measures is given. These are not specified in full, but this section can be used when designing security measures that protect the area.

Fig. 94 below shows the location of the "Evidence and Customer Relation" cluster within the *ESARIS Security Taxonomy*. The four *ICT Security Standards* are highlighted. This section is organized as follows:

- Sect. 12.1.1 describes the general environment, the scope and major activities.
- Sect. 12.1.2 contains information about major security measures.

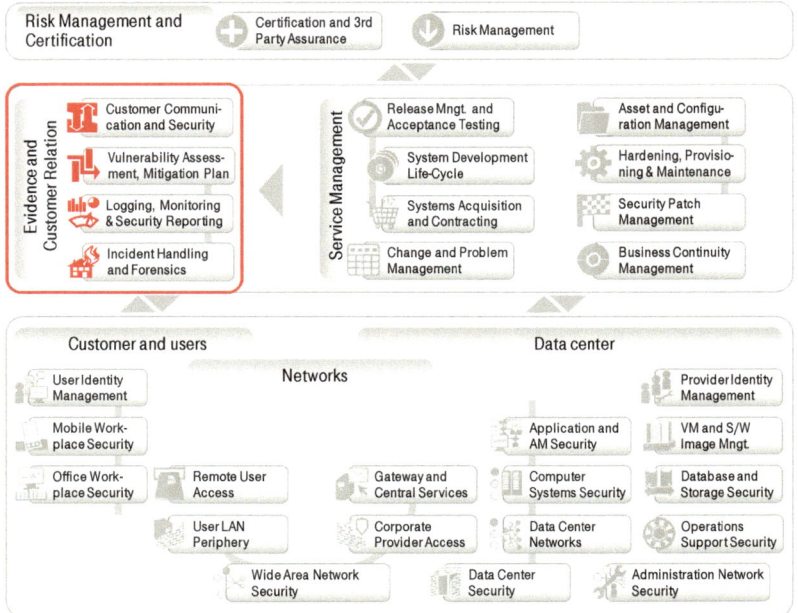

Fig. 94: Landing cluster of "Evidence and Customer Relation"

12.1.1   Match – (Im)Prove – Correct

ICT Service Providers operate data networks for customers and process data in their own or in customers' data centers. ICT security and data privacy are a top priority in all these activities. The survival of a company can depend on the security of data, how it is protected from manipulation and, last but not least, the high availability of this data. Appropriate security measures are necessary. These are stipulated in standards and implemented accordingly.

Match

In a complex IT outsourcing situation, the activities of an ICT Service Provider start with upon first contact with the customer, cover the entire sales process, including solution design and contract implementation, and comprise service set-up and service operations. The following four areas are identified (refer to Fig. 95):

- General communication between the ICT Service Provider and the user organization covers the day-to-day exchange of information for the purpose of managing the business relationship between them. The communication media include e-mail, telephone, file servers and groupware or even delivery of storage media. It is performed from the Manage the Deal phases through Transition and Transformation to Operations.

- Another type of information is being exchanged while new business is set up and major changes are performed. The exchange is required to allow the ICT Service Provider to design, implement and set up the requested ICT service.

Here, provider and user organizations work in projects with a definite starting point and an estimated end point.

- The migration is also a project. Here, data and ICT systems are transferred to the ICT Service Provider.

- Operations refers to day-to-day business. Here, primarily the ICT Service Provider provides information to the user organization. It must maintain the security of its ICT infrastructure and provide evidence that security requirements are met. In case of incidents, it might be necessary for the two parties to work together.

Each of these areas has its own challenges. They are outlined in slightly more detail below. Security aspects are considered in this process model as depicted by the eight activities on the bottom of the figure. They are provided as an orientation only and not being elaborated further in this book.

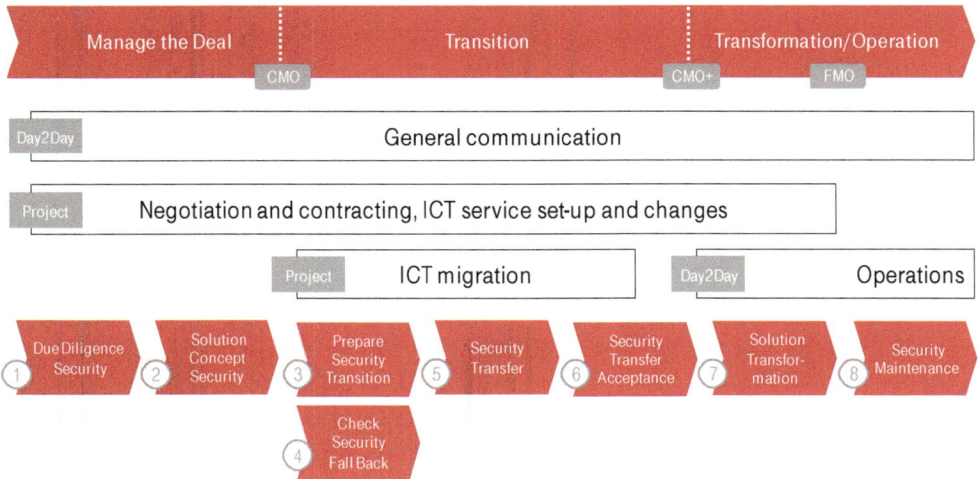

Fig. 95: Customer interaction from Manage the Deal all the way to Operations

In all phases including Manage the Deal, Transition, Transformation and Operations, provider and customer communicate and exchange relevant, sensitive, confidential or proprietary information. Such information comprises business-related information and other internal information of the customer as well as information about the ICT Service Provider and its ICT service delivery considered to be intellectual property or sensitive. This information needs to be kept confidential. As a minimum, the availability thereof is highly restricted to a group of people. Otherwise, one party can suffer serious economic loss, loss of reputation or other damage. It is also important that data integrity is ensured and that data originates as expected. Manipulations can lead to similar effects. Note that not only design information etc. is exchanged during sales and service delivery set-up. Moreover, information needs to be exchanged during Operations for effective Service Delivery Management and in order to make changes, treat possible problems and develop the cooperation.

However, large amounts of data and ICT systems are also transferred to the ICT Service Provider when the latter takes over ICT services from a customer or its previous provider. This is done in the so-called Transition phase. That migration is critical for the obvious reason that the customer's data and ICT might be accessed in an unauthorized, hostile way leading to a loss of confidentiality, integrity or availability. However, it is worth noting that additional and serious threat scenarios come into play since security measures of the existing environment are no longer effective during this intermediate situation whereas the planned security measures of the destination environment are not yet effective. Because of the temporality of this phase, implementation of extra protective measures may reach limits despite being very important.

Another problem area to be mentioned here is the lack of common understanding and binding clarity and uncertain or vague stipulation. The two parties must rely on each other. This requires mutual understanding and contractual clarity. Otherwise, business cannot be managed appropriately.

(Im)Prove

In the Operations phase, the ICT Service Provider operates ICT systems for user organizations. ICT systems and components as well as ICT security solutions operated to protect them may and will have vulnerabilities which could be exploited and may have a serious impact on the customers' business. Attacks may, for example, lead to a loss of availability, or may violate confidentiality, privacy and other requirements, e.g. as a result of gaining of unauthorized privileges. Vulnerabilities themselves may result from flaws in design, missed patches or updates, from unanticipated changes in use or to the operating environment, or technical progress that may provide new attack methods. ICT systems and components may also be misconfigured or their configuration tampered with. In addition, incorrect changes could be made, e.g. by applying patches which are not tried and tested, or by using patches which are not correctly serialized.

Just the appearance or knowledge of vulnerabilities can significantly change the anticipated risk and, therefore, requires the earliest possible detection, notification, thorough analysis and timely action. Therefore, a Vulnerability Assessment procedure is set up in order to detect existing and potential vulnerabilities from diverse sources and/or by different means as early as possible. Mitigation needs to be planned in order to remediate the vulnerabilities as quickly as possible in an efficient and effective manner.

If the required corrective actions are not performed for any reason (if a vulnerability goes unnoticed or a corrective action is postponed) the ICT service may suffer a loss of

▪ confidentiality — unwanted or unauthorized disclosure of information,

- integrity —unauthorized modification or corruption of information,
- availability — system or service cannot be accessed and used upon legitimate demand,
- control — system or service cannot be modified and adapted upon legitimate demand, or
- trust — there are doubts that the system or service meets requirements.

The relevance of a vulnerability has to be assessed within the individual customer context.

Most systems produce log data in order to provide "run-time information". Those generated by ICT security systems in particular are of great importance here where others may have another purpose such as capacity management. This log data is examined and specific tools are implemented to monitor ICT systems in order to gain information about possible attacks and abuse. This provides information about the security status of ICT systems and components in order to demonstrate adherence to policies and compliance with regulation, etc.

Log data is analyzed in order to allow system troubleshooting, check compliance with security policies and regulation, respond to security incidents and perform security investigations (forensics). Pattern recognition, normalization, classification and tagging as well as correlation analysis are typical examples of automated log data assessment. Such tasks should be performed on different system levels and consolidated centrally in order to generate a best possible overall picture. User monitoring covers the investigation of user access (rights and policies) and activity. It is important for threat management, fraud detection, breach discovery and compliance reporting. Applications also need to be monitored and other resource access monitoring may also be required. Improved threat management may require real-time data collection that enables immediate analysis. The most important data which needs to be collected and analyzed is security-critical events. This monitoring and alerting information from different sources is aggregated and then correlated. Notification should be supported in nearly real-time.

Both the user organization and the ICT Service Provider like to gather information about the security status or security quality of the ICT services they are consuming or delivering. There are two types of such information:

- snap-shot information about the design (construction) and set-up (configuration) of the ICT systems,
- run-time information about use and suspicious or malicious activity.

The first type of information, which is called snap-shot information, relates to the current construction and configuration of the ICT systems. The purpose of gathering this information is to discover and mitigate vulnerabilities. Appropriate security reports provide information about the vulnerability status and mitigation activities and their effect. The run-time information relates to the use of ICT systems and services. Suspicious, malicious or even hostile activities are analyzed. Appropriate security reports show if the countermeasures are working as expected and if attacks or other unwanted actions are being prevented.

Logging of information is the basis for all further activities. Only information being logged can be interpreted (in correlation to a system, process or business object). Logging itself is not just collecting the information, but may include also the activities for storing or processing information for later activities. Monitoring interprets log, event and configuration data, correlates information from different sources and relates results to targets such as ICT systems, services or processes. Security reporting finally makes the results of such evaluations and ratings visible. Security reporting may differ in terms of detail depending on the addressee: For the customer or the management, a higher level of abstraction may be the best choice. For those who have to deal with technology, a more detailed report will be essential. The content of a report may be different too, based on the fact that the information included must not be handed over to customers for confidentiality or data privacy reasons.

Logging and monitoring are considered to be the provider's internal activities. Security reporting is also used for internal purposes but the main objective is to inform customers.

Precautions during development and acquisition reduce the probability of security breaches. Moreover, ICT systems and components are to be maintained and kept up-to-date by applying security patches. Such corrective actions are the result of findings from the vulnerability management described above and of findings from logging and monitoring of ICT services and systems. Notwithstanding those day-to-day activities, circumstances may occur or be observed that require urgent counteraction. These are called incidents or here, more specifically, security incidents. Therefore, a so-called Incident Management process is needed in order to collect notifications of such circumstances and to mitigate the impact by remedying the weakness and through the timely restoration of the ICT service delivery in accordance with the requirements.

12.1.2 Accomplishing security

Cautionary note: This section provides examples of essential security issues. It is not the subject of this book to specify technical, procedural and organizational security measures in detail. However, the following section specifies major aspects that can be considered when designing security measures that protect the cluster "Evidence and Customer Relation" (described in Sect. 12.1.1). Note that security should also have a business case; the design, implementation and maintenance of security measures incur costs, but customers especially tend to look for lower prices. Thus, security needs to be carefully designed.

The *ICT Security Standard – Customer Communication and Security (CCS)* describes all the procedures that arrange the communication with customers and all means used to secure this electronic communication. This includes non-disclosure agreements and encryption technology for e-mails. Moreover, this standard covers the management of the relation between the customer and the ICT Service Provider and major security-related tasks in the Manage the Deal phase, during Transition and Transformation as well as in Operations.

A very basic obligation concerns confidentiality and the protection of intellectual property. The parties shall agree upon the classification of information before it is exchanged. Non-disclosure and other agreements may be signed. The use of communication resources should be discussed and agreed upon since media such as phone, e-mail, file servers and media exchange provide a different level of trust and risk exposure. In addition, all documents in any form shall be categorized in advance according to their level of confidentiality and labeled accordingly. This enables the other party to adhere to regulations that are agreed upon. Appropriate means may be necessary and used to securely exchange data, documents as well as e-mails. Here all phases of the cooperation, starting from the Manage the Deal phase, shall be considered where specific circumstances are to be taken into account. The means may include a technical infrastructure for encrypted e-mail communication. Such solutions can use a special gateway or an installation on workplace computers. Documents are often shared on collaboration platforms such as Microsoft's SharePoint. Security reporting may, for example, require means for secure data delivery, encryption, masking or pseudonymization[54]. The use of such platforms shall be agreed upon. It may be necessary to add security measures; at least the level of protection and possible risks should be transparent to both sides.

These examples also show that mutual agreements are a general foundation for the collaboration between the user organization and the ICT Service Provider. Regulations may be stipulated to ensure that essential and legitimate interests of both the ICT service consuming party and the ICT Service Provider are respected, maintained, considered and balanced. This requires appropriate transparency as well as clear statements and regulations, usually expressed in written or even signed agreements. In particular, the customer's security requirements shall be made explicit as required. This is a prerequisite for appropriate planning and secure ICT service delivery. The parties are reminded that definitions of security and ICT-related terms may differ in various organizations. Hence, alignment of understanding and practices is another essential prerequisite for comprehensive security. Complex services usually require a security concept to be developed based on the security measures, practices and processes stipulated in ESARIS. Regardless of

---

[54] also called "tokenization"

whether ICT systems and components are newly designed, procured off-the-shelf or taken over from the customer, their security status must be analyzed and understood in advance. Plans need to be developed and agreed to mitigate risks and to apply changes during Transition and Transformation e.g. in order to achieve conformity with provider standards.

Measures have to be taken during the migration of ICT systems or data[55] in order to ensure the protection of the migrated ICT systems and the customer's data. A security concept or plan shall be developed which is valid during the migration processes and appropriately considers applicable security policies and regulations. Such a concept or plan should define scope, actions, milestones, responsibilities, expected results and validation methods, agreements on risk treatment and transfer, troubleshooting and recovery planning, planning of technical process steps including freezing and testing, finalization and approval as well as possible rework. Migration is a critical process in the Transition phase since the security measures of the previous environment are no longer effective during this intermediate situation, whereas the planned security measures of the destination environment are not yet effective. Hence, appropriate planning and organization is essential in order to manage this step. This, in turn, requires knowledge of the critical assets in order to be able to provide appropriate protection. A risk analysis specific to this phase may be necessary. Risks must be identified but also acknowledged by the parties. A formal process for the transfer of hazard (or risks) shall be set up. Additional measures may be implemented in addition in order to mitigate identified risks.

The transfer of business and responsibility from the user organization (or its former provider) to the new ICT Service Provider needs to be planned, analyzed and tracked in a similar way. The status of migration and business transfer needs to be documented and tracked, verified and formally approved. Precautions are to be taken for troubleshooting and for recovery in case of interruption and relaunch of migration. Interfaces with roles and responsibilities as well as the interaction including the definition of deliverables are described and agreed upon. This particularly pertains to all phases after signing of the contract. The *Security Manager* and *Customer Security Manager* roles are introduced as described by the *ESARIS Collaboration Model* (Sect. 3.3).

The *ICT Security Standard – Vulnerability Assessment and Mitigation Planning (VAM)* describes all activities of regular security testing and scanning of systems software and their configuration, CERT services, evaluation of impacts and planning of corrective actions. The main objective is to ensure that all ICT systems and components operated by the ICT Service Provider maintain the appropriate securi-

---

[55] Migration means the transfer of equipment and data (if any) as part of the Transition.

ty level being assumed and agreed upon. As far as possible, vulnerabilities are fixed before corresponding attacks take place and try to exploit them. A high degree of proactive handling is required in order to achieve this. This area covers assessment and planning activities only. Remediation is conducted using the incident, change and patch management processes as shown in Fig. 35 on page 95.

First of all, means and processes are required for the identification of vulnerabilities. Vulnerability notification services and other sources such as announcements and release notes of manufacturers shall be utilized to gather information. Tools and testing shall be used to regularly search for vulnerabilities in ICT systems and components. This may include integrity scanning, detection of unauthorized or incorrect changes to software or configurations, version and patch status verification, automatic or manual testing of configurations and functions, penetration testing, identification and tracing of intrusions and possible misuse.

Then, processes shall be established and means provided for the assessment of vulnerabilities. This assessment requires identifying the parts of the ICT environment being affected. The possible impact on operations and possibly business is also determined. A risk-based approach may be used here. This assessment is needed to prioritize the defending and the remediation tasks that shall follow. It is additionally important to identify the root cause if intrusions, misuse or attacks are the reason for the correction regardless of whether they are security breaches or only attempts. A practical metric for managing vulnerabilities is a major component of the assessment. The metric may combine priorities (combination of possible damage and probability of vulnerability exploitation) and practicability (derived from the criticality and the agreed service level of the system, the application or the ICT service that is agreed with the customer). Timelines are developed based on the resulting valuation.

Finally, the ICT Service Provider must be prepared for the remediation of vulnerabilities and for the mitigation of their impact. Means and processes shall exist for the planning and implementation of corrective actions that either remediate or at least mitigate the vulnerabilities being identified and assessed in advance. To this end, interfaces to incident, change and patch management processes must exist. Critical vulnerabilities have the potential to greatly affect the ICT services being delivered. Precautions to handle them shall exist in particular. Preparatory activity includes at least plans for communication to responsible service delivery personnel and representatives of the user organization. Such a Vulnerability Assessment and Mitigation Planning considerably help to reduce risks for the ICT Service Provider and its customers to an acceptable level.

The *ICT Security Standard – Logging, Monitoring and Security Reporting (LMR)* comprises all activities and tools used for central log management and analysis, monitoring of systems, measurement and information provisioning to customers.

It includes Security Information Management (SIM) with log management, data collection, analysis and reporting of log data, privileged user und resource access monitoring as well as Security Event Management (SEM) with real time log and event data processing, correlation and analysis of events.

Log data is generated by almost all ICT systems and components. This data is analyzed in order to allow system troubleshooting, check compliance with security policies and regulation, respond to security incidents and to perform security investigations (forensics). Pattern recognition, normalization, classification and tagging as well as correlation analysis are typical examples of automated log data assessment. Such tasks should be performed on different system levels and consolidated centrally in order to generate a best possible overall picture. User monitoring covers the investigation of user access and activity with respect to rights and policies. It is important for threat management, fraud detection, breach discovery and compliance reporting. Applications also need to be monitored and other resource access monitoring may also be required. The systems must be identified for which log data are to be captured and the logging content need to be specified. A real technical discipline is the storage and centralized archiving of log data. Availability and integrity have to be maintained. Privacy requirements may also be taken into account.

Improved threat management may require real-time data collection that enables immediate analysis. Security critical events are primarily collected and analyzed. This monitoring and alerting information from different sources is aggregated and then correlated. Notification should be supported for security critical events in nearly real-time. The scope of monitoring must be determined together with the motivation for this activity or the goals to be achieved, respectively. Monitoring can require installing software agents on systems or network elements. They may run continuously or be used on demand. Logging and monitoring should be organized so that Incident Management and related workflows are appropriately supported. Operations personnel must be enabled to recognize and notify security incidents as part of their daily business. Logging and monitoring must provide the basis for Incident Management by effectively observing security violations (refer to Fig. 34 on page 92).

User organizations (i.e. customers of the ICT Service Provider) must be appropriately informed about the security status of the ICT services they are consuming (and of the ICT systems and components used for production as appropriate). This information is provided as a security report. Security reports can have different content and serve different purposes. Types, formats and content should be defined and agreed upon in advance. In particular, customers want to be informed about whether and to what extent contractual security promises are kept. That usually includes adherence to policies and regulations. Reports can be generated, for instance, about vulnerabilities and their remediation or mitigation, about the effectiveness of security solutions such as anti-malware software or about security incidents and their treatment. Security reports are usually provided in an electronic form. Often special servers are used to provide the information online. Such systems and the access to them must be adequately protected. The area of logging and monitoring helps to identify misuse and malicious activity so that counteraction can be initiated. Summary information in the form of security reports provides information to the user organization that allows evaluation if specific requirements are met by the ICT service. Security reports are also used by the ICT Service Provider in order to systematically identify gaps and to continuously improve the security of ICT service delivery.

The *ICT Security Standard – Incident Handling and Forensics (IHF)* describes all procedures and means for the handling of and responding to security-related circumstances that may have a significant impact and require timely resolution through the implementation of workarounds or by removing the root cause. Identification of the root cause may in certain cases imply forensics, which in turn may try to discover an offender's identity.

Means and processes shall exist that allow recognition and consideration of changes to the risk profile (e.g. as a result of the knowledge acquired) that may lead to a significantly higher impact on the customer's business. Indicators are vulnerabilities that are not fixed, malicious activity and the like. The sources of such indicators (e.g. vulnerability management, user help desk) shall be known and used. Even more critical than changes to the risk profile are actual or possible violations of security policies. Thus, appropriate preparations shall be made that allow recognition and consideration of security breaches that have already taken place and that are expected or already have a significant impact on the customer's business. The sources of such indicators (e.g. logging and monitoring, poor service delivery) shall be known and used.

The management of security incidents is integrated into the standard Incident Management process, e.g. according to ITIL. Thus, process and activities are decided upon and roles and responsibilities are defined and assigned. The management of incidents requires the support of workflow tools. There are several issues that distinguish security incidents from other incidents (such as lack of availability). These must be taken into account in the standard Incident Management process. Security-related issues need to be considered through the pre-qualification of incidents, their analysis and assessment as well as their rating or prioritization.

Means and processes shall exist to make a sound decision if reported incidents are to be handled or refused. They are categorized, understood and assigned for remediation. In the case of "known errors", the filed action for remediation is initiated. Others are further qualified. A first categorization can be conducted using a schema such as the one proposed by the Information Security Forum (ISF)[56]. Further analysis is required. The rating or prioritization, however, is something that requires specific attention in larger organizations. There are three quantities that need to be considered: the actual or possible limitation of ICT service delivery (service level), the severity of the actual or potential violation of security policies (security) and the criticality of the system or ICT service for the customer's business (dependency). Guiding metrics are required and need to be implemented for each of the three factors as well as for the combination thereof.

The ICT Service Provider shall then be prepared to deal with incidents and restore the status with an accepted level of risk. Actions have the purpose of mitigating the impact or minimizing the impact of secondary damage. Especially if only the risk profile has changed, actions are aimed at improving security measures in order to prevent future security breaches or mitigate their impact. Note that the possible actions can be very different. In most cases, remediation activities are initiated that result in either the removal of the root cause or in the implementation of a workaround. Though this is not performed as part of the Incident Management process, the review and the closing is. Refer also to Fig. 34 on page 92.

Especially in the case of major security incidents, the user organization needs to be informed and involved. The ICT Service Provider shall also be prepared to receive information from the customer and to start coordinated action of both the ICT Service Provider and its customer if required. Finally, the ICT Service Provider may be required to perform forensic analysis that discovers root cause and the offender's identity together with any accounting data and evidence required. Note that the above description concentrates on ICT and on security incidents resulting from a failure or breach of security measures. It is not possible to discuss incident handling and forensics in a comprehensive way here.

12.2   Service Management

Introduction and summary: This cluster comprises eight areas and addresses life-cycle issues and general aspects of operations security. The *Release Management and Acceptance Testing* standard describes the set-up of new ICT systems or ICT service delivery environments or major changes, respectively. *System Development Life-Cycle* describes requirements for systems being developed by the provider in particular. *Systems Acquisition and Contracting* describes specific requirements for systems and services being purchased from vendors for the purpose of ICT service provisioning. The *Change and Problem Management* standard describes how corrections are made and how possible problems are managed. The four remaining standards refer to general aspects of operations security: *As-*

---

[56] Information Security Forum (ISF): Information Security Incident Management, Establishing a Security Incident Management Capability; 2006 [27]

set and Configuration Management, Hardening, Provisioning and Maintenance, Security Patch Management and *Business Continuity Management*. – This section is split into two types of descriptions. First, the general environment, the scope and major activities are described in each area of the whole cluster. Thus, the context in the ICT service production and delivery is portrayed in order to highlight the security problems, issues or concerns which need to be addressed. Secondly, information about major security measures is given. These are not specified in full, but these sections can be used when designing security measures that protect the area.

Fig. 96 shows the location of the "Service Management" cluster within the *ESARIS Security Taxonomy*. The eight *ICT Security Standards* are highlighted.

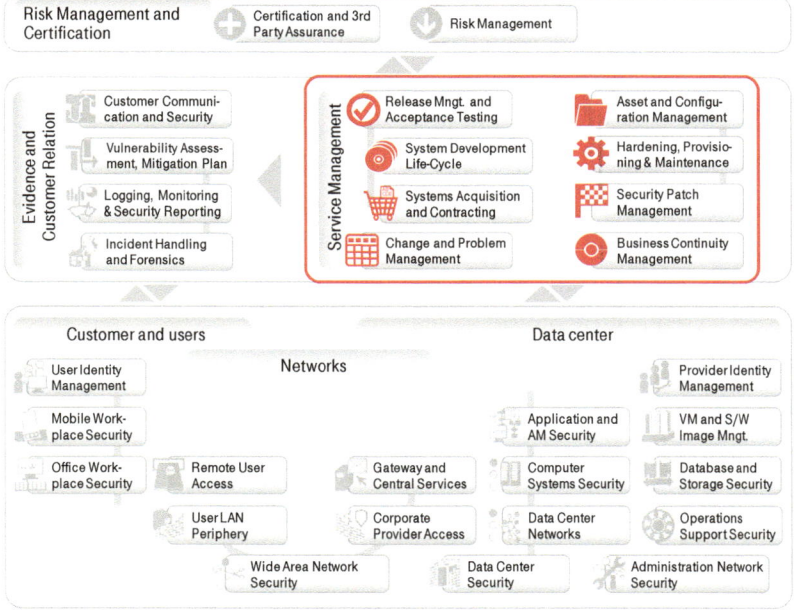

Fig. 96: Landing cluster of "Service Management"

This section is organized as follows:

- First column of standards ("plan – build – change"):
  - Sect. 12.2.1 describes the general environment, the scope and major activities.
  - Sect. 12.2.2 contains information about major security measures.
- Second column of standards ("stocktake – assemble – preserve"):
  - Sect. 12.2.3 describes the general environment, the scope and major activities.
  - Sect. 12.2.4 contains information about major security measures.

12.2.1 Plan – Build – Change

IT operations and service provisioning follows well-defined processes and procedures and the best practices stipulated in the IT Infrastructure Library (ITIL). They are proven and also contain a cycle of continuous improvement and adaptation. Refer to Fig. 31 on page 87 for a mapping between ITIL core processes and ESARIS.

Releases, changes, problems

New ICT service provisioning environments are set up and significantly changed since the ICT Service Provider wants to extend or modify its ICT service offering portfolio or improve its performance. Portfolio and Offering Management as well as Requirement Management have an influence on security issues, but cannot be explained in detail in this short summary of activities. These processes are part of the overall strategic alignment of the provider's business that includes market research, portfolio strategy and design, realization management, monitoring and performance review, making corrections and other activities. This area is far too complex to be covered thoroughly here. The same is true for all activities relating to Requirement Management, which collects, aligns and manages many requests often long before the realization or modification of a concrete ICT system is initiated. This complex of optimization, modernization and strategic alignment is also too complicated to be dealt with in full here. Specific security activities such as requirements engineering and portfolio and service catalog integration are part of the *ESARIS Attainment Model* (refer to Chapter 7). Other more life-cycle oriented activities are portrayed in the following since they are of primary importance in terms of security.

New ICT systems are set up in order to provide new services, and changes are applied to existing ICT systems or service provisioning platforms. In other words, the ICT Service Provider regularly generates new releases of its ICT service provisioning environment. A "release" is considered to be a set of pre-approved changes to the ICT service environment (i.e. ICT systems and components used to provide ICT services). A release is produced as part of the so-called Release Management process. Release Management plans, tests, communicates and coordinates the implementation of all releases, monitors the implementation of a specific release in the ICT service environment and ensures that all technical and nontechnical aspects are considered.

The incentive for new releases may come from
- customer requirements,
- need for (security) updates,
- demand from Business Development,
- request from Service Development or,
- changes resulting from incidents or problems.

The Release Management process ensures the bundling of changes and their orderly implementation in the ICT infrastructure. It extends from release planning, through to control of testing and acceptance procedures, to backout and rollout planning at organizational and technical levels. It is linked to Requirement Management, defines release policies, controls the interfaces for software deliveries, authorizes releases for use and archives master copies and reference configurations. Release and deployment management covers the whole assembly and implementation of new or changed ICT services for operational use, from release planning through to early life support.

Release Management is closely related to the Change Management process, because the latter is often the source of a new release. Both processes are interlaced as shown in Fig. 97. The changes are planned, assessed in terms of risks and approved by Change Management. Except for "normal changes", they are executed by the Release Management. Patch management and asset management issues are also managed in this way.

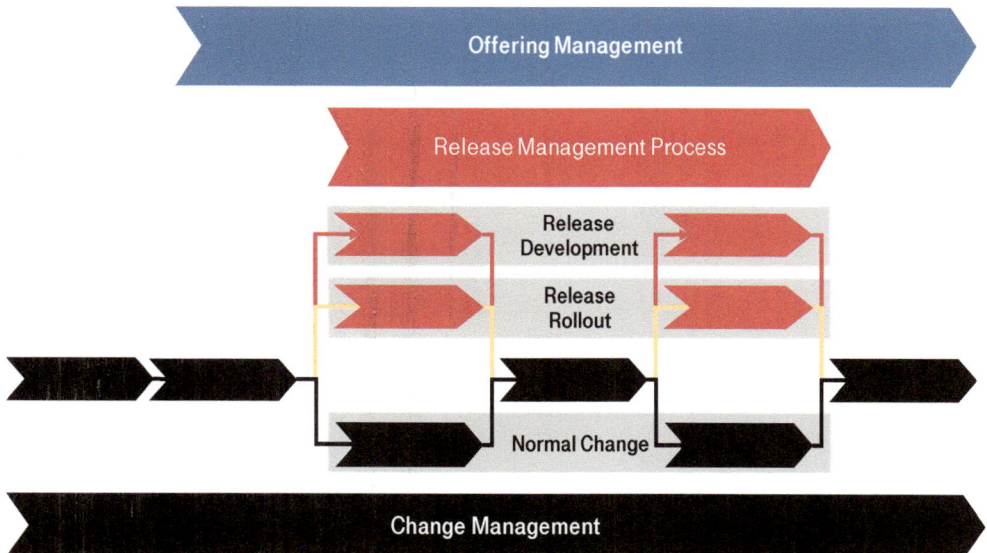

Fig. 97: Offering, Release and Change Management

Changes are alterations to ICT components which are mainly requested due to incidents or problems. Change Management is the life-cycle process of making modifications from request and analysis, to implementation and final verification. Thus, Change Management can broadly be defined as the process of requesting, analyzing, approving, developing, implementing and reviewing a change which has been planned in the long-term or one requested at short notice within the ICT infrastructure. Changes arise as a result of observed problems or incidents, but many changes can come from proactively seeking business benefits such as reducing costs or improving services.

Changes are planned and applied as a response to an observation, and the action or resolution is known. The ICT Service Provider knows how to react in advance or immediately. Situations, in which the root cause is not clear and the appropriate action or resolution has to be developed, are called problems. Such situations are managed through the Problem Management process.

Problem Management comprises the activities required to discover the root cause of incidents and to find a resolution. Problem Management also maintains information about problems, workarounds and resolutions. Thus, Problem Management maintains the so-called Known Error Data Base (KEDB). Nevertheless, the Problem Management consists of two major parts, the reactive Problem Management and the proactive Problem Management, both initiated in Service Operations[57].

Change Management and Problem Management usually follow the general approach of ITIL. The handling of changes and problems and the related activities comply with IT service management requirements. It focuses largely on the availability of ICT service delivery. It must be ensured that security-related issues are also considered.

The various activities necessary for an effective Change and Problem Management interact. A schematic representation of the integration of the (Security) Change and Problem Management in the overall process landscape and major relations to other activities is shown in Fig. 98.

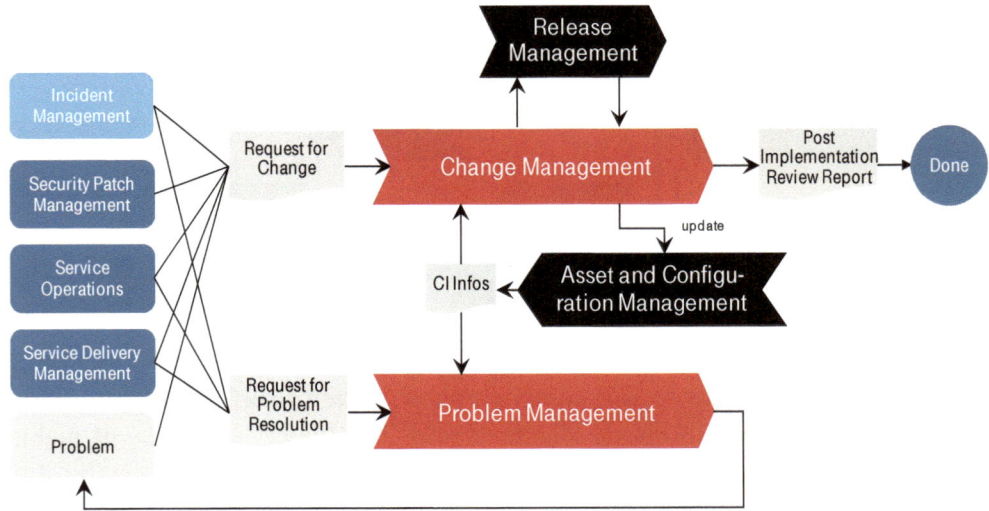

Fig. 98: Change and Problem Management

---

[57] The term Service Operations is used to specify all departments that are actively involved in the production and delivery of ICT services for customers.

There are several triggers for Change and Problem Management:

- Incident Management:
  Notifications of (security) incidents may require a change to be made to the ICT service provisioning environment. The appearance of a serious vulnerability may also be notified as a security incident. However, mainly actual attacks, cases of misuse or other security events result in a request for a change.

- Security Patch Management:
  Service Operations also receives notifications of flaws in ICT systems and components. Service Operations performs analysis and planning as part of its Patch Management process. However, the application of a patch requires prior issuance of a Request for Change (RfC) that appears in Change Management and will be processed in full there. Within the Change Management process, Service Operations is assigned to apply the patch as part of its Patch Management process.

- Service Operations:
  Service Operations may also observe other weaknesses in ICT systems and components, such as a lack of performance, a shortage of capacity or a failure in functionality. Such weaknesses must be remedied. Thus, the Change or Problem Management (CPM) is triggered to initiate resolution.

- Service Delivery Management:
  Similarly, the customer, the Service Delivery Management organization or the respective *Customer Security Manager* may observe defects in ICT services, systems or components. Then, the Change or Problem Management is triggered for resolution.

- Problem Management:
  The Problem Management seeks the root cause of a problem. If the root cause and a respective solution are found, the solution will be implemented through the Change Management process. Hence, the Problem Management process finally triggers the Change Management process.

It is important to differentiate precisely between incidents and problems, and the management thereof. Incident Management is described in detail in Sect. 12.1.

- Incident Management:
  The primary goal is to restore normal service operation as quickly as possible and to minimize the adverse impact on business operations.

- Problem Management:
  The primary process objectives are to prevent problems and resulting incidents from occurring, to eliminate recurring incidents and to minimize the impact of incidents that cannot be prevented.

The established standards and procedures for Change and Problem Management, including fallback and recovery procedures, will also be used for security issues.

First of all, the receiving and recording of change requests and problems is considered, followed by their identification and classification. The next step is the (security) impact assessment and prioritization of changes and problem resolutions before planning normal changes, releases and problem resolutions. After acquiring the formal approval and authorization, the proposed changes can be executed. Change testing and status tracking of problem resolutions is maintained by defined procedures and is documented appropriately.

It has already been stressed that final or acceptance testing is an absolute must and a mission-critical factor when providing ICT services. As a minimum, each new release has to undergo user acceptance testing, operational acceptance testing, as well as contract and compliance acceptance testing.

Development and procurement

A Release integrates ICT services, systems and components such as software

- that is developed by the ICT Service Provider or one of its subsidiaries, or
- that is procured from a vendor or another service provider.

In the first case, the ICT Service Provider must follow procedures in order to ensure quality that includes the appropriate consideration of security requirements. These practices are summarized under the heading "System Development Life-Cycle (SDL)", sometimes also referred to as "Security Development Life-Cycle (SDL)"[58] if security issues are mainly being considered. Here, general processes are used and security concerns are integrated so that the term System Development Life-Cycle (SDL) is used. If the ICT Service Provider develops systems or components including software, they are integrated into a Release as shown in Fig. 99. In the second case, ICT services, IT service management activities, ICT systems and components are procured from software vendors, hardware producers or service providing companies. The selection of partners and products has a significant influence on security and must therefore be performed carefully. This is the subject of practices summarized under the heading "Systems Acquisition and Contracting". Refer to Fig. 99. Note that the acquisition of ICT services and single IT service management activities shall also be included.

---

[58] Michael Howard and Steve Lipner: The Security Development Lifecycle, A Process to Develop Demonstrably More Secure Software; Microsoft Press, 2006, ISBN-10: 0-7356-2214-0 [42]

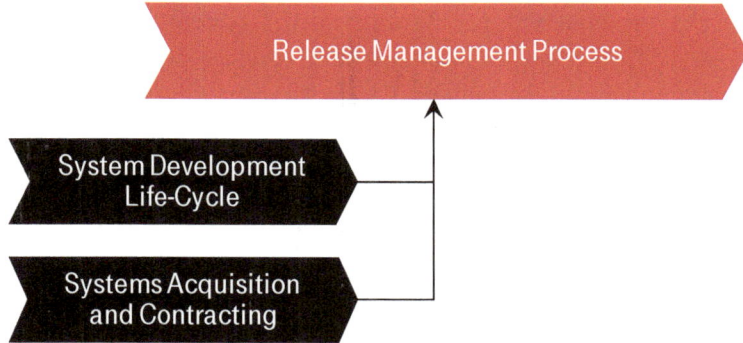

Fig. 99: Release Management and Secure Sourcing

A secure System Development Life-Cycle comprises all security measures that allow software and system engineers to identify and integrate an adequate level of security into the ICT system at all phases. Security aspects need to be considered early on and implemented in the design phase. A generic life-cycle is shown in Fig. 100.

Fig. 100: Generic ICT system life-cycle

At first glance, the broad coverage and generic nature of this life-cycle might be surprising. However, this generic model, or parts of it, can easily be matched against existing, established life-cycle models like those in service management, software engineering and solutions design. For example, quality gates which are typical for life-cycles are also known from service management.

The problems that may arise from an unsuitable life-cycle are diverse. Examples are as follows. A security-aware life-cycle starts with the identification of the security problem (risk analysis) and derives security objectives and requirements that are to be met. An inadequate analysis of the security environment results in incomplete requirements. Insufficient design documentation may result in the incorrect refinement of requirements, absence of measures, failures and vulnerabilities. Inadequate testing may mean that faults remain undetected. Poor configuration management may allow older, incorrect versions to be used, different ones to be mixed in and modifications to be made that are not allowed. Improper development tools may cause faults and vulnerabilities in the implementation. And, insufficient guidance may prevent users or administrators from installing, configuring, using and maintaining the system in a way that it is secure.[59]

---

[59] Refer to Part 3 of the Common Criteria which contains requirements for evaluating product security through analysis of the product's development life-cycle in its broad

The ICT Service Provider will not develop all ICT systems and components on its own. Instead, ICT systems, components and services are purchased from third parties (the manufacturer, the vendor, the distributor). Obviously, using the wrong supplier or product can have a negative impact and can cause risks that should be minimized.

Confidence in the fact that the security components or products will perform as expected and required is an important basis for the ICT Service Provider when delivering secure ICT services. Here, the ICT Service Provider is in a similar position to a user organization purchasing ICT services from the ICT Service Provider. The user organization can take advantage of ESARIS. The ICT Service Provider must define its own measures during systems acquisition and contracting. Otherwise, the following problems or threats may emerge: The ICT Service Provider may not be able to distinguish between valued vendors on the one hand, and those with fewer capabilities, a poorer reputation, lower dependability, viability, trustworthiness, and less experience, for example, on the other. The provider may not understand technology trends and may not be able to distinguish between useful products on the one hand and products with less functionality, lower quality and similar on the other. The ICT Service Provider may also fail to verify whether a product can meet the requirements; either if the latter are not explicitly documented or if the comparison or assessments cannot be conducted for some reason. Obviously, such issues may result in serious security problems with ICT service provisioning if inadequate systems, components or services are being integrated into the provider's ICT service provisioning environment.

Acquisition decisions need to find a balance between costs and timing. Furthermore, quality is an important parameter, which is understood to comprise all product-related characteristics. The acquisition of products is an investment that needs to give further consideration to short-term requirements as well as mid-term and long-term strategic considerations. An example of the latter is a standardization program.

Aspects that relate to the acquisition of ICT systems, components and services are outlined in Fig. 101. Note that the ICT systems, components and services that are purchased from a third party are integrated so that the System Development Life-Cycle (SDL) (Fig. 100) and the Systems Acquisition and Contracting process (refer to Fig. 101) are interwoven.

Fig. 101: Systems acquisition and contracting

---

meaning: ISO/IEC 15408 – Information technology — Security techniques — Evaluation criteria for IT security — Part 3: Security assurance components; 2008 [11]

Independent from the systems, products, components or services being procured, the acquisition process comprises the following, for example:

- preparatory, continuous activities such as market research, which includes investigations of demands, technologies, products, and vendors,

- supplier management activities which help to evaluate, select and develop vendors. The latter may include partner programs set up to develop and strengthen the cooperation between the ICT Service Provider and the vendors in order to improve the benefits gained from such a relationship,

- activities relating to contracting, which includes the preparatory tasks as well as the initiation and the conclusion of contracts. The business relationship is maintained through its life-cycle here.

- activities relating to quality inspection, in particular in the form of acceptance testing.

Systems, components and services from third parties and those being developed by the ICT Service Provider are used to carry out a new Release or to apply Changes. In terms of security, the changes made through a Release or a Change can primarily address known vulnerabilities or other weaknesses in ICT service delivery such as lack of performance and the like. The ICT services that are delivered to user organizations cannot be considered as secure if the planned systems and features are not set up or if the necessary modifications are not made, are postponed or are not adequately carried out. Required security measures may not be implemented in the ICT systems, vulnerabilities may not be removed or other vulnerabilities may be added, and security incidents may occur repeatedly because root causes are not removed or inappropriate workarounds are used.

The process of setting up ICT services and of making modifications needs to be well defined and controlled for reasons other than security. These include, but are not limited to, the following examples: availability of ICT service delivery and adherence to Service Level Agreements (SLA) as well as reasonable and cost effective resource utilization. Note that a complex ICT service provisioning environment can only be set up in a well-defined and organized way. Otherwise, it will fail completely.

12.2.2   Accomplishing security

Cautionary note: This section provides examples of essential security issues. It is not the subject of this book to specify technical, procedural and organizational security measures in detail. However, the following section specifies major aspects that can be considered when designing security measures that protect the cluster "service management" with "plan- build –change" (described in Sect. 12.2.1). Note that security should also have a business case; the design, implementation and maintenance of security measures incur costs, but customers especially tend to look for lower prices. Thus, security needs to be carefully designed.

The *ICT Security Standard – Release Management and Acceptance Testing (RMA)* describes the planning, testing, communication and coordination of the implementation of all releases, the monitoring of the implementation of a specific release in the ICT service environment and measures that ensure that all technical and nontechnical aspects are considered. A Release is a set of pre-approved changes to the ICT service provisioning environment.

The preliminary approval of changes includes the assessment of quality, benefit as well as impacts such as risks. The appraisal is conducted as part of the Change Management process. Thus, the contents of each Release, including the hardware, software, documentation, processes or other components, are managed, tested, and deployed as a single entity. Since a Release goes far beyond making a simple Change, the Release has to be assessed again to minimize the impact on the business service. Content and quality is to be evaluated in order to minimize impacts. This comprises acceptance testing including security assessments.

The Release Management shall be connected to the Offering Management of the ICT Service Provider in order to ensure that requirements are taken into account that are relevant to the market and express the actual demands of customers. In this way, the Releases are built to produce or improve ICT services that have the required characteristics, including security. Offering Management should be linked to an overall Portfolio Management, which also ensures that individual ICT services create a consistent whole and that standards are used. Generation and implementation of a new Release shall follow a defined process in order to ensure quality and integrity, prevent manipulation and ensure that all changes are authorized before being executed. The approval of a Release shall verify that security requirements are specified, reflected and actually respected. If not, the Release must not be approved for implementation.

Release Management is integrated with Change Management. This ensures that the same standards are used in both areas. Release Management, however, has its own defined roles and responsibilities. They are assigned in order to ensure the timely, correct and adequate execution of activities including mutual control. All associated updates to documentation shall be included in the Release, e.g. business processes, design documents, support documents and Service Level Agreements (SLA). This ensures further development and facilitates fault diagnostics. The design documents shall include security concepts as well. Guidance shall exist that instruct personnel to securely configure, operate and maintain the ICT service.

The goal of the Release Management (and deployment) process is to assemble and position all aspects of ICT services into production and establish effective use of new or changed ICT services. Effective release and deployment creates significant business value by delivering changes at optimized speed, risk and cost, and by offering a consistent, appropriate and auditable implementation of usable and useful business services. The key purpose of service validation and acceptance testing is to provide objective evidence that the new or changed ICT service supports the business requirements, including the agreed service level and level of security. The ICT service is tested explicitly against the specification set out in the ICT service design package, including business functionality, availability, continuity, security, usability and defect remediation.

Release Management coordinates the activities of the ICT Service Provider, a number of suppliers and the business to plan and deliver a Release across a distributed environment. A new Release integrates ICT services, systems and components that are developed and produced by specific departments or subsidiaries of the ICT Service Provider and internally purchased from there. It must be verified to some extent that the System Development Life-Cycle, with its security measures, were in place. The life-cycle and its measures ensure the integration of demonstrably more secure ICT systems into the Release. Details are given below. However, many ICT services, systems and components that are integrated into a Release are not developed by a specialized department or subsidiary of the ICT Service Provider but bought from the market. Here the ICT Service Provider has security measures in place that help to select the right suppliers and purchase the right products or services.

The *ICT Security Standard – System Development Life-Cycle (SDL)* describes a process for developing demonstrably more secure ICT systems. It includes activities performed with the goal that ICT systems respond to needs by providing the required functionality correctly and nothing more. That means that requirements are correctly being implemented without introducing vulnerabilities.

According to the ISO/IEC 27000 family of standards for information security management systems, security is an integral part of the operation, development, maintenance and use of ICT systems, and of the ICT system itself.[60] Unfortunately, these documents neither address the life-cycle nor the intended recipient. The Common Criteria[61] do address life-cycle aspects with very concrete security measures that need to be considered. A further very helpful source is the NIST publication about secure development[62], which is recommended for adoption. It can easily be extended to include evaluation and certification activities.

---

[60] for example: ISO/IEC 27002 – Information technology – Security techniques – Code of practice for information security management, 2013 [6]

[61] ISO/IEC 15408 – Information technology — Security techniques — Evaluation criteria for IT security — Part 3: Security assurance components; 2008 [11]

[62] Richard Kissel, Kevin Stine, Matthew Scholl, Hart Rossman, Jim Fahlsing, and Jessica Gulick: Security Considerations in the System Development Life Cycle; National Insti-

The standard helps to reduce the residual risks resulting from the ICT system's built-in security to a level that is both acceptable to the ICT Service Provider and its customers. The general system development life-cycle shall be seen from a security perspective and ensure that generally accepted industry best practices are applied appropriately. The main principles are as follows.

Requirements are identified up front and must be well-defined in terms of confidentiality, integrity and availability and may cover additional aspects such as privacy. It is best to understand and discuss the requirements up front in order to make appropriate management decisions and planning. Risks are continuously being analyzed and mitigating measures are taken early in the development phase. Then security design issues can be found and fixed before coding is committed. Processes or plans should be established to respond to new security vulnerabilities or situations. Design and implementation shall be done in a structured way to ensure that requirements are met and flaws are prevented. Secure coding best practices should be applied as well as proven testing processes and procedures. A final security review and testing shall be conducted before delivery. Guidance for customers shall be part of the product that helps to configure, deploy and use it securely. The development (and production) environment needs to be protected and appropriate tools shall be used in order to prevent manipulation, espionage or any other impact on the manufacturing process and its results. Especially in case of systems and components (with hardware), such requirements should be adapted as appropriate. Guidance can be gained from ISO 15408 (Common Criteria).

Often systems are developed for a purpose, an environment or risk profile but utilized in a different context later. Therefore, major assumptions must be documented. Moreover, it must be ensured that the ICT service, system or component is correctly be deployed in its environment. This includes but is not limited to a correct configuration which requires having appropriate guidance documents. Further life-cycle activities include the review of operational readiness, the integration into the configuration and operations management environment, continuous control and even precautions for a secure replacement or closing down at the end of life.

It must be emphasized that a security categorization is important. Thus, the ICT system and the data it processes need to be classified in terms of confidentiality, integrity, availability and business criticality. Such a categorization also gives high-level security requirements and indicates the level of effort (and costs) for security within the ICT system's life-cycle. Security requirements shall be understood and documented. The high-level and all refining design documentation shall explicitly

---

tute of Standards and Technology, NIST Special Publication 800−64 Revision 2, October 2008 [19]

address security issues. The testing concepts, plans and reports in particular shall ensure that testing is performed against security requirements.

The *ICT Security Standard – Systems Acquisition and Contracting (SAC)* describes measures for the selection of the right supplier and for purchasing ICT systems and components that are reliable and secure. This includes properties and other characteristics, the possibility of corrections and the process to achieve this. Most of these issues need to be fixed in a contract.

First of all, the ICT Service Provider should observe and know the market and therefore be able to identify and rate appropriate suppliers as well as goods and services. Larger companies usually have departments which specialize in these activities. It is critical, however, that the knowledge gained is distributed and actually utilized in design and purchasing processes. At least ICT service specific investigations[63] should reuse and consider the knowledge gained by the central marketing or offering management departments. The latter support the business success of the ICT Service Provider with the allocation of crucial market and sales information regarding a differentiated business analysis.

The purchasing processes range from quotation support to invoice settlement. Some processes are beyond the responsibility of the purchasing organization. The role of procurement is to ensure effectiveness and efficiency when procuring products and services. At the same time, it aims to respond flexibly to changes in the market and to lower supply chain costs. All contractual ties with payment obligations for the ICT Service Provider must be approved. This includes products, services and also nonmaterial goods such as patents, licenses, user rights, copyrights etc. Larger companies have a preselection process for suppliers and a supplier development process as well. Alliances and partnerships are managed in order to increase the benefit for the ICT Service Provider.

The security characteristics of goods and services being purchased shall be clear when taking a decision to purchase an ICT service, system, product or component. Security measures that need to be implemented are to be defined in a Product Requirements Document (PRD) which forms the basis for the contractual relationship between the ICT Service Provider and its supplier. Details are specified by the *ESARIS Third Party Integration Model* (refer to Chapter 9).

Security acceptance testing and other types of analysis provide evidence that the ICT service, system, product or component have the expected characteristics. Security must continuously be maintained. Suppliers should contractually be bound to fix security vulnerabilities or at least to support this. Corrections are therefore performed for errors which are made during development or manufacturing or in

---

[63] as performed when managing a specific offering or ICT service or even a Release

order to respond to changes in the environment. The latter may include, for instance, new attack methods or usage scenarios. The process and treatment of changes shall be regulated. An escalation process for problem resolution shall be established as appropriate. The definition of conditions for renegotiation and termination of agreements is required.

The ICT Service Provider may integrate third-party ICT services into the ICT service that is delivered to the customers (user organizations). Then, ICT service production is tiered in its supply chain. In this case, it may be necessary to monitor the ICT services from the supplier with respect to their characteristics and in order to prevent them from being abused in a way which would compromise the security of the ICT Service Provider or any of its customers. Specific agreements are required if suppliers are involved in the installation, operation, provisioning, management or maintenance of ICT systems and components used by the ICT Service Provider to provide ICT services to its customers. Specific agreements are also required if suppliers are involved in accessing, processing and managing data of the ICT Service Provider and of data accessed, processed and managed by the provider on behalf of its customers. Access to ICT systems and components shall be restricted and monitored as appropriate.

The responsibilities and the division of labor between the supplier and the ICT Service Provider shall be clear, transparent and adhered to at all times. This requires a description of the product or service. It also requires a description of the information to be made available along with its security classification. Verifiable quality or performance criteria should also be agreed upon. Liability should be regulated. Suppliers should be cooperative and obliged to report on observed or suspected security vulnerabilities of the systems, components or service they provide. Contractual binding non-disclosure agreements (NDA) shall be signed if required. Confidentiality and specific measures which ensure enforcement can be agreed upon.

The *ICT Security Standard – Change and Problem Management (CPM)* describes all security measures for applying Changes and for managing Problems. Changes are alterations to ICT components, which are requested due to incidents or problems. Change Management is the life-cycle process from request and analysis to implementation and final verification. Problems are the cause of any failure or of incidents in ICT service delivery. Problem management is the life-cycle process from occurrence, notification, analysis and identification of causes to planning of workarounds and changes.

The goal of the Change Management process is to ensure that standardized methods and procedures are used for efficient and prompt handling of all changes, in order to minimize the impact of change-related incidents upon service quality and consequently to improve the day-to-day operations of the organization. This requires a clear definition of the process and its activities and the inclusion of security as well. Roles and responsibilities are also not primarily designed to consider information security, but shall be chosen and enabled to deal with this subject. Both Change and Problem Management requires the support of workflow tools.

Changes require formal request and approval before being implemented. Here, the extent of the change and its impact need to be estimated and documented. It is checked if the organization or person which requested the change has verified possible impacts on meeting actual security requirements. If the change is requested to fix a security issue, this needs to be made clear by the requester too. When taking decisions it shall be guaranteed that both the required knowledge is available and the responsible decision makers are available. Precautions for a planned service outage (downtime) need to be considered. The result of a change is verified and also documented (refer to Asset and Configuration Management (ACM)). A risk assessment is mandatory within the Change Management process in order to minimize negative impacts. The focus should be on identifying the factors that may disrupt the business, impede the delivery of service warranties or impact corporate objectives and policies. This assessment considers several influencing factors. Mainly the criticality is considered that measures the dependency of a customer on the proper operation of the ICT service. The service restriction measures the impact that may occur if the change is made, or if it is not. The complexity also provides information about the possible difficulties, the size or dimension of the Change, the experience with such a Change and other preparations, as well as the existence of test options, fallback scenarios and alternatives. The planning to make the Change considers these risks as well as the priority. The priority is important with respect to IT security and provided by the requester in the Request for Change (RfC). Many RfC originate from an (security) incident or a (security) problem. The corresponding processes do perform a prioritization for implementing a workaround or for eliminating a root cause. This prioritization is fed to the Change Management process. The final decision, especially about major Changes (higher risks) and emergency changes (highest priority), is finally taken by a Change Advisory Board (CAB) to ensure decisions to be correct and reliable.

The goal of the Problem Management process is to prevent problems and resulting incidents from happening, to eliminate recurring incidents and to minimize the impact of incidents that cannot be prevented. Problem management shall learn from experience. Hence a record of known errors, causes and resolutions is kept. Actions such as the analysis of trends and correlations shall be taken in order to minimize response time and increase quality of result. If the problem originates from Incident Management, the Problem Management process can reuse the rating or prioritization made before. Otherwise, the problem manager shall determine this value accordingly. The prioritization is a combination of three quantities: the actual or possible restriction of ICT service delivery (service restriction), the severity of the actual or potential violation of security policies (security rating) and the criticality of the system or ICT service for the customer's business (dependency). The values may be changed in the Problem Management process. Guiding metrics are required.

12.2.3   Stocktake – Assemble – Preserve

ICT Service Providers set up new ICT systems in order to provide new services. The ICT systems and components are purchased from vendors and integrated into the ICT service delivery infrastructure. Others are developed by the ICT Service Provider. Changes are also applied. In other words, the ICT Service Provider regularly generates new Releases of its ICT service provisioning environment and applies changes for maintenance reasons. A Release is considered to be a set of pre-approved changes. Refer to Sect. 12.2.2.

Operational ICT systems may have vulnerabilities that could be exploited and may cause a serious impact on the customers' business. Such systems may also feature a lack of performance, a shortage of capacity or a failure in functionality. In all these cases, modifications need to be applied to the ICT systems and components in order to repair, correct or improve their functionality and adherence to expectations and requirements.

All changes that make corrections or improvements require the analysis of existing ICT systems and components. Therefore, an inventory is needed which provides all the required information. It needs to be kept up-do-date at all times. Ultimately, such an inventory is also the basis for any Risk Management, which requires knowledge of the existing assets. Such information is handled by the Asset and Configuration Management process.

Any Change generates new information about a so-called Configuration Item (CI) as shown in Fig. 102.

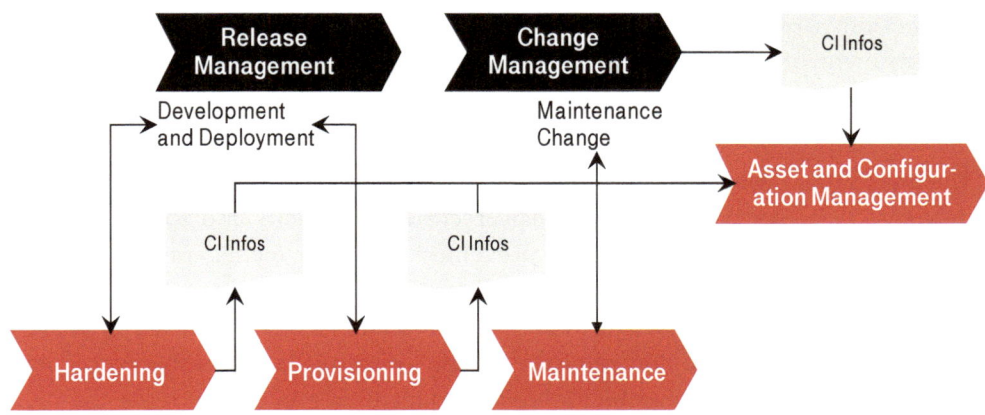

Fig. 102: Setting up ICT systems

A Configuration Item (CI) is a component that needs to be managed in order to deliver an ICT Service. Information about each CI is recorded in a configuration record and maintained throughout its life-cycle in a data base. Examples of Configuration Items (CI) are computing systems (e.g. hardware, operating systems, middleware, and application software) and associated centralized services (e.g. data bases, directories and authentication) on the one hand and equipment for operations support (e.g. capacity and performance management, monitoring systems, update server and repositories) and networking (e.g. firewalls, routers or switches) on the other.

In this way, Configuration Management provides a logical model of the ICT infrastructure. It contains all Configuration Items (CI) as an inventory with identification, definition and status and is used to control and monitor all changes by means of a Configuration Management Data Base (CMDB). The Change Management process provides CI Information but it also receives information about the Configuration Items (CI) to allow preparation and planning of changes. Other major processes that require information about Configuration Items (CI) are the Problem Management and the Incident Management processes.

Note that genuine Asset Management has the primary purpose of providing an inventory for general Risk Management and of enabling the tracking of financial values. In ESARIS, ICT systems and components are mainly considered so that Asset Management is closely related to the Configuration Management aspects.

If the information about the assets (required for ICT service delivery) and their configuration (characteristics and relationships) is not available, incomplete or incorrect, the analysis is performed based on the wrong information, which could lead to defective, inadequate or missing results. In particular, vulnerabilities may not be identified and therefore not thoroughly remediated, an incident's root cause may not be identified with the result that incidents accumulate, or changes are not applied as required, are imperfect or may even produce a change for the worse. These are only examples. The dimensions of failure are conceivable if the provider does not know the object of the investigation and change.

Release Management and Change Management are processes that deal primarily with the organization of work on ICT than actually tackling the administration of the ICT components. The highly technical, concrete tasks to be carried out on each ICT component are described under the heading "Hardening, Provisioning and Maintenance". Refer to Fig. 102. The ICT systems and components need to be set up according to specifications. They need to be deployed and put into operation. And later they need to be maintained. This results in the following activities:

- Hardening comprises all methods applied to ICT systems, software and components that reduce the possibility of vulnerabilities and susceptibility to attacks. General configuration requirements such as the removal of test data and software before deployment for production are also considered.

- Provisioning comprises all methods of deployment and activation of ICT services, including conception, installation, configuration and approval. That includes technical life-cycle issues, approval and ownership issues and general configuration requirements for final deployment.

▪ Maintenance comprises technical support to ensure continued operation and actuality, including the help desk. Specific attention is paid to the life-cycle of data that is stored and processed and which may require secure deletion at the end of a component's life.

The initial set-up of ICT systems and components is critical since a configuration must be established that meets the specifications exactly. Otherwise, the ICT system or component will fail to meet the requirements including its security target. An important part of this initial set-up is the so-called hardening. If not adequately being carried out, the ICT system or component may unnecessarily contain software with vulnerabilities or simply provide functionality which is not needed and which exposes the ICT to risks. Hardening also reduces the attack surface.

After this set-up, the ICT systems and components are deployed and put into operation. Obviously, this process requires accuracy. Otherwise, the status of the installation may not be clear, for example, which leads to the risk of using ICT systems and components for production that are not set up and approved for production. This could lead to assets and their configuration not being documented, which could hinder later modifications and mean that vulnerabilities are not removed as required.

Finally, continuous maintenance is essential. Flaws need to be remediated, which may fail if the right experts or vendors are not committed or not available. Security problems may also rise if other resources are not available for the necessary repairs during the operational period of the ICT systems and components.

Hardening, Provisioning and Maintenance can be considered as a technical, more implementation-oriented level of development and deployment on the one hand and of normal changes in the operational phase on the other (Fig. 102). Asset and Configuration Management plays an important role in all these phases since information about the ICT systems and components and their configuration is maintained there.

Patch Management is another technical, more implementation-oriented discipline. The application of (security) patches is so important that it is considered as an extra area with a distinct *ICT Security Standard*. ICT systems and components may have vulnerabilities. Vulnerabilities could be exploited and may cause a serious impact on the customers' business. Attacks may, for example, lead to a loss of availability. Other attacks may violate confidentiality, privacy and other requirements. Examples include theft and espionage.

In order to penetrate the corresponding target system and thereby cause a security breach, attackers can exploit security vulnerabilities in any ICT systems and components. Software updates or patches remove many of these vulnerabilities. Security Patch Management covers all ICT systems and components used by the ICT Service Provider to provide ICT services to customers. This includes office workstations (e.g. desktop computers, laptops) and related central ICT services (e.g. file servers, mail servers, domain controllers) on the one hand and equipment for central ICT services (e.g. Unix/Windows servers, web and application servers, data bases) and networking (e.g. firewalls, routers or switches) on the other.

The application of security patches is performed in accordance with the overall processes and procedures for applying changes, including patches to ICT systems and components. However, the vulnerability management process plays an important role in this context and must be considered too. A schematic representation of the integration of the (Security) Patch Management process into the overall process landscape is shown in Fig. 103.

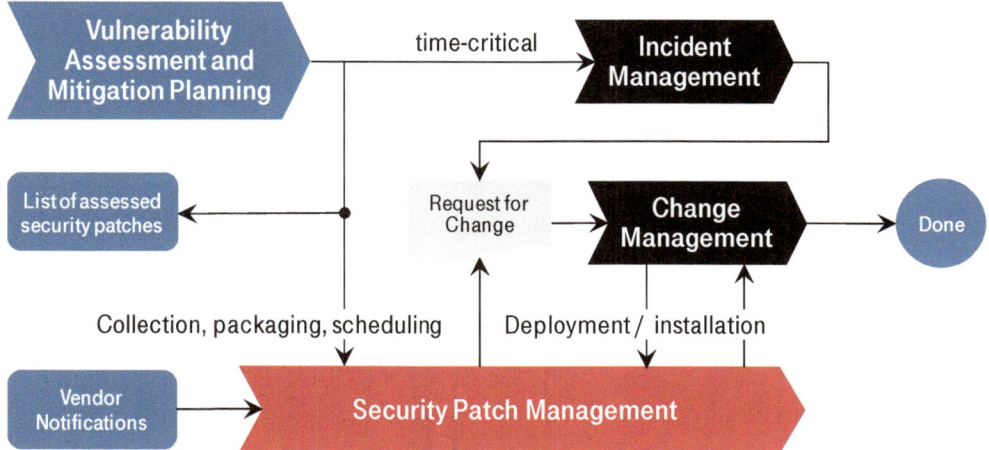

Fig. 103: Security Patch Management

In principal, Security Patch Management is part of the Change Management process: All changes to ICT systems and components are made following the Change Management process and through a formal Request for Change (RfC). Change Management comprises the steering activities whereas Security Patch Management pertains to the actual doing. The actual doing comprises two phases: the preparation (collection, checking, packaging, testing and scheduling) and the deployment or installation (initiated by the RfC and ended with the closing report). Generally, the overall process has two starting points (refer to Fig. 103):

- Vulnerabilities are analyzed and assessed with respect to their possible impact as a central service. In case that the vulnerability is found to require immediate remediation, the process flow branches to Incident Management. Otherwise, lists of assessed security patches are forwarded to the Security Patch Management.

- Operations departments receive vendor notifications (refer to Fig. 103) also directly. They receive notifications of flaws in ICT systems and components as well as software updates and patches from vendors and possibly other sources. The information includes notifications for functional repair (bug-fix, hot-fix, update, service pack, etc.) as well as notifications about vulnerabilities and software patches for repair (security patches).

Duplicate requests will be dealt with by Change Management or by Security Patch Management at latest. Change Management will also ensure that the configuration data base is updated. Note that ITIL does not describe vulnerability management so that the above description is ESARIS specific and already part of the solution which is summarized in the next Sect. 12.2.4.

ICT systems may fail and data might be lost as the result of, for example, natural disasters, accidents, equipment failures and deliberate actions. In this case, normal operation must be restored and resumed. Fig. 104 shows the phases that follow a possible disaster which disrupts normal operation:

- After the disaster, ICT service provisioning is interrupted or critically affected.

- Immediate measures are taken (after a delay). Systems are restarted or recovered in the original location, in a backup location or services are replaced by an alternative. But operation is still reduced.

- Some systems may sustain with operation, whereas other systems and data may be restored in the middle stages. Business processes must also be sustained.

- Typically, this restoration takes time if operation is to be restored from the emergency operation level back to the normal level. Finally, business is resumed to normal operation.

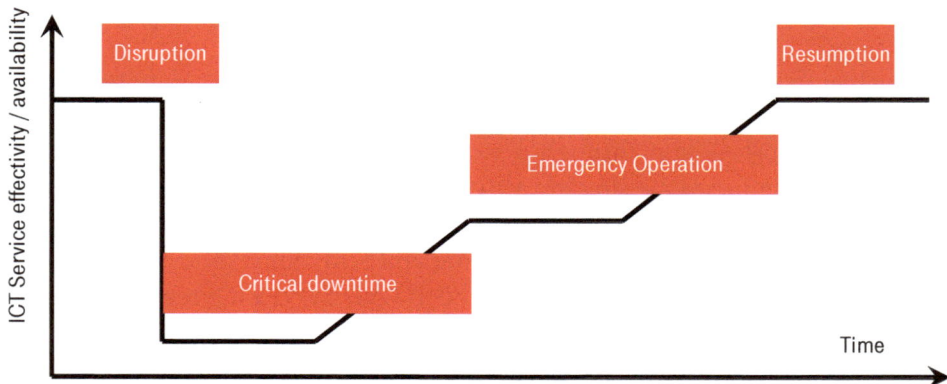

Fig. 104: From disruption to resumption

Disruptions to ICT service provisioning have a variety of consequences for the ICT Service Provider and the customer:

- System outage affects the customer's business and can cause financial loss, impact on reputation, breach of laws, regulations and obligations and other consequences.

- Loss of data can lead to similar situations for the customer.

- The ICT Service Provider may fail to fulfill the contract with the customer. That may result in a penalty, loss of future business, impact on reputation or even breach of laws, regulations and obligations.

The impact of possible disruptions or loss of data should be low. A combination of preventive and recovery measures is required to achieve this.

Business Continuity Management is standard for professional ICT service delivery. The volume Service Design of ITIL [64] defines the "IT Service Continuity Management" process. In ISO/IEC 27002 [65], Business Continuity Management is one of the fourteen security control clauses. Strictly speaking, the ICT Service Provider cannot resume the customer's business or ensure its continuation. The provider can only resume ICT service delivery and ensure continuation of ICT service delivery. Following the ISO standard, the term Business Continuity Management is used. It is considered synonymous with Service Continuity Management here.

12.2.4   Accomplishing security

Cautionary note: This section provides examples of essential security issues. It is not the subject of this book to specify technical, procedural and organizational security measures in detail. However, the following section specifies major aspects that can be considered when designing security measures that protect the cluster "service management" with "stocktake – assemble – preserve" (described in Sect. 12.2.3). Note that security should also have a business case; the design, implementation and maintenance of security measures incur costs, but customers especially tend to look for lower prices. Thus, security needs to be carefully designed.

The *ICT Security Standard – Asset and Configuration Management (ACM)* describes the process that is responsible for tracking and reporting the value and ownership of ICT systems and components throughout their life-cycle. It also comprises the process responsible for maintaining information about any component required to deliver an ICT Service, including their relationships.

---

[64] ITIL: IT Infrastructure Library, version 3

[65] ISO/IEC 27002 – Information technology – Security techniques – Code of practice for information security management, 2013 [6]

Changes are alterations to ICT components which are mainly requested due to incidents or problems. Change Management is the life-cycle process of making modifications from request and analysis to implementation and final verification. Tracking and inventory of all assets and their characteristics is essential and an integral part of these activities. (Service) Asset Management tracks and reports the existence, value and ownership of ICT systems and components throughout their life-cycle. The inventory of ICT systems and components must be integrated with procurement and order management processes since new items are dealt with here. The inventory must also be integrated with Change Management processes since modifications including withdrawal from service are initiated through Changes.

Asset and Configuration Management covers different disciplines: It identifies requirements, specifies interfaces and relations, and develops a plan and implements a Configuration Management System (CMS). The CMS is a complex IT system. As part of these activities, data structures, naming conventions, identifiers and attributes are determined in particular. This includes relationships. Roles and responsibilities should be clear and assigned. Configuration of all critical ICT systems and components must be documented or made available as appropriate (outside the ICT systems or components). Other materials also required for ICT service delivery and maintenance are also subject to inventory and configuration control as appropriate. Most of these activities are not specific to security, though they essentially contribute to maintaining the security of the ICT. It is, for instance, important that ownership and criticality can be retrieved at any time. Both values are important for Incident and Change Management. Moreover, security-related configuration or security settings must also be documented and made available.

Modification of the inventory or of configuration information content must be approved, shall be limited to authorized operations personnel and must reflect the status of the corresponding ICT components and other material being required for ICT service delivery and maintenance. Requests primarily originate from Change and Problem Management, although a large amount of information about configurations is generated during Hardening, Provisioning and Maintenance and Security Patch Management activities. The requests and the data should be validated and integrity must be ensured. Typical data to be tracked may include identifier, description, category and type, product and manufacturer, version, location and responsible person, change history, relation to other Configuration Items (CI), licenses, settings, and records.

The *ICT Security Standard – Hardening, Provisioning and Maintenance (HPM)* describes real, practical, hands-on activities. Hardening comprises all methods applied to ICT systems, software and components that reduce the possibility of vulnerabilities and susceptibility to attacks. Provisioning comprises all methods of deployment and activation of ICT services including conception, installation, configuration, and approval. Maintenance comprises technical support to ensure continued operation and up-to-dateness, including the help desk.

Only those versions of ICT systems and components should be used which are approved for IT production (at least by the manufacturer). They should only be used within the period of active manufacturer support. Test data sets, software components installed for testing, default data sets and default (or initial) accounts or passwords and the like shall be removed from ICT systems before switching to ICT service delivery for customers. Such software or data may remain on the ICT systems where they are necessary for power-on or regular self-testing.

ICT systems, software and components should be configured in a way that reduces the possibility of vulnerabilities and susceptibility to attacks. One way of achieving this is the so-called system hardening in which for example software components or services are removed which are not required and will never be used. Baseline policies, guidelines and working instructions shall exist to ensure appropriate hardening. Note that dynamic computing and virtualization may impose restrictions on the hardening of platforms since different applications may use the platform software systems. ICT systems should be assigned to classes which express different levels of control, trustworthiness and attack potential depending on the network zone in which they are operated. For instance, ICT systems in the DMZ and in the data center LAN may belong to different classes and may be treated differently.

Provisioning comprises all methods of deployment of ICT systems and components and activation of service. This may include conception, installation, configuration, and approval. Such tasks shall be organized so that there are no configurations which could compromise security. Example measures to achieve this are as follows. People assigned such tasks should be trained and approved in order to ensure that the likelihood of flaws is minimized that could have negative impact on security. Appropriate tools should be used for the same reason. Methods and processes should be approved before being deployed as standard. ICT systems, software and components shall be configured so that applicable security policies are met. ICT systems and components shall run with the least possible privileges as appropriate. Rights are configured according to applicable policies and consider the segregation of duties, for example. ICT systems and components used for development, testing and ICT service delivery to customers (production) shall strictly be separated. Acceptance testing must include security checks.

Maintenance comprises technical support to ensure continued operation and actuality. Help desk services are most often the entry gate for basic maintenance. Maintenance-related tasks shall be organized so that the secure state is maintained and so that no configurations are produced which may compromise security. Maintenance shall be performed in a way that confidentiality, integrity and availability of user data is ensured. It is worth noting that the users' data needs to be considered in the life-cycle. The storage, backup, restoration or recovery as well as final deletion and removal of this data must be taken into consideration. When removed from the data center, all items and equipment containing sensitive data shall securely be disposed of in order to maintain the confidentiality of data and any other restrictions to their use. The same applies if items and equipment such as storage media are reused for different customers or services.

The *ICT Security Standard – Security Patch Management (SPM)* describes the process responsible for the consolidated proactive update of ICT systems for which new potential vulnerabilities are discovered and their fixes are available. It is applicable to all ICT systems, both customer-specific installations and general infrastructure. Even though patching seems to be a standard procedure in maintaining ICT systems, it is not explicitly described in ITIL or ISO/IEC 20000 and a few security considerations may be worth mentioning as well.

Manufacturers often fix vulnerabilities by providing software updates or patches. The proactive installation of critical security patches within a specified period considerably reduces the likelihood that a known vulnerability is exploited. Hence, Security Patch Management contributes to effectively guaranteeing the operational availability, confidentiality and integrity of ICT systems. The process covers IT systems patched at runtime as well as software images patched before being deployed and executed in a cloud computing environment. ICT systems shall also carefully be designed and tested. Hence, even if patches are to be applied soon, control, testing and precautions for rollback are essential too. This trade-off needs to be dealt with carefully.

Security Patch Management shall ensure that all ICT systems have the right security level at the right time. The process shall be simple and standardized as much as possible for all ICT systems, using the standard Change Management process that triggers the application of security patches. Patches must be collected from authentic sources in a secure way. They are checked, approved and stored in patch register. Packaging, testing and scheduling are important. The patch levels of all ICT systems shall be visible at all times (refer to Configuration Management). The reporting of patch levels is demanded by many user organizations.

The business impact caused by system downtime shall be minimized. A standard downtime cycle must be agreed between the ICT Service Provider and the customer. During standard downtimes, standard patches will be installed in a smooth manner with minimal business impact. Precautions for urgency patching (patching outside the normal interval) and for applying emergency patches are to be taken. Emergency patches require shortening the overall procedure primarily by setting short-term deadlines. Necessary patches that are not installed for any reason shall be identified and treated as risks.

The most important measure with respect to security is the integration of the Vulnerability Assessment and Mitigation Planning (often also referred to as CERT services). The corresponding activities can realistically not be conducted as part of the Change Management process. The activities are usually also not performed by Operations personnel and the scope of vulnerability management is wider than that of Security Patch Management.

The *ICT Security Standard – Business Continuity Management (BCM)* defines precautions that minimize the impact of possible disruptions to ICT service provisioning or loss of data, which includes a timely and full recovery of service and data.

Business Continuity Management is a complex matter. Hence, only a few examples of security-related issues are provided in the following. Designing any precaution requires an understanding of the subject and priority. Hence, critical business processes shall be identified and made known together with the ICT systems and components and other resources necessary for them. The criticality of the processes, services and resources needs to be assessed in terms of the business impact. This requires the identification of reasons for discontinuity and analyzing the consequences of disasters, security failures, loss of service and service availability. A plan should be developed and implemented to ensure the timely restoration of essential operations. ICT security must be an integral part of the overall business continuity process like other management processes within the organization. The plan should consider management requirements as well as resource and capacity planning relating to such aspects as operations, staffing, materials, transport and facilities. The use of backup locations or services must not lead to situations where the systems are exposed to severe security risks. This must be considered during planning. The plan should also establish measures to identify and proactively reduce risks or mitigate the impact of damaging incidents. A process should be implemented, trained and repeatedly tested to counteract interruptions and recover from disaster or other major failures of information systems.

More detail about Business Continuity Management is provided in the literature.[66]

---

[66] Marianne Swanson, Pauline Bowen, Amy Wohl Phillips, Dean Gallup and David Lynes: Contingency Planning Guide for Federal Information Systems; National Institute of Standards and Technology, NIST Special Publication 800-34 Rev. 1, May 2010 (updated Nov. 2010) [20]
Aligning Business Continuity and Information Security; Information Security Forum (ISF), Special Project Report, March 2006 [28]
ISO 22301 – Societal security – Business continuity management systems – Requirements; 2012 (replacing BS 25999-1:2006); and ISO 22313 – Societal security – Business continuity management systems – Guidance; 2012 (replacing BS 25999-2:2007 [12]

12.3   ICT Service Access

Introduction and summary: This cluster comprises eight areas. *Wide Area Networks* connect users (or user organizations) with ICT services from the ICT Service Provider. Users use their workplace to access the ICT services that are provided remotely. *Office Workplace Security* and *Mobile Workplace Security* address the corresponding security issues of protecting these workplaces and the information and applications being used and processed with them. In mobile usage scenarios in particular, the workplaces need be enabled to securely connect via *Remote User Access*. In the office usage scenario, it is the *User LAN Periphery* that establishes the connection from the user's side. This part comprises the corresponding ICT security solutions such as firewalls and VPN. The user organization requires the management of users, equipment and their access to ICT components and services. If provided by the ICT Service Provider, this is described in *User Identity Management*. The elements on the user's side require their counterpart on the provider's side where the data center is located. *Corporate Provider Access* comprises all network and IT elements required to protect the provider's computing periphery and to provide VPN capabilities. The standard *Gateway and Central Services* comprises elements residing on top of a sole connection such as e-mail security services. – This section is split into two types of descriptions. Firstly, the general environment, the scope and major activities are described in each area of the whole cluster. Thus, the context in the ICT service production and delivery is portrayed in order to highlight the security problems, issues or concerns which need to be addressed (Sect. 12.3.1 through 12.3.3). Secondly, information is provided about major security measures. They are not specified in full but these sections can be used when designing security measures that protect the area (Sect. 12.3.4 through 12.3.6).

Fig. 105 below shows the location of the "ICT Service Access" cluster within the *ESARIS Security Taxonomy*. The eight *ICT Security Standards* are highlighted. In this section and the one that follows, two clusters are defined: "ICT Service Access" (Sect. 12.3) and "IT Service Production" (Sect. 12.4).[67] This section is organized as follows:

- Transportation (covering Wide Area Networks, WAN):
  - Sect. 12.3.1 describes the general environment, the scope and major activities.
  - Sect. 12.3.4 contains information about major security measures.
- Customer side and endpoints (covering the five standards to the left of the WAN):

---

[67] Note that the *ICT Security Standards* associated with ICT services and their functionality are organized differently in Sections 4.2 and 4.3. There are three clusters, i.e. "Customer and Users", "Networks" and "Data Center".

- Sect. 12.3.2 describes the general environment, the scope and major activities.
- Sect. 12.3.5 contains information about major security measures.
- Connectivity (covering the two standards to the right of the WAN):
  - Sect. 12.3.3 describes the general environment, the scope and major activities.
  - Sect. 12.3.6 contains information about major security measures.

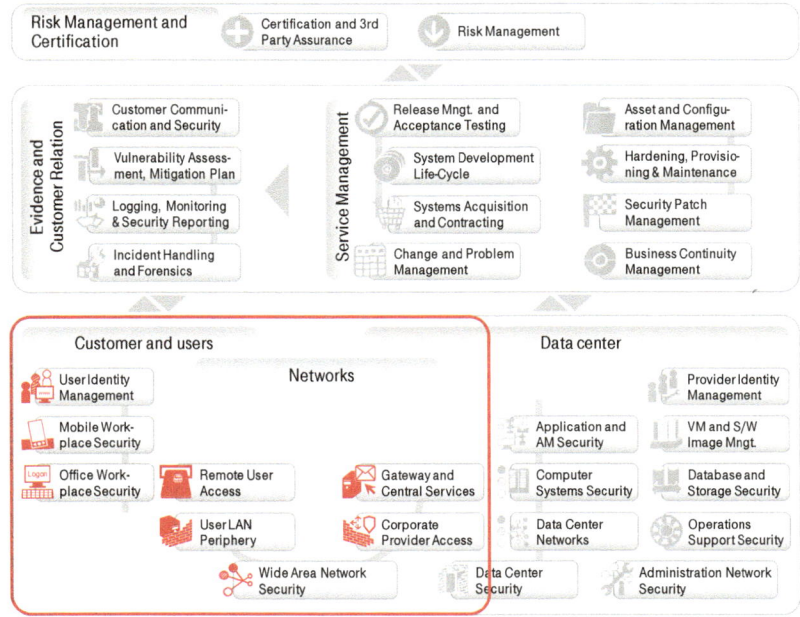

Fig. 105: Landing cluster of "ICT Service Access"

12.3.1 Transportation

Global cooperation and services from the web are a matter of course in today's world. High-performance network infrastructures and flexible applications are a prerequisite for this. Companies are centralizing more and more ICT services and connecting sites to their head office with high bandwidths. Customers are connecting their sites (head offices and branch offices). This allows communication between them. Depending on the geographical situation, this requires a connection to be set up via Wide Area Networks (WAN). Customers connect their sites with data centers of ICT Service Providers in order to consume the ICT services produced there. The Wide Area Network (WAN) is the sole connection between the users and the data center systems.

The communication between the customer's site via a WAN can be implemented differently (refer to Fig. 106). First, a Direct Network Link (DNL) can be established where one customer site is connected to another (No. 1 in Fig. 106). Usually this is implemented with a Layer 1 connection. The network or communication service provider (referred to as "carrier" in the figure) can furthermore interconnect sites of its customers while using the same physical network infrastructure for different customers. The Virtual Private Network (VPN, No. 2 in Fig. 106) separates the data streams of different customers and is built on Layer 2 or Layer 3.

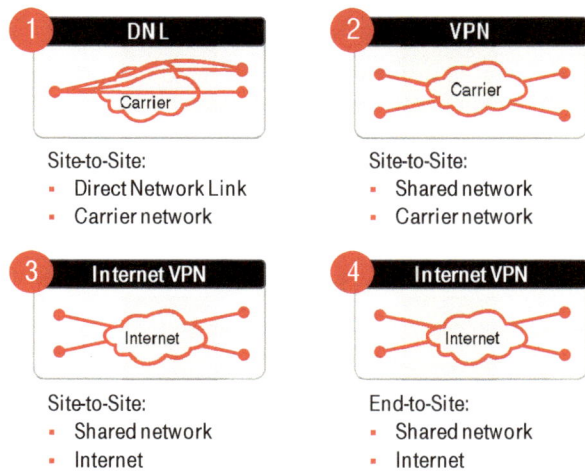

Fig. 106: Connections via the WAN

In order to be accessible, the provider's network needs to be present (that is, the ICT Service Provider must have a so-called Point of Presence, PoP). The edge where the customer accesses the provider's or carrier's network is called Provider Edge (PE) or Service Point (SP) with an appropriate PE router which establishes the connection. At the customer's side, some Customer Premises Equipment (CPE) is required in order to connect. This is considered to be part of the WAN, although physically this equipment (a router) is often located at the customer's premises (called User LAN Periphery below).

Some ICT Service Providers provide a variety of WAN communication services. The site-to-site connection over a shared network of the carrier is mostly implemented through MPLS (Multiprotocol Label Switching). MPLS is a technology that separates the data transmittal of different users by using labels and thereby allows the communication of different users over the same physical network. Legacy transport platforms, ATM (Asynchronous Transfer Mode) and Frame Relay exist as well. All these types of connection are based on networks owned and operated by the ICT Service Provider. There are core technologies that are directly integrated into the networks, which are operated and maintained by the provider. The ICT Service Provider also has central platforms which are used for management, including service delivery.

In other cases, the WAN is only a means for data transport. Especially if public or third-party networks are used, no specific security features can be assumed. In this case, the security is solely implemented at the endpoints (No. 3 and 4 in Fig. 106).

A distinction is made here between two cases. A site (i.e. a User LAN) is connected to a public network (Internet) and the communication is tunneled and, at the end, reaches the provider's data center (Nr. 3 in Fig. 106). In the other case, a user's workplace connects to a public network (Internet) and the communication is tunneled and, at the end, reaches the provider's data center (No. 4 in Fig. 106). This second variant is called Remote User Access in the following.

The different connections over the WAN (see Fig. 106) provide different levels of trustworthiness. In the case that a public network (Internet) is used, generally speaking, no specific security level or security measures can be assumed. Here, the security must solely be provided by the endpoints (both for end-to-site and site-to-site connections).

If the networks are operated by named carriers, then more trust and knowledge is available. If the networking capability is provided by a single service provider (carrier), the situation can be even better. If the ICT Service Provider provides the networking service, the user organization can rely on the existence of security characteristics as part of the WAN connectivity such as separation of user traffic through MPLS.

If there is no protection, the communication in the WAN can result in security issues:

- Information is not properly routed so that it does not reach its correct destination.
- Information is not properly separated so that unauthorized users can access the information being transmitted.
- Information can be manipulated without being noticed by the authorized recipient.
- The communication of users interferes with that of another authorized user.

These are examples only.

12.3.2 Customer side and endpoints

Users work on a computer (client) equipped with a keyboard and a display. Software and data can be stored locally on that machine (thick client), or the client computer is used to access programs provided by remote data centers, where the data is also stored. The workplace computer systems are located at the customer's premises but often managed by an ICT Service Provider. Set-ups also exist whereby parts of the management environment reside on the customer's site. Regardless of the details of the service model, the workplace computers are handed over to the customer so that the ICT Service Provider does not have physical control over these systems. Therefore, at least some of the measures for securing the operation of the workplace may be under the responsibility of the user organization itself.

Typical security issues associated with the use of workplace computers include the following:

- Unauthorized persons gain access to functionality provided by the system or to data stored on that machine.
- The configuration of the workplace computer may be manipulated in order to fraudulently obtain privileges. Or, persons may change or add functionality, for instance, by installing software that is not intended for use or which is explicitly forbidden for some reason.
- The integrity of the system is compromised through infection by malware.
- The integrity or confidentiality of data being communicated or stored locally is lost.

The list of security concerns, threats, risks or problems that are relevant when using a workplace computer can be made much longer since this front-end is usually a focal point of many use cases. It is the way in which most users consume centrally provided ICT services. Depending on the connectivity, it can access a large amount of functionality and data provided remotely. It provides important functionality locally and stores important data persistently or at least temporarily in its internal storage facility.

There are two basic types of workplace computers which are referred to as the following, in this book:

- Mobile Workplace and
- Office Workplace.

The difference is the way in which it is used, or more precisely, the connectivity which is used. The form factor is therefore not important here,[68] although the usage environment which determines threats, etc. is. This is shown in Fig. 107.

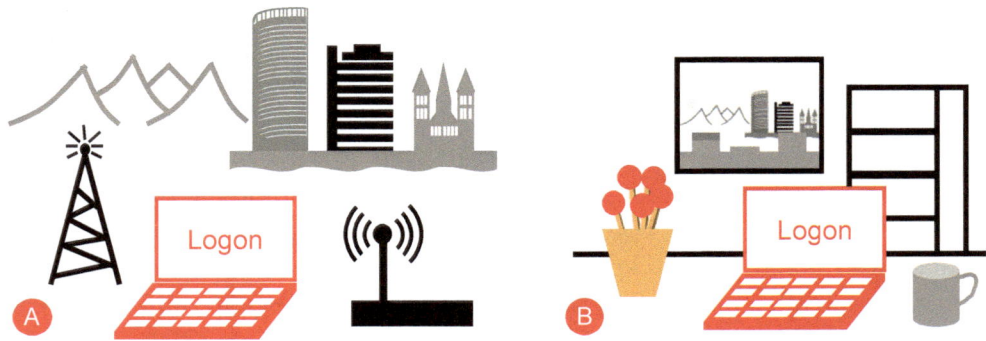

Fig. 107: Mobile (A) versus Office Workplace environment (B)

---

[68] This does not mean that the device and its construction do not influence security. However, in this section the environment is analyzed in order to identify the security concerns and sources for requirements. These are independent of whether the device may or may not allow a threat to be counteracted or help to clear a vulnerability.

The following terms are used in order to differentiate between the types of connectivity:

- The term "User LAN" refers to local area networks of the user organization. The User LAN is located at the user's site. Workplace computers that are located in offices of the user organization are directly connected to the User LAN.

- The term "public network" or "Internet" is used for all noncorporate networks. Public networks do not belong to the user organization; they are also not owned or managed by the ICT Service Provider who provides ICT services. Public networks and the Internet are third-party networks in which no specific security control can be assumed or is agreed upon.

Furthermore, the following is stated:

- Users are anyone who is designated by the user organization to access the ICT services provided by the ICT Service Provider. The group of users mainly comprises the employees of the user organization. However, users may also be customers of the user organization. If the latter runs an Internet business, for instance, consumers or citizens of a country belong to the group of users.

- A Mobile Workplace is a computing device that is not solely used inside an office of the user organization. Instead, it connects to public networks first in order to be put through to the ICT services being provided. This includes notebook computers, tablets and smartphones.

- An Office Workplace is a computer that is only used inside an office of the user organization. This computing device only connects to the "User LAN" from which it is put through to the ICT services being provided.

- An office is a location providing reasonable protection against theft and direct access to equipment (including User LAN network components). The protection is provided by physical security measures, including access control to the building, floors and rooms as appropriate as well as suitable supervision by guards or other means.

There are three ways of using a Mobile Workplace:

- The users (e.g. employees) connect their Mobile Workplace devices to public and other noncorporate networks. Thus, they are "mobile" and work "anywhere". This access is directed in full to the corporate network or, more precisely, to corporate services and applications being produced in a data center.

- But the users may also be enabled to use public and other services (which are not corporate but usually provided on the Internet). In this second usage scenario, the Mobile Workplace device is used outside of any corporate ICT.

- The Mobile Workplace device is used offline (no data connection) or on the user organization's premises. On the premises, the device may be connected to the User LAN (mostly via WLAN) or to an Office Workplace for the purpose of data synchronization (via Bluetooth or cable).

In the first usage scenario, the Mobile Workplace device uses a special software system called Remote User Access (refer to Fig. 108) to connect to a public network and to be put through to the ICT services being provided remotely in the ICT Service Provider's data center. Many enterprises do not use or do not allow the second usage scenario. Critical enterprise services are usually not provided on public networks such as the Internet. The use of public services is out of scope or they are provided using the first usage scenario. In the third usage scenario, the Mobile Workplace device uses the so-called User LAN Periphery to establish a connection to the outside and to be put through to the remote ICT services.

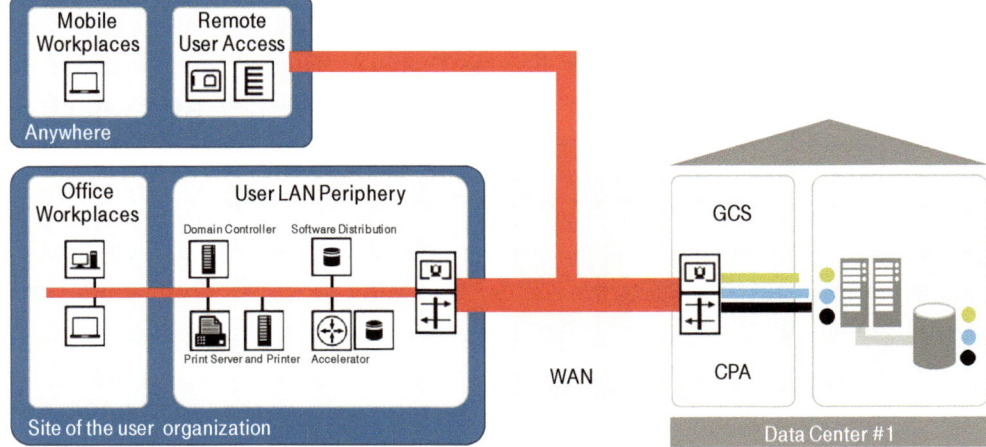

Fig. 108: Accesses to ICT services[69]

This model therefore includes:

- workplaces (two types: Mobile and Office),
- connectors to the WAN (two types: Remote User Access and User LAN Periphery) that provide a connection to the WAN or another public network first of all,
- WAN connectivity (two types: firstly a network controlled by a "carrier" who is an ICT Service Provider of the user organization and secondly a public network or the Internet), and
- ICT services (one type: those being provided by the ICT Service Provider in the remote data center).

This differentiation is needed in order to understand the different security concerns that are to be encountered.

The situation of an Office Workplace is easily characterized:

---

[69] CPA (Corporate Provider Access) and GCS (Gateway and Central Services) are described below. CPA and GCS enable accessing ICT services from the WAN.

- The Office Workplace is a personal computer which is considered to be connected to the User LAN.

- The Office Workplace is physically located in an office. Theft or unauthorized removal is not considered.

Situations are not foreseen in which an Office Workplace establishes a connection, which is not or not thoroughly controlled by the User LAN. If such situation is possible, the analysis for Mobile Workplaces may also be used. Though designed to connect to the corporate network (User LAN) first, Office Workplaces may also utilize virtual private network technology (e.g. using TLS, SSL) to connect securely to remote ICT services. In this case, they use technology from Remote User Access in the User LAN (not shown in Fig. 108).

Users access their Workplace computers, functions provided by them and data stored there. Users also consume ICT services and thereby access applications, servers, networks and other equipment. Such access shall be enabled in a controlled way while preventing abuse and hostile action, especially unauthorized access. Therefore, digital identities including rights and other attributes for users are required. Organizational, procedural and personal means are also necessary. Identity management and account management procedures and techniques, including rights management and user provisioning for users on the customer's side, are therefore required. These users are typically employees of the ICT Service Provider's customer. More specifically, these users are all individuals who the customer anticipates will access the ICT systems and components. Operations personnel (administrators) of the ICT Service Provider are explicitly not included in this group and are not taken into consideration here.

Examples of risks or threats that encourage the need for correct identity administration are:
- Compromised integrity and privacy of customer information when accessed by non-authorized individuals.
- Need-to-know principles cannot be enforced.
- Non-authorized access to customer systems occurs.
- Litigation issues in the case of security breaches or failures.
- The management of entitlements and access covers the provisioning with identities and passwords or tokens and the assignment of duties and rights, and finally requires the maintenance of all means.

12.3.3 Connectivity

Office Workplace computers are directly integrated into the User LAN and connected to it. The User LAN Periphery is the bridge between the User LAN and the Wide Area Network (WAN). Users (of customers) come from the User LAN. The ICT services are provided from the WAN side. All ICT equipment, which is used to provide and secure this bridge, is seen as part of the User LAN Periphery. The

User LAN is to be protected from the potentially hostile WAN environment by components in the User LAN Periphery. The availability of a communication line between the User LAN and a WAN, including the Internet, is associated with several security risks and threats which have to be considered and controlled.

If the User LAN Periphery is not being properly protected,

- unauthorized users may gain access to the User LAN and its ICT systems or services,
- the User LAN Periphery and the ICT equipment it consists of are vulnerable and susceptible to attacks if single ICT systems and components are not properly managed,
- the User LAN and its ICT systems or services may be subject to manipulation or other hostile activity,
- the communication of authorized users may be subject to eavesdropping or manipulation, or
- the communication of authorized users may interfere with that of other authorized users.

These are examples of possible security issues that are to be addressed by appropriate protection of the User LAN Periphery.

Note that a large variety of ICT services and solutions may be provided in the User LAN by equipment installed at the customer site. However, it is assumed here that all essential ICT services are provided from within the data center. Essential services comprise, but are not limited to, e-mail services (such as Microsoft Exchange), file server and storage, complex collaboration platforms (such as Microsoft Share-Point) as well as specific business applications. Consequently, the User LAN Periphery only contains a typical (minimal) set of services required for workplaces to be used in the User LAN and to consume the ICT services provided from the remote data center.

Key ICT elements that are used for a secure connection between users and (remote) ICT services include

- MPLS routers, VPN gateways,
- firewalls and Intrusion Detection and Prevention Systems (IDS, IPS).

Note that other ICT elements might be required to support communication. Furthermore, the User LAN Periphery may comprise domain controllers, print servers and software distribution services.

Communication both from the User LAN Periphery (fixed connect) and from anywhere (Remote User Access) to the data center requires appropriate router or gateway functionality on the data center site.

Data centers are the heart of any IT production and ICT service delivery in general. Almost all ICT systems and components, except for external networking, for example, are located in data centers. Applications which support business processes are hosted in data centers. They store critical data in storage systems which are also located in the data center. The applications and ICT services are accessed from outside the data center. User organizations or individuals such as employees of the customers connect to the data center infrastructure in order to consume the ICT services being produced there. Consequently, this access to the data center needs to be appropriately protected. The technical ICT equipment that is installed in order to protect the access to and the electronic communication with the ICT services in the data center, is also located in the data center. This part is called Corporate Provider Access (denoted by CPA in Fig. 109). The Corporate Provider Access is the user-side interface or periphery of the data center and provides the communication bridge between users (coming from the WAN) and the ICT services produced by the ICT Service Provider with ICT systems located in a data center.

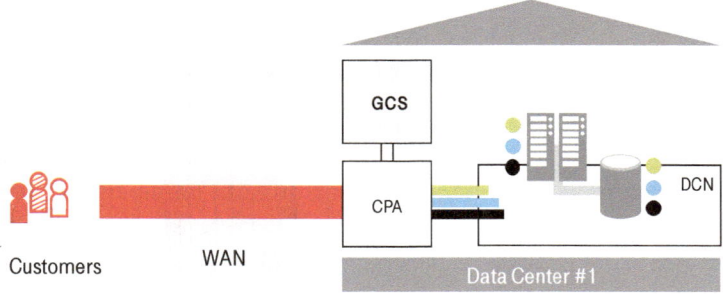

Fig. 109: External WAN interface of a data center

The ICT systems and components for ICT service production are connected directly to an internal Data Center Network (denoted by DCN in Fig. 109). The ICT systems are to be protected from the potentially hostile WAN environment by components in the Corporate Provider Access area. This is the main task of the Corporate Provider Access. It also comprises central services for communication and the required management systems. Thus, the Corporate Provider Access is the bridge between the Wide Area Network (WAN) and the Data Center Networks (DCN). Users come from the WAN. The ICT systems are connected to the Data Center Network.

If this "bridge" is not properly protected,

- unauthorized users may gain access to the ICT systems or services,
- ICT systems or services may be subject to manipulation or other hostile activity,
- the communication of authorized users may be subject to eavesdropping or manipulation, or
- the communication of authorized users may interfere with that of other authorized users.

These are examples of possible security issues that are to be addressed by appropriate protection of the Corporate Provider Access.

The Corporate Provider Access comprises all ICT equipment between the WAN and the Data Center Network, i.e. the communication periphery of the data center (refer to Fig. 109). That includes packet filter firewalls, switches and routers, VPN gateways and intrusion detection / prevention (IDS/IPS) solutions. Other central equipment is required for relaying the communication. This equipment is summarized under the heading "Gateway and Central Services" (denoted by GCS in the figure). First, the ICT systems and components in the Corporate Provider Access area require specific security services which should be centrally provided. Typical examples are authentication or domain name system (DNS) services. In addition, communication and front-end services may also be provided to customers. These are application-oriented services or services which need to be centrally available and perhaps equally accessible both from WAN and from applications in the data center. They are placed in the Gateway and Central Services area in order to be easily accessible from the WAN. Examples are services for e-mail security and other such communication. The third group of equipment comprises general security services at an application level, including the Internet. Typical examples are proxies, reverse proxies, and load balancers.

If central services such as authentication or domain name system (DNS) services do not function properly, the access from the WAN to the data center internals may not be properly protected. If communication and front-end services are not properly protected they may not be reliable, the data being exchanged may, for instance, be infected with malicious code or Internet communication may provide undesired content. Similarly, specific applications may require central protection by means of a gateway or reverse-proxy system. Otherwise, sensitive information about network or application internals may be gathered from the WAN, complex functionality may feature too many vulnerabilities, applications in the data center may be easier to attack, or peak loads may affect performance and availability. The use of a "gateway system" can, in turn, also protect the client accessing the application in the data center. These examples are not exhaustive.

12.3.4   Securing transportation

Cautionary note: This section provides examples of essential security issues. It is not the subject of this book to specify technical, procedural and organizational security measures in detail. However, the following section specifies major aspects that can be considered when designing security measures that protect the cluster "transportation" (described in Sect. 12.3.1). Note that security should also have a business case; the design, implementation and maintenance of security measures incur costs, but customers especially tend to look for lower prices. Thus, security needs to be carefully designed.

The *ICT Security Standard – Wide Area Network Security (WAN)* comprises all means to securely transport data between users and between users and IT systems in data centers including direct network links, Internet access, bandwidth and MPLS.

There is no standard set of requirements for WAN communication services. The requirements may depend on

- the existence and quality of security measures at the endpoints,
- the complexity and distribution of the WAN, which includes the existence of subnets, geographical distribution and distance,
- the ownership and the level of control of subnets.

Whereas consumers solely use the Internet to connect to remote IT services, enterprise users may not, since many applications require a quality of service which cannot be guaranteed by public networks. Connections such as MPLS moreover provide features that are advantageous for user organizations since they often require flexible cross-linking of different sites and data center locations.

Since Wide Area Networks are diverse in nature, security objectives are to be defined that reflect the customer's needs for confidentiality, integrity, authenticity, and quality of service (including availability). Reasonable measures shall then be selected to protect the WAN service being provided.

Protection of networking shall be effective and purposeful and precautions shall be taken so that possible impacts are isolated as far as possible. Therefore, networks should be segmented into subnets, where each answers a specific or similar purpose and meets similar security needs. Parameters that guide such segmentation include security objectives, types and rights for access, purpose and users as well as the relation of such users (e.g. differentiation into customers, organizations, groups etc.). Or, depending on the security objectives being defined, the appropriate network connection is chosen featuring the required protection or risk profile, respectively.

Parts of the total network, such as segments, differ in the level of control, trustworthiness and attack potential. It is therefore necessary to perform an analysis of these parameters and assign each part or network segment to a category. For example, wireless networks are usually considered to be unsecure because communication can easily be intercepted. Networks with different security levels or risk profiles shall be separated by firewalls, routers or gateways. Networks with an inappropriate level of security can still be used if the data is, for example, encrypted so that the total traffic is tunneled through the potentially unsecure network. Such control may include intelligence and filters as appropriate. The security gateways and other network components shall themselves be appropriately protected. Interference with measures taken on the application level in particular shall be avoided in order to limit or prevent impacts.

The possibility and probability of attacks shall be reduced by a means that reduces the attack surface. Hence, network segments with a higher level of control, trust-worthiness or a potentially lower attack potential shall disclose as little information as possible to other networks, especially those of third parties or to the Internet. Services and protocols that are not used should not be made available. It can be necessary to protect routing information when it is exchanged and to allow the proof of its origin through digital signatures. Commercially provided networks should be monitored continuously in order to identify malicious or suspicious activity.

Authorized operations personnel (administrators) shall have the means to conduct the administration of the networks securely and consistently. Unauthorized indi-viduals are excluded from accessing administrative functions and services. In par-ticular, device management traffic may be encrypted. All network elements must be securely configured. This needs to be maintained in the case of automated con-figuration of network components in particular. Configuration information needs to be protected and backed up.

Public network segments are owned and operated by an ICT Service Provider (car-rier), often called an Internet service provider (ISP) in this context. The Internet service providers provide a communication service by establishing the best route through the Internet or to the next Internet service provider[70]. This chain is con-trolled by BGP (Border Gateway Protocol, which is the Internet's routing protocol). The destinations are resolved using DNS (Domain Name System, which is a worldwide directory service that provides the IP address for a host name). These services are necessary for any Internet communication and are mostly taken for granted by users. Internet services and their security are not considered in this book. Thus, the Internet is taken as an opaque data transport service. User organi-zations may, however, take related risks into account and consider related threats and current attacks. However, protective measures are beyond the scope of this description. For example, effective protection against Distributed Denial-of-Service Attacks (DDoS) can only be implemented in an Internet backbone. The receiving endpoints (Internet users including ICT Service Providers) have limited ability to do this.

12.3.5   Securing workplaces

Cautionary note: This section provides examples of essential security issues. It is not the subject of this book to specify technical, procedural and organizational security measures in detail. However, the following section specifies major aspects that can be considered when designing security measures that protect the cluster "customer side and endpoints" (described in Sect. 12.3.2). Note that security

---

[70]   more precisely to the next or through a chain of Autonomous Systems (AS)

should also have a business case; the design, implementation and maintenance of security measures incur costs, but customers especially tend to look for lower prices. Thus, security needs to be carefully designed.

Logon

The *ICT Security Standard – Office Workplace Security (OWS)* describes all the software and equipment that is used to protect office computers and the data and software stored and processed there. Office Workplaces connect to remote IT services via the User LAN.

The Office Workplace offers the user significant functionality to support his daily business. From the user's point of view, it is also the entry point to the ICT infrastructure of the user organization. As a side effect, this entry point may also be subject to attacks. Therefore, effort is taken to keep such workplaces under control of the IT administration and to add and maintain the security functionality that is required. In the following, it is assumed that the Office Workplaces are company-owned and controlled and managed by the ICT Service Provider (on behalf of the user organization). Individual users are considered to have limited entitlements.

Users shall not be able to access Office Workplace computers other than their own. Access to and usage of Office Workplaces requires authorization. Users shall be equipped with a credential (means for authentication) that is compliant with the security requirements of the use of the Office Workplace and data and applications being processed. Re-authentication may be required after a certain period or time of user inactivity.

The correct configuration of Office Workplaces shall be maintained. Changes to the configurations and settings of an Office Workplace should require authorization. In other words, access to all administrative functions (especially of the BIOS and of the operating system) requires authorization. Users are not intended to perform administrative tasks and must not have administrative privileges. User-defined software shall not be executed since this may cause security breaches or at least violate corporate policies. Hence, the installation of privileged software requires authorization or is performed by a privileged administration process remotely. Software in centrally managed Office Workplaces is not updated using services in the public Internet and related communication channels, as well as error messages are not submitted to external parties. Office Workplaces shall only be used as intended. Remote control, e.g. of cameras and other recording devices, is completely disabled or restricted to prevent abuse.

The integrity of Office Workplaces shall be maintained through the use of anti-virus and malware scanners. The latter cannot be disabled by users without notice and must regularly be provided with appropriate update information. Their status needs to be reported. Office Workplace computers communicate with the external (its environment) which they do not control. As a result, they may control inbound and outbound traffic and decide which protocols and services can be used and by which applications. Office Workplaces may be equipped with the means to detect attacks (i.e. potentially hostile access). Negative effects may then be mitigated or avoided as appropriate.

Office Workplaces may be equipped with means for encrypting files, file containers, virtual drives, hard disk partitions or the entire hard disk. Hard disk encryption (either partitions or in its entirety) must be enforced so that users are prevented from disabling this function. Implementation of such features depends on the criticality of the Office Workplace and data and applications being processed as well as on the office environment and risks associated with it. Web browsers are powerful tools and work as a presentation layer, application front-end or multimedia player. Malicious communication, data or executable code should be detected. Negative effects shall be mitigated or avoided as appropriate.

E-mail client software and office software may be supplemented by encryption functions, the means to apply digital signatures or tools to control information flow (known as data leakage or loss prevention or as Enterprise Digital Rights Management (EDRM) solutions). The necessity of such features depends on the security policies to be applied. E-mail client software may also provide functions for the automatic treatment of unsolicited or undesired e-mail messages (known as spam).

Office Workplaces should be provided with the ability to backup and restore of data. The necessity depends on the criticality and the amount of this data being stored locally. If Office Workplace computers are used outside the internal corporate network, connections to networks should be set up through an encrypted channel for secure remote access to the required ICT service. Physical locks and screen privacy filters may also be provided.

The *ICT Security Standard – Mobile Workplace Security (MWS)* describes all software and equipment that is used to protect mobile computers and the data and software stored and processed on them. There are notebook computers and different types of smartphones. Mobile Workplaces connect to remote IT services also via Remote User Access, possibly using public networks.

Notebook computers are examples of Mobile Workplaces. These computer devices are fully equipped personal computers with a hard disk and operating system. But they are mobile and can be used on the move or in an office environment to serve as an Office Workplace. Because of this dual use, notebooks should feature the same protection as defined above for Office Workplace. The description will not be duplicated here. Tablet computers and other such form factors may be treated accordingly where possible.

Notebook computers (or even tablets) require the base protection referred to above. However, they are used in a mobile, unsecure environment which requires additional protection. The level of protection and the concrete security measures strongly depend on this environment, namely the physical environment, the connectivity and the risk profile of the networks being used. The description in this section will therefore be limited to provide general recommendation only.

Since the environment and the usage scenarios are diverse, security objectives are to be defined that reflect the needs of the user organizations in terms of confidentiality, integrity, authenticity, and accountability. Thereby "types of usage" should be defined, for example office bound, home worker, and occasionally mobile, or "road warrior". Security is implemented accordingly. It is also important to understand how the mobile device connects (locally, wireless LAN, wireless UMTS/LTE, etc.) and what kind of data is stored, processed and transmitted.

The correct configuration of Mobile Workplaces shall be maintained. Changes to configurations and settings for a Mobile Workplace should require authorization. Configuration includes but is not limited to logon and device unlock, network and other log requirements, synchronization and connection facilities, backup, and application installation and management. Note that the synchronization with other computers and web or cloud services should be controlled as appropriate. Precautions shall be taken if a Mobile Workplace computer is lost in order to prevent a security breach or mitigate the possible impact. It must be clear what kind of data is stored on which devices. Strategies for backup and, possibly, recovery shall exist. The goals and objectives developed for the Office Workplace security shall be examined in order to find out which are valid, which should be applied and which can reasonably be afforded for Mobile Workplaces.

Note that smartphones and other "embedded systems" feature limited capabilities to add security features. If the device lacks an expansion slot (such as micro SD) then it may not be possible to add hardware-based key storage for encrypted e-mail and other purposes. More critically, most of these devices are developed for a consumer market. Therefore, they do not feature functions that are required in an enterprise context. They are equipped with functions for easy repair which can unfortunately also be used to compromise the device's security. This trend is called consumerization. It also considers dual-use scenarios where people start to use their private equipment for business application or vice versa. In this case, it can be necessary to adapt the usage scenario of the device including data and applications in order to avoid violation of corporate policies. Other devices such as flash drives, portable disks and multimedia devices should also be treated. Security measures should combine user education, device protection, connection security and data protection as appropriate. Other literature than this book should be consulted regarding appropriate strategies for dealing with these trends.

The *ICT Security Standard – Remote User Access (RUA)* describes all client components that are used in a mobile usage scenario to securely communicate via the possibly unsecure WAN and establish a connection to remote IT services. This includes VPN clients, authentication tokens and other such client tools.

Selected employees or even the entire staff of the user organization shall be able to connect to the company network and use all or some of the corporate infrastructure, services and applications.[71] A "mobile" or "home office" usage scenario is considered where the Workplace computer connects directly to a network other than a corporate User LAN (i.e. usually to the Internet). This opens the door to various new threats. These threats can occur anywhere on the end-to-end remote connection, beginning at the remote user's device, up to the data center periphery. The threats have to be considered and controlled by taking the following into account.

Users shall be allowed to connect securely to specific ICT services produced in the data center. Non-authorized individuals shall not gain access to these ICT systems and functions. This feature cannot be guaranteed by the client side. But users shall be equipped with a credential (means for authentication) that is compliant with the security requirements of the ICT service being consumed. It is the customer's decision if and which additional means for authentication are necessary. A special case is the remote access for the purpose of administrating an application. In this case, strong authentication may be used and logging should be mandatory.

If connections are made in different usage scenarios (i.e. to networks with a different risk profile), it can be necessary to securely reconfigure security solutions such as the personal firewall to allow and secure the type of current connectivity. All data being transferred between the user and the ICT service shall be protected from manipulation and eavesdropping. Note that all these security services shall be provided independent of whether the ICT service or application provides additional security services such as authentication and encryption or not. That means that secure communication is terminated at a "central service area" (SSL/TLS or IPSec) in front of the ICT service.

Remote User Access can also provide a complete desktop functionality remotely. This is called desktop virtualization. In this case, users are equipped with software or a token with software that establishes a tunneled connection to a remote ICT service. The Mobile Workplace is only used for data input and data display. Storage of user data and its processing is performed within the data center. Such an approach has several advantages in terms of security. Only a small portion of the

---

[71] Note that due to the underlying model, the corporate infrastructure (of the user organization) is located in the data center of the ICT Service Provider. The provisioning of ICT services is conducted by the ICT Service Provider on behalf of the user organization.

information is transported to the outside (to the Workplace which can be located anywhere). Backup and software maintenance can be provided centrally.

The *ICT Security Standard – User LAN Periphery (ULP)* describes all ICT equipment between the User LAN and the WAN. That includes site-to-site gateways, firewalls, intrusion detection / prevention systems (IDS/IPS) and domain services. Office Workplace computers connect directly to the user organization's LAN. It is the User LAN Periphery that puts the user through to remote IT services. Some information is provided on how this information is protected at the user's site.

The corporate network and the public network or WAN differ in terms of the level of control, trustworthiness and attack potential. Hence, inbound and outbound traffic shall be controlled by security gateways which separate the two. Secure communication is also possible over public, potentially unsecure networks. In order to maintain confidentiality, integrity and authenticity of transmission at a high level, all data transfer between the corporate network and a gateway shall be encrypted after authentication of the remote gateway, which will mediate the access to the sought ICT service. In most cases, it is decided to implement a two-way authentication. Then the gateway in the User LAN Periphery needs to have a unique digital identity too. Appropriate key management, registration and identity management facilities must be implemented.

Attacks (here understood as potentially hostile access, mostly from the WAN) shall be detected as far as possible. Malicious communication, data or executable code shall be detected. Negative effects shall be mitigated or avoided as appropriate. The possibility and probability of attacks (mostly from the WAN) shall be reduced by means that reduce the attack surface of the customer's corporate network periphery and its elements. Specific information about the network internals, such as internal addresses and the like, shall be hidden or protected from the WAN so that this information cannot be retrieved from the WAN side.

An inventory shall be provided of all ICT equipment (in particular office workplaces) that is authorized to be connected to the User LAN. It shall provide the means to control membership and access to the User LAN and the resources it provides. Authentication and name resolution services are typically also provided. These services are set up and used to guarantee controlled use of the User LAN's resources while preventing unauthorized access. All ICT security solutions (including further services such as software distribution services) shall be actively managed in order to maintain their level of security.

The *ICT Security Standard – User Identity Management (UIM)* describes all procedures and regulations, systems and services that are used to create and manage the digital identities, including rights and other attributes for users. The digital identities can be used to protect the access to Workplaces, the User LAN and remote ICT services. The digital identities of a person are described as "personalized identity objects" which are assigned to other identity objects such as location, organization, legal entity and others. These identities are managed in the so-called Identity Management life-cycle. Identity Management services are the basis for real-time Access Management. Note that in the case of accesses to remote ICT services, all authentication services (and Access Management) are performed in the remote data center.

In order to reduce the risks associated with the user access to ICT systems and services, a variety of security measures are put in place. They are designed to achieve the correctness, quality and reproducibility of the user access. The assignment of digital identities with roles, rights (entitlements) and other attributes shall follow a controlled process with application, check-up, clearance, and provisioning. User registration and approval is one key element which also determines the quality of security that can be achieved.

Reproducibility and accountability are essential when controlling user access to ICT resources. Hence, the management of digital identities with roles, rights (entitlements) and other attributes shall be conducted with tools for workflow and administration and using at least partly automated means for provisioning (of identities, rights etc. to target components).

Credentials are chosen and may be changed according to the corresponding security policies. This includes the strength of authentication methods. Help desk and user self-services (if any) shall be designed not to undermine security. Roles and responsibilities shall be defined and documented in accordance with business and the user organization's ICT security policies. Entitlements shall be designed for business (on some abstract "role" level) and then assigned to individuals. Business tasks or roles shall be described and approved before being implemented in access rights.

Users shall be given appropriate guidance as well as education, training and the like in order to enable them to use the means being provided appropriately and to follow the rules and procedures and to adhere to policies. Consequences and disciplinary action in case of violations should be known.

Important note: The user organization remains responsible for human resources management, user registration and other internal processes of the customer's organization. The ICT Service Provider can only provide regulation and management tools according to policies and practices which the customer is responsible for. The customer must also ensure that data is complete, correct and up-to-date.

12.3.6   Securing connectivity

Cautionary note: This section provides examples of essential security issues. It is not the subject of this book to specify technical, procedural and organizational security measures in detail. However, the following section specifies major aspects that can be considered when designing security measures that protect the cluster "connectivity" (described in Sect. 12.3.3). Note that security should also have a business case; the design, implementation and maintenance of security measures incur costs, but customers especially tend to look for lower prices. Thus, security needs to be carefully designed.

The *ICT Security Standard – Corporate Provider Access (CPA)* describes all ICT equipment between the WAN and the data center networks. That includes packet filter firewalls, switches and routers, VPN gateways and intrusion detection / prevention (IDS/IPS) solutions.

As described above, customers of the ICT Service Provider shall be able to connect their own entire LAN to ICT services provided from within the data center of the provider. And, mostly in a mobile usage scenario, individual users shall be able to connect to such ICT services. The ICT Service Provider must provide this connectivity but simultaneously ensure that the outer edge of its computing environment is protected from third-party access, hostile action and malfunction of communication. Some rather general issues are mentioned below in order to characterize this complex subject.

The data center network and the WAN differ in terms of the level of control, trustworthiness and attack potential. Hence, inbound and outbound traffic shall be controlled by security gateways which separate the two.

An encrypted communication channel shall be terminated if user organizations require such a secure tunnel for WAN transfer in order to ensure the confidentiality, integrity and authenticity of data being exchanged. This includes appropriate key management and a unique digital identity for a VPN gateway. Users shall be allowed to connect securely, whereas non-authorized individuals shall be excluded. In most cases, authentication of the requesting party is required.

Attacks (here understood as potentially hostile access mostly from WAN) shall be detected as far as possible. The impact of Denial-of-Service attacks shall be minimized. Malicious communication, data or executable code shall be detected. Negative effects shall be mitigated or avoided as appropriate. The possibility and probability of attacks (mostly from WAN) shall be reduced by means that reduce the attack surface of the data center periphery and its elements. Specific information about the data center internals such as internal addresses and the like shall be hidden or protected from the WAN so that this information cannot be retrieved from this side.

The *ICT Security Standard – Gateway and Central Services (GCS)* describes all ICT equipment that is centrally provided for specific communication such as e-mail and user authentication. That includes e-mail security and archiving, other communication services, file sharing as well as directory services, LDAP, other authentication servers, web SSO and identity federation services, application level gateways including proxies and reverse proxies and web application firewalls (WAF).

The "transport-oriented" issues are addressed by the Corporate Provider Access. Gateway and Central Services focuses on "application-oriented" issues as described in full above. Secure communication and usage of ICT services requires the prior authentication of users or of the user's side. Hence, these services are provided to calling parties that allow the validation of credentials and the authentication of users or user side gateways, respectively. Their use is restricted to authorized ICT systems which are located in the "central service area" (Corporate Provider Access). Similar services may also be provided for other authorized ICT entities (such as applications and possibly computer systems) located in the data center. The functionality for (server-based) single sign-on enhances ease of use and possibly also security since it makes it easier for users to handle passwords.

ICT services or applications such as e-mail, web services and others shall be protected from being tampered with using malicious code, malicious communication requests and the like. Hence, specific services are provided that filter and clean data streams transferred through the "central service area" (Corporate Provider Access) and that remove or repair, or at least signal suspicious, dangerous or illicit requests and communication. Additional services may also remove unsolicited, undesired or disruptive messages (in the case of e-mail known as spam) from the data stream being forwarded and, in this way, also help to maintain the availability of the ICT services.

The confidentiality, integrity and authenticity of e-mails shall be maintained in the case of critical business communication. Hence, specific services can be provided that feature encryption functions or apply and validate digital signatures on behalf of the sender or recipient.

Sensitive information about network or application internals shall be hidden from the WAN whenever possible. Complex application functionality shall be reduced in order to reduce the possible occurrence and exploitation of vulnerabilities. Applications located in the data center can be isolated from direct access from the WAN in order to make attacks harder. Loads shall be shared in order to avoid peak loads that affect performance and availability. Clients that utilize applications in the data center from the WAN can reduce the associated risks by using a known gateway system (as proxy).

12.4   IT Service Production

Introduction and summary: This cluster comprises nine areas. ICT services are produced in data centers of the ICT Service Provider but accessed remotely. A connection is required to the *Data Center Networks* within the data centers, which also connect physical computer systems, these computer systems to storage and administrators to both computers and storage systems. *Computer Systems Security* comprises at least the computer hardware and operating systems. In dynamic computing environments, hypervisors and such virtualization means are part of the computer systems. *Database and Storage Security* is considered as an extra discipline. *Operations Support Security* pertains to all security aspects of supporting technology such as servers and utilities needed for data center operations. *Virtual Machine and Software Image Management* addresses the security issues relating to the engineering (creation and configuration) of software images, their handling and deployment to machines as well as moving them and other management activities including the management systems required for this. The access of operations personnel (administrators) to those and other critical systems or systems functions needs to be controlled with care. The related security issues are summarized in *Provider Identity Management*. Management of the ICT is performed from operations centers remotely. *Administration Network Security* defines security requirements for such administrative access. *Data Center Security* comprises all aspects of physical and environmental security relating to the data center as a whole. Software applications are located on the top of the IT stack. *Application and Application Management Security* describes this subject. – This section is split into two types of descriptions. First, the general environment, the scope and major activities are described in each area of the whole cluster. Thus, the context in the ICT service production and delivery is portrayed in order to highlight the security problems, issues or concerns which need to be addressed (Sect. 12.4.1 through 12.4.3). Secondly, information about major security measures is given. They are not specified in full but these sections can be used when designing security measures that protect the area (Sect. 12.4.4 through 12.4.6).

Fig. 110 shows the location of the "IT Service Production" cluster within the *ESARIS Security Taxonomy*. The nine *ICT Security Standards* are highlighted. This section is organized as follows:

- The lower IT stack:
    - Sect. 12.4.1 describes the general environment, the scope and major activities.
    - Sect. 12.4.4 contains information about major security measures.
- IT management and data center premises:
    - Sect. 12.4.2 describes the general environment, the scope and major activities.

- ▪ Sect. 12.4.5 contains information about major security measures.
▪ Applications:
  - ▪ Sect. 12.4.3 describes the general environment, the scope and major activities.
  - ▪ Sect. 12.4.6 contains information about major security measures.

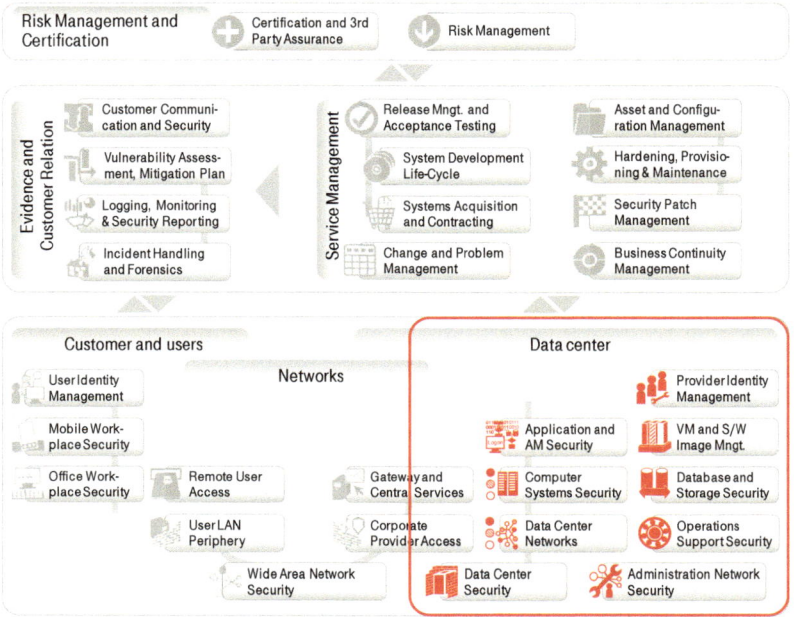

Fig. 110: Landing cluster of "IT Service Production"

12.4.1   The lower IT stack

The "lower IT stack" roughly consists of all elements below the application:
- ▪ networks (cabling, switches, routers),
- ▪ computer systems (hardware with operating system and possibly a virtualization layer), and
- ▪ central storage in the case of industrialized computing.

Application software (with middleware) is considered in Sect. 12.4.3.

User organizations access their ICT services, including applications, from outside the data center, which requires appropriate protection using additional systems. This communication between the users and the data center is conducted over Wide Area Networks (WAN) such as the Internet. This communication must find the way from the WAN to the ICT systems actually providing the ICT services required by the user organization. The crossover from the WAN to the data center's internals is managed by the so-called Corporate Provider Access area (see CPA in Fig. 111). Then communication is distributed to the ICT systems by the Data Center Networks (denoted by DCN in Fig. 111).

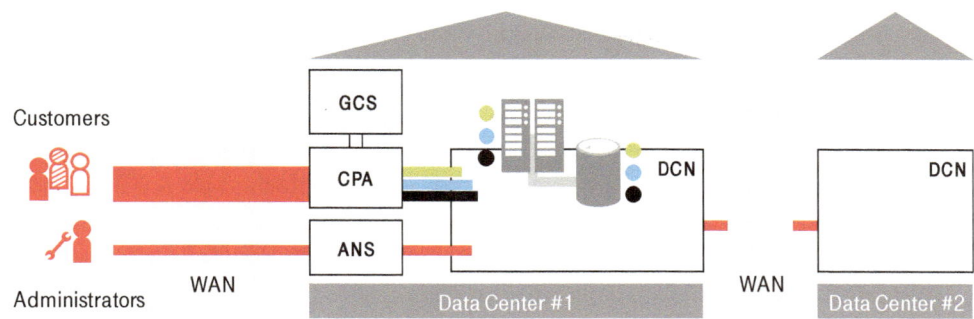

Fig. 111: Data Center Networks (DCN) and data center accesses

Administration of ICT systems and components is conducted remotely. A specific Administration Network is used for this communication (denoted by ANS in Fig. 111). Potentially, operations personnel (administrators) must be able to access all ICT systems and components which require management. The communication to the data center's internals is managed by the Administration Network. Then communication is distributed to the ICT systems by the Data Center Networks (DCN in Fig. 111). Furthermore, data might be exchanged between data centers of the ICT Service Provider to allow disaster recovery or to enhance performance or resource utilization. Despite being located outside the data center, these networks are also considered to be Data Center Networks.

The Data Center Networks serve different purposes, they:
- allow users to communicate with Computer Systems (applications),
- connect Computer Systems with other Computer Systems to support distributed applications,
- connect Computer Systems with central storage systems for persistent storage,
- allow administrators to access Computer Systems and storage systems.

Sharing a computing infrastructure and storage requires that every user must potentially have the ability to connect to every system. Consequently, all ICT systems must be interconnected. This is the function of the Data Center Networks (DCN in Fig. 111). The networking within the data centers (and between those of the ICT Service Provider) is a critical issue. If it is not properly protected,
- the communication of authorized users may interfere with that of other authorized users,
- the communication of authorized users may be subject to eavesdropping or manipulation,
- the communication of different groups or for different purposes (e.g. administrators versus users; outbound customer communication versus entirely internal traffic) may interfere and violate the segregation of duties and other rules,
- unauthorized users may gain access to the ICT systems or services, or
- ICT systems or services may be subject to manipulation or any other hostile activity.

These are examples of possible security issues that are to be addressed through the adequate design and protection of the Data Center Networks.

Computer systems are highly standardized and installed in rack cabinets. These racks are usually placed in long rows forming aisles between them. The Computer Systems do not usually have any keyboard or display attached to it. All communication is carried out through networks. Computer systems form the central part in the IT stack consisting of all elements from the computer hardware up, but except for applications and middleware and centralized storage. Computer systems provide the solid ground for implementing ICT services and running applications.

In traditional computer systems, monolithic or distributed applications are installed on one specific physical computer system. (Refer to Case A in Fig. 112; Computer Systems as defined here comprise the elements below the green arrow.) This computing model is characterized by the fact that application software is located on one physical machine during operations. Mobile code as used in web applications is also covered by this model. In this model, a computer system and its application is assigned to a customer. Compensation is provided for this whole IT stack, its data center environment and all the (ICT) services being provided in addition.

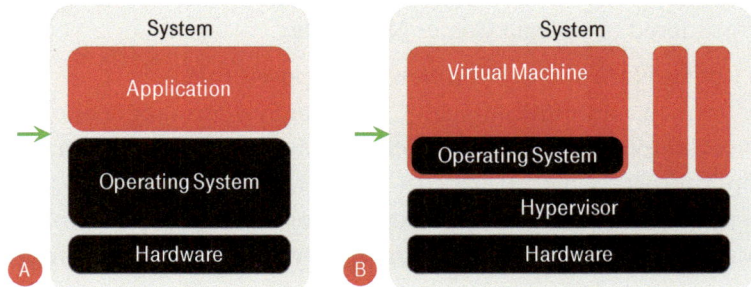

Fig. 112: Traditional computer system (A) and system with virtualization (B)

In dynamic computing environments, operating systems and applications are not installed in the traditional way. These environments use different virtualization technologies to separate hardware, operating systems and applications. This is done to generate economies of scale that result from sharing resources between user organizations. In order to distribute the costs of acquisition (and operations) over user organizations, the latter have to share hardware and software. In this dynamic computing model, computer systems consist of hardware, operating systems and virtualization layers (refer to Case B in Fig. 112). The hardware and virtualization layer (hypervisor) form one part; and the hypervisor software is installed in the traditional way and remains on the physical machine. The other software (combined in a so-called Virtual Machine, VM) can move. The software is prepared as an executable image (memory copy). For execution, it is copied onto one physical machine, the environment is configured and the hypervisor is instructed to start the software. Details regarding the management of Virtual Machines are provided in the next Sect. 12.4.2.

A dynamic computing environment with virtualization allows sharing of resources and their dynamic allocation to Virtual Machines (VM). This is shown in Fig. 113, where the hypervisor or Virtual Machine Monitor (VMM) allocates CPU time and memory resources which are shared by several VM. If a VM requires more resources but resources run out on the physical machine (No. 1), the VM must be moved to another physical machine (No. 2 in Fig. 113). The management of Virtual Machines (VM) uses the hypervisor.

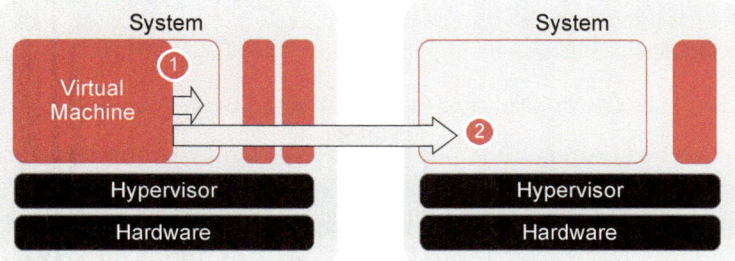

Fig. 113: Dynamic resource allocation

Computer Systems need to be installed, configured, maintained, and operated in a secure way. Appropriate security functions need to be added. Computer Systems are highly critical; if not properly protected, the following may occur:

- Intruders or malicious software (viruses, malware and the like) may gain access to these ICT components and the software and data being processed.
- These and other scenarios may lead to a manipulation of data and software.
- Data being processed, stored, or transmitted may be disclosed to unauthorized users.
- Customer applications and data communication may interfere with those of other ICT services or customers.
- Modifications may be made that facilitate or even enable subsequent attacks that violate a security policy. They may be made in a way that is neither reproducible nor traceable so that adherence to rules and compliance with requirements cannot be proven.
- Computing performance and Service Level Agreements cannot be met.

This list provides examples for possible security issues that are to be addressed by appropriate security measures.

Computer Systems and their operating systems usually do not use local hard disks for persistent storage but use centralized storage solutions. This storage can be constructed differently. Two major types are Network Attached Storage (NAS) and Storage Area Networks (SAN).

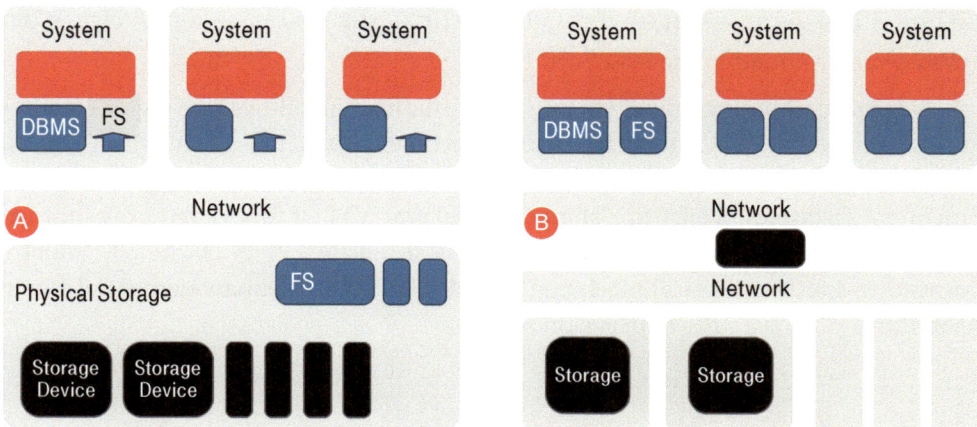

Fig. 114: Network Attached Storage (A) and Storage Area Network (B)

Network Attached Storage (NAS) is a concept whereby Computer Systems mount a remote storage volume and thereby get access to files. Refer to Case A in Fig. 114. The file system is exported from the storage system. So-called virtual filers are used to support sharing of physical storage in a multi-tenant environment. This virtualization and the associated segmentation of storage are essential in terms of security. In this way, each customer computer system uses its own file system. Mechanisms of the computer system's operating system can be used for authentication on the remote storage system. Different customers or ICT services use their own Virtual Local Area Network (VLAN) to access storage. This separation is used to map customers or ICT services to virtualized file systems in the storage. The secure administration of the components is critical to ensure security.

A Storage Area Network (SAN) connects the storage devices over a network (often Fibre Channel) which is separated from the Virtual Local Area Network (VLAN) connecting the computer systems. Refer to Case B in Fig. 114. The Computer System connects to a specific remote storage volume (e.g. via SCSI on top of IP). Hence, the file security is established by the operating system and file system of the computer system. The storage itself, however, is separated into different zones (subnets) and logical units (LUN). A unique identifier (World Wide Name, WWN) is assigned to the Computer Systems accessing storage. In this way, it is decided which storage volume can be accessed by which Computer System. The secure administration of the components is critical to ensure security.

Data bases are used to store structured data. They comprise the Data Base Management System (DBMS) and the actual data storage. Data bases are used for storing data, even though the DBMS runs on the individual Computer Systems (refer to Fig. 114).

A close technical and organizational integration within network services, operating systems, automation and provisioning results in a huge challenge in terms of customer separation, while sharing as many resources as possible between customers.

The importance of being fundamental to other services makes central data services especially critical in terms of availability. Data bases and storage systems are a highly attractive target for attackers because critical business information is usually centrally stored and represents a valuable asset. Due to scalability and cost reduction, data services like storage are usually operated in shared mode with other customers. This actually increases the risk, as the target becomes more valuable for attackers.

The handling of disasters is also of major importance. A possible data center disaster requires proper recovery planning in terms of data base and storage design, as well as operational steps. Depending on customer requirements for availability, data services usually have to run without interruption in order to avoid business impact on customers. Because of these security concerns, several security measures are in place for data bases and storage to prevent against attacks. Other security measures are implemented to reduce the impact of possible failure.

There are systems for Operations Support aside from Computer Systems, data bases and storage. An ICT Service Provider delivers different ICT services to a variety of customers often on a global basis. Economies of scale and other such benefits are the main motivation for user organizations to use third-party ICT services. Consequently, ICT services must be produced in an industrial way with a one-to-many business model. This means that ICT equipment and tasks are centralized whenever possible, and that processes and procedures are standardized and applied in the same way if possible.

In particular, the management of the ICT systems and components is conducted in this way. Specific ICT systems and components are used as a means to manage the ICT systems and components used to provide ICT services to customers. These specific systems are called systems for Operations Support here. They are also located in the data center. They are needed for IT production, to make updates, to manage resources or to adapt configurations. ICT systems must also be monitored in order to be able to verify the status of the overall security, to discover possible violations of security policies and to generate security reports for different purposes. These tasks also require central Operations Support.

It is easy to see that the ICT service delivery and its security strongly depend on the availability, functionality and successful operation of many supporting ICT systems and components. The centralization of Operations Support can also be seen as a bottleneck, but the performance requirements are often not very high; availability is critical if the Operation Support is being used. Notwithstanding, failure of such systems may have critical consequences including the following:

- ICT services may not be available or feature a lack of performance since resources are not correctly assigned or exhausted before this is observed.
- Resources are not optimally allocated, which may cause additional costs or result in latencies, downtimes and the like.

- Disruptions, failures and also security breaches may not be discovered, or not discovered in time, so that remediation activities are not started or are postponed.
- There is no ability to analyze the current operations status including the fulfillment of Service Level Agreements.
- In the case of failure of ICT supporting systems that maintain asset inventories, configuration data or workflow information, the corresponding processes may fail, be inefficient or lead to incorrect results.

The concrete possible security issues and their impact depend on the purpose of the element and its cross-linking and integration into the whole ICT infrastructure.

12.4.2   IT management and data center premises

The increasing customer requirements for scalable ICT services, which can handle different workloads as needed, are met by using dynamic computing environments. These environments use different virtualization technologies to separate hardware, operating systems and applications. In dynamic computing environments, operating systems and applications are not installed in the traditional way. Instead, an executable image (memory copy) is produced, adapted and then archived. For execution, it is retrieved from the archive and copied onto one physical machine. Computing and networking resources are configured, software variables are set and the hypervisor is instructed to start the software.

While the software is running, resources such as computing cycles or main memory are dynamically associated to a running software image as required since different software (Virtual Machines) can simultaneously run on one physical machine. If a Virtual Machine requires more resources than available, it can be moved to another physical machine with the available resources. From a technical perspective, the virtualized environment and the ICT infrastructure that is used for managing the virtualized environment include the following ICT objects:

- Virtual Machines,
- Virtualization layer (here implemented by a Virtual Machine Monitor also known as hypervisor),
- Virtual Service Console (administrative interface of the hypervisor),
- Management Server and supporting ICT systems (e.g. for automation), and
- Virtual Networking Layer.

The Virtual Machines and the virtualization layer are part of the Computer Systems (Sect. 12.4.1). This section considers the elements used to provide and control the Virtual Machines (VM) as shown in Fig. 115. The elements considered are those above the "Systems" in the figure as well as the activities shown in blue.

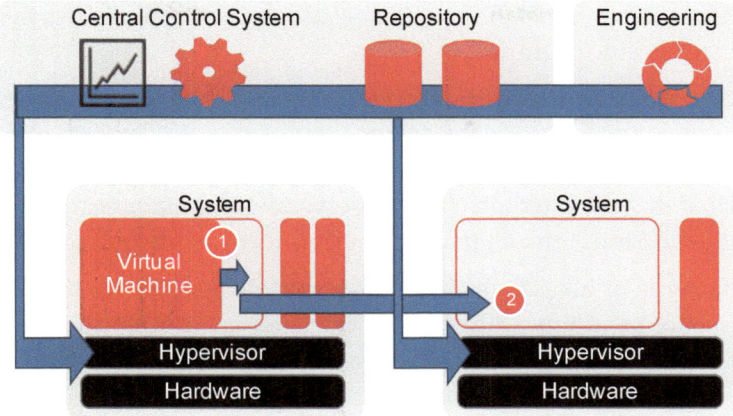

Fig. 115: Virtual Machine and Software Image Management

Management or operation of a dynamic computing environment includes

- management of software images (for operating systems as well as applications; engineering and administration of repositories),
- central control of Virtual Machines at run-time (start, stop, move, allocate resources etc.),
- monitoring and logging of the virtualization layer,
- authorization and authentication issues with regard to the separation of duties

plus the processes and tools that are used. The required security measures cover the virtualized environment itself (lower IT stack, Sect. 12.4.1) and the ICT infrastructure that is used for managing the virtualized environment (upper elements in Fig. 115).

There are some advantages with respect to quality which has also an effect on security. Examples are

- consolidation and standardization of the hardware and software landscape,
- shorter restore times,
- central administration and monitoring,
- easier implementation of redundancy and fall back mechanisms,
- central patch management possible (though actual execution may not be easy).

However, adding a new technical layer (e.g. Virtual Machine Manager) and introducing a new administrative layer (management of the virtualization infrastructure) changes the environment and associated risks compared to the "traditional" computing concepts. Specific disciplines become more complicated or have to change when virtualization technology is used. Examples are as follows:

- The dynamic character (e.g. ease of deployment of new servers) is a main benefit but makes Configuration and Change Management far more critical.
- The possibility to move virtual machines between different servers respectively locations is associated with the risk of failure to comply with regulations

(e.g. data privacy legislation), which could for example restrict the processing of data to specific countries.

Applications, Computer Systems, networks and storage are usually managed by different teams which ensure the segregation of duties. The consolidation of the server and network infrastructure in the virtualization infrastructure (virtual server and virtual switches) requires the preservation and maintenance of the separation of duties and must ensure that all concepts form an integral secure whole.

A particular type of access which requires specific attention is that which allows the performance of administrative tasks. The latter are diverse and cover the provisioning of devices, configuration of networks and storage, operations management including dynamic resource allocation, as well as central management activities such as service management, operations control and monitoring, including log and event management. Hence, a precise assignment of responsibilities and tasks as well as an Identity and Access Management system is essential to ensure that security requirements are met. Note that this crucial part consists of managing the provider's personnel, the organization of business and processes relating to IT production and the management of IT accounts with all the data required. Fig. 116 shows some of the principles of Identity and Access Management (IAM) on the one hand and business and process organization on the other. The management of privileged user access goes far beyond having an Identity and Access Management system. Moreover, it comprises many activities relating to Human Resources, is influenced by and integrated into the internal organization of the whole corporation and IT production in particular, and it covers cooperation aspects organized in a variety of business processes of the ICT Service Provider.

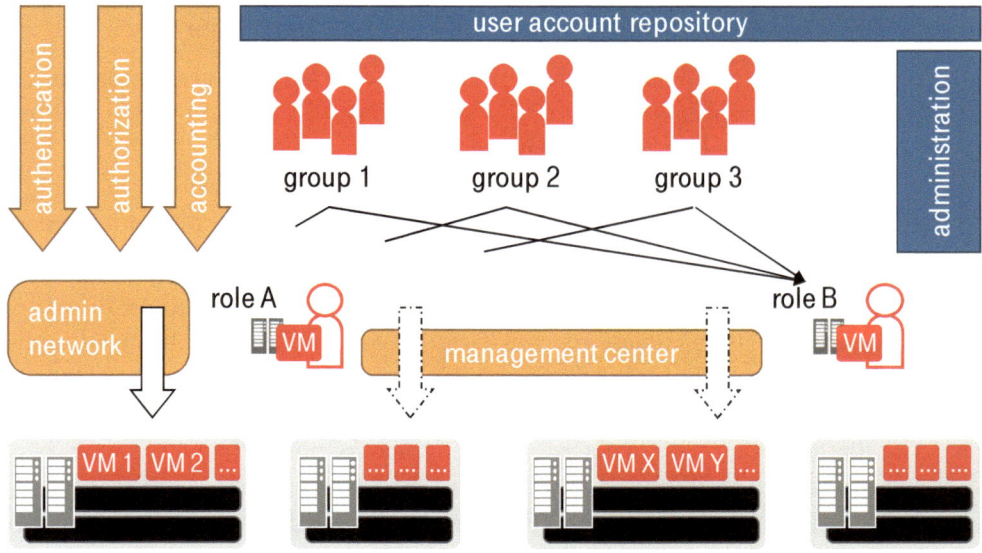

Fig. 116: Privileged user access

The provisioning of entitlements as well as measures for controlling their use are essential for secure operation and achieving customer confidence. The management of entitlements and access starts selecting the right people and their training, covers the provisioning with passwords or tokens and the assignment of duties and rights, and finally requires the maintenance of all means. Two infrastructures are required,

- one for the management of digital identities including roles and rights and
- one for the processing of administrative accesses in the ICT service provisioning infrastructure.

The first infrastructure (Identity Management) is denoted by the blue boxes in Fig. 116; the second one (called "Administration Network") by the yellow elements. The "management center" indicates that there is a specific system for managing Virtual Machines in dynamic computing environments.

From a technical perspective, network equipment such as firewalls and switches is core to an Administration Network, including an administration firewall or security gateway at the edge of this network. Jump and management servers[72] are needed for tasks relating to the management of ICT systems. Network and firewall management servers as well as log servers are necessary for the management of the administration network. This reminds us that there are two levels of administration. Firstly, there is operations personnel (administrators) who administer the ICT systems and components that are used to produce and deliver the ICT services for customers of the ICT Service Provider. They have more privileges than standard users. Secondly, there are operations personnel (administrators) who administer the administrators (identity management) and the administration network and its components (administration network management). They have more privileges than standard administrators.

Here are some examples of risks or threats that underline the need for proper protection. Major security risks or problems include:

- compromised privacy or integrity of customer information when accessed by non-authorized individuals from the administration network,
- ICT service outage after a deliberate attack or manipulation from the administration network,
- non-authorized access between systems operated for different customers of the ICT Service Provider,
- manipulation of log data, thus concealing attacks in general or more specifically misuse of administration rights,
- litigation issues in case of security breaches or failures, and
- loss of operation stability and business continuity.

---

[72] A Jump Server is a computer system typically used to administer computer systems. Administrational access can only be gained through the Jump Server. The latter provide a well-defined set of functions only.

The relevance of each risk may differ between the individual customer contexts.

Data centers are the heart of any ICT service production and ICT service delivery in general. Almost all ICT systems and components, except for external networking, for example, are located in data centers. Applications which support business processes are hosted in data centers. They store critical data in storage systems which are also located in the data center. The applications are accessed from outside the data center which requires appropriate protection using additional systems which in turn are located there. Ultimately, all the supporting systems which are necessary for IT production, to make updates, to manage resources or to adapt configurations are located in the data center.

All technical equipment in the data center (computers, storage etc.) has a very high economic value. The costs of acquisition and replacement are huge. Consequently, the equipment must be protected from theft and from any damage that may arise from fire, ingress of water and other natural disasters. However, the equipment also plays an essential role in supporting the business processes of the user organizations. Availability is therefore very important. If equipment is removed or damaged, a user organization is partly, temporarily or even irrecoverably taken out of business. Finally, data located in data centers may have its own economic value as intellectual property or competitive information. Hence, data must be kept confidential and protected from physical theft and manipulation. It would not help to have appropriate ICT security measures in place in order to control logical access to and telecommunications with the ICT systems, but allowing physical access and direct damage.

Availability and confidentiality as well as security in general are the main aspects which customers demand. Their requirements pertain to the ICT service as a whole, but availability and physical protection of technical equipment is the basis for this. Major threats, which generate risks, are environmental influences (such as flood, earthquake, lightning etc.), man-made threats (e.g. assault, theft and vandalism) and security of supply aspects (such as power failures and out of range temperature).

A schematic design of a data center is shown in Fig. 117. It shows that a major section of the entire data center premises is taken up by power supply and other supply services, as well as by air conditioning and ventilation. This is a total of around two-thirds. Note that even these (non-ICT) areas are essential for ensuring continuous and undisturbed operation. "Computer rooms" comprise the actual ICT systems and components that are used to produce the ICT services for the customers of the ICT Service Provider. Building security is required to control access to these areas. Interfaces such as delivery and loading areas also need to be controlled. There are several perimeters which require protection in order to guarantee appropriate protection of this complex.

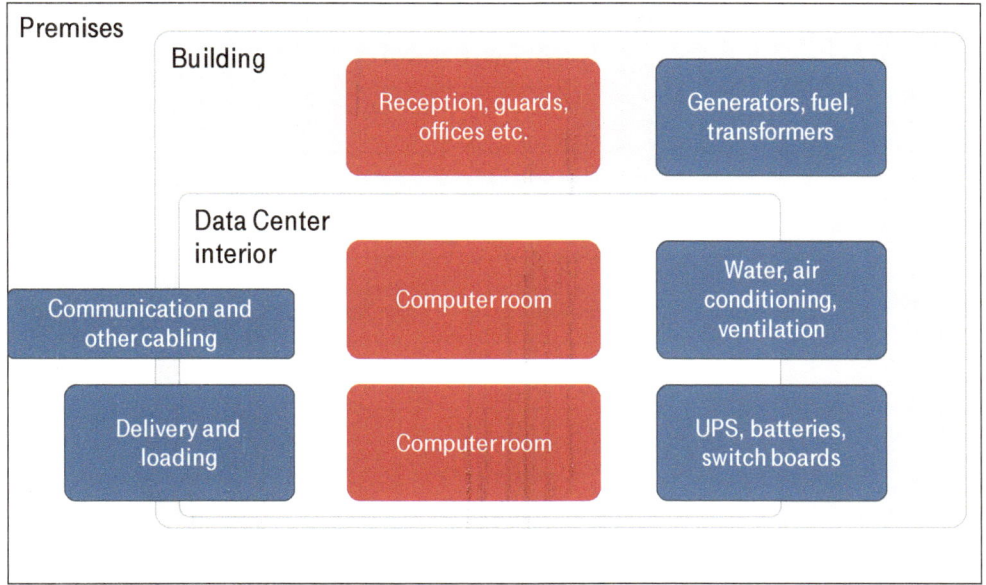

Fig. 117: Schematic diagram of data center premises

Such real physical aspects show that securing ICT service delivery requires a comprehensive approach.

12.4.3   Applications

An ICT Service Provider provides ICT services using ICT systems which are located in data centers owned and operated by the provider or at the customer's premises. These ICT systems run applications. The applications may execute complex computations and store results for further processing and use. In this way, ICT services are provided that result in datasets, data for subsequent jobs (such as print jobs), or that are used by customers and other users from their remote location (head office, branch offices, mobile, Internet). Applications sit on top of Computer Systems (Sect. 12.4.1 describing the lower IT stack) and provide ICT services for customers in accordance with their business requirements. All other ICT systems and components can be seen as being a platform only. This includes the ICT systems and components for administration and maintenance (Sect. 12.4.2).

Applications provide the interface users are working with and perform operations on data depending on user interactions according to predefined business rules. In this sense, an application can be regarded as "the real and sole entity that users are interested in and working with". This results in a difficulty since it may not be straightforward to precisely define the external boundary of an application. Modern applications are also distributed over a number of Computer Systems, span end users' workplaces and store their abstract logic in data bases located elsewhere. Modern applications are not therefore a monolithic block. Notwithstanding such methodical difficulties, applications may be "located" in the context of an ICT landscape. This is shown in Fig. 118. The application covers the central part (shaded area) in the figure; the operations environment is grouped around it.

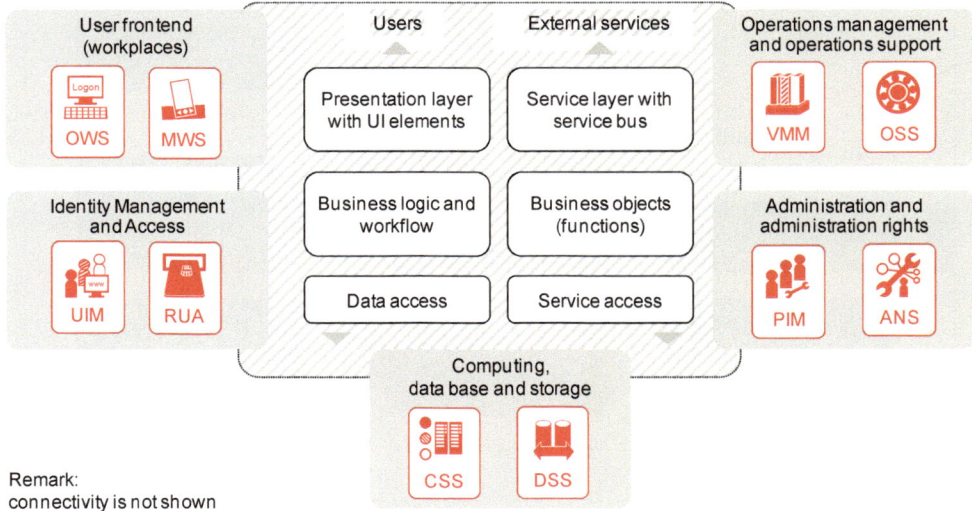

Fig. 118: Application architecture and operations environment

Applications are executed by Computer Systems (denoted by CSS in Fig. 118) and use centralized storage for persistent data (DSS in Fig. 118). Users use their workplace computers to access and interact with the application. The Office Workplaces (OWS) and Mobile Workplaces (MWS) are shown on the left-hand side of Fig. 118. These devices are not considered to be part of the application. The registration of users and their provisioning with identifiers and credentials is likewise largely not part of the application itself. These tasks of User Identity Management (denoted by UIM in Fig. 118) and of token provisioning for Remote User Access (RUA in Fig. 118) are also considered to be a central work area which is independent from an individual application. The same is true for operations personnel (administrators of the ICT Service Provider) that may access the application or a related functionality. The management of identities for operations personnel (administrators) and related means and procedures are referred to as Provider Identity Management.[73] The Provider Identity Management (PIM in Fig. 118) and the necessary infrastructure for administrative access (with the Administration Network; denot-

---

[73] The identity management and all related means and procedures come in two variants. On the one hand, there are users (employees of the ICT Service Provider) who access ICT systems and components in order to perform administrative tasks, monitoring and the like. This is summarized as Provider Identity Management (PIM) which may also be read as privileged identity or user management. On the other hand, there are users (employees of the user organization or other people authorized to consume ICT services) who access ICT services. The issues of registration, identities, credentials, roles, rights, verification and attestation are summarized as User Identity Management (UIM).

ed by ANS in Fig. 118) are also not part of an application. Finally, if the application runs in a virtualized environment it will be managed accordingly (referred to as Virtual Machine and Software Image Management, VMM, in Fig. 118). Operations require facilities for logging, monitoring and maintenance. These are provided centrally and referred to as Operation Support (OSS in Fig. 118).

Back to the application itself (shaded, central area in Fig. 118), it typically consists of different layers and elements as follows.[74] Basically, an application

- contains a Presentation Layer that defines the behavior and structure of the application and provides this according to the end-user frontend (workplace) that is used,
- contains a Business Logic or Workflow component that defines, orders and coordinates single user interactions in order to build a well-defined business process,
- provides functions realized in so-called Business Objects that manage business data based on business rules depending on users' requests,
- uses a Data Access component to access the underlying data store,
- uses a Service Access component to access data provided by an external service, and
- contains a Service Layer that allows to communicate with external services.

Connectivity and any networks are not shown in Fig. 118.

Applications are very different with respect to scope, functionality and complexity. They range from the provisioning of a single function for a single user to support of a core business process within an industry community. Hence, security-related problems and threats also differ. General threats include[75]

- spoofing identity,
- tampering with data,
- repudiation,
- information disclosure,
- denial of service, and
- elevation of privileges.

This may pose a risk for the business, since

- actions may not be performed (application is not available),
- operational sequences can be messed up (unauthorized people or people with the wrong entitlements participate),
- operational sequences cannot be proven (missing or unsecure proof; people dispute action),

---

[74] Microsoft Application Guide, Patterns and Practices; Microsoft, 2nd Edition, 2009 [43]
[75] A Guide to Building Secure Web Applications and Web Services 2.0; The Open Web Application Security Project (OWASP), Black Hat Edition July 27, 2005 [44]

- the user organization may suffer a financial loss or loss of competitive advantages or of reputation (intellectual property or other confidential data is disclosed).

These are only the important examples. If applications fail, they may pose a risk for everything associated with using them.

12.4.4   Securing the lower IT stack

Cautionary note: This section provides examples of essential security issues. It is not the subject of this book to specify technical, procedural and organizational security measures in detail. However, the following section specifies major aspects that can be considered when designing security measures that protect the cluster "lower IT stack" (described in Sect. 12.4.1). Note that security should also have a business case; the design, implementation and maintenance of security measures incur costs, but customers especially tend to look for lower prices. Thus, security needs to be carefully designed.

The lower IT stack consists of Data Center Networks, Computer Systems, Data base and Storage, and Operations Support.

The *ICT Security Standard – Data Center Networks (DCN)* describes all networks and network equipment within the data center that is used to connect Computer Systems (to each other, to external users and to Storage) as well as to connect operations personnel (administrators) to Computer Systems, Storage and Operations Support equipment. Note that all that networks and network equipment is "inside the firewall". Connectivity between different data centers of the ICT Service Provider is included in addition.

User organizations connect their entire network and individual users consume ICT services being provided from within the data center. This communication must be distributed within the data center. Ultimately, there is internal communication within the data center, for instance, when ICT systems store data in a central storage area. All networking within the data center (and between data centers) must be protected against third-party access, hostile action and communication failure. Specific security issues are as follows. However, the subject is far too complex to be dealt with comprehensively here.

Systems of different customers or different services may use the same physical data center network. In order to ensure confidentiality and integrity and prevent any other interference, different customers (or services) and their communication must be separated (using VLAN, VXLAN or a similar technology). Further separation into multiple segments (security zones) might be required. Operations personnel (administrators) shall be able to administrate customer and other ICT systems and therefore have the ability to access them. In order to maintain the aforementioned separation, the administration network is segmented (using the above mentioned technology) to distinguish access to different (customer) systems. Note that such access can originate from shared or dedicated networks and components. The Computer Systems need to be connected to the central storage. In order to maintain the separation when sharing the access to central storage, a storage network is used and segmented (using the above mentioned technology) to distinguish access between different customers, systems and services. If applications require services to be provided to the Internet via a public interface, an additional network may be set up and protected e.g. using a DMZ.

The Data Center Networks have a complex topology. Typically, they use OSI Layer 2 [76] to connect, forward and separate user communication and OSI Layer 3 to create subnets using Virtual Routing and Forwarding (VRF) or VLAN with Switched Virtual Interfaces (SVI), respectively. The abovementioned three or four networks (customer data, storage data, administration, and, possibly, the Internet) form different zones or domains in the network. Physical or virtual switches are used to separate them.

Information about the network segmentation and ways to access this (notably IP addresses) are provided for the administration of the Corporate Provider Access area to allow user access and for the administration to allow operations personnel (administrators) to securely access ICT systems, including storage. Requests for changes in the Data Center Networks may come from those adjacent areas (Corporate Provider Access area and Administration Network).

The correct and secure use of such a complex network infrastructure requires network address and naming schemas, which includes Link layer, IP naming and routing, VLAN ID assignment and segmentation and the management of these elements. Networks and network segments that are located in the data center are protected from physical access to a far greater extent than those outside it. Hence, the latter are considered as not secure and all communication via external networks (such as traffic between twin core data centers) shall be adequately protected against eavesdropping and manipulation.

The *ICT Security Standard – Computer Systems Security (CSS)* describes all parts of the IT stack except user applications, centralized storage and middleware including runtime environments and data bases. Computer Systems comprise physical computer machines with operating systems and system virtualization software such as hypervisors.

---

[76] OSI: Open Systems Interconnection model which consists of seven layers (physical, data link, network, transport, session, presentation, application)

Major security issues include the following: Changes to configurations and settings which have a potential effect on multiple users or comprehensive services or entire subsystems, must be subject to authorization. In other words, access to all administrative functions of operating systems, hypervisors etc. requires authorization. Users who are not intended to perform administrative tasks must not have administrative privileges. Computer Systems communicate with other ICT systems, which they do not control. As a result, they may control inbound and outbound traffic and decide which protocols and services can be used and by which applications. In order to prevent any interference, customer data communication, communication with storage and access for administration should be separated using separate network interfaces. Computer systems that do require direct access to the Internet may have an additional and separate interface for that purpose.

Different applications that simultaneously run on one computer system (typically Virtual Machines, VM, each comprising one or more applications and an operating system) are separated securely, which allows the sharing of resources without any unwanted or illegal flow of information or any other illegal interference between them. Access to and communication with any virtualization software (hypervisor or Virtual Machine Monitor) shall be strictly controlled and only accessible by authorized operations personnel (administrators). Virtual Machines that are no longer needed on a physical machine shall immediately be deleted from the computer system and resources such as the main memory shall be cleaned from residual data before being assigned to another Virtual Machine.

The integrity of Computer Systems shall be maintained by using anti-virus and malware scanners which must regularly be provided with appropriate update information. Incorrect configurations and tampering with the configuration and other settings of operating systems and virtualization software is detected so that corrective measures can be initiated.

The *ICT Security Standard – Database and Storage Security (DSS)* describes all centralized storage equipment and software (that is accessed by Computer Systems via Data Center Networks) plus Data Base Management Systems, even if they run on the individual Computer Systems. It also contains all means for backup and disaster recovery.

Although storage and data base security is far too complex to be covered in this section as well, some important security concerns are as follows: Mounting, dismounting and other installation, moving or removal of media, as well as physical and logical partitioning of storage, must be controlled and executed with authorization only. Administrative access shall be separated from other information exchange.

Data in storage systems can be business-critical and shall be maintained or recovered even if the data center operation has been disrupted, for instance, by fire. This may be achieved by using redundant storage systems which are located in different fire zones or even data centers. Data recovery requires the existence of a backup that is stored safely and ready for recovery. Data in storage systems shall only made available to the authorized user, customer, application or service. Other entities shall not be able to access or influence this data. Hence, storage is securely separated using means such as access control, including tagging of data for storage and physical and logical segmentation of the storage system. Storage arrays shall support the encryption of storage media. Encryption keys are securely stored e.g. in a Trusted Platform Module (TPM).

Changes to configurations and settings of data bases require authorization. In other words, access to all administrative functions requires authorization. Entities and users accessing data bases that are not intended to perform administrative tasks on the data bases must not have administrative privileges.

Attacks (i.e. potentially hostile access) shall be detected whenever possible. Malicious communication, data or executable code shall be detected. Negative effects shall be mitigated or avoided as appropriate. Activity in the data base and compliance with configuration might be monitored or checked regularly to provide evidence and enable corrective actions where appropriate. The integrity of software components and of major settings and the actuality of software should be maintained by using appropriate means such as scanners. Data bases are accessed from other systems which cannot be controlled by the data bases. As a result, data bases may control communication and decide which functions and services can be used and what entities are authorized to do so.

The *ICT Security Standard – Operations Support Security (OSS)* describes the security of all supporting technology such as servers and utilities that are used by operations personnel (administrators) for basic data center operations. That includes software for systems management, ICT asset and life-cycle management, IT service management as well as for service availability and performance management.

Major security-related issues can be found below. Configuration Management is essential. The corresponding process is described in Sect. 12.2.3. However, the systems being used must also meet security requirements. The availability of ICT systems and components, services or features is often an essential requirement for security too. Therefore, required ICT equipment shall be made available (procured, installed and integrated) and can, in principle, be used. An inventory is required to be able to control that process and to maintain the integrity and the configuration of ICT equipment. The configuration of ICT systems and components is critical with respect to security. It shall be ensured that a configuration can be created, changed or deleted only by operations personnel (administrators) authorized to do so. Secret configuration data such as cryptographic keys must be kept confidential.

Configuration must be documented and all configuration data and information made available and stored centrally (outside the ICT systems and components concerned).

Capacity management ensures that resources (such as ICT equipment, ICT services) are usable and provided optimally so that demands can be met. This requires appropriate controls as well as the ability to track availability and the utilization rate, analyze historic data and make evaluations for future planning. Performance management aims to optimize the efficiency and quality of an ICT service through the management of resources. As a result, latencies, downtimes and the like are low and accessibility of ICT services is high. This is achieved with appropriate controls for resource management.

Monitoring capabilities are the basis for operations, capacity management, performance management and any troubleshooting. Disruptions and failures shall be analyzed so that corrections can be made. Fulfillment of Service Level Agreements must be monitored and appropriate information must be gathered and maintained in order to measure the level of achievement and improvement with appropriate key performance indicators. Notification, data analysis, decision-taking, remediation and review are key steps in many areas. Processes are designed and standardized and roles and responsibilities are assigned in order to ensure accuracy and quality as described elsewhere. Moreover, automation is important. This requires the provisioning of appropriate ICT supporting systems and tools, the function of which needs to be maintained.

Note that many of these objectives primarily aim at ensuring quality of ICT service delivery. However, operational security management and related activities are closely linked to these issues, whereas others solely depend on the appropriate provisioning of Operations Support. Operations Support also provides the ICT systems necessary for effective service management and incident handling. Hereby, different tools are not only provided but must be orchestrated and connected in order to allow an overall management. Operations Support also provides the technology for provisioning, e.g. of Virtual Machines as well as diverse software repositories including those to apply updates and security patches.

12.4.5   Securing IT management and data center premises

Cautionary note: This section provides examples of essential security issues. It is not the subject of this book to specify technical, procedural and organizational security measures in detail. However, the following section specifies major aspects that can be considered when designing security measures that protect the cluster "IT management and data center premises" (described in Sect. 12.4.2). Note that security should also have a business case; the design, implementation and maintenance of security measures incur costs, but customers especially tend to look for lower prices. Thus, security needs to be carefully designed.

The *ICT Security Standard – Virtual Machine and Software Image Management (VMM)* describes all procedures, tool sets and utilities that are used by operations personnel (administrators) to deploy, start, stop, move and otherwise manage Virtual Machines that run on Computer Systems. This also includes all procedures, tool sets and utilities that are used to generate and configure software images (engineering of images) and for archiving as well as the inventory of these images. Software images comprise those for operating systems and applications.

The following enables the ICT Service Provider to deploy and manage virtual environments efficiently and securely. It aims at achieving an appropriate security level for the customer consuming dynamic computing services from the ICT Service Provider. Only a few issues can be mentioned here.

The integrity and correct configuration of software images is not only essential for correct operation of the software. Moreover, this shall ensure that different security policies are observed, namely those of the customer, of the application and of the service provider as well as any regulation specific to the corresponding ICT service delivery infrastructure. Hence, the engineering process (creation, production of images) shall correctly identify and assign images in all management activities, prevent unauthorized changes and manipulations and maintain relations between files, descriptive information, scripts, configurations and the like. Image engineering considers the necessity of patching and related management activities.

The integrity and correct configuration of computing and networking resources is not only essential for correct operation of ICT services. Moreover, this shall ensure that different security policies are observed, namely those of the customer, of the application and of the service provider as well as any regulation specific to the corresponding ICT service delivery infrastructure. Hence, resource configuration shall be as designed and unauthorized changes and manipulation prevented. Configuration includes network interfaces and addresses, memory and other resources being allocated, parameters and variables of operating systems, middleware and applications and other setting as required.

Similar due care is required in the provisioning or distribution of images onto physical machines, when starting or stopping them, or when moving them from one physical machine to another. The ability of the ICT Service Provider to fulfill contractual duties and Service Level Agreements heavily depends on the assurance that the requested computing resources for a Virtual Machine are available if needed. Hence, security measures should be implemented that prevent resources from being exhausted through other Virtual Machines on the same physical host. A decision may be taken to run Virtual Machines that feature different levels of criticality or accessibility on physically separate systems or on different platforms. Examples are business-critical back-end systems versus less critical supporting ones or business-critical back-end systems versus systems that can directly be accessed from the WAN.

The *ICT Security Standard – Provider Identity Management (PIM)* describes all procedures and regulations, ICT systems and services that are used to create and manage the digital identities including rights and other attributes for operations personnel (administrators).

In order to reduce the risks associated with the administration of or administrative access to ICT systems and components, a variety of security measures are put in place. They are designed to accomplish correctness, quality and reproducibility of the administration of or the administrative access to ICT systems and components. This standard describes the Identity Management part. The infrastructure being set up for secure administration (called Administration Network) is described later.

The assignment of digital identities with roles, rights (entitlements) and other attributes shall follow a controlled process with application, check-up, clearance, and provisioning. User registration and approval is one key element, which also determines the quality of security which can be achieved. Reproducibility and accountability are essential when controlling access of users to ICT resources. Hence, the management of digital identities with roles, rights (entitlements) and other attributes shall be conducted tool-based using solutions for workflow and administration and at least partly automated means for provisioning (of identities, rights etc. to target components).

Credentials are chosen and may be changed according to the corresponding security policies. This includes the strength of authentication methods. Usually two-factor authentication is the minimum. The help desk and user self-services (if any) shall be designed not to undermine security. Roles and responsibilities shall be defined and documented in accordance with business and the ICT Service Provider's security policies. Entitlements shall be designed for business (on some abstract "role" level) and then assigned to individuals. Business tasks or roles shall be described and approved before being implemented in access rights.

Administrators shall be given appropriate guidance as well as education, training and the like in order to enable them to use the means being provided appropriately and to follow the rules and procedures and to adhere to policies. Consequences and disciplinary action in the case of violations should be known. Screening, authorization and disciplinary action shall be integrated into all Human Resources management processes. This begins with checking before employment and hiring. Terms and conditions of employment shall consider security obligations, etc. Termination or change of employment shall also be taken into consideration since rights must be securely revoked and assets must be returned, for instance.

The *ICT Security Standard – Administration Network Security (ANS)* describes all networks and other equipment that allow operations personnel (administrators) to connect to the data center and its components remotely and to perform management and maintenance tasks. That includes network security plus jump servers for SSH/RDP and centrally provided services such as authentication services. Note that the use of such equipment is confined to administrators only.

This part describes the technical infrastructure used by administrators to access ICT systems that are located in the remote data center. There are several security aspects that need to be considered, including the following: Operations personnel (administrators) shall be allowed to connect securely to selected data center areas and their components in order to perform management and maintenance tasks. Non-authorized individuals shall not gain access to such systems and functions. Users of ICT services shall not be able to access the Administration Network though being connected to the data center. The integrity of customers' systems and information shall be retained when accessed by individuals from the Administration Network. Continuity of service is retained by averting deliberate attacks or manipulations through the Administration Network, which could cause a system outage.

Systems operated for different customers, for different security zones of a customer or for different services shall be separated so that they cannot interfere with or compromise one another. In particular, the authorization for one customer or customer security zone may not automatically allow access to another. The ability of the ICT Service Provider to fulfill contractual duties may depend on the availability and correct functioning of the IT management facilities including the Administration Network. Hence, critical systems and functions shall be available in a way that allows appropriate service delivery. Precautions to restore settings or components might be needed. The ability of the provider to fulfill contractual duties may also require the confinement of the impact of possible security incidents. Hence, it may be necessary to take further precautions such as the separation of elements with different levels of trust or functionality and the like. Misuse, deliberate manipulation or other hostile activity shall be adequately logged so as to allow the supervision of status and corrections if required. Integrity of such evidence data shall be maintained. This also applies to configuration data. Litigation shall be avoided or supported, as appropriate.

The *ICT Security Standard – Data Center Security (DCS)* describes physical and environmental security aspects of a data center. It does not include ICT security equipment except for that relating to entrance control, etc.

In order to reduce the risks associated with data center operations, a variety of physical security measures are put in place. They are designed to achieve the availability of technical equipment and data. Examples include the following: Theft of and damage and unauthorized interference to ICT systems and data located in the data center shall be prevented. Security barriers (such as walls, controlled entry gates and reception desks) and secure areas (with specific entrance and access control) are examples of security measures used to ensure this. Regarding entrance and access, all groups of individuals are considered, including guards and other onsite workers, maintenance and support personnel, guests or visitors from the ICT Service Provider and other companies, as well as possibly the rescue services and members of the government. Security checks of people or a code of conduct may also be applied. Physical barriers are not limited to entry. For instance, adequate measures are taken to prevent the interception of and damage to internal cabling, e.g. by physical means. Supervision or surveillance might also be used on the premises and inside.

Delivery and loading areas in particular shall be protected to prevent theft and the unauthorized installation of equipment. Import into and removal of items and equipment from the data center shall be controlled. Offices and desks and cabinets located there shall be adequately protected in order to prevent the theft of or damage to material and data. This applies especially to the reception desk since this room or area may contain critical equipment such as access control cards and computers with access to security systems.

ICT systems shall be protected from power failures and other disruptions caused by failures in supporting utilities. Their operating environment shall be controlled in a way that allows undisturbed operation. In particular, uninterruptible power supply (UPS) shall be installed. The data center and its components shall be adequately protected against damage caused by fire, ingress of water, earthquake, explosion, civil unrest and other forms of natural or man-made disaster. This starts with, but is not limited to, the appropriate choice of location for the data center. Fire zones, fire prevention and protection are mandatory.

12.4.6   Securing applications

Cautionary note: This section provides examples of essential security issues. It is not the subject of this book to specify technical, procedural and organizational security measures in detail. However, the following section specifies major aspects that can be considered when designing security measures that protect the cluster "applications" (described in Sect. 12.4.3). Note that security should also have a business case; the design, implementation and maintenance of security measures incur costs, but customers especially tend to look for lower prices. Thus, security needs to be carefully designed.

The *ICT Security Standard – Application and Application Management Security (AMS)* deals with all software that produces the primary ICT services for user organizations. It does not include platforms and infrastructure services. Applications reside on top of Computer Systems. Middleware such as runtime environments (e.g. .NET) is also included, with the exception of Data Base Management Systems.

Applications provide a tool to users that is accessed and used directly. Applications may potentially harm all activities supported by them. These activities differ greatly in scope and complexity. Applications may also be distributed, technically over several systems and furthermore with respect to users which may be situated in an organization with multiple branches. This opens the door to various threats. They must be considered and controlled as regards the customer's specific needs. For this purpose, major security objectives are as follows:

- Reflecting the customer's needs, security objectives for the confidentiality, integrity, authenticity, accountability and quality of service (including availability) are to be defined. In so doing, compliance requirements shall be considered.

- The security of applications depends on the environment in which they are used. Hence, security objectives shall be split into those for the application itself and those for its environment. The latter may include requirements for secure networking with, e.g. encryption of transmitted data, filtering of data streams or limitations for using specific networks.

- Changes to configurations and settings, which have a potential effect on multiple users or on general functionality, that go beyond the intended usage must be subject to authorization. In other words, access to all administrative functions requires authorization. That also applies to support and monitoring.

- The confidentiality of each part of executable code is not ensured. Therefore, confidential data such as credentials (e.g. passwords) shall not be hard-coded. In order to minimize errors or failure (and to facilitate industrialized production), all information and parameters about the computing environment should be externalized and set as variables which can easily be changed. Applications should support backup and recovery of their data with a defined runtime status, if any. Stopping the system should not lead to an unrecoverable or unsecure state.

- Web services are provided to the calling party or requester only. This may require prior authentication and should allow logoff. The web service may be totally stateless. Otherwise, different sessions of different users or of the same user shall be separated and transactions be correctly identified.

A more detailed structuring of security objectives or related security tasks can be found in Fig. 119. Fourteen aspects of application security have been identified.[77] They are assigned to groups and explained in the following.

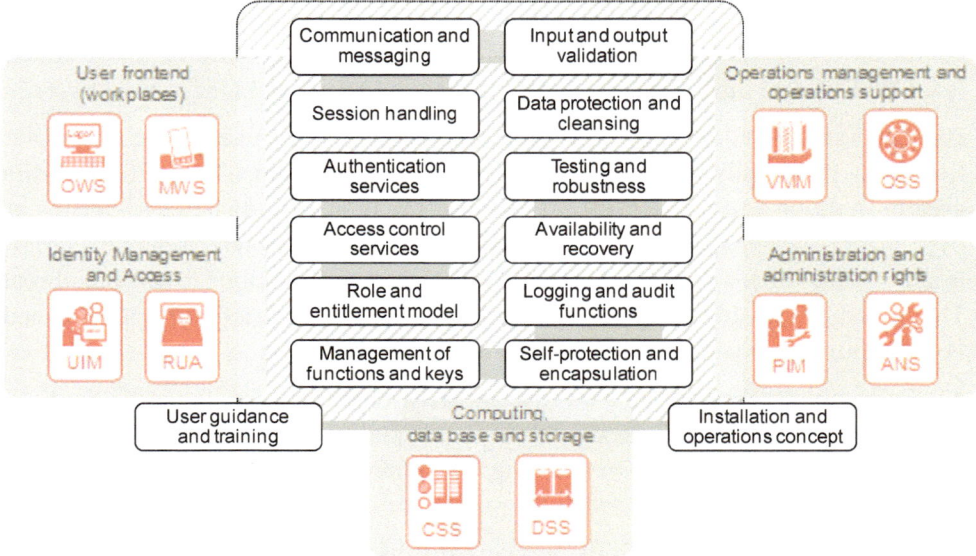

Fig. 119: Application security architecture

Interface control

Communication and messaging: The user accesses the application remotely. The exchange of information must be translated into an ordered sequence of messages, called protocol, and converted into a format that can be submitted over the communication channel being used and understood by both parties on the ends of the channel. Data often needs to be transformed, wrapped and protected. The application programmer cannot assume the world outside the application can be trusted. Hence, the communication between the user (or the user's workplace, respectively) and the application, in particular, is to be protected.

Session handling: There is not only one single user who accesses the application. Typically, a number of users (or even other entities) access the application simultaneously. Hence, the corresponding conversations have to be separated from each other so that they do not interfere and so that a user is not able to access or tamper with anyone else's information. This must be ensured regardless of whether the access is realized as a stateful or stateless session. Session handling also ensures

---

[77] The catalog of functional requirements of the Common Criteria provides useful information on how to secure software. Refer to: ISO/IEC 15408 – Information technology – Security techniques – Evaluation criteria for IT security – Part 2: Security functional components; July 2008 [10]

that a distributed application cannot be compromised by redirecting or otherwise manipulating the communication with external services.

Input and output validation: The processing of unexpected data content or format may cause the application to act irregularly. Such data may be interpreted incorrectly, causing erratic behavior. The processing thereof may cause the application to crash or violate security policies. Or, unexpected input data may set the application or parts of it to a state that is not secure. Hence, input data is to be validated in order to eliminate such cases. The data that is output by the application should also be validated in order to protect the user and its workplace and to prevent data that may not be provided from being disclosed. Input and output validation is sometimes realized in extra software modules since it cannot be assumed that the core software code of an application is perfect and error-free.

Access control

Authentication services: The access to and the use of an application is restricted to a group of authorized users and/or authorized IT entities such as services or other applications. This is to protect confidential data and to limit the use of the application, but also to keep attackers away. The accessing parties (users or IT entities) must prove their claimed identity before being granted access. This is called authentication. This is generally realized as a central service. Authentication must consider security policies such as password policies and support the authentication methods being used. The latter include knowledge of passwords, possession of tokens, biometrics or a combination thereof. The group of authorized users may not be homogenous, coming from a single registering organization. In this case, authentication has to support federation, which is a separate complex matter.

Access control services: Users and/or authorized IT entities may have different tasks. Accountability or segregation of duties may be other requirements. Hence, users will be assigned to different roles and entitlements. The entitlements are used by the application to assign functionality and to control business and workflow processes within the application. Entitlements or rights may also be used to consider confidentiality and integrity requirements for information.

Role and entitlement model: Access can be controlled if users are assigned to roles and entitlements. Many applications allow the administration of such roles and rights and the dynamic assignment thereof. The assignment must follow predefined rules. It is also subject to access control in order to prevent the elevation of privileges. But moreover, access control often affects the structure of the application itself since functions must be separated into modules in order to allow strict enforcement of applicable policies.

Application model and management

Management of functions and keys: The application or parts of it are modified in their appearance and internal performance in order to meet different requirements or to allow adaptation to different operational environments. Such administration manages the availability and behavior of functions and changes attributes or functional parameters as required. This management is a specific functionality of an application which must meet specific requirements. – The protection of functions and data is often realized by using cryptographic algorithms, which may have internal parameters such as cryptographic keys. The management of such parameters and keys is an extra discipline which requires specific care.

Self-protection and encapsulation: First of all, software codes may be separated into parts that provide functions for users on the one hand and those that require distinguished privileges to be executed and used on the other hand. This principle reduces the attack surface and is a best practice since complex code may not be perfect. There are other coding principles that need to be observed. Development shall aim to ensure that knowledge of the internal design will provide as little help as possible to anyone wishing to compromise application security. For instance, secret parameters are not hard-coded since then they cannot be changed and the software will not provide sufficient protection. The application shall not provide functionality that is not required and shall not output information about internals unless required. This also reduces the attack surface. In some cases, it may not be sufficient to encapsulate code in separate modules. Instead, they are isolated in a hardware module such as a smart card or a security module with another form factor. These architectural features are also included under this subject.

Logging and audit functions: An application records and stores information about security-related activities. This is often called security logging. Later inspection and analysis of such data provides information about activities that have taken place and who is responsible for it. This enables vulnerabilities to be identified and dealt with and allows countermeasures to be put in place. The application often provides a means for determining the purpose, content, format or amount of information being logged. Applications may also analyze the information and generate alarms to selected users or privileged users. Such automated audit analysis looks for possible or real security violations. Rules for such analysis may also be manageable by authorized users. In addition, an application may also provide dedicated auditing functions that allow reading, processing and analysis of audit data.

Data protection and cleansing

Data protection and cleansing: Functions and data of an application are subject to access control. Refer to above. The issues raised in this section go much deeper and can be seen as a basis for or reinforcement of access control. Thus, data protection can be reinforced if data is always kept encrypted or is encrypted before being transferred outside of the applications. Such issues are addressed in coordination with the security measures of communication and messaging. Another important point is cleansing. Resources such as memory are reused. In order to prevent an illegal flow of information, resources are cleaned or reset before being reused. Another issue that falls into this category is the consideration of privacy regulations.

Robustness and availability

Testing and robustness: Any malfunction of an application's function, especially of security functions, can significantly reduce the level of security or even result in a security failure. Testing is an effective measure to prevent, or at least detect, a function's failure. An application can perform self-tests and integrity control of code and data, and provide means that supervise or test the internal performance. Using similar methods and good coding practices, the software is made robust against changes to the environment, single failures as well as unexpected resource allocation or exhausting resources. In the case of a malfunction, an application must not enter an undefined state. Power outages should be taken into consideration here. The application may prioritize its service provisioning in order to avoid problems. All internal error states in particular must explicitly be handled putting the application back into a secure state without disclosing sensitive information to possible unauthorized users. Robustness may also be enhanced, for instance by setting data to read-only.

Availability and recovery: Availability starts with the appropriate planning (and integration) of resources. This comprises internal resources such as main memory, as well as external ones such as persistent storage, computing power or communication bandwidth. Such resources and their utilization are monitored in order to prevent resources from being exhausted. The application may create copies or backups of data automatically at run-time, or provide the means for, or at least allow creation of, backups. The latter are only useful if the application allows recovery. System recovery may be supported as an automated process, which must not lead to an unsecure situation where the system can be attacked. Backup data may be transferred to another environment. This may require other measures such as separation of data and keys, additional access control etc.

Usage and operations

User guidance and training: Guidance documentation is considered as part of the application. Guidance shall exist for all types of users, including the authorized "normal" users and privileged users such as application administrators. Guidance is also given by the application at run-time by displaying help and advisory warning messages to users regarding the appropriate use of the application. Guidance documents describe all aspects for the secure handling of the application. Users may also include programmers if the application is built to interface with other services or applications. The guidance helps to understand security-critical issues, to identify critical states and to act appropriately. The documentation aims to reduce the risk of human and other error. It also aims to ensure the user's support necessary to maintain the application's security.

<u>Installation and Operations Concept:</u> Guidance shall also be provided for the installation (including hardening) and operations. This guidance is separated into target groups, which may include people who set up or reinstall the application, those who are responsible for operations and others which look after maintenance. The guidance describes all aspects for the secure handling of the application. The guidance helps to understand security-critical issues, to identify critical states and to act appropriately. The documentation aims to reduce the risk of human and other error. It also aims to ensure the user's support necessary to maintain the application's security. – The application software must be maintained in the operations phase. There are two ways of doing this. Routine adaptations are initiated and organized through a standard change process. If observations of operations personnel or users indicate that significant re-engineering is required, the systems development phase is re-initiated.

Such issues are to be observed for an application which is developed, installed and operated. Note that life-cycle issues are not addressed here. A life-cycle is outlined in Fig. 120.

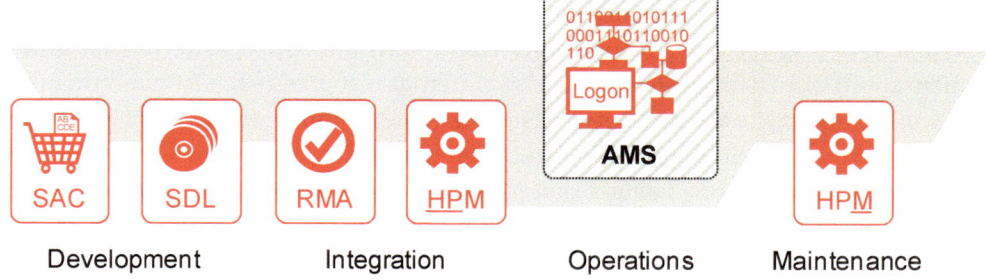

Fig. 120: Application security in its life-cycle context

Applications may not be developed from scratch, but utilize components that are purchased. Security aspects that relate to the security of such third-party components and their acquisition are described in Sect. 12.2 (Systems Acquisition and Contracting, SAC in Fig. 120). The actual process of developing the application is critical for the security of the final result. These security aspects are addressed in the System Development Life-Cycle (SDL). Complex systems and applications are put in place as part of a Release Management process with Acceptance Testing (RMA). The actual installation is performed as part of this process but the technical realization includes hardening and provisioning. Maintenance activities follow the initial set-up for operations. Thus, Hardening, Provisioning and Maintenance (HPM) comprise life-cycle activities before and during operations.

12.5   Risk Management and Certification

Introduction and summary: This cluster comprises two areas: *Certification and 3rd Party Assurance* describes the general approach of the ICT Service Provider to certifications. It also describes how third-party assurance, gained through audits and assessments, is planned, conducted and integrated into the provider's business strategy and communication. The *Risk Management* standard describes the procedures for making decisions on the implementation of security measures. On the one hand, this section describes the general environment, the scope and major activities in each area. On the other hand, it provides information about major security measures. These are not specified in detail.

Fig. 110 shows the location of the "Risk Management and Certification" cluster within the *ESARIS Security Taxonomy*. The two *ICT Security Standards* are highlighted.

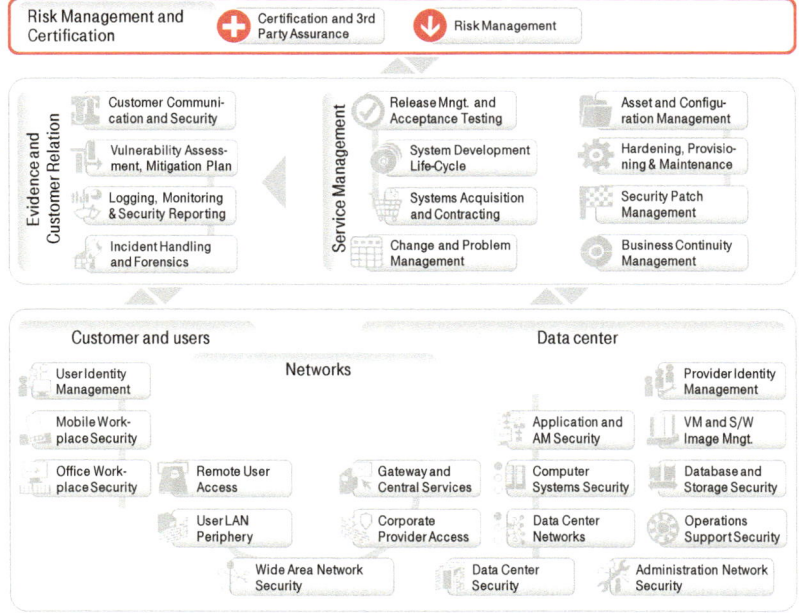

Fig. 121: Landing cluster of "Risk Management and Certification"

Certification and Third-Party Assurance

User organizations require evidence that the ICT services they are consuming are as secure as expected or, more precisely, that the security risks are reduced to an acceptable level. The "measurement" of security requires the definition of some kind of security target, which in turn should be agreed upon between the user organization and the ICT Service Provider. Based on such an agreement, assurance is produced which is essential for the Risk Management of the user's organization.

It is the main aim of the *Enterprise Security Architecture for Reliable ICT Services (ESARIS)* to produce assurance and to organize the process of exchanging information between the ICT Service Provider and its customers. However, the ICT Service Provider must have a policy and related security measures in place that ensure the effective production and delivery of assurance (see Chapter 1). The ICT Service Provider must provide different information or support the provisioning of information so that the required assurance is established. Customers may additionally require that assessments and validations are performed by third parties since this provides a greater level of independence and acceptance. Assessments and validations by the ICT Service Provider are still helpful and required. They will not be replaced. The results of this may be inspected by the user organization. However, often user organizations insist on performing their own assessments and validations. More specifically, they like to perform audits. All these activities provide assurance.

The ICT Service Provider should be interested in using the expertise and experience covered by industry and other standards. In turn, customers have more confidence if the ICT Service Provider uses such practices. This also reduces the effort involved in validation, which may or may not utilize formal certification processes.

If user organizations have no assurance, they will not consume any ICT services from third parties. If user organizations have a nonrealistic perception of the security level of the provider's ICT services, they may fail to meet their security objectives. If assurance is established from scratch for each customer of the ICT Service Provider and each service, the cost for both the user organization and the ICT Service Provider will be too high. Thus, the ICT Service Provider shall be prepared to support the above with the minimum security measures.

The *ICT Security Standard – Certification and Third-Party Assurance (CTP)* basically defines two principles that are put into practice by corresponding policies. Firstly, third-party assessment and validation may provide a greater level of independence and acceptance in a wider market. The ICT Service Provider should support this. Utilization of security practices from industry standards provides benefits since expertise and experience from a wider market is used. The ICT Service Provider should therefore utilize this.

In general, assurance and certifications are a means for corporate Information Risk Management of user organizations which consume ICT services from an ICT Service Provider instead of providing these services themselves. User organizations (and the ICT Service Provider itself) require "written confirmation" which, for instance, is mandated by their customers, by law or any other regulation. Independent validation provides strong evidence of the security level being achieved and maintained. Appropriate measures are to be taken to establish an appropriate level of confidence in security. An approach needs to be established so that users' business and security objectives can be met at acceptable costs for both the user organization and the ICT Service Provider. The ICT Service Provider should have the policy that its standards and practices are made transparent to its customers or other trustworthy entities. The ICT Service Provider should develop a plan for periodic external verification and inspection of its security measures. The provider shall develop the precautions for such evaluations or audits.

Security measures described in all other *ICT Security Standards* shall correspond to industry standards rather than being home-grown in order to utilize and take advantage of the high expertise and experience available elsewhere. Hence, national and international standards are applied to security and quality standards of the ICT Service Provider. Security is not an off-the-rack solution. But rather, security is connected to cyclical processes which themselves must be constantly further developed. Therefore, regular checks as well as inspection of the ICT systems by customers and independent bodies are performed. It is ensured that all security processes and procedures as well as the effectiveness of their implementation are verified periodically.

But security starts in the minds of the employees and requires everyone's support. Hence, the role of security and privacy must be stipulated in written documents and communication to employees. Executive management commitment is required. Security is everyone's responsibility. This needs to be enabled through appropriate organization, processes and tools. Moreover, the employees need to be trained to develop their knowledge and skills and made suitably aware of security and privacy issues.

Risk Management

For ICT service provisioning different information is created, read, changed, stored and communicated. That information is processed by applications, ICT systems and components to support business processes. Each entity has protection requirements with regard to its security objectives. Compliance with these security objectives can be put at risk by different circumstances. Information Security Risk Management comprises the identification of risks, the analysis and categorization of risks and the determination of countermeasures to reduce the risks to an acceptable level.

Risk Management as addressed here focuses on risks in information processing. But to be more precise, the scope is ICT service provisioning for customers. Consequently, Risk Management is performed in different contexts as outlined in the next two paragraphs. The two perspectives are similar to the ones described in Sect. 2.2.

Many risks are dealt with as appropriate by the ICT Service Provider independently from customer requirements. The motivation is standard due care and own business reliability and resilience, which includes compliance with legal requirements. A holding company (where this exists) may additionally enforce this and have additional standards and requirements which are to be met. A second source of motivation is the fact that the ICT Service Provider is committed or feels committed to implement a certain standard and, for instance, provide compliance with national or international standards, regulations and the like. Customers can rely on both. The differentiation between them is not of great importance, but in the second case obligation is publically visible and apparent.

The ICT Service Provider designs its business and ICT infrastructure to deliver ICT services that meet "standard" customer demands regarding the security level to be provided. Customer demands exceeding that security level have to be identified and agreed upon jointly during the sales and contracting phase and may be subject to adjustment during the Transition and Transformation phase. An acceptable and agreed level of risk is part of the contract. The ICT Service Provider's challenge is twofold: First, the provider must anticipate typical applications with their environment and risk appetite (or level of required control and protection). In so doing, typical or suggested risk scenarios, business impact and risk threshold levels are used in the Risk Management as described below. The situation is similar to that above since the Risk Management is performed independently from customer projects. The second challenge, however, is that adjustments may be required during the sales and contracting phases, as well as in the Transition and Transformation phase. Hence, Risk Management is performed in the context of a concrete customer project.

Note that the exact business impact is only known by the customer (user organization). As a result,

- it is the customer's responsibility to identify and manage its very own security risks, and
- the provider should support that by default only through the provision of evidence of the security level of its ICT services.
- In addition, fixing a threshold requires making a tradeoff between costs and risks with the possible consequence that the customer may need to order optional ICT services in order to meet its specific demands. Refer to the *ESARIS Industrialization Concept* (Sect. 6.2).

The *ICT Security Standard – Risk Management (RMP)* describes the treatment of risks. ICT risks put business at risk. The major aim of Risk Management is, therefore,

- the identification, understanding and estimation of existing risks with their probability and possible impact on the business,
- the provisioning of a sound, reliable and objective basis to make a decision on how to treat those existing risks,
- the delivery of a process for risk communication and for monitoring of realization and effectiveness.

Risk Management is important for and directly linked to the security level being achieved. Security is the absence of unaccepted risks. This condition is seen as the result of implementing and maintaining security measures (technical, procedural, and organizational in nature).

Risks are a function of the business impact due to a threat, which could – with a given probability – exploit an existing vulnerability.[78] Risk Management comprises the identification of risks, the analysis and categorization of risks and the determination of countermeasures to reduce the risks to an acceptable level. The identification of risks requires the prior understanding of their origin, which leads to a definition of the scope of potentially different areas of Risk Management. Risks should be grouped and organized in hierarchies and so on. The analysis of risks comprises a business impact assessment with the determination of probability or likelihood and determination of criticality or risk potential. The comparison with the predefined acceptable level leads to risk treatment. There are several ways to treat risk; one of them is mitigation through the addition or modification of security measures.[79]

The Risk Management process enables the costs for the implementation and operation of security measures to be balanced and achieves gains in achieving business objectives by protecting the ICT systems and data that are used thereby. This process is not unique to a specific ICT environment.

Risk Management is performed with very different scope and on different levels, such as
- equipment and component level,
- systems and services,
- applications and business processes, or
- departments and whole organizations.

Risk Management shall maintain confidentiality, integrity, availability and authenticity of data and ICT services.

---

[78] refer to NIST: Guide for Conducting Risk Assessments; NIST Special Publications 800-30, Gaithersburg, Sept. 2012 [17]

[79] More details on these procedures can be found in ISO/IEC 27005 – Information technology — Security techniques — Information security risk management, 2011 [7]

13 Routine – day-to-day security management using ESARIS

Introduction and summary: Larger IT departments and specialized ICT Service Providers must be able to define, communicate and correctly apply hundreds and thousands of single security measures in a large-scale, industrial environment with thousands of employees located in many countries. The IT production is characterized by standardization and a rigorous division of labor within the ICT Service Provider and its supplier network. The ICT Service Provider offers its ICT services to many customers (user organizations). There are new challenges with respect to IT security in such an environment. The *Enterprise Security Architecture for Reliable ICT Services (ESARIS)* is built to meet these challenges. This chapter investigates and summarizes effects on the security management. Essential tasks for the Security Management organization are highlighted. First, the focus is on differences at the provider's side caused by meeting the new challenges by using ESARIS (Sect. 13.1). The actual implementation of the concepts and methods defined in ESARIS is a pre-condition for reaping the benefits of ESARIS, primarily higher efficiency and improved security. A primary task of the Security Management organization in day-to-day business is therefore to ensure that the company adheres to the security standards. There are different techniques for verifying if and to what extent security standards are actually applied (Sect. 13.2). The use of ESARIS decreases the effort for managing security but the Security Management organization of the ICT Service Provider will still have trouble and see confusion. A considerable portion of the security management activities must therefore be dedicated to motivation, cultural change, convincing, training and the like. Some important tips are provided to deal with trouble and confusion (Sect. 13.3). The security management of a user organization undergoes a big change when ICT services are outsourced for the first time. The last section focuses on major activities for the user organization's Security Management organization. Together with the huge amount of detail about the provider's side given in other chapters of this book, a portrait of a joint security management is drawn (Sect. 13.4).

13.1 Fourteen tasks for managing security using ESARIS

Introduction and summary: The *Enterprise Security Architecture for Reliable ICT Services (ESARIS)* comprises a variety of concepts and methods for managing IT security in a large-scale, industrialized IT production. ESARIS supports the division of labor, standardization and efficiency. It integrates security in the core business of an ICT Service Provider and considers Portfolio and Service Catalog Management for example. It helps to organize and to orchestrate security beyond the ICT Service Provider's boundary and improves the management of supplier networks. ESARIS reorganizes the interaction of the ICT Service Provider and the user organizations (customers) and much more. This section investigates and summarizes the effects on and the consequences for the Security Management organization.

Obviously, the *Enterprise Security Architecture for Reliable ICT Services (ESARIS)* changes the way security is managed in a large-scale IT production. Otherwise such a new approach would not be necessary. But what are the main effects?

Fig. 122 shows major tasks for the Security Management organization.

Fig. 122: Essentials tasks for the Security Management organization

Align corporate and product security; determine risk appetite

First, the Security Management organization must align corporate security on the one hand and product security on the other hand. The difference of the two perspectives has been discussed in Sect. 2.2 by means of the *ESARIS Duplex Security Management Concept*. Especially in case of an ICT Service Provider, it is very important to balance between the two perspectives and to distribute attention, skill and effort amongst them in a way that the core business of the company is supported appropriately. In other words, providing secure ICT services for customers is strategic from a business and market perspective though corporate security must also be ensured because the company must not be put at risk in this area either. It is necessary to adjust the requirements and the level of security in both areas because there are interdependencies. This adjustment starts with a determination of the organization's risk appetite which may deviate between market leaders and corporations which are rather start-ups.

Operate the ISMS in a manner that is "service-driven" (ICT is core business)

Second, the ESARIS security standards and all the methods of utilizing them do not cover each and every activity relating to security management. This has been emphasized in Sect. 2.1 where the *Enforcement Framework for ESARIS* and the *Endorsement Framework for ESARIS* have been described. The first framework relates to establishing, implementing, operating, monitoring, reviewing, maintaining and improving an *Information Security Management System (ISMS)* as described in ISO/IEC 27001.[80] The design and implementation of an enterprise's ISMS strongly depends on its specific situation and requirements and therefore may vary significantly between different enterprises. This is why the ISO standard mainly provides general guidelines. ESARIS adds a requirement for ICT Service Providers and thereby changes the focus a little bit. ICT Service Providers must operate and maintain the ISMS in a way that it is "service-driven". This means that the organization and the processes are enabled and directed to care for the provisioning of secure ICT services by using the methods stipulated with ESARIS.

Maintain a Control Framework which also compares various control sets

Third, the ICT Service Provider's customers come from different industries; have different businesses and different risk appetites. Hence, they have different security requirements or, more precisely, use different security standards and frameworks and therefore express their security requirements differently. This is why an ICT Service Provider should maintain an Internal Control Framework that also matches the ESARIS security standards with other sets of requirements (such as ISO/IEC 27002, ISF SOGP). This is the subject of the *Endorsement Framework for ESARIS* (refer to Sect. 2.1).

Support cooperation of security functions in different work areas

Fourth, the *Enterprise Security Architecture for Reliable ICT Services (ESARIS)* is made for managing security of ICT services in a large-scale, industrialized IT production. Such an IT production is characterized by a high degree of division of labor within the corporation and its subsidiaries. Activities, skills and resources are geographically distributed and spread amongst departments and teams each being specialized to a range of technologies, to executing a procedure or process and so on. The Security Management organization must ensure that each department, team and employee is provided with the appropriate guidance which in turn is orchestrated in a way that the sum of activities results in having a secure integrated whole. There are many tools in ESARIS which provide valuable assistance here. Examples include the *ESARIS Dimensions* (Sect. 3.1) and the *ESARIS Work* Areas (Sect. 3.2). The *ESARIS Collaboration Model* (described in Sect. 3.3) guides and steers security functions in different *ESARIS Work Areas*. It supports and fosters cooperation and

---

[80] ISO/IEC 27001 – Information technology – Security techniques – Information security management systems – Requirements, 2013 [5]

ensures the use of common security standards. The Security Management organization must understand the ICT Service Provider's business and internal organization. But moreover, it must implement and support roles in the IT production to ensure that the ESARIS security standards are actually applied.

Steer collection of best practices; turn the best into ESARIS standards

Fifth, a large-scale, industrialized IT production is also characterized by a high degree of standardization in order to ensure a consistently high quality at reasonable costs. The Security Management organization must support the standardization of security measures covering technological areas as well as procedural ones. Standardization is a main objective of ESARIS. As a result, a specific chapter is dedicated to standardization (Chapter 6). But moreover, standardization is mentioned and a subject of discussion in many chapters and sections. Activities relating to responsibilities of the Security Management organization include steering the collection of security requirements, of state-of-the-art solutions as well as of best practices. Such issues are part of the *ESARIS Attainment Model* (Chapter 7). Feedback from the customer's side (market) is included in the *ESARIS Fulfillment Model* (Chapter 8). Treating feedback from the supplier's side is part of the *ESARIS Third Party Integration Model* (Chapter 9). All input needs to be analyzed and then brought into the form of ESARIS security standards. This is a subject of the *Maintenance System for ESARIS* (Chapter 10) where the Security Management organization is directly involved in and mainly responsible for. Necessary additions to and updates of the ESARIS security standards are identified and carried out. In each case it must be decided if a measure is intended to become a default (standard) or predefined as option only.

Assure quality of specification; foster a standardization culture (efficiency)

Sixth, supporting standardization goes far beyond having processes for document management in place and tools like templates defined. It requires much more than that to assure great quality of specification, to prevent inconsistencies, and to take care of regular review and update. The Security Management organization must be able to steer a process that looks for the feasibility of realization and costs. The Security Management organization must primarily foster a standardization culture in which almost everything is (at least for a couple of minutes) examined if it could be of value for other departments, teams and other areas of the ICT Service Provider and beyond. Refer to Sect. 6.

Ensure verification of compliance with ESARIS standards; track deviations

Seventh, standards are only useful if they are actually applied. This is the main subject of the *ESARIS Attainment Model* (Chapter 7). This model emphasizes that the Security Management organization must not only concentrate on technology, it must, moreover, ensure that also operations (including all deployment and maintenance processes) use and adhere to ESARIS security standards. The *ESARIS*

Attainment Statements provided in form of Aces are very important since the compliance with ESARIS security standards must be verified and documented. It is worth noting, that the Security Management organization must support the development and management of *ESARIS Attainment Statements* (in form of Aces). Based on them, the Security Management organization can track deviations and care for their remediation if required. The organization can register them as risks if needed and obtain management attention in this way. Details are provided in Chapter 5 providing a background for the description of the *ESARIS Attainment Model* in Chapter 7.

Ensure that security is considered in service descriptions and catalogs

Eighth, the Security Management organization must also ensure that Portfolio and Catalog Management use and adhere to ESARIS security standards and incorporate security into service descriptions and catalogs. If necessary, the Security Management organization must support the modular composition of ICT service elements. The maintenance of service catalogs is a very specific task and typical for ICT Service Providers and large IT departments. This is a complex area since Portfolio and Catalog Management more or less directs the core business which is the provisioning of ICT services for user organizations (customers). Security experts can no longer concentrate on technology and other single areas and stay in the background as long as no critical security incident drags them onto the illuminated corporate stage. Security experts must deal with the development of the ICT Service Provider's business and help to shape the service offering portfolio with respect to IT security. This is also a subject of the *ESARIS Attainment Model* described in Chapter 7.

Ensure suitable support of customer deals and for day-to-day Operations

Ninth, the ICT services are made for customers. They must meet market requirements also with respect to security. IT outsourcing is a specific type of business where the interaction with customers is very important since the user organizations depend on the reliability of the ICT services they obtain from the ICT Service Provider. The exchange of information with customers ("transparency") and appropriate interaction between the two parties ("interfaces") require having the right people (roles) at the right time in the process. The sales and contracting phase ("Deal management" for the ICT Service Provider) are complex and critical for both parties. As a consequence, the Security Management organization must foster the support of customer deals as depicted by the *ESARIS Collaboration Model* (Sect. 3.3). Here security experts are involved in sales activities which may require a quite different behavior and conduct than expected from administrators. Security agreements are only paper if not being considered also in subsequent phases of the IT outsourcing deal. That's why teams in Transition and Transformation need also be supported appropriately. But experienced security experts are also required in day-to-day Operations. All activities need to be aligned; agreements need to be forwarded to the next phase in the process. The Security Management organization must support a culture of "solve as early as possible". If possible the security issue should be solved in the sales phase and not when the time is limited in a deal. If an agreement is possible while discussing the contract, it keeps the topic away from the projects in Transition and Transformation. And it is worst to wait until the ICT service is actually delivered.

Ensure that security is carefully considered in customer contracts

Tenth, security shall carefully be considered in the contract. This avoids repairing or correcting activities with extra costs that are neither calculated by the ICT Service Provider nor by the user organization. The Security Management organization must therefore encourage people that a good contract is clear and covers all relevant security aspects. This is detailed in the *ESARIS Fulfillment Model* described in Chapter 8. The solution developed for the contract should be based on standards as much as possible. The Security Management organization must therefore support a culture of "standardization brings ease and customer satisfaction". The Security Management organization should try to actively talk about the costs of security though there is the risk that security is not integrated to reduce costs. The message should be: IT security is demanded by the customer anyhow and sooner or later this gets apparent to all. It is much cheaper and easier to sell the ICT Service Provider's security standards and use them as the basis for contractual agreements.

Organize regular feedback from customer deals (in any phase)

Eleventh, an ICT Service Provider acts market-driven. Competitive advantages are required to stay successfully in the business. This includes knowing what customers require, expect and want. The ICT Service Provider will not be successful if the security standards do not reflect the demands of the user organizations. It is quite obvious that ICT Service Providers should learn from their customers. The Security Management organization should support receiving regular feedback from customers in deals (in any phase). The organization should collect and analyze this feedback and improve the security standards accordingly. This is emphasized e.g. in Chapter 1 and Chapter 8.

Make sure that security is considered in the sourcing strategy and procurement

Twelfth, the ICT Service Provider does not everything alone. Instead, hardware, software and single ICT services are provided by suppliers and integrated into the composite ICT service that is delivered to the user organization. Nevertheless, the ICT Service Provider is still responsible for the security of the composite ICT service including all its constituents. Hence, the ICT Service Provider must also care for the security of components and services from third parties. This is the subject of the *ESARIS Third Party Integration Model* described in Chapter 9. It is up to the Security Management organization to make sure that security is considered in the sourcing strategy of the ICT Service Provider and during all relevant procurement activities. The procurement department needs to understand that technology can make the difference, that quality requirements also include security and that insufficient security can considerably harm the company.

Verify that security is considered in sourcing contracts

Thirteenth, ESARIS concepts and security standards shall be used and adhered to also in sourcing activities. Note that it is not sufficient to have an ESARIS security standard about this and the concept just mentioned. The Security Management organization must additionally verify if and to what extent those concepts and standards are actually applied. In particular, it needs to be ensured that security is considered in sourcing contracts. In this way, the Security Management organization must step into areas which belong to the financial department and are often far from the IT business.

Ensure that people's knowledge is sufficient, renewed and kept up-to-date

Fourteenth, securing a large-scale, industrialized IT production is a complex undertaking. The ICT Service Provider and the employees must learn how to act and what to use. The introduction of ESARIS must carefully be planned and executed. This is the subject of the *Transformation towards ESARIS* described in Chapter 11. This program splits into the *Transformation of organizational units* (stream 1) and the *Transformation of ICT services* (stream 2). It needs to be planned and executed. The Security Management organization takes the responsibility for this although being backed by the top management, by human resources and other departments. In addition, the Security Management organization must ensure that the people's knowledge is sufficient, renewed and kept up-to-date. This is the subject of a standard qualification or training program but is made more complex due to the complexity of securing a large-scale, industrialized IT production.

13.2   Three ways of verifying compliance with security standards

Introduction and summary: A main goal of the *Enterprise Security Architecture for Reliable ICT Services (ESARIS)* is the standardization of security in order to raise the efficiency and the level of security. The development and application of security standards is organized according to the *ESARIS Attainment Model* which also defines methods for verifying if and to what extent security standards are actually applied. This section discusses the role of the Security Management organization in this context.

The *ESARIS Attainment Model* entails developing and managing security standards as well as means for comparing if they are actually implemented. The ICT Service Provider must apply its own security standards and also verify this for itself. The result is called *ESARIS Attainment Statement* and documented in form of an Ace. The results of the Attainment process are centrally filed and made available for re-use in the context of the *ESARIS Fulfillment Model*. The customer security requirements are matched against the security features of the proposed ICT solution and it is shown to the customer how the ICT Service Provider diligently takes care of its customer's security requirements. The result of that evaluation is the *Customer Security Arrangement (CSA)*.

Hence, the ICT Service Provider deals with two types of compliance. Firstly, the ICT Service Provider needs to comply with a wide range of (its own) security standards and safeguard its ICT services accordingly. This is the subject of *Attainment*. Secondly, the ICT Service Provider must also ensure that the user organization's security requirements are complied with. This is the subject of *Fulfillment*. The ICT Service Provider needs to verify and ensure both aspects separately.

What does this mean for the Security Management organization? It is very clear that the *Fulfillment* part does not work without the *Attainment* as its basis. It may also be rather impracticable for the Security Management organization to verify hundreds of customer contracts and direct all business in this context. The Security Management organization should focus on *Attainment* and struggle to identify and to remediate deviations.

The division of labor between the IT business units on the one hand and the IT security management on the other was already discussed in great detail in Sect. 5.2. Specific tasks and responsibilities of the Security Management organization were already explained in Sect. 5.3. What has been said in these sections shall not be repeated here. Instead, it is analyzed how compliance with ESARIS security standards can actually be verified.

Fig. 123: Day-to-day business of the security management

Fig. 123 shows how compliance is verified. There are three techniques or activities. The verification of compliance ("*Attainment*") is a comparison between the security features of a real ICT service (left in the figure) and the security standards (on the right-hand side of the figure). The three cases or techniques are discussed in the following.

Fig. 124 shows that the ESARIS security standards are used as design patterns for the actual ICT service. The IT business unit (more specific the "service owner") is responsible for documenting the compliance with ESARIS security standards and possible deviations in form of an Ace. The "service owner" formally confirms its content. Aces are *ESARIS Attainment Statements*. They contain information about ESARIS security standards which are correctly applied and about deviations (if any). The Security Management organization must inspect these Aces and identify, collect and analyze gaps. Deviations which cannot be tolerated are tracked as described in Sect. 5.3. Critical deviations can lead to the creation of a risk record. The Security Management organization must demand corrections (remediation) if needed.

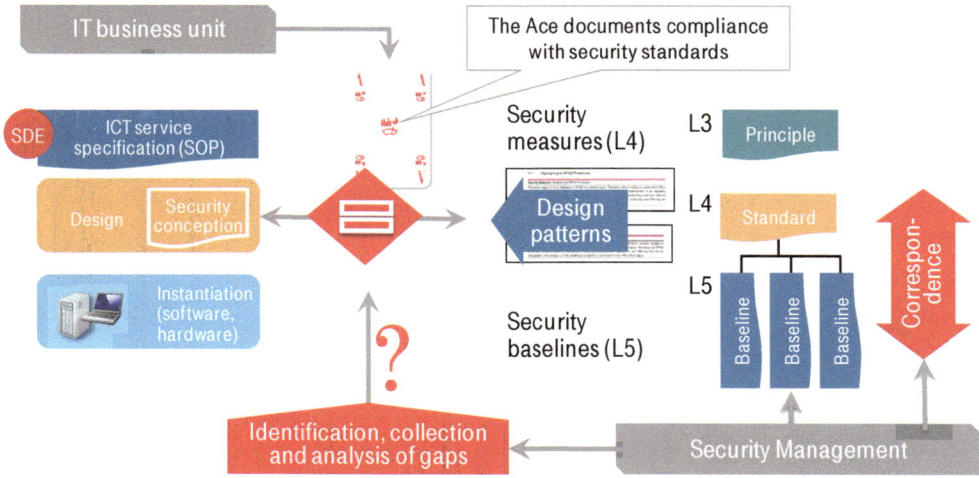

Fig. 124: How compliance is verified (1/3)

The Security Management organization can also make a deeper dive (refer to Fig. 125) and inspect the design and implementation. This is mostly conducted in form of spot checks. The design is studied and checked against the ESARIS security standards. Differing implementations of security standards or potential gaps are identified and documented. Note that the inspection does not only relate to the technical design and its implementation. The design of IT service management activities and their performance in all phases of the life-cycle is also inspected and analyzed. Deviations which cannot be tolerated are tracked. Critical deviations can lead to the creation of a risk record. Corrections (remediation) are demanded if needed.

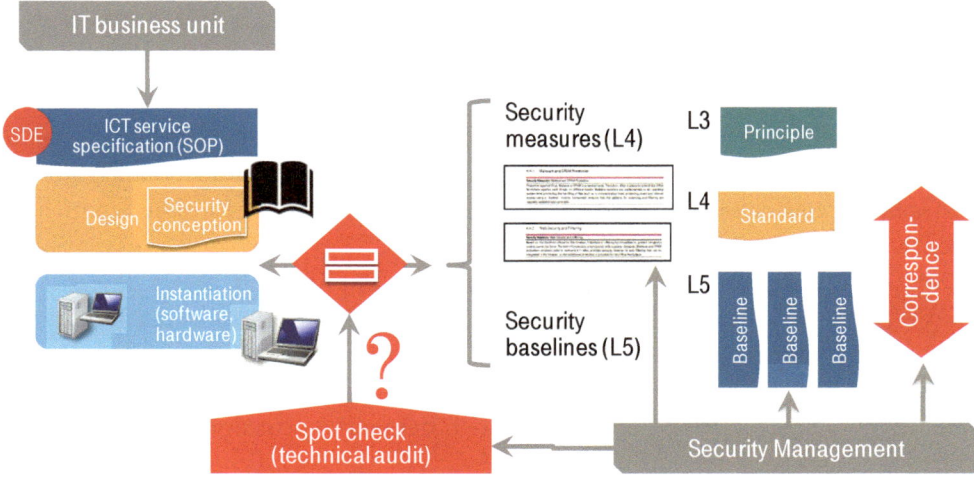

Fig. 125: How compliance is verified (2/3)

Fig. 126 shows the last technique or case. The ESARIS security standards contain security measures and features that provide information if other security measures or features are effective or not, respectively. This is extensively discussed in Sect. 8.3.2. Refer to Fig. 67 on page 153 and Fig. 68 on page 154 for example. The information about effectiveness of other security measures or features is e.g. provided in the form of log data and monitoring information. If being analyzed, such information can help to discover deviations from ESARIS security standards.

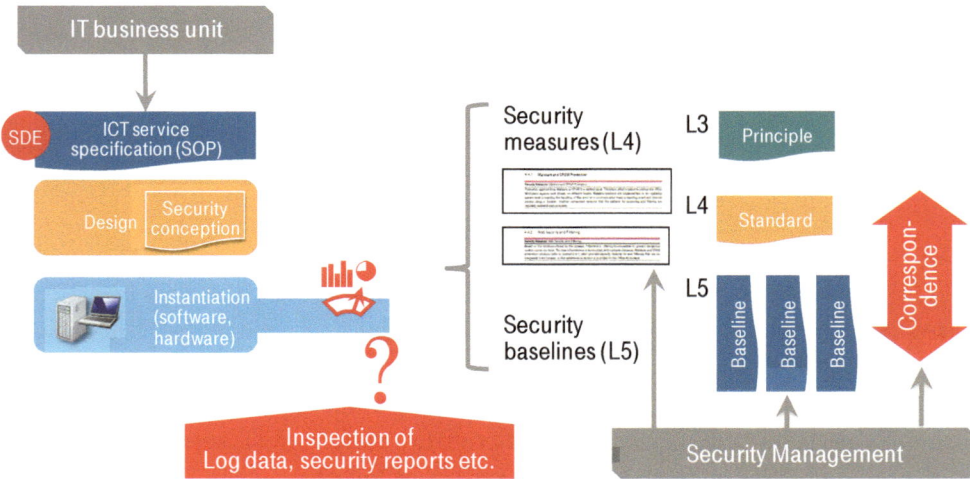

Fig. 126: How compliance is verified (3/3)

Note that a considerable portion collecting, aggregating, correlating and assessing log and event data is performed automatically. Security Information and Event Management solutions (SIEM) can process log and event data from security devices, network devices, systems and applications in real time. Standard threat management activities are performed by the personnel of a Security Operations Center

(SOC). Results are summarized in form of security dashboards and security reports. The more detailed ones are inspected by the Security Management organization. Deviations which cannot be tolerated are tracked. Critical deviations can lead to the creation of a risk record. The Security Management organization must demand corrections (remediation) if needed.

Fig. 127 provides a summary. Six elements are shown that ensure that the ESARIS security standards are actually applied.

Fig. 127: Ensuring that ESARIS security standards are applied (summary)

Note that the verification of compliance with the ESARIS security standards and the initiation of corrective measures is not the only main task of the Security Management organization. A summary of other essential tasks is given in the last Sect. 13.1.

13.3   A number of tips to deal with trouble and confusion

Introduction and summary: The use of ESARIS decreases the effort for managing security but the Security Management organization will still have trouble and see confusion. Employees are creatures of habit: Many of them have problems to realize the cultural change, are reluctant to accept the new methods and hesitate to adopt different practices. A considerable portion of the security management activities must therefore be dedicated to motivation, cultural change, convincing, training and the like. This book can only provide a limited number of tips. It takes time fostering a "standardization culture" and a culture of "solve as early as possible" so that great staying power is required. People learn the "theory" if they are told "examples". People learn from their peers so that success stories should be collected and distributed. But the security experts must change their behavior too. They shall neither act as a fire brigade, nor as police men and never as politicians or a court of justice. They must beware of underestimating the proportion of the necessary changes or the amount of knowledge to be learnt. Other tips relate to the popular project mode, role models and rationalization in general.

Employees do not act as planned or expected. They are very different and not machines. The key element is *motivation*. The security managers must try to understand the motivation of the employees and try to motivate them. This needs to be done differently because people are different. The best way to motivate the general management is to convince them that "Security is an investment in the brand" and say "Security is anyway a must (customers demand this)" followed by "ESARIS helps to reduce the costs for security". Technicians may not be convinced by such arguments. But saying "ESARIS provides you with all the stuff" and "Reuse of design patterns makes life easier for you" could help (refer to Sect. 11.3).

But it is not that easy. Many employees are creatures of habit and reluctant to act differently. People tend to hesitate changing their habits. This is a problem for fostering a "standardization *culture*" (Sect. 6.4 and Sect. 13.1) and a *culture* of "solve as early as possible" (Sect. 13.1). Don't despair! The Security Management organization must be patient. A change is to be managed for the whole corporation. This takes time. Great staying power is a prerequisite to be successful. The security experts must be aware that the organization is about to learn much when introducing ESARIS. Moreover, every employee must learn much. The material includes things that appear to be difficult and complex. The security experts should do three things. First, *communication* is essential in general: repeat, repeat with slightly different words and then say it again. Repetition is the basis for learning sustainably. Second, people learn the "theory" if they are told "examples". People adopt practices that are successfully applied by their peers. The Security Management organization should collect *success stories* as much as possible, real ones and others which could have happened in this way. These stories should be told again and again when explaining the concepts, methods and measures. Third, many companies engage persons which have a job title "evangelists" or similar. Though the term is deceptive and may sound arrogant in many ears, ICT Service Providers need something like this not only to convince customers. The best people are required which are real motivational speakers, trainers which make the audience understand the topic, and recognized subject matter experts with a teaching ability. Especially in Asia, well recognized people are needed as the guarantor before content is accepted. In other parts of the globe, hierarchical authority is important so that one need to involve and primarily activate the management. People in central Europe like to put things into their own hand; they like to primarily follow their own ideas. Then it may help to give people the feeling they are leading. In all cases, it is necessary to understand the employee's motivation to be reluctant or to act in any other way that is not wanted or planned. It helps to know the background and history of teams and organizational units. Especially in larger organizations, many people experienced changes in the past. This often explains their current behavior.

But the work actually begins with forming the Security Management organization. Similar people work here though they could also be quite different. Security managers should be shining examples. First, this means they should not act as "fire men" because it is the goal that the ICT services are "secured by definition". To stay in the metaphor, they should help to prevent fire.[81] The organization should cultivate the attitude that "silence" (no incidents, no complaints, no escalations etc.) is best. Although it is important in that moment that the business is saved, security is restored and so on; the organization must not focus on praise the "heroes" which managed the exception. Instead, the silent workers should be incentivized. Second, this means that they should not act as "police men" because everybody shall take his or her responsibility and act on its own according to the predefined methods, procedures and standards. The security experts should not be perceived as agents of a criminal investigations department that tries to identify individuals violating corporate rules. Third, security managers should also not act as "politicians" because they are not only directing and governing; they should act as partners and as a helping hand too.

One of the major pitfalls is to *underestimate* the proportion of *the necessary changes* or the amount of knowledge to be learnt, respectively. It is very clear to everybody that one must take up a course in e.g. Java or C++ in order to learn programming in such a language. Experts hold such courses which last a few days or even longer. Many other IT disciplines (and ESARIS too) are treated differently. PowerPoint slides are sent around. People are invited to attend one hour training sessions. Such trainings are attended e.g. between two other project meetings so that many people are stressed before and after. But ESARIS is a rather complex matter for many employees. People need time and a relaxed learning atmosphere. Especially the "shining examples" and "evangelists" should get familiar with the new approach when they have the time to do so, perhaps also outside their day-to-day working environment. This means that security managers should invest a few fulldays to get familiar with ESARIS and to exchange experience they gained in working with the new approach.

There are many things where the Security Management organization must set a good example. Many people, especially those on corporate functions, are used to think solely in terms of *projects*. This may hinder the integration of new methods into the day-to-day activities called the mode of "silence" or the mode of "secured by definition" above. Useful projects transfer their results into the day-to-day practices. They must be measured against this objective.

---

[81] This does not mean that no incidents occur which need to be "extinguished" like a fire. Nowadays, most companies are attacked and "hacked". The example shall emphasize that the corporation shall not be in a state of emergency. Incidents shall instead be managed "as a matter of routine".

The definition of processes, procedures and activities uses *role models* in order to differentiate responsibilities (segregation of duties) and to describe the division of labor. Unfortunately, role models are often not understood and applied properly. People mix roles with persons. It may help to speak about work areas and activities instead of roles and to explain that people are assigned to do the work and perform the activities in the second step.

People like to know why! That's why security managers must spend a considerable portion of the time to talk about reasons, goals and benefits. The other portion can then be dedicated to explain the methods. Without the first part, the second will not be understood. This does not mean that the new methods are easy to comprehend. Many security experts must learn much about today's information and communication technology and the IT service management processes. Technicians must learn much about IT service management processes and their role for achieving the overall business goals of the ICT Service Provider.

The introduction of ESARIS in a larger organization is complex and takes time. A cultural change is required to ensure that the new methods are continuously applied. The change begins with the Security Management organization. These security exerts must be shining examples and experienced in playing their modified role actively. A strong Security Management organization is the basis for dealing with trouble and confusion.

13.4   Buyers and providers: joint security management

Introduction and summary: The Security Management of a user organization undergoes a big change when ICT services are outsourced for the first time. The ICT Service Provider is obviously responsible for maintaining the agreed level of security. Typical representatives of the two parties are looked at. Their skills and the way of their interaction are analyzed. Both parties must join their security management activities. This last section focuses on major activities for the user organization's Security Management organization. Together with the huge amount of detail about the provider's side given in other chapters of this book, a portrait of a joint security management is drawn.

IT outsourcing of rather complex ICT services entails that IT-related skills and resources are reduced at the user organization's side. Less people (a smaller portion of the total staff) are engaged with ICT services. The user organization is no longer occupied with the design, implementation and operation of the information and communication technology (ICT) since this is "outsourced" to the ICT Service Provider. The latter requires many different IT-related skills and larger resources since ICT services are produced on a large scale and provided to various customers simultaneously. Hence the distribution of skills and occupations on both sides is different. Refer to Fig. 128. The user organization is shown on the left, the ICT Service Provider on the right-hand side. Obviously, the user organization requires less people in the IT than the ICT Service Provider. Nevertheless, the user organization still needs an "IT department" since the ICT services must be chosen, purchased and integrated into the business processes of the user organization. IT skills are required in order to choose the right provider and the right ICT services, to close the contract properly and to steer and agree upon necessary changes during operations. However, these required skills are rather steering qualities (management level) and less related to hands-on implementation (technical level). Refer to the blue shape in Fig. 128. At the ICT Service Provider's side this is quite different. Obviously, all types of IT skills are required; and hopefully there are fewer managers than technicians and fewer decision-makers than performers. Refer to the amber shape in the figure.

Fig. 128: Distribution of IT-related skills at the buyer (left) and the provider (right)

This distribution of IT-related skills is important since both parties must exchange information, negotiate, and agree and so on. What does this mean with respect to the security management? A lot, since in the more complex IT outsourcing situations, the security management of the ICT Service Provider (producer) and that of the user organization (customer) are interwoven. Both parties are specialized in different ways but must cooperate in order to make the best for both of them.

Fig. 128 can be used to imagine a meeting taking place. What are the roles that typically represent the user organization on the one hand side and the ICT Service Provider on the other hand? Table 14 shows a fictive gathering of roles from both the user organization and the provider organized in three columns that match with the two vertical sections in Fig. 128. (The rightmost column in the table contains people without direct customer contact. They can be disregarded for the moment.) There is one thing that becomes immediately apparent: There are different roles or job titles on both sides. The user organization focuses on the business integration, on maintaining and developing the agreed status, as well as on compliance and costs. The ICT Service Provider is strong in IT service management (operations), technology and service design (portfolio). The user organization's IT skills and resources do not cover a broad range and do not reach all of the very details. The user organization perfectly understands how to utilize the ICT services in their business and knows the requirements for being successful with this. The ICT Service Provider is just the "opposite". Hopefully, the provider knows the industry of its customer a bit and is able to understand the main requirements. Otherwise it is hard for the user organization to get the required ICT services with the necessary maintenance and support.

Table 14: Typical roles representing the buyer and the provider (contract renewal)

	User organization	Provider (front end)	Provider (back end)
1	Business process manager Application manager	Service delivery manager	IT experts
2	IT service manager	Service delivery manager	Realization manager
3	Change manager Project manager	Service delivery manager IT project manager	IT operations Administrator
4	IT architect/expert	IT architect; (Contract) solution designer	IT experts
5	Compliance manager IT security manager	IT security manager	IT security subject matter experts
6	Procurement IT controlling	Account manager Deal manager	Portfolio manager

It is definitely not sufficient if the user organization would only be represented by a business process manager (#1 in Table 14) and the procurement department (#6). IT experts (#2 and #4) are required to express the requirements and to assess the solution proposed by the ICT Service Provider. The IT service manager controls the ICT services at the user's side, integrates them into the business processes and assists in limiting possible impacts e.g. due to outages. The change manager and project manager supports migration activities at the user's side in case of major updates and new releases and synchronize them with the activities at the ICT Service Provider's side. The compliance manager (in addition often also a privacy manager) as well as the IT security manager are important roles. The latter represents the Security Management organization of the user organization (customer) which often comprises various roles each being specialized to one subject matter. The Chief (Information) Security Officer (CISO/CSO) may not participate in all rounds of negotiations though finally being responsible for the agreement.

Technology and IT service management processes are the core business of the ICT Service Provider. IT security should be integral and important too. The challenge is to understand the language of the user organization and to be able to meet the requirements with ICT services which are produced in a standardized manner. Both partners must learn to speak the same language. This means that the user organization must abstract its key security objectives and express them in a largely implementation independent manner since it cannot and will not control the implementation. On the other hand these security requirements must be concrete enough to ensure that they are suitably implemented and met by the ICT Service Provider. Both extremes, requirements being too general or too specific, rather hinder successful IT outsourcing. The ICT Service Provider, on the other side, may tend to prefer general requirements since they leave more freedom for the implementation. Transparency is a key element of ESARIS (e.g. Sect. 1.2.1). ICT Service Providers must provide as much information as actually being required by the user organization. Both parties must take costs into account. Standardization is a key element of ESARIS (e.g. Sect. 1.2.3). User organizations must understand that standardization potentially increases the level of security. The user organization and the ICT Service Provider must regard IT outsourcing as being a partnership with different interests but primarily with common goals.

This is not only required during negotiations. Moreover, there are various situations during Operations where both parties must interact. These interfaces (e.g. Sect. 1.2.2) are important and need to be maintained. IT outsourcing does not mean to give everything away. But it also does not mean to still be responsible for all. As a matter of fact, the user organization's business depends on the reliability of the ICT services delivered by the ICT Service Provider. Hence, the security managers on both sides of the desk must cooperate in developing and maintaining the level of security. For the user organization this includes funding of innovations and development of new security solutions if this is not already covered by the contract. The user organization must study security reports and verify if their security requirements are still current and met. They must also become active in case of major security incidents which requires the provider to inform its customer appropriately. Both parties must cooperate in order to mitigate impacts. The IT is not on one side only. It is operated by the provider and used by the user organization. Risks are also distributed. Both parties must join their security management activities accordingly.

Fig. 129 shows major activities for the user organization's Security Management organization. The activities are briefly explained below the figure.

Fig. 129: Major activities for the user organization's security management

Here is a list of major security management activities to be performed by the user organization:

- Examine the *security reports* received from the provider; check scope and quality; assess content and draw conclusions,
- Judge and *manage risks* associated with the use of the ICT services,
- *Integrate the ICT services* in the user organization's business processes and ensure their proper use in order to avoid vulnerabilities on this side,
- *Support the provider* when necessary which mean e.g. authorizing changes, especially emergency changes; planning maintenance windows,
- Collaborate in *managing security incidents* and support or initiate forensic analysis; conduct the activities required on the user organization's side,
- *Enforce the contract*: demand regular delivery of security reports, impose penalties etc. if needed,
- *Perform audits* corresponding contractual agreements (if any) in order to verify that the provider is still on the right track,
- *Review the division of labor* between the user organization and its provider; adjust if necessary,
- Continuously *check* if *the contract* is still appropriate and fit for purpose; initiate contractual changes if necessary,
- Identify and *initiate improvements and innovations* with respect to IT security which were found necessary in the risk assessment,
- Set-up and *support projects* that improve and innovate IT security,
- *Update the knowledge* about IT production, IT security, the threat landscape, and compliance requirements; feed this knowledge back to the activities above.

Note that these activities are representative examples only which do not provide an exhaustive description of what the Security Management organization has to do. While the user organization works in the mode "observe" (Fig. 129), the ICT Service Provider is primarily in the mode "enforce security". While the user organization works in the mode "support", the ICT Service Provider is in the mode "maintain and repair". When the user organization approaches the provider in the mode "review", the latter may be seen in the mode "support" (the customer). In the stage "improve", the two parties finally shall act similarly though in most cases it's up to the ICT Service Provider to implement the changes whereas the user organization is mainly in a buying position.

Now security management activities from both the ICT Service Provider and the user organization are put together. Refer to Fig. 130.

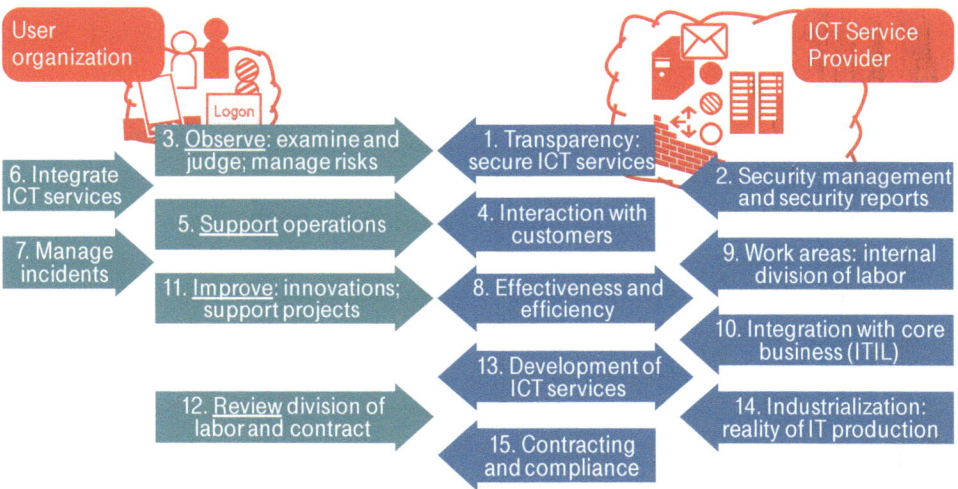

Fig. 130: Joint security management

The ICT Service Provider is shown on the right-hand side. For the sake of clarity, activities relating to the implementation of security measures ("Attainment") and the management of supplier networks ("third party integration") are left out. Instead, major activities relating to the customer (user organization) are shown. This explains the difference to Sect. 13.1 (with Fig. 123 on page 310) in which fourteen essential tasks for managing security using ESARIS were described. The selection of tasks in Fig. 130 is easier and more straightforward. On the left-hand side, the activities of the user organization are shown similar as in Fig. 129. The twelve activities are combined and reduced to six. Both sides work together and interact which form the joint security management briefly explained in the following. Fig. 130 shows activities which are numbered from 1 to 15 in order to facilitate their explanation.

It has been emphasized that reliability and transparency (No. 1 in Fig. 130) are of particular importance. The ICT Service Provider must deliver secure ICT services and sufficient information about implemented security measures and the level of security as well. One element of the transparency is the generation of security reports based on obtaining and processing information from many sources in the course of day-to-day security management activities (No. 2). The user organization examines and utilizes these security reports. It judges and manages risks associated with the use of the provider's ICT services (No. 3). In rather complex IT outsourcing situations, the ICT Service Provider must maintain "living interfaces" to its customer. The interaction (No. 4) is needed e.g. when the user organization (No. 5) shall authorize changes, help to plan maintenance windows etc. The integration of the ICT service (No. 6) is also important: The user organization must integrate the ICT services into its business appropriately and support their use in order to avoid unnecessary risks (No. 3) and to allow upkeep and maintenance during operations to be effective and fit for purpose as well (No. 5). It is worth to emphasize that collaboration in managing security incidents (No. 7) can be a necessary task in order to reduce impacts for the user organization.

The ICT Service Provider must provide for effectiveness and efficiency (No. 8). The security measures must be effective. They must also efficiently be implemented and maintained in order to satisfy the customer and to offer ICT services that are competitive on the market. Though not explicitly mentioned in the figure, standardization is the main measure for more efficiency. Efficiency also requires an appropriate definition of work areas and a suitable internal division of labor (No. 9 which is also necessary for the interaction with customers, No. 4) and the integration of the security management with the core business (No. 10) or IT service management activities (mostly ITIL processes). The Security Management organization must continuously take care of division of labor and business integration. Adjustments and reorganization are always required since the business develops rapidly. The rapid development of business, process optimization and major improvements require adjustments and the reorganization of roles and responsibilities and of procedures as well. That's why these two tasks are incorporated in this list of activities which contribute to deliver ICT services with security measures which are both effective and efficient (No. 8). Effectiveness and efficiency need to be continuously worked on. But also the customer (user organization) can demand improvements and innovations (No. 11), mostly with respect to security measures but also procedures can be concerned. Though, it is up to the ICT Service Provider to implement most changes, project support from the user's side may be required, e.g. if ICT services or their provisioning is modified. Such improvements or innovations may be triggered by suffering security incidents (No. 7).

A major activity on the user organization's side (refer to No. 12 in Fig. 130) is to continuously check if the contract is still appropriate, fit for purpose and if contractual changes are possibly required. In particular, the division of labor should be reviewed since many problems result from missing or insufficient definition or from misunderstanding of agreements. Neither the user nor the provider is or feels responsible so that nobody becomes active when needed. Note that it is almost impossible to anticipate each and every situation in a complex IT outsourcing relationship and to predefine suitable follow-up activities. That's why the user organization (and the ICT Service Provider) must keep an eye on developing their relation. The user organization's reviewing tasks also cover performing audits etc. What does the ICT Service Provider have to do? Effectiveness and efficiency with respect to security were already mentioned (No. 8). As a consequence, the ICT Service Provider must standardize and optimize its IT production and the way in which the ICT services are made secure. This in turn relates to and affects the ICT services and their development (No. 13). The Security Management organization must observe the development of the ICT services. Important modifications must be considered in the service catalogs and communicated to the customers. Contractual changes may be necessary. Though improving the efficiency and reducing costs is eventually in the interest of the user organization, standardization may also constitute a source of difficulty giving rise to discussions between the two parties. Standardization generally relates to two other areas: the already mentioned integration of security activities in the core business (No. 10) and the modernization and development of IT production (No. 14) including changes e.g. in the organization of the supply chain. Such optimization may affect the user organization e.g. if functionality or specific characteristics change which are either contractually agreed or implicitly expected to remain stable and unchanged. Both cases require interaction between the two parties. Hence, significant effects of standardization need to be managed and discussed with the user organization (No. 13). If required, the ICT Service Provider must initiate a contractual change; but the provider's Security Management organization must primarily support contract fulfillment (No. 15).

Note that the joint security management is different from the one within a single corporation even if it is large. In an IT outsourcing situation, two legally and economically independent companies are making business with each other. The user organization has no authority to directly issue instructions for the IT staff of the ICT Service Provider. There is no common boss who can act as the mediator between diverging interests. The ICT Service Provider, moreover, has a one-to-many business model. Standardized ICT services are delivered to many customers with diverse businesses and different expectations. This results in a usually larger IT production environment that in turn leads to a stricter organization. The two parties couldn't be much more distinct than they are.

The joint security management requires exchanging information and agreeing solutions. The basis is to understand each other. However, it is already hard to achieve having a common language within the own corporation. Thus, it is more complicated to find this common ground with another corporation. IT outsourcing of rather complex ICT services will not work without having a joint security management. The joint management requires a common language including a classification scheme that supports any type of division of labor. It requires security practices that are aligned with industrialized IT production and interfaces between the two parties in all phases of their business. ESARIS provides all this. The *ICT Security Standards* (Level 4, *ESARIS Orchestration Layer*) comprises the security measures that are relevant for both sides and therefore presented and written so that they can be used for mutual contractual agreements. Security measures are also integrated into the core business processes of the ICT Service Provider; they enhance them and ensure that IT security really works. Rigorous standardization ensures that costs are minimized. ESARIS provides a full featured methodology for implementing the security standards. As a result, security is also considered in the service catalogs which are the basis for the ICT services delivered to user organizations. Another methodology ensures that these ICT service are proven to meet the customer's security requirements and that evidence is also provided during Operations. It ensures that the contract contains all necessary detail and that it is updated according to the actual needs. The whole architecture is modular and all its constituents are aligned with the reality of today's IT industry. Hence, relationships between buyers and providers, including those in the supplier network, can be managed suitably. To put it in a nutshell: ESARIS is built to manage IT security within an industrialized IT production environment and to balance between the interests of supplying parties on the on hand and of consuming parties on the other.

14   Conclusion

Introduction and summary: This chapter does not provide a summary of the *Enterprise Security Architecture for Reliable ICT Services (ESARIS)*. Instead it looks onto the challenges from a different angle. Then the development of major IT security methodologies from the early 1980s till today is briefly reviewed. The industrialization of IT and its effects have not or not appropriately been considered in the literature about IT security management. ESARIS has been developed in order to fill identified gaps by providing numerous concepts, methods and measures that help managing the challenges of the industrialization of IT with respect to information security. Highlights in the development of ESARIS are summarized. Finally, the contribution to quality is highlighted: The "zero impact philosophy" behind ESARIS can also be read as a "mission statement" or a highly compressed version of the numerous solutions presented in this book.

Synopsis of IT and IT security methodologies

Information security historically originates from protecting military secrets and diplomatic messages. Cryptography, steganography and physical security were the most important measures used. This changed with the upcoming IT. In the 1960ies, central computing emerged. In the following decades, especially banks and assurance companies began to deploy their own systems which required a specific protection. The development of secure payment systems till the 1990s provides examples for this. Security technology was advanced but also methods for the evaluation and certification of security systems and products were developed and implemented. But also governments developed similar schemas. In the 1980s, the Personal Computer changed the IT dramatically and pushed it towards decentralized computing. But already in the 1990s the Internet connected them all with central computing services. As a result, the need for security solutions increased everywhere. The ever larger number of mobile devices increased this trend. But by the end of the 2000ths the IT came back to central computing services consumed by numerous distributed end-user devices. Central computing was reinvented again and again by using virtualization technologies which also required new security technologies. But maybe more important, business models and deployment models changed too. The term *cloud* summarizes those rather new developments. The IT is invented again and again.

This story was told many times in the literature about IT security. Why? The shared use of central computing resources made "access control" important to have. Networking of devices required to separate communication by means of tunneling techniques and other means for "secure communication". Moreover, "perimeter protection" had led to the development of many security solutions required to shield the internal IT from outside threats. Especially the use of mobile devices required to add specific security solutions such as "data at rest" protection. The interconnection of computers via the Internet made them vulnerable to remote attacks and infections so that e.g. "malware protection" became an issue. Today many of the following disciplines are to be applied almost everywhere in IT: controlling access, secure identification, controlling and blocking software execution, filtering and modifying data and code, drawing up inventories, checking integrity, encrypting data and connections, checking rules, searching for anomalies, alarming etc. This results in numerous security solutions each being required to prevent a specific threat which in turn may lead to an impact. The strategies and methodologies for prevention, detection and reaction changed too and required different action since attacks became more sophisticated than ever.

Security managers, strongly supported by vendors, consultants and researchers, learned to implement and to maintain all these solutions and related practices: Till approximately 2008, IT security kept up with the development of IT shown on the top of Fig. 131. But not only security technologies evolved, several security methodologies were developed too. Some of the most important ones are shown in the lower part of Fig. 131. (The length of the boxes approximately span the period in which they were developed and introduced.)

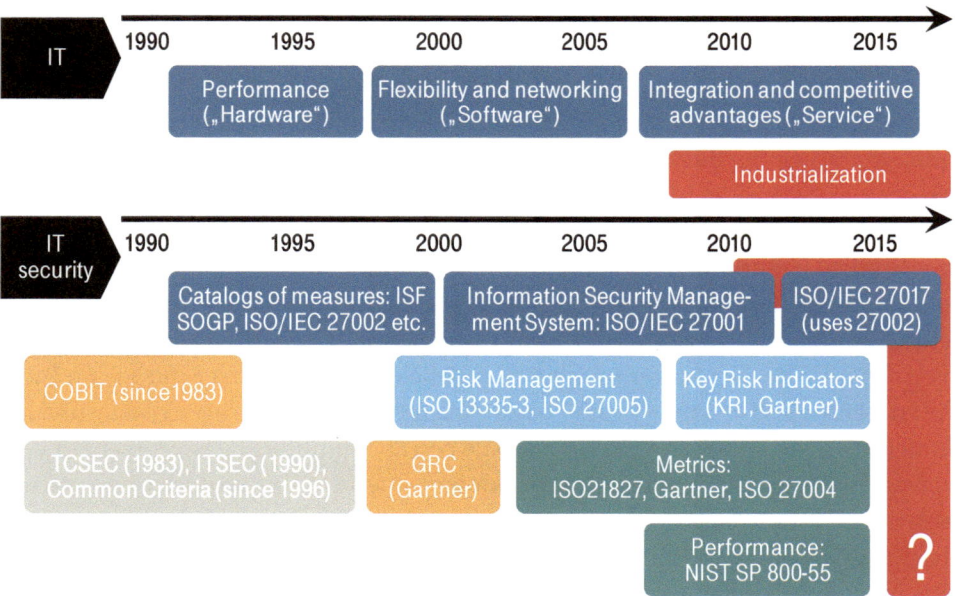

Fig. 131: Development of IT and IT security methodologies

Here are some details: The Information Systems Audit and Control Association (ISACA) developed COBIT 5 to provide enterprises with a comprehensive framework that enables them to govern and manage information and related technology in a holistic manner – including security.[82] Also in 1983, TCSEC[83] (also called the Orange Book) was published by the Department of Defense (DoD) of the U.S.A. as one of the first standards for computer security. A major step was the provisioning of best practices for securing corporate ICT from the mid-1990s till today. The British Standard BS7799-1 was elaborated by industry peers, became ISO/IEC 17799, was revised several times and eventually took its final form as ISO/IEC 27002[84] at the beginning of the 2000s. At this time a standard for the Information Security Management (BS7799-2) was published which became the international standard ISO/IEC 27001[85] in 2008. One of the most influential concepts is GRC ("Governance, Risk Management and Compliance") which was developed since 1996. It defines a management and controlling structure necessary to achieve corporate goals. In this context, the management of IT risks became specifically important. At the beginning of the 2000s, ISO/IEC 13335-3 defined a systematic approach which was continued and improved by ISO/IEC 27005.[86] The model of Key Risk Indicators (KRI) from Gartner, introduced 2011, connects information security risks more tightly with an enterprise's core business. Another area is measurement of success. Gartner presented metrics in 2004. ISO/IEC 21827[87] was first published already in 2002. The National Institute of Standards and Technology (NIST) of the U.S. Department of Commerce developed several guidelines including the Performance Measurement Guide for Information Security.[88] There are several papers about almost all of these topics from the Information Security Forum (ISF).

Appraisal of other frameworks and the development of ESARIS

However, there is one trend that has not or not appropriately been considered: the industrialization of IT. Refer to the red boxes in Fig. 131. Major effects include (1) larger-scale ICT, (2) necessity for rigorous standardization, (3) process-oriented organization of ICT service provisioning, (4) different work organization following a more horizontal model, (5) a higher degree of division of labor in the supply

---

[82] COBIT: Control Objectives for Information and Related Technology; COBIT 5, A Business Framework for the Governance and Management of Enterprise IT; ISACA [1]

[83] TCSEC: Trusted Computer System Evaluation Criteria

[84] ISO/IEC 27002 – Information technology – Security techniques – Code of practice for information security management, 2013 [6]

[85] ISO/IEC 27001 – Information technology – Security techniques – Information security management systems – Requirements, 2013 [5]

[86] ISO/IEC 27005 – Information technology — Security techniques — Information security risk management, 2011 [7]

[87] ISO/IEC 21827 – Information Technology – Systems Security Engineering – Capability Maturity Model (SSE-CMM), 2008 [3]

[88] Elizabeth Chew, Marianne Swanson, Kevin Stine, Nadya Bartol, Anthony Brown, and Will Robinson: Performance Measurement Guide for Information Security, NIST Special Publication 800-55 Rev. 1; NIST, Gaithersburg, July 2008 [14]

chain, (6) strong separation of consuming and supplying party and mediation of their relationship via the open market. There are strategies for implementing and maintaining security measures. There are methods for quality management in its broader sense. Industrialization is not considered. There is e.g. ISO/IEC 27017[89] which is only an interpretation of ISO/IEC 27002 for cloud service customers and cloud service providers. Other papers about cloud security are similar; they mainly relate to technology and basic deployment models or describe risks.[90]

The above concepts lack the following: (1) integration of information security in industrial operational processes which includes procedural security measures beyond design phases and a concept for integration into the IT production environment as well, (2) a concept for increasing efficiency and for allocating resources accordingly that goes beyond prioritization, (3) a classification and organization schema that provides a common language that can be understood by IT managers and is suitable for managing security in a complex ICT environment, (4) a customer-provider model which defines appropriate interfaces and modes of interaction between the consuming and the supplying parties in complex IT outsourcing situations and the supplier network as well, (5) a concept how assurance or grounds for confidence is provided to the consuming parties (especially user organizations) that there are no risks which are not accepted.

The *Enterprise Security Architecture for Reliable ICT Services (ESARIS)* has been developed in order to fill those gaps. ESARIS introduces several concepts, describes methods and defines numerous measures that help to manage the challenges of the industrialization of IT with respect to information security.

The development of ESARIS began in 2010. Whenever a new demand turned up, a new concept was developed to respond to it. Practical experience obtained by using existing concepts was used for continuous improvements. In 2014, the large ICT Service Provider, that developed ESARIS, started a longer lasting program to introduce ESARIS in its departments and subsidiaries. While performing this Transformation program the company gained other valuable experience which led to further improvements. Nonetheless, the ICT Service Provider's customers are the most important source of information. These customers include huge corporations with a global footprint in different industries. Though, ESARIS is rather complex and hard to grasp at the first go, these larger corporations got deeply involved and provided helpful and very positive feedback. ESARIS was used while managing numerous big and complex deals throughout their IT outsourcing phases including Sales, Manage the Deal, Transition and Transformation as well as Operations. At the end of 2016, the *Zero Outage Industry Standard Association* was founded

---

[89] ISO/IEC 27017 – Information technology — Security techniques — Code of practice for information security controls based on ISO/IEC 27002 for cloud services; 2015 [8]

[90] Refer to the literature listed in Annex C.

by major tech-companies which want to start an industry-wide discussion and collaborate to define an industry standard for IT quality based on the four pillars security, processes, platforms and people. The group analyzed the challenges with respect to information security and came to the conclusion that existing standards need to be enhanced: ESARIS was chosen as the starting point for this ambitious project. The current status of the industry standard is available on the web site of the association.[91]

The zero impact philosophy

What is the main contribution of ESARIS with respect to improving quality? Main points of the "zero impact philosophy" behind ESARIS, which can also be read as a "vision and mission statement", are:

Secured by definition: The implementation of security measures is completely and seamlessly integrated into the ITSM processes. In this way, IT security is merged into the area of the ICT Service Provider's "core competencies" (management concept from 1990). Following the example of "Total Quality Management" (TQM) from the 1980s, IT security is actively produced as a result of culture, commitment and adherence and not primarily achieved through quality control.

Security is everybody's business and responsibility: This means that the implementation of security will stop to be a dedicated discipline. Only strategic and preparatory tasks as well as steering and executive activities may remain delegated to what was called the Security Management organization. The IT staff is enabled (and empowered) to care for IT security and follow technical and procedural instructions sovereignly. The IT staff considerably contributes to the specification of such instructions and will finally elaborate them on their own. "Empowerment"(1980s) was an influential management concept with a similar intention.

One step at a time and just see the accomplishment: Quality gates are a major instrument for controlling if important tasks are successfully accomplished. They should be implemented in project as well as in continual businesses in order to verify if corporate IT security rules and objectives are met and if the security measures are correctly implemented. The principle follows "Management by objectives" (MBO, 1954) since the focus is set to achievements and not to activities. The management concept „Balanced Scorecard" (BSC, 1992) reminds that there are several dimensions, perspectives and target figures to be considered and used.

Master complexity using architecture: A large-scale IT production is complex with respect to organization and technology and characterized by a high degree of division of labor. This makes securing ICT services a big challenge. Architecture (classification and organization schemas) helps mastering this complexity and ensuring that effective security measures are defined and appropriate guidance is made

---

[91]   Refer to https://www.zero-outage.com/

available in each area of IT production. Architecture also helps to ensure that all parts integrate to a secure whole. "Complexity management" is a business methodology from the early 2000s which identified complexity as a factor that drives costs up and maybe also degrades quality.

Excellence through standardization: IT production gets industrialized in order to raise the efficiency. IT security must follow this trend. IT security needs to be standardized in order to reduce costs and to increase quality. IT security needs to be organized in a modular way in order to preserve business flexibility. This approach is related to the management concept "Lean manufacturing", in particular with respect to eliminating wasting (Japanese "muda") e.g. by avoiding overburdening of people ("muri") and unevenness in operations ("mura").

Balance between buyers and providers: The chain is only as strong as its weakest link. The success strongly depends on each party participating in the supplier network. IT security must become an element of genuine "supply chain management". A modular architectural approach must support the decomposition of security requirements for supplying parties as well as the composition of the security services for the consuming party. Interfaces between the parties need to be defined in each phase of their interaction together with methods to negotiate, agree and control IT security and to provide assurance together with ICT services and technology especially to the user organization.

Speak a common widely understood language: Experts tend to organize their discipline according to their own needs. They also define terms that outsiders often do not understand. The above requires a change. IT security should be IT related. IT security management should be service-driven. On the whole, it's the business which must derive benefit from secure ICT services.

In this context, ESARIS defines numerous concepts, methods and measures which are explained in this book. The architecture does not only tell "what", but provides detailed guidance "how" to treat IT security in today's large-scale IT industry with complex technology and a high degree of division of labor in order to meet the diverse security requirements of numerous user organizations at reasonable costs.

Annexes

A   Authors and acknowledgement

Acknowledgement

The *Enterprise Security Architecture for Reliable ICT Services (ESARIS),* with its architectural approaches, concepts and models, as well as all the specific measures, is the result of a project started by T-Systems' Security Management in order to develop the general treatment of ICT security issues following the trend towards industrialized IT production and delivery. The authors would like to thank T-Systems for having been charged with the development of the architecture and its components. This was and still is an undertaking which is both fascinating and challenging. It is fascinating from a scientific or technical point of view since T-Systems was open to the introduction of new models, the integration of these into common practices and the use of a systematic holistic approach, which was built to collect and organize all the individual parts in one model. It was and still is a practical undertaking since ESARIS was built to secure T-Systems' real ICT business and there was no option for a green-field approach since T-Systems has been in the business for a long time. The authors would like to thank T-Systems for its decision to publish parts of the work and for being given the opportunity to develop a large section of the manuscript for this book as part of their work as permanent, paid employees.

It is discussing problems that often leads to new innovations. Thus, a long time ago a small group of security professionals and leaders sat down together to talk about the difficulties once more, but ended up stepping aside from these and going far beyond this task. This group, together with the authors, did something radical: The authors would mainly like to thank Thomas Speichert, Jörn Garbers and Thomas Breitenbach, who opened the door to a real change towards strategic and structural thinking. This later led to a fundamental change in the mode of operation. Thomas Speichert especially devoted himself to the development and introduction of ESARIS. The authors would also like to thank their other main supporters, including Heike Bayerl and Sebastian Winterstein, for their contribution to the transformation of local practices into global standards. Thank you.

The authors would like to thank their many colleagues who have been consulted and who have contributed either by providing sources and tips, performing reviews or by writing standards or parts thereof. Meanwhile, ESARIS has been introduced in T-Systems. Thomas Ade, Walter Sedlacek and others considerably contributed to distribute the ideas of ESARIS and to implement the methodology in day-to-day businesses. Thank you. The authors and surely many of their peers admire the general management of T-Systems for having the principles and the courage to start the huge undertaking of making ESARIS mandatory and to initiate the Transformation project.

One of the authors (Eberhard von Faber) would like to point out that this book, and possibly the entire architecture, might not exist in this form without his extensive thinking on information security in general, and the security aspects in outsourcing models in particular which he did in his sideline job as professor for IT Security at Brandenburg University of Applied Science. The author would like to thank T-Systems for supporting him and granting him permission to maintain this "hobby". More importantly, he would like to say thank you for the intensive and fruitful close collaboration during the elaboration of ESARIS and the writing of this book. It is a pleasure working with you, Wolfgang.

The other author (Wolfgang Behnsen) would like to express his deepest gratitude to Eberhard von Faber for his excellent and purposeful teamwork and for the many hours of inspiring discussions: designing and building ESARIS was – besides being hard work – a type of intellectual adventure. It is worth pointing out that security is not an easy task. In one sense, he considers somebody working in security to be like Sisyphus, a king in Greek mythology who was condemned to rolling a rock up to the top of a hill repeatedly without a break or a chance to change his situation. In using this metaphor, ESARIS is the tool that enables Sisyphus to end his dilemma.

This book – written by humans – may contain errors. However, we know that computer programs do not make their job any easier, since ultimately these are also man-made. Interested readers are nonetheless invited to provide their valuable comments to the authors.

Curriculum vitae of Eberhard von Faber

Eberhard von Faber from T-Systems studied electrical engineering and obtained a doctorate in the field of semiconductor physics. He is a professor for IT Security at Brandenburg University of Applied Science. In this sideline job, he teaches the Security Management Master's degree course.

In January 1992, he started his career as a developer for security products. He developed the first hardware-based security system for notebook computers. This security system was made available in the form of a credit card-sized PC Card and featured a full size microcomputer with battery

Source: private

backup secure key storage.

One key element was a highly integrated circuit (ASIC) especially developed for this product in order to manage the integration into the card's small form factor. It also featured the world's fastest integrated circuit for DES encryption.

He left the company in 1994 and moved to debis Systemhaus, where he worked in various fields of security engineering, security consulting and security evaluation.

Mr. von Faber developed the basic conception for a sophisticated electronic car immobilizer system – still in existence today – for a leading automotive company. Another large security engineering project was the development of an infrastructure for secure communication for a German banking consortium in around 1996. The system was designed from scratch.

Eberhard von Faber demonstrated in 1995 till March 1996 that the Data Encryption Standard (DES) is no longer secure against a brute-force attack. As a result, the German financial industry decided to replace this algorithm in all payment systems and components. This issue was kept strictly confidential and was completed long before the "Deep Crack" brute-force attack of June 1998.

Mr. von Faber has conducted security evaluations, especially of integrated circuits used in international payment systems. He invented several highly sophisticated techniques for attacks. He is the main author of the international standard for the security of smart card integrated circuits.

He set up and developed the Commercially Licensed Security Evaluation Facility of debis Systemhaus. Mr. von Faber headed this lab and was active as an evaluator until 2003.

Mr. von Faber now works for T-Systems, where he has held various positions. He has made a significant contribution to the company's security portfolio strategy, formed and shaped the structure of the security offering portfolio, worked on the go-to-market strategy and supported marketing activities. He was also involved in developing prize-winning, innovative solutions.

In 2010 Mr. von Faber was assigned the task to improve and reorganize the management of securing ICT services for customers which result in ESARIS, the subject of this book. He is a valued security strategist and executive consultant. His special subjects are security strategy, enterprise security management, identity and access management, as well as IT security solutions and components. His current special interests are security aspects in outsourcing models including cloud computing, measuring security and assurance models as well as enterprise security architectures. Mr. von Faber is an internationally recognized security expert, responsible for more than 150 public talks and publications.

Curriculum vitae of Wolfgang Behnsen

Wolfgang Behnsen, being retired now, was Senior Security Manager at T-Systems. He studied mathematics and graduated with a diploma from the University of Hagen (FernUniversität (FU) in Hagen) in 1995. He holds several internationally recognized security certificates, including Certified Information Systems Security Professional (CISSP), Certified in Risk and Information Systems Control (CRISC), Certified Information Security Manager (CISM) and Certified Information Systems Auditor (CISA).

Source: private

After completing his vocational training as a Mathematical Technical Assistant at the RWTH Aachen University (Rheinisch-Westfälische Technische Universität) in 1982, he started his career as a Technical Employee at the Chair of Programming Languages of the Friedrich-Alexander Universität Erlangen-Nürnberg. His main tasks included software development as well as operations (from planning up to administration) of the IT infrastructure of the Chair.

In 1996, he moved to debis Systemhaus where he worked as an IT Systems Specialist & Consultant. He dealt with the management of complex client/server environments, operations of security systems such as firewalls and authentication servers (from planning up to administration) and security consultancy for customers with respect to topics such as secure Internet access, secure remote access and similar.

From 1999 to 2002, he held the position of IT Security Manager and representative of the Head of IT Security of debis Systemhaus, later in this period also of T-Systems ITS. He was responsible for the creation and coordination of security policies, standards and guidelines, coordination of the overall strategic and operational security issues and Europe-wide performance of security audits of company units on behalf of the board of management.

From 2003 to 2007, he worked as Senior Security Consultant at T-Systems. He was mainly responsible for consultancy on security strategy, corporate-wide information security management, enterprise security architectures, management of (IT) security projects and the performance of security audits and reviews at enterprise-level for a variety of large companies from different sectors.

From 2008 to 2014, he worked as Senior Security Manager at T-Systems Production. One aspect of this role was to assume responsibility regarding security governance in all phases of Big Deals. The other aspect was the development of security practices in ICT Service Delivery. As from end of 2010, Mr. Behnsen was involved in the development and implementation of T-Systems' "Enterprise Security Architecture for Reliable ICT Services (ESARIS)".

He is a member of "Deutsche Mathematiker-Vereinigung (DMV)", "Information Systems Audit and Control Association (ISACA)" and "Gesellschaft für Informatik (GI)". From 2002 to 2007 he was Vice Chairman of GI's professional group "Management of Information Security". His special subjects and interests include security strategy, security governance, enterprise security management, enterprise security architectures, security assurance and auditing, and all kinds of enterprise-level security frameworks such as COBIT, ISO27000-series and ITIL.

B   Glossary (terms and definitions)

Terms and definitions can also be found in the literature:[92]

B.1   Fundamental terms

Goals of Information Security (CIA)

Confidentiality The confidentiality of information expresses the need to be protected from being accessed by or disclosed to unauthorized subjects (individuals or systems). Confidentiality is preserved, e.g. by restricting access, readability and flow of information.

Integrity The integrity of information, systems and services is the property of not being altered or corrupted, or tampered with, in an unauthorized manner or accidentally. Integrity can be preserved, e.g. by limiting the ability to make modifications. Integrity can be detected, e.g. by comparison.

Authenticity The authenticity of information is the property of being genuine. This encompasses integrity but additionally means that its origin is verified. Authenticity can be preserved, e.g. through the authentication of remote subjects or through the authentication of data (e.g. using signatures).

Availability The availability of information, systems and services is the property of being accessible and usable upon legitimate demand. Availability is preserved, e.g. through redundancy, capacity and resilience.

Accountability Accountability is the property that actions of an entity can be uniquely traced back to that entity which can be identified. The purpose can be different. Examples include non-repudiation, forensics, billing, as well as resource allocation and optimization.

---

[92] Kissel, Richard (ed.): Glossary of Key Information Security Terms; National Institute of Standards and Technology, U.S. Department of Commerce, NIST IR 7298, Rev. 2, May 2013 [16]
Chrissis, Mary Beth; Mike Konrad and Sandy Shrum: CMMI – Guidelines for Process Integration and Product Improvement; Addison-Wesley, 2003, ISBN 0-321-15496-7 [34]
ISO/IEC 27000 - Information technology — Security techniques — Information security management systems — Overview and vocabulary; 2016 [4]

Threats and risks

Threat A threat is an anticipated scenario or circumstance with the potential of violating a security policy. A threat requires a vulnerability to be utilized or exploited before the business is impacted. Threats are directed towards assets.

Vulnerability Vulnerabilities relate to the absence of or defect in appropriate security measures (or *security control*). Technical vulnerabilities are gaps in technology which – if exploited – lead to a breach of *security* or violation of a *security policy*. For more detail refer to the definitions in Sect. B.3 on page 342.

Security Security is the absence of unaccepted *risks*. This condition is seen as the result of implementing and maintaining security measures (technical, procedural and organizational). Security will allow an organization to perform as desired despite the risks its ICT is exposed to.

Risk A risk is generated if a threat can – with a given probability – utilize or exploit a *vulnerability* (absence of or defect in appropriate security measures), which has an impact on business.

Asset An asset is anything that has value for the organization and is critical for being able to meet the business objectives. Therefore, assets need to be protected from being put at risk.

Goals and measures

Security objective A security objective is a statement of the desired state to be achieved. Usually it combines a specific subject and environment with declarations of *confidentiality*, *integrity*, *authenticity*, *availability*, *accountability* and the like. More specifically, a security objective can determine the outcome of an action.

Security measure A security measure is any means that is suitable to mitigate risks. Security measure is synonymous with security control. Security measures can be administrative, organizational or procedural, technical or legal.

Security requirements Security requirements describe the characteristics of *security measures*. This is done in a way that allows flexibility in selecting and designing the measures. Security requirements reply to *security objectives* that in turn are formulated as response to identified *threats*.

Security target A security target is a comprehensive security specification that includes the identification of *threats* in a defined environment (problem statement), the description of *security objectives* defined as responses to that problem statement, as well as a description of *security requirements* which are chosen in order to achieve the *security objectives*.

Assurance Assurance is the level of confidence that the "entity under consideration" meets its *security target*, in particular that the *security objectives* are met.

Assurance is established by applying assurance measures (e.g. by following specific security procedures in the life-cycle) and by providing transparency about and third-party assessment of these measures.

Certification Certification is the confirmation that *assurance* has been established in a defined process using predefined criteria. The confirmation is issued by an independent certification authority or certification body. Often this certification authority basically confirms that *assurance* has been established in accordance to the certification requirements (i.e., the above conditions of applying a "defined process" and "predefined criteria"). The assessment against the "predefined criteria" is then conducted by another party called the evaluation facility. The evaluation facility needs to be accredited by the certification authority, which requires approval and continuous monitoring of the business and activity.

Process and improvement

Compliance For an organizational unit or for people, compliance means that they act according to certain defined standards. This is usually achieved by the definition of processes and procedures that are actually used. – A physical entity is compliant if its characteristics match predefined characteristics or properties or have predefined quality or attributes. Characteristic may also mean to be constructed in a predefined way.

Capability Capabilities are the means of an organization or people to master anticipated situations and gradually improve them. Capabilities usually apply to an individual, well-defined area. Capabilities can be determined. Their quality can be measured, e.g. by reflecting on how the result is achieved and how this can be proven to an audience.

Maturity Maturity allows predictions of general outcomes of upcoming or future projects, activities etc. This requires maturity to be measured. Maturity usually applies to multiple areas.

Procedure A procedure is a specific and usually specified way to carry out a process or parts of it.

Process A process is a set of subsequent or interrelated activities that serve an overall common purpose.

B.2   Terms relating to security organization

Security architecture

Enterprise Security Architecture (ESA) An Enterprise Security Architecture (ESA) is a rigorous structured approach built to achieve an adequate level of (information or ICT) security in an enterprise. The security architecture defines and comprises elements (e.g. the methods and security measures), their relations (e.g. interfaces, interactions and dependencies) and a taxonomy that provides a rigorous structure and a classification and organization schema (e.g. hierarchies, organization, conventions). The means or security measures that are applied comprise technological, organizational and procedural means. The term is synonymous with Enterprise Information Security Architecture (EISA) where the focus is on mitigation of ICT or information-related risks.

Enterprise Security Architecture for Reliable ICT Services (ESARIS) An Enterprise Security Architecture for Reliable ICT Services (ESARIS) is an Enterprise Security Architecture (ESA) made for ICT Service Providers. An Enterprise Security Architecture (ESA) has the general goal or purpose of protecting an enterprise or, more specifically, the information and IT being used. It can be built and maintained by any enterprise that processes information. – An Enterprise Security Architecture for Reliable ICT Services (ESARIS) is built and maintained by ICT Service Providers with the clear goal, purpose and focus to deliver ICT services to customers with an adequate level of security. Thus, an ESA protects an enterprise and its business, whereas an ESARIS is built and maintained in order to reduce risks for customers who consume any ICT service from the ICT Service Provider.

Information Security Management System (ISMS) An Information Security Management System (ISMS) is a model that enables an enterprise to cope adequately with information security. It comprises policies, procedures and guidelines and is used to establish, monitor and improve an enterprise's overall information security. An ISMS is an enablement, governing and management framework. An Enterprise Security Architecture (ESA), moreover, comprises the individual, very specific measures that enforce security by averting threats.

Security Management

Security policies Security policies express intention and direction through the definition of rules and criteria. Usually policies abstract from technology. They are often put into force by the management.

Security record A security record is a document in any format that provides evidence of activities. Activities can be automated (operation and usage of ICT) or manual (human intervention). Evidence can pertain to the activity itself or to its result. Automatically generated records are also called log data. They are also called audit data, audit logs or audit trails if systems activities are recorded chronologically.

Security report A security report is a reply to a specific request and not just evidence like a security record. Usually, a security report is provided in order to provide evidence of a provided service or its quality. A security report is created to leave the department or domain it is created in. Its purpose is third-party notification. Security reporting is the process of communicating to contracting bodies and the like based on security reports.

Security audit A security audit is an independent review and examination of records, reports or observed facts by people. Audits can be conducted to verify the existence and effectiveness of measures, to check compliance with policies and procedures, and to identify and recommend necessary changes in measures, policies, or procedures. An audit usually includes practical tests. – For information on automated "observation", refer to security record and log data.

Security testing Security testing is an independent review, "hands-on" trial and examination of ICT security measures by people. Testing is conducted to verify the existence and effectiveness of measures, to check compliance with policies and procedures, and to identify and recommend necessary changes in controls, policies, or procedures. Security testing is also performed as part of a security evaluation; and penetration testing or ethical hacking are specific types of security testing.

Service Management

Change A change is the alteration to ICT, more specifically to a Configuration Item (CI). This includes the addition, modification or removal of ICT services, approved or supported hardware, network, software, applications, environments, systems, desktop workplaces or associated documentation.

Configuration Item (CI) A Configuration Item (CI) is any component that needs to be managed in order to deliver an ICT service. Information about each CI is recorded in a configuration record in a data base and maintained throughout its life-cycle by Configuration Management. Examples of Configuration Items are ICT services, hardware, software, buildings, people and formal documentation such as process documentation and Service Level Agreements (SLA).

Criticality The criticality measures the dependency of the customer on the proper operation of an ICT service. The value is assigned to the ICT elements (Configuration Items) used and which are necessary to provide the ICT service.

Customer Business Impact (CBI) The Customer Business Impact (CBI) measures the degree of impact caused due to an incident. It combines the measured loss of availability (see service restriction) and the measured dependency of the customer to maintain the business (see criticality). Thus, the CBI does consider the use of the ICT service or systems in the customer's business context. The CBI does not consider security aspects such as the loss of confidentiality or integrity of data.

Release A Release is a collection of hardware, software, documentation, processes or other components required to implement one or more approved Changes to ICT Services. The contents of each Release are managed, tested and deployed as a single entity.

Request for Change (RfC) A Request for Change (RfC) is a formal proposal to initiate a change. It contains a description about the action requested. This term does not describe the change itself or records of it.

Service restriction The service restriction measures the degree of impact caused due to an incident. The service restriction solely considers the loss of availability. It does not consider the use of the ICT service or systems in the customer's business context. The service restriction is used to determine the Customer Business Impact (CBI).

The ICT Service Provider and its business

Transition Transition is the process of moving ICT service provisioning to an ICT Service Provider. The Transition is the execution of a set of contractually defined projects to take over operational responsibility for the customer's services that are in scope. ICT services are taken over without any change (also called "as-is") which defines the so-called Current Mode of Operation (CMO). However, Transition also allows for making adjustments and limited improvements, which turns the IT operation from CMO into a different mode of operation managed by the ICT Service Provider (CMO+). During transition, the transfer of all defined CMO assets, staff and/or services to the ICT Service Provider is prepared and performed.

Transformation Transformation is the modernization of ICT service provisioning at the ICT Service Provider. The Transformation is the execution of a set of contractually defined projects to implement the Service Level Agreement (SLA), to reduce the total cost of ownership (TCO), and to enhance or implement new services. Emphasis is on standardization, centralization and integration. Transformation moves the ICT service into its so-called Future Mode of Operation (FMO).

Current Mode of Operation (CMO) The Current Mode of Operation (CMO) is the mode of IT operation before Transition starts. In other words, the customer's ICT systems are operated "as-is" and without any change being made by the ICT Service Provider.

Current Mode of Operation plus (CMO+) The CMO+ is the mode of IT operation after Transition ends and before Transformation starts. The CMO+ is different to the CMO since the ICT services are adapted and improved to some extent when moved to the ICT Service Provider and operated under the provider's responsibility.

Future Mode of Operation (FMO) The Future Mode of Operation (FMO) is the mode of IT operation after Transformation has finished. That means that optimized operation is achieved after the implementation of all agreed projects. The CMO+ is changed to the FMO during Transformation.

B.3   Terms relating to difficulties and restoration

Vulnerabilities, events and incidents

Patches Patches are pieces of software that are developed to expand or replace existing code because the latter is defective. Patches address and remove existing defects in software or enable additional functionality.

Problem A Problem refers to the cause of (security) incidents or a lack of performance, a shortage of capacity or failure in functionality. A Problem requires a repair. The cause, however, is usually not known at the time a problem record is created, and the Problem Management process is responsible for further investigation.

Vulnerability (general) Vulnerabilities relate to the absence of or defect in appropriate security measures (or security control). The term "appropriate" refers to the fact that threats and risks are analyzed and security objectives are defined. Then security requirements and security measures are designed that are intended to meet the security objectives, counter the threats and mitigate the risk.

Vulnerability (technical) Vulnerabilities are gaps in technology which – if exploited – lead to a breach of security or violation of a security policy. Gaps are caused by defects in software, misconfiguration or general or architectural design errors. Day-to-day corrective measures are patches (which remove defects in software) and changes in the configuration (removing or replacing equipment, changing the equipment setup). – Gaps may also be caused by unanticipated changes in the usage and operating environment and by technological progress which may, for instance, allow or provide new methods of attack.

Vulnerability Assessment Vulnerability assessment requires prior identification of vulnerabilities, e.g. using vulnerability notification services (CERT advisory services), release notes from manufactures, other sources of announcements, as well as results from any security testing, which includes integrity scanning, detection of changes, automated and manual penetration testing. Vulnerability assessment includes identification of root cause, evaluation of impact and mitigation planning. Mitigation planning includes the planning of any corrective action and the evaluation of anticipated and achieved results.

Logging Logging is the process of producing log data. Log data are records being produced by ICT systems and components at run-time in order to report on usage and operation. Log data which are most relevant for managing security are that which relate to security events.

Monitoring Monitoring is any observation of ICT systems and components during run-time. The result is data which are usually logged. Whereas genuine log data are produced by the ICT systems or components itself (own records), monitoring is supervision at run-time and produces records (or log data) externally.

Log management Log management is any analysis and processing of log data in order to allow system troubleshooting, checking of compliance with policies and regulation, to identify and respond to security events and security incidents and to perform security investigations (forensic analysis).

Security events Security events are any security-related or security-relevant action that is made visible by a log entry, an alarm or any other observation that has been tracked. A security event is "neutral" or not yet measured in terms of its effect. It may represent a critical security breach or just an authorized use of the ICT.

Security incidents Security incidents are security events that violate a security policy and require human intervention which is beyond applying day-to-day corrective measures. Security incidents also consider the event of an imminent threat of violating a security policy. A security incident can be caused by an exploitation of a (technical) vulnerability, of another weakness in organization or processes; it may utilize human failure or misbehavior or a combination thereof. ICT security incidents are security incidents that affect the ICT (and therefore the ICT services) and possibly the information being processed.

Security incident response Security incident response comprises notification to users and other groups as well as any actions taken in order to minimize losses, destruction, systems outage or any other business impact.

Forensic analysis Forensic analysis is the process of reconstructing past events from the analysis of traces being produced or recorded during the event and to identify the root cause. Forensic analysis tries to avoid any alteration to systems and data being involved or used in the event. Forensic analysis should provide evidence and accounting data.

Business Continuity Management Business Continuity Management provides precautions that minimize the impact of possible disruptions to ICT service provisioning or of a business-critical loss of data, which includes a timely and outright recovery of service and data. Business Continuity Management comprises Business Continuity Planning that utilizes a Risk Management approach. Business Continuity Management also comprises practical execution, or emergency management. ESARIS deals with ICT services. Strictly speaking, it concerns (ICT) service continuity.

B.4   Major concepts and models at a glance

This section provides a "fast track to ESARIS" by delivering definitions or short explanations for major concepts or models of ESARIS.

The figures are reproduced from the previous sections in order to ease the use of this glossary.

ESARIS Standardization Philosophy (Fig. 132)

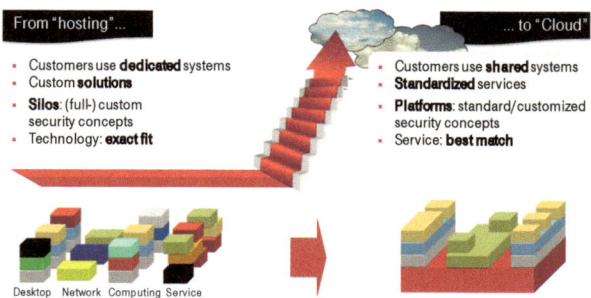

Fig. 132: ESARIS Standardization Philosophy (Fig. 7 on page 19)

"IT outsourcing" started with moving systems from customer premises to large data centers of specialized ICT Service Providers. New systems were developed as dedicated systems to fit the specific requirements of the customer. At this time, silos were set up which resulted in heterogeneous environments. – In order to reduce costs and improve flexibility, today's "outsourcing" uses shared systems and demands largely standardized services. ESARIS follows this trend and supports industrialized IT production and delivery.

ESARIS Duplex Security Management Concept (Fig. 133)

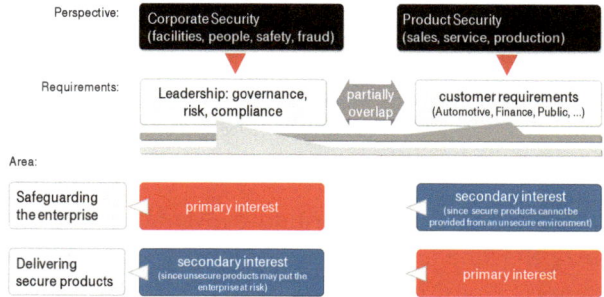

Fig. 133: ESARIS Duplex Security Management Concept (Fig. 12 on page 31)

The *ESARIS Duplex Security Management Concept* firstly recalls that there are, for ICT Service Providers, two distinct goals in the field of information security: the protection of the enterprise as a whole and of the service or product being provided. Both areas can cause risks to both the enterprise and its customers. Hence, the two areas are interwoven. The *ESARIS Duplex Security Management Concept* indicates the necessity and existence of two different security organizations or perspectives. Each one will concentrate on one scenario while supporting the other. The interrelation is called "duplex" since none of them should actively control an issue that is already and actively controlled by the other party.

ESARIS Governance Model (Fig. 134)

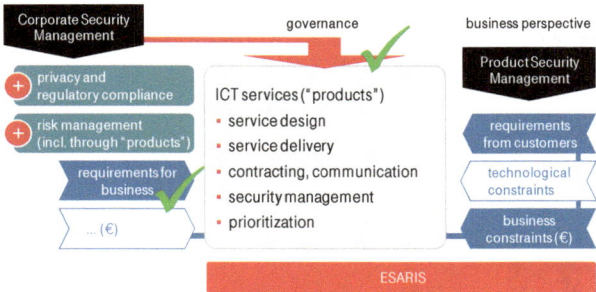

Fig. 134: ESARIS Governance Model (Fig. 13 on page 32)

The *ESARIS Governance Model* combines and aligns the two perspectives and tasks described in the *ESARIS Duplex Security Management Concept*. The two perspectives are called governance, risk and compliance (GRC) perspective and business perspective here, whereby the first clearly controls the second. Note, however, that there can be conflicts and other constraints such as funding of security measures and others resulting from the actual practice thereof.

Approach

ESARIS Industrialization Concept (Fig. 135)

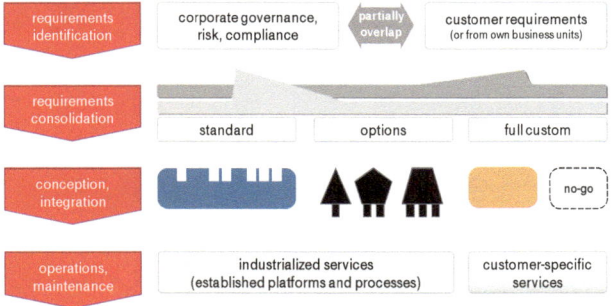

Fig. 135: ESARIS Industrialization Concept (Fig. 39 on page 104)

It is a major goal of ESARIS to increase the degree of standardization. ICT services shall be produced in an industrialized way that requires embedded and related ICT security measures to be standardized as well. ICT services provide a minimum, baseline or standard security (blue). Requirements that are not common to all customers are met by adding predefined options (black). Customer-specific services that meet full custom requirements are considered as exceptional cases. The different types of solutions consider both the provider's and the customer's requirements.

ESARIS Composition Model (Fig. 136)

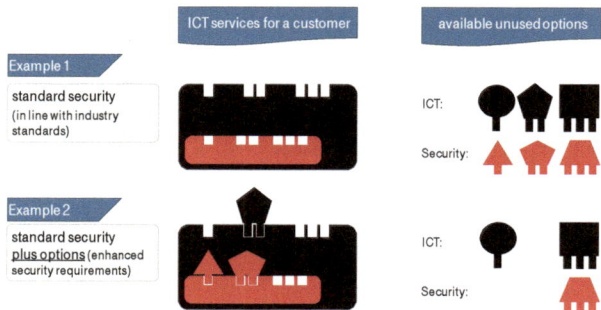

Fig. 136: ESARIS Composition Model (Fig. 40 on page 106)

ESARIS is built to support the ICT core business. The provider follows a modular approach in providing ICT services and the embedded or associated ICT security measures. Each ICT service consists of a baseline service (rectangle with interfaces) but allows options to be added (shown as plugs). The ICT security measures are provided in the same manner. There is a baseline security which can be enhanced using options. Many of the security options are also available as dedicated security services and therefore part of the ICT Security Service portfolio.

Framework for ESARIS Fig. 137

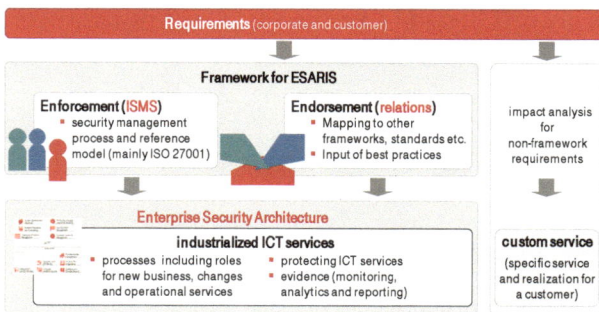

Fig. 137: Framework for ESARIS (Fig. 9 on page 27)

The ESARIS approach – the subject matter of this book – does not cover all the activities within an enterprise that relate to information security and risks. Firstly, a Security Management organization and processes for it on a corporate level are required. This Information Security Management System (ISMS) build or maintain the so-called *Enforcement Framework for ESARIS*. Secondly, one must manage the relations to standards, industry and other best practices. The collection and classification of security measures is the subject of the so-called *Endorsement Framework for ESARIS*. This framework also maintains a mapping between all existing security measures from the different sources as required for the Internal Control Framework of the ICT Service Provider and its customers.

Enforcement Framework for ESARIS (Fig. 138)

Fig. 138: Enforcement Framework for ESARIS (Fig. 10 on page 28)

The *Enforcement Framework for ESARIS* can be considered the Information Security Management System (ISMS) of the ICT Service Provider since it provides the organization, the processes and other resources and is built to establish, implement, operate, monitor, review, maintain and improve information security. An ISMS which is largely defined in ISO/IEC 27001 [93] is used by many large organizations and implemented on a corporate level.

Endorsement Framework for ESARIS (Fig. 139)

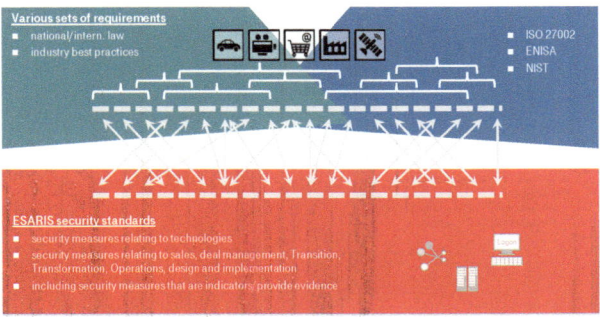

Fig. 139: Endorsement Framework for ESARIS (Fig. 11 on page 30)

The *Endorsement Framework for ESARIS* builds the part that manages relations of ESARIS to norms, industry standards and best practices as well as legislation and regulation. This framework looks in detail at security implementation standards such as ISO/IEC 27002 [94] or the ISF's SOGP.[95] It also comprises a mapping between the security measures defined in ESARIS and the security measures stipulated in the environment.

---

[93] ISO/IEC 27001 – Information technology – Security techniques – Information security management systems – Requirements, 2013 [5]

[94] ISO/IEC 27002 – Information technology – Security techniques – Code of practice for information security management, 2013 [6]

[95] Information Security Forum (ISF): The Standard of Good Practice for Information Security 2016 [25]

Content

ESARIS Dimensions (Fig. 140)

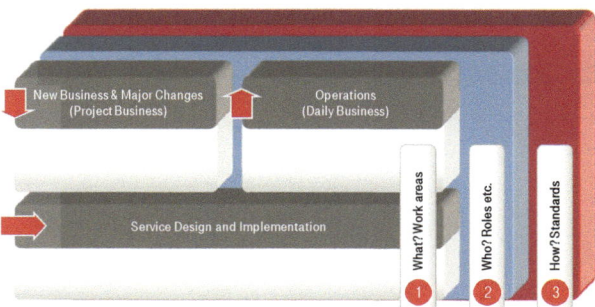

Fig. 140: ESARIS Dimensions (Fig. 14 on page 34)

ESARIS spans three dimensions and thereby responds to three questions: What? – ESARIS comprises all components that are needed to deliver secure ICT services and dedicated security services to customers. Who? – ESARIS comprises definitions of roles and responsibilities as well as of processes and practices. How? – ESARIS comprises the security standards showing how security is "achieved" and allow for "assessing" the level being achieved.

ESARIS Work Areas (Fig. 141)

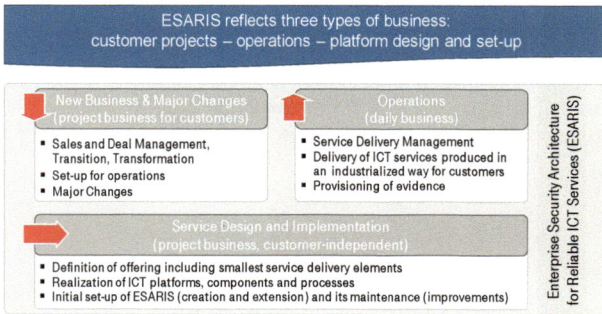

Fig. 141: ESARIS Work Areas (Fig. 15 on page 35)

The *ESARIS Work Areas* are one of the *ESARIS Dimensions* (i.e. No. 1). ESARIS considers the whole life-cycle. Consequently, there are three work areas that are considered. Service Design and Implementation comprises all elements that are prepared and available to deliver ICT services in a secure way. Secondly, there is the Project Business in which new business is prepared and major changes are made. The third dimension is Operations, where ICT services are actually delivered to customers in a secure way.

ESARIS Collaboration Model (Fig. 142)

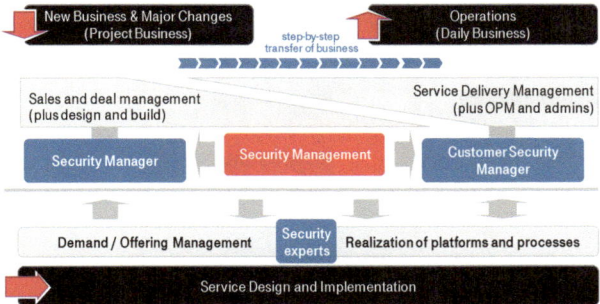

Fig. 142: ESARIS Collaboration Model (Fig. 17 on page 39)

The *ESARIS Collaboration Model* fills one of the *ESARIS Dimensions* (i.e. No. 2) and describes the roles and their interaction in Project Business and Operations (refer to *ESARIS Work Areas*). In particular, it features the *Security Manager* who is responsible for security issues in the Project Business (plan – build) and the *Customer Security Manager* who does perform this task in Operations.

Hierarchy of Security Standards (Fig. 143)

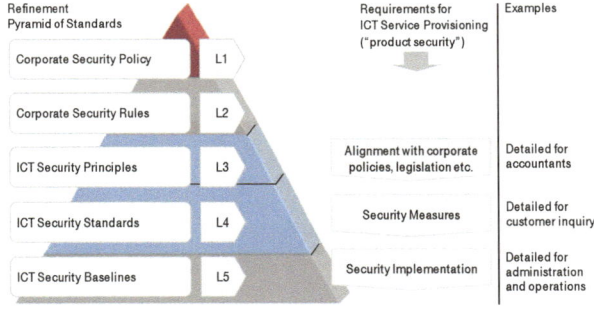

Fig. 143: Hierarchy of Security Standards (Fig. 19 on page 43)

The *Hierarchy of Security Standards* fills in one of the *ESARIS Dimensions* (i.e. No. 3). This hierarchy comprises an overall security policy on the top (Level 1) and more detailed security rules below (Level 2). These two concern the whole enterprise and its business. The next levels (3 to 5) deal with the ICT service delivery. They describe security principles and standards that are built and maintained in order to deliver ICT services in a secure way. Such a hierarchy may look different and use other terms.

ESARIS Concept of Double Direction Standards (Fig. 144)

Fig. 144: ESARIS Concept of Double Direction Standards (Fig. 20 on page 48)

ESARIS aims to standardize the security measures and to provide information, transparency and evidence to customers that security is actually being achieved. In order to ensure unambiguity, Level 4 of the *Hierarchy of Security Standards* is chosen to provide information to customers and simultaneously to provide directives for ICT service delivery and production. The *ESARIS Concept of Double Direction Standards* stipulates that the same text is used for both purposes. The security measures of Level 4 (*ESARIS Orchestration Layer*) therefore address a concrete security issue and respond to a question or concern that is of interest for customers. The context, purpose and effect become clear from studying the security measure. The security measures, moreover, provide directions for implementation, formulated as clearly and specifically as required in order to ensure that security objectives are achieved.

ICT Security Standards (Fig. 145)

Level 3: ICT Security Principles	• Alignment with corporate policies • Alignment with international frameworks, industry standards etc. • Overall security principles that apply to all ICT services and technology and process areas
Level 4: ICT Security Standards	• Implementation independent specification of security (e.g. independent from product version, product, manufacturer) • Communicating, negotiating and agreeing security issues with customers • Synopsis of all security aspects relevant in ICT production; level that allows to verify completeness and dependencies and provisioning of an integrated mutually supporting whole
Level 5: ICT Security Baselines	• Instruct people how to implement the security measures • Instruct people how to act (during development, implementation and operations)

Fig. 145: Three levels with the *ICT Security Standards* on Level 4 (orchestration layer)

The *ICT Security Standards* are the ESARIS security standards on Level 4 of the Hierarchy of Security Standards. They form the *ESARIS Orchestration Layer* and specify security features protecting the provider's ICT services in the form of security measures. There are 31 *ICT Security Standards* which are organized according to the *ESARIS Security Taxonomy*. The set of all *ICT Security Standards* (or the security measures they describe) is qualified to respond to the security-related requirements that originate from both the ICT Service Provider and the user organization (customer). The *ICT Security Standards* are the most detailed ESARIS security standards which are foreseen for communication to customers. Refer to the *ESARIS Concept of Double Direction Standards* for details.

ICT Security Baselines (Fig. 146)

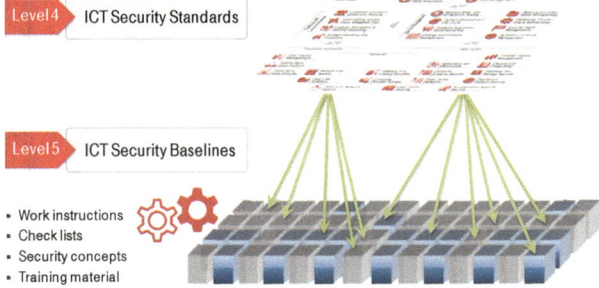

Fig. 146: Refinement to the most detailed *ICT Security Baselines* (Level 5)

The *ICT Security Baselines* are the ESARIS security standards on Level 5 of the Hierarchy of Security Standards. They refine the security measures stipulated in the *ICT Security Standards* and specify security features protecting the ICT services in the form of technical policies and concepts, work instructions and checklists, and comprise also tutorials and guidance. In this way, they cover all information necessary to implement the security measures from Level 4 in technology and processes.

Specification

ESARIS Security Taxonomy (Fig. 147)

Fig. 147: ESARIS Security Taxonomy (Fig. 21 on page 56)

ESARIS describes security measures in a structured and totally modular way. The security measures had been distributed amongst several *ICT Security Standards* since both the ICT services and the security requirements are manifold. The *ICT Security Standards* provide transparency to customers by explaining how the ICT Service Provider achieves and guarantees security. They are also directives for production and service delivery. The structure of the *ICT Security Standards* has therefore been designed to serve three objectives: Customers shall obtain answers on how their requirements are addressed. The individual departments and teams of the ICT Service Provider shall easily find the guidance relevant for them. Thirdly, the *ICT Security Standards* shall cover all relevant aspects, i.e. "the whole world of IT and TC security" with all the details and variants across all technical disciplines and throughout the entire life-cycle. This structure is called *ESARIS Security Taxonomy*.

Clusters of ICT Security Standards (Fig. 148)

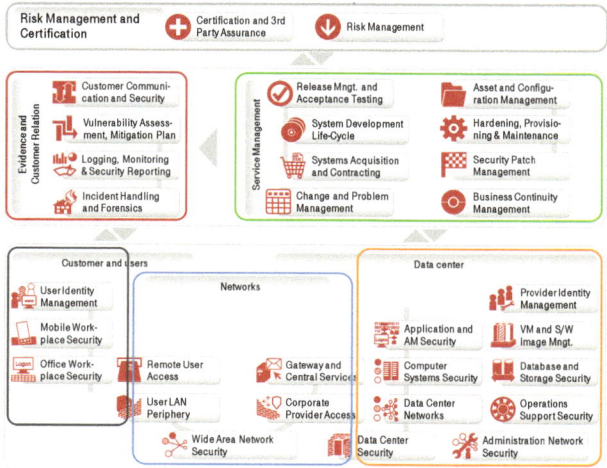

Fig. 148: Clusters of ICT Security Standards (Fig. 22 on page 59)

The *Clusters of ICT Security Standards* are one element or aspect of the *ESARIS Security Taxonomy*. Areas can be grouped into so-called clusters. The diagram shows six clusters as used in the original map of *ICT Security Standards*. Other clusters can be defined in order to combine areas which, from a specific perspective, belong together.

ESARIS Security Specification Concept (Fig. 149)

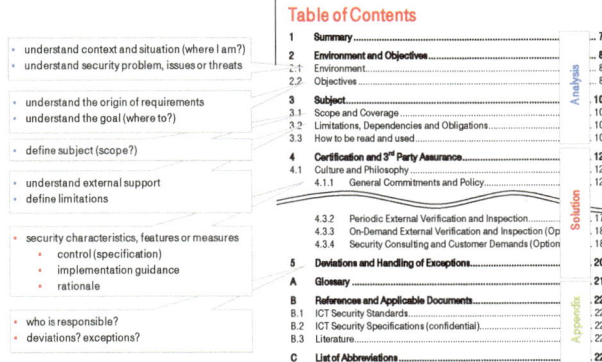

Fig. 149: ESARIS Security Specification Concept (Fig. 42 on page 108)

The *ESARIS Security Specification Concept* provides guidance for the authors of *ICT Security Standards* and ensures that the latter have the same structure and content and integrate into the overall *ESARIS Security Taxonomy* while describing dependencies etc. All standards have the following structure and content: security problem definition, security objective identification, scope and coverage clarification, identification of external support (dependencies with other standards), definition of security measures with implementation guidance and rationale. The approach is related to the one described in Common Criteria (ISO/IEC 15408).

Compliance

Provider Scope of Control (Fig. 150)

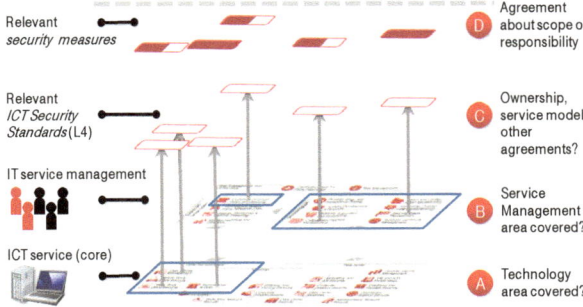

Fig. 150: Provider Scope of Control (Fig. 28 on page 76)

Provider Scope of Control describes a method for selecting the right and relevant information for a customer, an individual service or a specific deal. This starts with selecting the technological elements and the related *ICT Security Standards* that are associated with the delivered ICT service. Then operations and the division of labor between the ICT Service Provider and the customer are considered, and specifically, services are selected with the related *ICT Security Standards*. Next, specific responsibilities are checked which provides additional filters. Finally, parameters such as ownership and contractual details are taken into account. The method of selection works at the level of security measures.

Taxonomy of Service Models (Fig. 151)

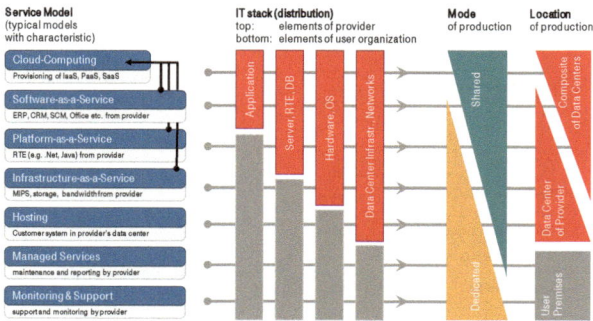

Fig. 151: Taxonomy of Service Models (Fig. 29 on page 77)

In ESARIS, the *Taxonomy of Service Models* helps to determine the *Provider Scope of Control*. It relates the Service Model to the possession of elements in the IT stack (provider or user organization). The model also differentiates between the dedicated and shared mode of production and helps to discuss the location of production. The taxonomy considerably helps to characterize an ICT service to the required level of detail.

Compliance (ESARIS) (Fig. 152)

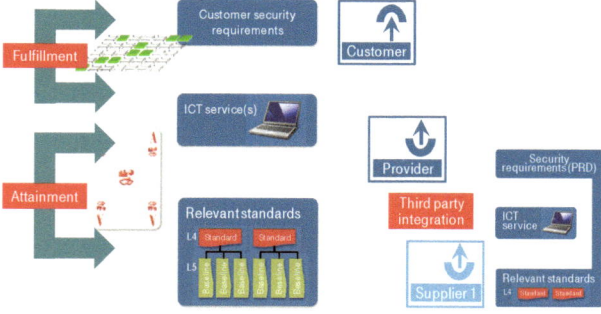

Fig. 152: Two types of compliance (ESARIS)

In ESARIS, compliance refers to two different areas. 1) The *ESARIS Compliance Attainment Model* measures if ICT services are compliant with relevant ESARIS security standards. It is verified if the security features are correctly implemented in technology and processes used for delivering the ICT service. The result is documented in form of an Ace. 2) The *ESARIS Customer Fulfillment Model* measures if an ICT service is compliant to the customer's security requirements. It is verified if the customer's security requirements are met by the ICT service being the subject of the contract. This duality is also the subject of the *ESARIS Concept of Double Direction Standards*. The *ESARIS Third Party Inte-*

gration Model combines the two models: The requirements are specified using the standards.

ESARIS Customer Fulfillment Model (Fig. 153)

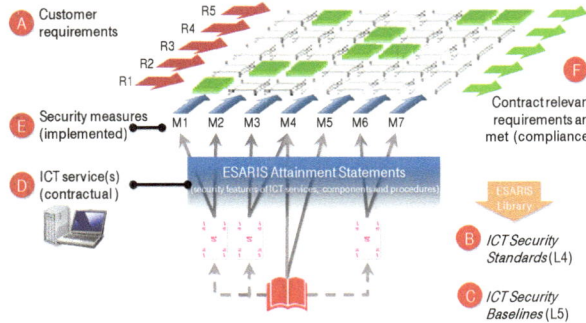

Fig. 153: ESARIS Customer Fulfillment Model (Fig. 66 on page 152)

The ESARIS Customer Fulfillment Model (or: ESARIS Fulfillment Model) describes a method to demonstrate that the customer's security requirements are met and how. Large enterprises in particular take a comprehensive risk-oriented approach. They have different requirements due to the fact that their business differs. The model describes five steps: (1) the collection and analysis of the customer's security requirements, (2) the categorization of customer requirements and the matching of the more general ones to policies, rules, and schemas, (3) the matching of detailed customer requirements with security features of the provider's ICT services using Aces, (4) the treatment of possible differences and contradictions, and of gaps through acceptance or design of custom or new solutions, and (5) the synopsis, verification of composition and summary or results.

ESARIS Compliance Attainment Model (Fig. 154)

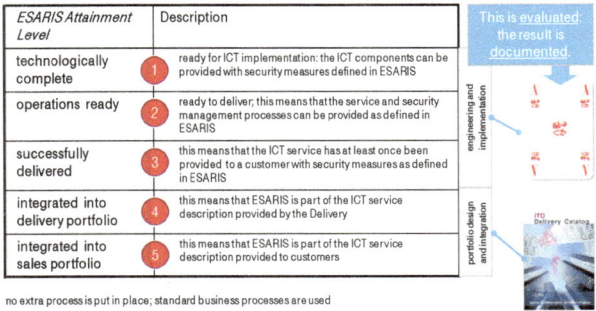

Fig. 154: ESARIS Compliance Attainment Model (Fig. 53 on page 129)

The *ESARIS Compliance Attainment Model* (or: ESARIS Attainment Model) describes a method to verify if and to what extent an ICT service complies with ESARIS and its *ICT Security Standards*. The result is documented in form of an Ace. The "attainment" is organized into five *ESARIS Attainment Levels* which relate to the achievement of milestones in delivering ICT services according to the methods, procedures, and standards of ESARIS. The first three levels are related to more technical tasks (IT engineering and implementation). Level 1: The technical components integrate the security measures that are stipulated in the ESARIS security standards. Level 2: The IT service management processes also integrate security as defined in the ESARIS security standards. Level 3 is "successfully delivered" which means that the ICT service has at least once been provided to a customer with security measures as defined in the ESARIS security standards. The last two stages are related to the management of the service portfolio (called Service Catalog Management in ITIL). Level 4: integrated into delivery portfolio means that ESARIS is part of the ICT service description provided by the delivery units. Level 5: integrated into sales portfolio means that ESARIS is part of the ICT service description provided to customers.

Ace (Fig. 155)

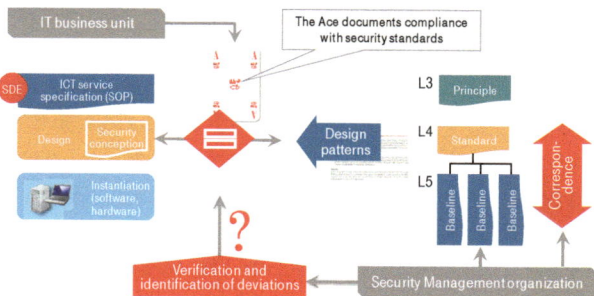

Fig. 155: Aces document compliance with security standards (Fig. 54 on page 131)

Using the *ESARIS Attainment Model* it is measured if and to what extent an ICT service meets the security standards stipulated in ESARIS. The result is documented in form of an Ace. An Ace usually refers to an ICT service, but the scope can also be any component (that can be reused in an ICT service) or an activity (like incident handling). An Ace contains a statement of compliance with respect to the relevant security measures (Level 4), describes deviations and may also enlist the ICT Security Baselines (Level 5) that are considered.

Introduction of ESARIS and Maintenance

Transformation towards ESARIS (Fig. 156)

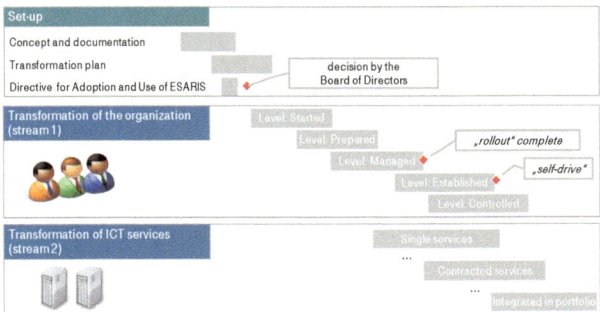

Fig. 156: Transformation towards ESARIS with two streams (Fig. 85 on page 193)

Transformation is the act of revising or altering into a different form (involving reconsideration and modification). The change (revision or alteration as used in this book) has a significant effect so that the starting and the ending point significantly differ in terms of maturity or attainment. The change lasts a period of time and usually has an anticipated ending as projects have. So, transformation is not considered to be a continuous process. – The *Transformation towards ESARIS* is the process that introduces ESARIS in IT production. The Transformation comprises the (i) Transformation of organizational units and the (ii) Transformation of ICT services.

Transformation of organizational units (Fig. 157)

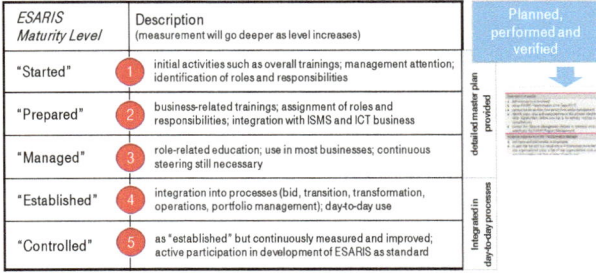

Fig. 157: Transformation of organizational units (stream 1; Fig. 86 on page 194)

The Transformation of organizational units is stream 1 of the *Transformation towards ESARIS*. It is organized into five *ESARIS Maturity Levels*. The organizational units introduce ESARIS and raise the maturity of using the concept, methods, standards and tools of ESARIS. Employees are trained to this end. The organizational units work along a predefined ESARIS Transformation Master Plan (ETMP) which is modified and complemented by the organizational unit.

Transformation of ICT services (Fig. 158)

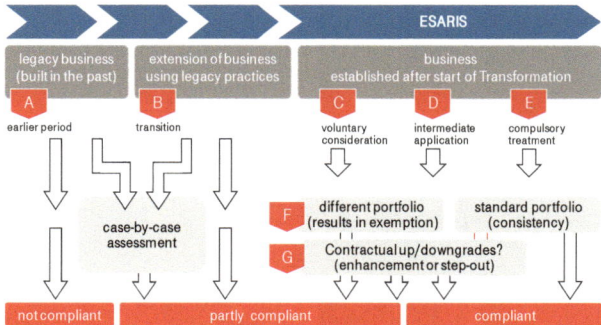

Fig. 158: Transformation of ICT services (timeline stream 2, Fig. 93 on page 207)

The Transformation of ICT services is stream 2 of the Transformation towards ESARIS. It is organized into five *ESARIS Attainment Levels*. After having achieved an appropriate *ESARIS Maturity Level* (stream 1 of the Transformation towards ESARIS) the organization starts to apply the ESARIS security standards and to use the *ESARIS Attainment Model* in order to document if and to what extent they have actually used the ESARIS security standards during design, realization and provisioning of an ICT service.

Maintenance System for ESARIS (Fig. 159)

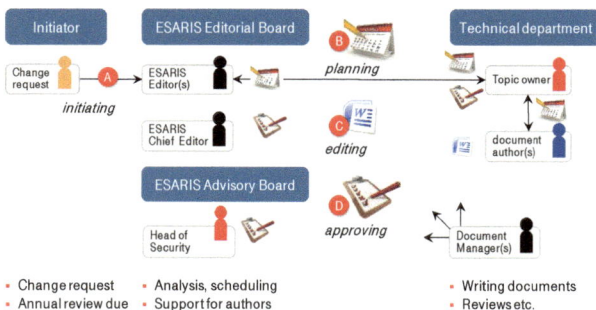

Fig. 159: Process of managing ESARIS documents (Fig. 80 on page 180)

The process of modifying a system or component after delivery or initial introduction to correct flaws, improve performance or other attributes, or adapt to a changed environment. – The *Maintenance Systems for ESARIS* defines processes, procedures and roles for the process of developing, modifying, releasing and distributing the ESARIS documentation. Maintenance is a continuous activity. It refines the standard document management process and introduces e.g. the *ESARIS Editorial Board* and the *ESARIS Advisory Board*.

C   Literature

Standards

[1]   COBIT 5, A Business Framework for the Governance and Management of Enterprise IT; ISACA

[2]   ISO/IEC 20000 – Information technology – Service management – Part 1: Service management system requirements, Part 2: Guidance on the application of service management systems; 2012

[3]   ISO/IEC 21827 – Information Technology – Systems Security Engineering – Capability Maturity Model (SSE-CMM), 2008

[4]   ISO/IEC 27000 - Information technology — Security techniques — Information security management systems — Overview and vocabulary; 2016

[5]   ISO/IEC 27001 – Information technology – Security techniques – Information security management systems – Requirements, 2013

[6]   ISO/IEC 27002 – Information technology – Security techniques – Code of practice for information security management, 2013

[7]   ISO/IEC 27005 – Information technology — Security techniques — Information security risk management, 2011

[8]   ISO/IEC 27017 – Information technology — Security techniques — Code of practice for information security controls based on ISO/IEC 27002 for cloud services; 2015

[9]   ISO/IEC 15408 – Information technology — Security techniques — Evaluation criteria for IT security — Part 1: Introduction and general model; 2009

[10]   ISO/IEC 15408 – Information technology — Security techniques — Evaluation criteria for IT security — Part 2: Security functional components; July 2008

[11]   ISO/IEC 15408 – Information technology — Security techniques — Evaluation criteria for IT security — Part 3: Security assurance components; 2008

[12]   ISO 22301 – Societal security – Business continuity management systems – Requirements; 2012 (replacing BS 25999-1:2006); and ISO 22313 – Societal security – Business continuity management systems – Guidance; 2012 (replacing BS 25999-2:2007

[13]   PCI Standards Council: PCI DSS (PCI Data Security Standard); Version 3.2 as of 2016

Publications of governmental agencies

[14] Elizabeth Chew, Marianne Swanson, Kevin Stine, Nadya Bartol, Anthony Brown, and Will Robinson: Performance Measurement Guide for Information Security, NIST Special Publication 800-55 Rev. 1; NIST, Gaithersburg, July 2008

[15] Pauline Bowen, Joan Hash and Mark Wilson: Information Security Handbook: A Guide for Managers, Recommendations of the National Institute of Standards and Technology; NIST Special Publication 800-100, October 2006 (updated 2007)

[16] Kissel, Richard (ed.): Glossary of Key Information Security Terms; National Institute of Standards and Technology, U.S. Department of Commerce, NIST IR 7298, Rev. 2, May 2013

[17] NIST: Guide for Conducting Risk Assessments; NIST Special Publications 800-30, Gaithersburg, Sept. 2012

[18] Paul Cichonski, Tom Millar, Tim Grance and Karen Scarfone: Computer Security Incident Handling Guide, Recommendations of the National Institute of Standards and Technology; NIST Special Publication 800-61 Revision 2, August 2012

[19] Richard Kissel, Kevin Stine, Matthew Scholl, Hart Rossman, Jim Fahlsing, and Jessica Gulick: Security Considerations in the System Development Life Cycle; National Institute of Standards and Technology, NIST Special Publication 800 — 64 Revision 2, October 2008

[20] Marianne Swanson, Pauline Bowen, Amy Wohl Phillips, Dean Gallup and David Lynes: Contingency Planning Guide for Federal Information Systems; National Institute of Standards and Technology, NIST Special Publication 800-34 Rev. 1, May 2010 (updated Nov. 2010)

[21] European Network and Information Security Agency (ENISA): Cloud Computing – Benefits, risks and recommendations for information security; November 2009

[22] European Network and Information Security Agency (ENISA): Cloud Computing Information Assurance Framework; November 2009

[23] Federal Office for Information Security (BSI): White Paper Security Recommendations for Cloud Computing Providers (Minimum information security requirements); 2011

[24] Federal Office for Information Security (BSI): IT-Grundschutz-catalogues; Version 13, 2013

Industry associations and initiatives

[25] Information Security Forum (ISF): The Standard of Good Practice for Information Security 2016

[26]   Information Security Forum (ISF): Security Architecture, Navigating Complexity; March 2016

[27]   Information Security Forum (ISF): Information Security Incident Management, Establishing a Security Incident Management Capability; 2006

[28]   Aligning Business Continuity and Information Security; Information Security Forum (ISF), Special Project Report, March 2006

[29]   Information Security Forum (ISF): Security Implications of Cloud Computing; July 2009

[30]   Information Security Forum (ISF): Securing Cloud Computing: Addressing the seven deadly sins; January 2011

[31]   Cloud Security Alliance (CSA): Security Guidance; Version 3.0, Nov. 2011

[32]   Cloud Security Alliance (CSA) Trusted Cloud Initiative (TCI): TCI Reference Architecture; Quick guide, 2011

[33]   BITKOM: Cloud Computing – Was Entscheider wissen müssen, Ein ganzheitlicher Blick über die Technik hinaus Positionierung, Vertragsrecht, Datenschutz, Informationssicherheit, Compliance; Leitfaden; 2010

Books

[34]   Chrissis, Mary Beth; Mike Konrad and Sandy Shrum: CMMI – Guidelines for Process Integration and Product Improvement; Addison-Wesley, 2003, ISBN 0-321-15496-7

[35]   Ahmad K. Shuja: ITIL: Service Management Implementation and Operation; Auerbach Publications, 2010

[36]   TOGAF Version 9.1 Enterprise Edition; Van Haren Publishing, 2011

[37]   The Open Group Security Forum: Guide to Security Architecture in TOGAF ADM; November 2005

[38]   The Open Group: Open Enterprise Security Architecture (O-ESA), A Framework and Template for Policy-Driven Security; Van Haren Publishing, Zaltbommel, 2011, ISBN 978 90 8753 672 5

[39]   John Sherwood, Andrew Clark and David Lynas: Enterprise Security Architecture, A Business-Driven Approach; CRC Press, Boca Raton, 2005, ISBN 978 1 57820 318 5

[40]   Eberhard von Faber: How Economy and Society affect Enterprise Security Management; in: N. Pohlmann, H. Reimer, W. Schneider (Editors): Securing Electronic Business Processes, Vieweg (2009), ISBN 978-3-8348-0958-2, p. 17 – 26

[41]   Eberhard von Faber and Michael Pauly: User Risk Management Strategies and Models – Adaption for Cloud Computing; in: N. Pohlmann, H. Reimer,

W. Schneider (Editors): Securing Electronic Business Processes, Vieweg (2010), ISBN-10: 3834814385, p. 80 – 90

[42]   Michael Howard and Steve Lipner: The Security Development Lifecycle, A Process to Develop Demonstrably More Secure Software; Microsoft Press, 2006, ISBN-10: 0-7356-2214-0

[43]   Microsoft Application Guide, Patterns and Practices; Microsoft, 2nd Edition, 2009

[44]   A Guide to Building Secure Web Applications and Web Services 2.0; The Open Web Application Security Project (OWASP), Black Hat Edition July 27, 2005

[45]   Eberhard von Faber and Michael Pauly: How Cloud Security strongly depends on Process Maturity, Automation and Scale; in: N. Pohlmann, H. Reimer, W. Schneider (Editors): Securing Electronic Business Processes, Vieweg (2011), ISBN-10: 3834819115, p. 23 – 33

[46]   Eberhard von Faber: In-house standardization of security measures: necessity, benefits and real-world obstructions; in: ISSE 2014 Securing Electronic Business Processes, Highlights of the Information Security Solutions Europe 2014 Conference, Springer Vieweg, Wiesbaden, 2014, ISBN 978-3-658-06707-6, p. 35-48

[47]   Eberhard von Faber: Changing the security mode of operation in a global IT organization with 20000+ technical staff; in: ISSE 2015, Highlights of the Information Security Solutions Europe 2015 Conference, Springer Vieweg, ISBN 978-3-658-10934-9, p. 286 – 304

[48]   Eberhard von Faber: Organisation und Absicherung einer industriellen IT-Produktion, Drei Handlungsfelder jenseits von „Protection, Detection, Reaction"; in: Datenschutz und Datensicherheit - DuD, October 2016, Vol. 40, Issue 10, pp 647–653, ISSN 1614-0702, Springer Fachmedien Wiesbaden 2016

D   Abbreviations

ATM   Asynchronous Transfer Mode
BCM   Business Continuity Management
CBI   Customer Business Impact
CERT   Computer Emergency Response Team
CMDB   Configuration Management Data Base
CI   Configuration Item
CIA   Confidentiality, Integrity, Authenticity
CMO   Current Mode of Operation
CMS   Configuration Management System
CPE   Customer Premises Equipment
DDoS   Distributed Denial-of-Service Attack
DMZ   Demilitarized Zone
DNL   Direct Network Link
DoS   Denial-of-Service Attack
ESA   Enterprise Security Architecture
ESARIS Enterprise Security Architecture for Reliable ICT Services
FMO   Future Mode of Operation
GRC   Governance, risk and compliance
ISMS   Information Security Management System
ICT   Information and Communication Technology
IDS   Intrusion Detection Systems
IPS   Intrusion Prevention Systems
IT   Information Technology
LAN   Local Area Network
MPLS   Multiprotocol Label Switching
RfC   Request for Change
OSI   Open Systems Interconnection (model)
PoP   Point of Presence
SDE   Service Delivery Element
SDL   System Development Life-Cycle
SDM   Service Delivery Manager, or Service Delivery Management
SLA   Service Level Agreement
UPS   Uninterruptible Power Supply
VPN   Virtual Private Network
VLAN   Virtual Local Area Network
VM   Virtual Machine
WAN   Wide Area Network

E   Index

— A —

Acceptance testing.......................... 167
Access Management....................... 264
Accountability.......................... **336**, 337
Ace....131, 132, 151, 164, 168, 169, 306,
    355, **356**
Acquisition of ICT etc. 228, 233
Administration network........ 277, 289
Administration of ICT... 269, 274, **276**,
    287, 289
Applications 279, 291
Architecture...... **10**, See: ESA, ESARIS
Asset 337
Asset and configuration
    management **236**
Asset Management................. 237, 241
Assurance 16, 50, 102, 298, **337**, 338
Attainment...See: ESARIS Attainment
    Model
Attainment Levels ....See: ESARIS ~
Audit ....See: Security audit
Audit data, logs, trails....See: Security
    record
Authenticity............................ **336**, 337
Availability...................... **336**, 337, 341

— B —

Bibliography of documents........... 184
Business Continuity Management
    .... 240, **343**

— C —

Capability **338**
Certification............................ 298, **338**
Change **340**
Change Management92, **223**, 234, 239
CISO 100, 102, 115, 119
Cloud computing........................ 19, 77

Cluster of ICT Security Standards **352**
CMO...................................36, 208, 341
CMO+.. **341**
Common Criteria 16, 109
    Assurance 227
Competitive advantages............... 100
Complexity
    reduction of… 101
Compliance 16, 310, **338**
Compliance (ESARIS).................... **354**
Composition.................................... 168
Computer systems 270, 283
Confidentiality.................186, **336**, 337
Configuration Item (CI)..........236, 340
Configuration Management ..**236**, 241
Consistency 184
Consumerization 261
Contract 144, **145**
Contractual compliance................. 148
Contractual evidence 148
Control .... See: Security measure
Costs..............18, 84, 102, 103, 115, 275
Critical downtime 240
Criticality..........217, 220, 232, 235, **340**
Culture... 314
Current Mode of Operation.......... **341**
Current Mode of Operation +....... **341**
Customer Business Impact (CBI) . **340**
Customer Security Arrangement
    (CSA) 152
Customer Security Manager 40
Customer specific documents....... 183

— D —

Data bases.................................272, 284
Data center 254, 289
Data center networks..............268, 282
Data center security 278

Deal management 36, 144, 146, 210
Dependencies.................................. 111
Desktop computers 251
Deviations from standards..... 91, 113, 310
Direct Network Link...................... 247
Directive (board level) 193
Disaster recovery........................... 240
Division of labor ...3, 88, 101, 159, 234, 305
Document IDs................................ 174
Document library 173
Document repository 174
Due diligence................................ 144
Dynamic computing 243, 270

— E —

Economies of scale 4
Efficiency... **18**
Emergency operation..................... 240
Endorsement Framework for ESARIS 26, 149, 305
Enforcement Framework for ESARIS 26, **28**, 88, 305, **347**
Engineering of software images... 287
Environmental security 289
ESA..**23, 338**
ESARIS...**23, 339**
ESARIS Advisory Board................ 179
ESARIS Attainment Levels ...**128, 355**, 358
ESARIS Attainment Model ...**121**, 140, 164, 306, 309, **355**, 358
ESARIS Attainment Statement 121, 128, 132, 151, 169, 306
ESARIS Collaboration Model .. **37, 41**, 305, 307, **349**
ESARIS Compliance Attainment Model.......See: ESARIS Attainment Model
ESARIS Composition Model..**105, 346**
ESARIS Concept of Double Direction Standards **47**, 140, **350**, 351, 354

ESARIS Customer Fulfillment Model ...... See: ESARIS Fulfillment Model
ESARIS Dimensions..........**33**, 305, **348**
ESARIS Duplex Security Management Concept ..**31**, 304, **344**
ESARIS Editorial Board..................179
ESARIS Enforcement Framework.155
ESARIS Fulfillment Model....139, 141, 168, 306, 308, **355**
ESARIS Governance Model **32, 345**
ESARIS Industrialization Concept **103**, 123, 300, **345**
ESARIS Library 122, 125, 173, 174
ESARIS Maturity Levels.194, 357, 358
ESARIS Orchestration Layer ..48, 113, 140, 154
ESARIS Security Specification Concept **106, 353**
ESARIS Security Taxonomy13, 51, **55**, 163, 350, **351**
ESARIS Standardization Philosophy **344**
ESARIS Third Party Integration Model 163, 306, 308
ESARIS Transformation Master Plan (ETMP)..196
ESARIS Work Areas 34, 305, **348**
Ethical hacking ...See: Security testing
Evidence **16**
Exceptions 113

— F —

FMO 36, 341
Forensic analysis 219, 343
Framework for ESARIS **26, 346**
Fulfillment...See: ESARIS Customer ~
Full-custom 27, 105
Future Mode of Operation.............**341**

— G —

GRC...32, 104

— H —

Hardening, provisioning and maintenance **237**
Hierarchy **12**
Hierarchy of Security Standards ... 34, **42**, **349**, 350, 351
Hypervisor 271, 284

— I —

ICT Security Baselines 46, **351**
ICT Security Standards . 46, 48, 51, 55, 62, 106, **350**, 351
    Clusters of… 56, 58
    Groups of… 56
    Taxonomy of… **55**
Identity and Access Management253, 276
Identity Management 253, 264, 288
Implementation of ESARIS 190
Incident Management 92, 214, 219, 225, 235
Industrialization 3, 101, 133, 159
Information Security Management System (ISMS) 26, 347
In-house standardization 99
Integration of security **82**
Integrity **336**, 337
Intellectual property 186
Interaction 8, **14**, 18, 141, 307, 317
Interfaces 8, **14**, 18, 141, 317
Internet 251, 258
Introduction of ESARIS 190
Investment 115
ISMS 88, 155, 305, **339**
ISO/IEC 15408 109
ISO/IEC 27002 51
IT business 3, 19, 78, 81, 89
IT outsourcing ... 4, 7, **14**, 139, **142**, 316
IT production . 3, 19, 82, 100, 101, 190, 328
IT stack 78
ITIL ..14, 19, 37, 58, 81, 85, 88, 134, 190

— L —

LAN 253
Level of detail or abstraction 48
Library history 184
Log management 218, 312, **343**
Logging 213, 218, **342**

— M —

Maintenance System for ESARIS .. 92, 124, 306, **358**
Managed services 78
Maturity **338**
Maturity Levels .... See: ESARIS ~
Migration 144, 211, 216
Mobile Workplace 250, 260
Monitoring 213, 218, 312, **342**
Motivation 314
MPLS 254, 257

— N —

Naming convention 178
Network Attached Storage 272

— O —

Objective .... See: Security objective
Offering management 40
Office Workplace 251, 259
Operations 36, 145, 211
Operations support 273, 285
Options
    ICT services 105
    Security requirements 104
    Security services 105

— P —

Patch management 95, 238
Patches **342**
PDCA 28
Penetration testing .... See: Security testing
Physical security 289
Policies .... See: Security policies
Policy violation 91

Portfolio management 40
Privileged user access 276, 288
Problem **342**
Problem Management 92, **224**, 235
Procedure **338**
Process **338**
Procurement.................................... 166
Product Requirements Document
   (PRD) 165
Provider Scope of Control...... **74**, 126,
   131, 150, 167, **353**, 354
Provisioning of ICT systems 237
Public network................................ 251

— **R** —

Records ....See: Security record
Release **340**
Release Management **222**, 230
Remote access 249, 251, 262
Report .... See: Security report
Request for Change (RfC) **341**
Request for Information (RfI) 143
Request for Proposal (RfP)............ 144
Requirements.................. See: Security
   requirements
Requirements engineering 123
Risk..................................109, 337, 342
Risk management........................... 300

— **S** —

Sales process 36
Secured by definition..81, 88, 315, 329
Security **337**, 339, 342
Security analysis............................ 108
Security architecture ....See: ESA,
   ESARIS
Security audit................................. **340**
Security Development Life-Cycle 226
Security environment 109
Security events........................342, 343
Security experts 40
Security incidents 214, 340, 341, 343
Security Manager 38

Security measure....108, 112, **337**, 340,
   342, 350
Security measure IDs...................... 178
Security objective 110, **337**, 342
Security patch management **238**
Security policies 337, **339**, 342, 343
Security record **339**
Security report.........**213**, 218, 312, **339**
Security requirements 103, **337**, 342
Security Target 109, 167, **337**
Security testing **340**, 342
Service Continuity Management .240,
   343
Service Delivery Element (SDE)......35
Service Delivery Management 145,
   211, 321
Service Delivery Manager................40
Service Design and Implementation
   ....**35**
Service Level Agreement (SLA) 145
Service models................................77
Service offering (portfolio).............134
Service restriction....................340, **341**
Service versus product 143
SIEM...217, 312
Software Development Life-Cycle226
Specialization...3
Standardization .9, **18**, 20, **99**, 141, 306
Standards
   ICT services 105
   Security requirements 104
   Security services 105
Statement of Work 146
Storage 271, 284
Storage Area Network....................272
Supplier networks...........................159
Supply chain 159
System Development Life-Cycle..**226**,
   231
Systems acquisition........................**228**
Systems Acquisition and Contracting
   (SAC) 163, 166

– T –

Taxonomy .... See: ESARIS Security
    Taxonomy
Taxonomy of Service Models.. **77**, **354**
Third party . See: ESARIS Third Party
    ~
Threat 109, **337**, 339, 342
Transformation 36, 210, **341**
Transformation of ICT services ... 194,
    358
Transformation of organizational
    units 194, **357**
Transformation plan 193
Transformation towards ESARIS 190,
    357
Transition........... **36**, 145, 211, 216, **341**
Transparency............. 8, **9**, 14, 140, 307

– U –

Unit specific documents 183
User LAN................................ 251, 263

– V –

Virtual Machine.......270, 274, 284, 287
Virtual Machine Monitor 271
Virtual Private Network................ 248
Virtualization 287
VLAN.....................................272, 282
VPN.. 254
Vulnerability 337, **342**, 343
Vulnerability (general) **342**
Vulnerability (technical)................ **342**
Vulnerability assessment**212**, 216, **342**
Vulnerability management 95

– W –

Wide Area Network........247, 253, 257
Workplace computers
    Mobile workplace 250
    Office workplace........................ 251